Handbook of the Economy of the German Democratic Republic

prepared by

Doris Cornelsen, Jochen Bethkenhagen, Rainer Hopf,
Horst Lambrecht, Maria Lodahl, Heinrich Machowski,
Manfred Melzer, Peter Mitzscherling, Charlotte Otto-
Arnold, Maria Elisabeth Ruban, Angela Scherzinger,
Heinz Vortmann and Herbert Wilkens

a research team of the German Institute
for Economic Research, West Berlin

edited by

Reinhard Pohl

translated from the German by

Lux Furtmüller

SAXON HOUSE

Published by

SAXON HOUSE, Teakfield Limited,
Westmead, Farnborough, Hants., England

British Library Cataloguing in Publication Data

Deutsches Institut für Wirtschaftsforschung
    Handbook of the economy of the GDR.
    1. Germany, East — Economic conditions
    I. Cornelsen, Doris II. Pohl. Reinhard
    III. Furtmüller, Lux
    330.9´431´087   HC290.78
    ISBN 0-566-00256-6

Printed in Great Britain by Biddles Ltd, Guildford, Surrey

Contents

Figures

Charts

xiv

Tables

Contributors

Authors	Chapter
Dr Doris Cornelsen (Head of the project)	1.1
Dr Jochen Bethkenhagen	1.2.1, 4.1.3 (z. T.) 7.2
Dr Rainer Hopf	4.4
Dr Horst Lambrecht	4.3, 6
Ing. Maria Lodahl	5.3.4
Dr Heinrich Machowski	7.1
Dr Manfred Melzer	1.2.4, 2.1, 2.2, 2.4, 2.5, 4.2, 5.1
Dr Peter Mitzscherling	5.2.2
Dipl.-Kfm. Charlotte Otto-Arnold	5.3.2.1, 5.3.2.2
Dr Maria Elisabeth Ruban	4.5, 4.6, 4.7, 5.2, 5.3.5
Dr Angela Scherzinger	1.2.2.2, 1.2.5, 2.3, 2.5
Dipl.-Ing. Heinz Vortmann	1.2.2.1, 1.2.3, 5.2, 5.3.1, 5.3.2.3, 5.3.3
Dr Herbert Wilkens	3, 4.1

Other contributors

Hans Martin Duseberg, Ruth-Ingetraut Giese, Helga Kleidt, Elisabeth Lange, Iris Mundt, Hans Schmitz, Axel Schumacher, Wolfgang Steinbeck, Angelika Tuschy and Ilse Walborn.

Foreword

To the Federal Republic of Germany, the GDR invites comparison in a way in which no other social example does. Its economic structure and productivity serve opponents, such as advocates of our capitalist system, as a medium for argument. Frequently however expert knowledge is lacking.

The domestic economy of the GDR poses many questions: How did the planning and organisation develop? Where do the successes and failures lie? How will bottlenecks be overcome? How large are the energy sources, the reserves of raw materials, the construction capacity and the output level? How does a system of controlled consumer prices function? How high are the wages, the rents and the purchasing power? What do collectivity and industrialised production methods mean to agriculture? What role is played by export trade, involvement in the Eastern Bloc, the pressure of rising energy and raw materials prices on the world market?

In the 'East Germany and Eastern Industrial States' department of the German Institute for Economic Research (Deutsches Institut für Wirtschaftsforschung — DIW), the domestic economy of East Germany has been carefully analysed for many years: its system of administration and planning, its economic basis, the production of the individual regions, the distribution of income, the system of social security, the export trade — in short, all relevant economic facts.

The results of this work are to be found in a concise and clearly arranged form, written for students, teachers, journalists and for all who are interested in events in the GDR — in the 'Handbook of the Economy of the German Democratic Republic', which will be re-edited at intervals as new facts are available.

The DIW was founded in 1925 by Prof. Ernst Wagemann, currently president of the Statistical Bureau of the German Reich, as the Institute for the Study of Trade Fluctuation (Institut für Konjunkturforschung). In 1945 the leadership was handed on to Prof. Ferdinand Friedensburg. His successor in 1968 was the then Parliamentary Secretary of State to the Federal Minister of Economics, Dr Klaus Dieter Arndt, after whose death in 1974 the long standing Berlin Senator of Economics, Dr Karl König, took over the leadership of the Institute.

The DIW has preserved an unbiased position up to the present day. The Institute serves economic objectives beneficial to the community and has a duty to research economic performance at home and abroad, to publish the results of its work and to assist government, science and economics through the delivery of reports and opinions.

The 'East Germany and East Industrial States' is one of 10 research departments and has a staff of 18. The crucial point of their work lies in the analysis and prognosis of the economic development of the GDR and in the observation of the Eastern European states, particularly their external economic involvement. Head of the department is Dr Doris Cornelsen.

1 Economic development and basic factors

1.1 Economic development

1.1.1 The situation at the outset

At the end of the war, in 1945, the situation was much the same in all four occupation zones of Germany: the productive potential was largely destroyed, the population stricken by the direct and indirect effects of the war, acute material distress was widespread. Yet, there were differences of degree. The process of reconstruction had to contend with greater difficulties in the East than in the rest of Germany.

These disadvantages of the Soviet Zone of Occupation (SZ) would not have been apparent in a stocktaking carried out immediately after the end of hostilities. Air raids had been directed with particular severity against Berlin and the industrial centres of the Rhine-Ruhr region. Estimates of the damage caused by air raids and the fighting on land in the closing stages of the war agree in attributing higher losses of industrial capacity to the Western regions than to the territory of the present GDR. For Germany as a whole, the losses of capital assets in all branches of the economy are put at about 15 per cent of the stock available in 1939. In the SZ the loss ratio lies slightly below, in Western Germany slightly above this average figure.

On the other hand, the SZ suffered substantially more from *dismantling* than did the Western Zones. Like the Western Powers, the Soviets dismantled not only industries of military importance, but also capacities serving the peace-time economy. The following picture emerges for the decrease in capital assets of industry as a whole (loss ratio in per cent of the 1939 stock):

	Western Zones	SZ
through war damage	21	15
through dismantling	12	26
Total	33	41

Here, allowance must be made for the fact that while dismantling was of necessity confined to movable assets, the sequestration of

1

machinery, even of a single subsection of a production line, was liable to paralyse a whole factory, so that the losses of productive capacities were substantially higher than the losses of capital assets. Contemporary estimates put the loss of industrial capacity in the SZ through war damage and dismantling at well over half by comparison with the situation in 1939.

Another form of reparation — unknown in the Western Zones — consisted in *imposts on current production*. Such deliveries, repeatedly demanded by the Soviet Occupying Power in very forceful terms, began to be exacted as soon as production got going, and came to an end officially with the German-Soviet agreement of 1953. The original demand was for deliveries totalling 10,000 million dollars 'at 1938 world market prices', part of which, however, was later remitted. Since those deliveries out of current production were never accounted for officially, and subsequent statements referring to their value were contradictory, no precise value can be attached to them. A tentative estimate puts the total of such imposts, including deliveries from the enterprises of the Soviet Joint Stock Companies, in the region of 15 per cent of the domestic product during the early post-war years. Later on, this proportion declined steadily. During the first three years the levies on current production actually exceeded gross investment expenditure (including build-up of stocks); only after that was it possible for investment activity to take off.

Whereas the economy of the SZ thus had to cope with substantial levies on current production, the Western Zones — later on the Federal Republic of Germany — benefited under the aegis of the Marshall Plan and various other American relief programmes from gratis deliveries of foodstuffs, raw materials and machinery. These relief supplies boosted the process of reconstruction in Western Germany to such an extent that a veil of oblivion came to be drawn over the harshness and futility of the dismantling policy applied by the Western Powers during the initial stage.

Moreover, the partition of Germany and the break-up of the country's integrated economy left the territory of the SZ as a separate economic region largely isolated from the Western part. But the economy inherited by the SZ was to a vital degree dependent on supplies from the West. There was a virtually complete lack of raw materials and semi-manufactures for the most advanced industrial processes in the chemical industry, mechanical engineering, vehicle and aircraft construction, electrical engineering, precision engineering and the making of optical instruments. The territory of the SZ had accounted for a negligible proportion of the output of hard coal, iron ore, pig iron and crude steel produced in the German Reich as a whole, and its links with the Western part of Germany were correspondingly close and intricate.

No attempts were made at first to compensate the SZ for the break-up of Germany's integrated economy and the territory's separation from its Western markets by seeking alternative foreign trade links. Up to about 1956 economic policy in the Eastern camp had to conform to the Soviet maxim that it was incumbent on each socialist country to develop all branches of production, in particular industrial production. The GDR was thus obliged to resort to self-help and devote a large proportion of available funds to the development of basic industries instead of specialising in branches of manufacture with a long tradition in the territory. Later on, when foreign trade began to develop, the GDR's political alignment with the East led to its economic integration with the East European region. From that time on the Soviet Union accounted consistently for two fifths of the GDR's foreign trade. But the economic structure of the foreign trade partners of the GDR within the CMEA region offered the country no benefits remotely comparable to the advantages accruing to the Federal Republic from its links with the highly developed industrial economies of the West.

1.1.2 Property relations and economic controls

The manifest differences between the economies of the GDR and the Federal Republic derive from the fundamental divergence of the two economic systems. Whereas in the West a market economy was introduced in 1948, in the Soviet Zone a complete transformation of the social order in accordance with communist principles was ushered in through the dominant influence of the Soviet Union. The main features of this order were taken over from the Soviet model:

a) Political and economic power vested in the Communist Party;
b) social — i.e. state or collective — ownership of the means of production;
c) central planning, administration and supervision of the economy.

In September 1945 a land reform was promulgated as the first of a series of measures intended to transform the relations of ownership. All estates and agricultural establishments with an agricultural area exceeding 100 hectares, as well as all those, irrespective of size, owned by persons classified as war criminals or leading National Socialists were expropriated and distributed among over 200,000 'new peasants'. Simultaneously the first step towards a socialisation of agriculture was taken with the establishment of publicly owned estates (*volkseigene Güter*, VEGs). The 'socialist transformation' of agriculture was continued with the

3

collectivisation campaign, which began in 1952 and was completed in 1960. By that time over 90 per cent of the total agricultural area was farmed by agricultural producer co-operatives (*landwirtschaftliche Produktionsgenossenschaften*, LPGs). Since 1960, this proportion has continued to increase, though only to a slight extent.

The nationalisation of industry was initiated by several orders of the Soviet Military Administration in Germany (SMAD). Political support was provided by a plebiscite conducted in Saxony in the middle of 1946. Nearly 4,000 industrial enterprises whose proprietors were held to be politically incriminated were nationalised. In addition, over 200 large enterprises were taken over by the Soviet Union and converted into 25 Soviet Joint Stock Companies (SAGs). All of these enterprises, with the exception of the SDAG Wismut, the uranium ore mining combine, had been returned to the GDR by 1953 and set up as publicly owned enterprises (VEBs).

In the following years the socialisation of industry was continued by means of economic and, in particular, fiscal measures. Many employers evaded such pressures by escaping to the West, and their enterprises were promptly transferred to public ownership, i.e. nationalised. Other enterprises entered into partnership with the state by adopting the statutory form of a *Kommanditgesellschaft* (KG), a type of company serving that purpose. The formation of such semi-state enterprises was promoted by the granting of numerous concessions in matters of taxation, allocation of materials and the provision of capital.

Similar arrangements encouraged individual artisan enterprises to form artisan producer co-operatives (*Produktionsgenossenschaften des Handwerks*, PGHs), while private retailers entered into contractual relations with state-owned or co-operative trade organisations (HO and consumer co-operatives). In the spring of 1972 the industrial semi-state enterprises were nationalised; at the same time about 1,600 artisan producer co-operatives engaged in industrial production were converted into publicly owned enterprises. Thus the share of 'socialist forms of ownership' was increased substantially over the years.

It is only in the artisan trades that private businesses have survived to any significant extent.

In contrast to the shifts in the ownership of the means of production, the transition to 'socialist economic planning' proceeded without profound changes in existing relationships. Retaining many of the wartime economic controls, the Soviet Military Administration in Germany, assisted by the economic planning authorities of the individual states (*Länder*) and by the Central Administrations (e.g. for Industry, Trade and Supplies, Transport), assumed the role of central direction. In 1948 the authority to issue decisions with the force of law throughout the Soviet Zone was vested in the German Economic Com-

4

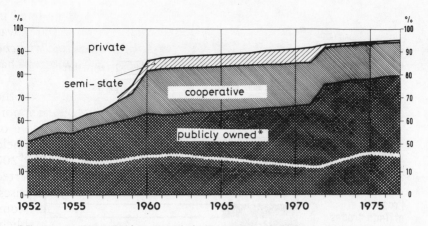

DIW 79

Figure 1   Development of forms of ownership in the GDR economy

mission (*Deutsche Wirtschaftskommission*, DWK), a body that had been set up the year before by merging the Central Administrations, and that was later, after the foundation of the GDR, transformed into the 'Provisional Government of the GDR'. Finally, in 1950, the State Planning Commission was established as the supreme planning authority, and has remained so since.

1.1.3   Medium-term plans

Economic planning is governed by the targets set by the top-level political authorities. The planning process starts with the drafting of medium-term plans or 'perspective plans' which specify targets, assess capacities and dovetail developments. These plans, covering a number of years, are in principle the foremost planning instruments, providing a solid basis from which the annual economic plans are to be derived. The first economic plan was drawn up for the second half of 1948; this was followed by a succession of plans covering two to seven years.

The Two-Year Plan 1949 to 1950   The chief purpose of limiting this plan to so brief a period was to synchronise GDR planning with that of the other countries of the Eastern bloc. The principal aims of the plan were to get industrial production going in an orderly fashion, to ensure supplies for the population, and, above all, to comply with the schedules of reparations deliveries. Priority was given to the development of the basic industries (expansion of the raw materials basis and

5

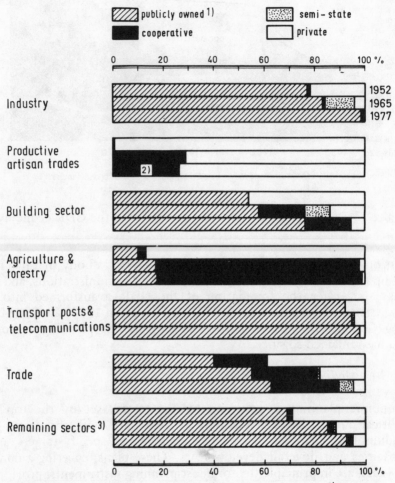

Figure 2   Forms of ownership in individual sectors (percentage shares
of economically active persons engaged in each sector)

the iron and steel industry).

The first Five-Year Plan 1951 to 1955 Although the technique of planning was still imperfect at the time, this plan, based on detailed computations, set the course for the generation, distribution and utilisation of the total economic output. The principal aim was the continuation of the restructuring of the economy started by the Two-Year Plan: the increase of productive capacities in the basic sector. Priority was given to the expansion of the fuel and power industries, the metallurgical industry, steel works and rolling mills (Eisenhütten-Kombinat Ost), of mechanical engineering (machine tools and industrial plant) and of the chemical industry.

These projects were promoted at the expense of the manufacture of consumer goods and of private consumption which ranked last in the scale of priorities. Wage increases combined with shortages led to considerable difficulties in the consumer goods sector, which the authorities tried to tackle by halting the upward trend of wages through higher production norms while simultaneously increasing the supply of goods through the introduction of the so-called 'New Course'. After the disturbances of June 1953 all industrial enterprises were ordered to produce additional consumer goods. Loans and imports from the Soviet Union and the formal termination of reparations deliveries from current production enabled the state, though only for a short spell, to adopt a policy more favourable to the consumer.

The second Five-Year Plan 1956 to 1960 This plan was not enacted with the force of law until December 1957, and the plan promulgated then differed from the first draft in that the original plan targets had been substantially reduced. It may be presumed that during the final stages of compiling the plan, change was indicated by considerations touching on the economic integration of the CMEA member states as well as by the events in Poland and Hungary. The important new departure was the promotion of specialisation within the CMEA region. The GDR was to give priority to the development of the coal, power, and chemical industries, investments to be concentrated on the last named. The plan centred on a long-term programme for the chemical industry, which was completed in detail in 1958. Another programme was drawn up with a view to raising labour productivity which at the time, according to official figures, was still 15 per cent below that in West Germany. Individual enterprises as well as entire industries were to be rationalised in the course of a 'socialist reconstruction'.

The second Five-Year Plan did not remain operative for its full term, owing partly to the surprisingly favourable economic development in 1957 and 1958, and partly to the need to dovetail GDR planning with

7

that of the Soviet Union, where the case for increasing the customary five-year periods of the economic plans had been under discussion since the autumn of 1957. The new approach aimed above all at bringing planning into line with the lengthy periods required on technological grounds for the construction of modern production plant. In January 1959 the CPSU Congress approved the Soviet Seven-Year Plan. At the same time the Five-Year Plan was terminated in the GDR and preparations were taken in hand for a Seven-Year Plan.

The Seven-Year Plan 1959 to 1965   The foremost aim of this plan, the 'principal economic task', was to serve the consumer; that is, 'by raising labour productivity and expanding production to catch up with and overtake West Germany by the end of 1961 as regards the per-capita consumption of the majority of industrial consumer goods and foodstuffs'. The new priorities were set against the background of ever-growing numbers of East Germans making their escape to the West. Allocation of investments was to be governed by the principle that preference should be given to the development of those industries for which prospects were most promising in the light of existing natural and economic conditions. This was meant as a corrective to the one-sided investment policy of the past. The concentration of investments on selected basic industries and the neglect of necessary complementary investments had brought about a situation in which some of the newly constructed plants could not be fully integrated into the process of production. The plan also envisaged an accelerated growth of exports.

The targets of the Seven-Year Plan soon turned out to be unrealistic. At the end of the 1950s private per capita consumption was between 25 and 30 per cent below that of the Federal Republic. In order to close the gap it would have been necessary to combine a high overall growth rate with an increase in the private consumer's share in the social product. But that was not feasible owing to the shortage of resources. The planned expansion of all possible uses of the available resources at the same time led to conflicting claims. It was like tugging in all directions at a blanket that is too short and too narrow. Instead of increasing, the overall economic growth rate declined. There were renewed shortages, partly due to a bad harvest. This downturn and the intensified collectivisation measures of 1960 swelled the numbers of refugees escaping to the West until the building of the Berlin Wall on 13 August 1961 stopped the exodus.

The disproportions in the development of the economy which had been inherent in the very conception of the plan became apparent in 1961. The annual plan for 1962 set new targets — independently of the Seven-Year Plan — for the development of supplies to the private consumer. Towards the end of 1962 the Seven-Year Plan was formally repealed. During the ensuing interim period planning was carried on from year to year. The failure of the Seven-Year Plan had an important effect. After the spectacular planning errors, which had even led to a crisis of growth, a serious discussion was initiated as a result of which the system of direction and planning was modified.

The Perspective Plan 1964 to 1970   The basic aims of the 'Perspective Plan 1964 to 1970 for the Development of the National Economy of the GDR' were laid down by the Sixth SED Congress at the beginning of 1963. In its approach to planning the Perspective Plan was more realistic than its predecessor. The final production targets for 1970 were fixed with considerable caution. Capital investment was to increase again at an above-average rate.

But the plan was never given the force of law. Indeed, the planning authorities made a point of characterising the plan figures as non-mandatory guidelines, leaving room for modifications and new departures. At a time when the debate on the most effective planning methods was in progress, the permissive character of the long-term plan was more in keeping with the new system about to be developed. After years of cautious self-restraint, a lively discussion on planning reform was sparked off in the GDR by the novel ideas which the Soviet economist, Professor Libermann, had been able to propound without interference from the Party leadership. This discussion led to the adoption of the 'New Economic System' (for which see sections 2.2 and 2.3 below).

The Perspective Plan 1966 to 1970   The introduction of the New Economic System gave rise to some uncertainty on a number of points in the early 1960s. It was in particular the industrial price reform which confronted enterprises and the economic authorities with contingencies, the detailed effects of which both on the individual enterprise and on the economy as a whole could not be calculated in advance. The third and final stage of the industrial price reform was concluded on 1 January 1967. Later in the same year the new Perspective Plan, this time reverting to the five-year planning period, was promulgated as a law. The starting position was given by the actual production figures of 1965. The plan targets were set in a sober spirit, in keeping with the real development prospects. As a matter of principle, the new Perspective Plan continued to grant priority to the increase in investments. Noteworthy shifts occurred, however, in the relative investment allocations within the industrial sector, with the share of the mining, power and metallurgical industries being reduced in favour of the rest.

During the period covered by this Perspective Plan further decisions were made which brought changes in the planning and administrative machinery. Of particular importance was the directive on the delimitation of competencies issued in 1968. Under it, the central authorities were again vested with increased powers in certain production sectors deemed important for economic growth so as to cope with structural key tasks. This measure, foreshadowing a return to centralisation, entailed numerous difficulties for the smooth meshing of interdependent production processes, and is today by common consent regarded as the beginning of the end of the New Economic System.

The Five-Year Plan 1971 to 1975 The drafting of this plan, too, was not completed until nearly a year of the period it was to cover had elapsed. While the plan was being prepared, important changes took place in the top leadership of the GDR. On 3 May 1971, only a few weeks before the Eighth SED Congress, the Party leadership passed from Walter Ulbricht to Erich Honecker.

Centralisation in directing and planning the economy was again substantially strengthened. The sanguine expectations of the 1960s were abandoned. The immediate aim of the Five-Year Plan was the elimination of the existing disproportions: safeguarding and expansion of the power and raw materials base; extension of the technological infrastructure; strengthening of the industries supplying semi-manufactures for further processing and scaling down of foreign debts by raising exports. All in all, it was a programme for the consolidation of the state and the economy in all spheres, to be achieved even at the price of reduced growth rates. To safeguard the system was also the intention behind the principal aim of the plan: inspired by the Twenty Fourth CPSU Congress, the Eighth SED Congress proclaimed the 'raising of the people's material and cultural living standards' as the principal task of the new Five-Year Plan, 'on the basis of a rapid development of socialist production, increased efficiency, scientific-technological progress and growing labour productivity'. The choice of priorities was governed in part by the effect of the tensions in neighbouring socialist countries, but it was also influenced by the recognition that the increases in labour productivity envisaged for all branches of the economy could not be achieved unless incomes and private consumption were also going up at least to some extent.

The plan's investment policy was marked by a note of caution. Enterprises were enjoined to 'elaborate an optimum balance between maintenance, disposal and renewal, as well as expansion'. Expansion of the basic funds would only be sanctioned when all other possibilities — improved plant utilisation, repairs, rationalisation — had been exhausted.

In contrast to the previous planning period from 1966 to 1970, during which imports rose more rapidly than exports, export promotion was now declared a primary task. In discussing the production of individual industries the plan stressed the importance of export production again and again. The development of the world markets during the five-year period covered by the plan lent new urgency to this task. In mid-1973, the world market prices of raw materials experienced a spectacular rise, leading to a permanent worsening of the terms of trade of the GDR (cf. chapter 6).

The Five-Year Plan 1976-1980 The basic features of economic planning for this period were largely determined by the changed growth prospects of the seventies. Measures had to be taken to absorb the substantial increase in import prices, in particular for energy sources and raw materials. In theory there were three options, that is to say, increasing indebtedness, higher exports or lower imports. Although in their published form the Five-Year Plan as well as the annual plans have little to say on the subject of foreign trade, the basic features of the plan suggested that the GDR economic authorities included all three possibilities in their planning, with the main accent, however, on the raising of exports.

In theory it might have been possible to cope with the increased demands in the foreign trade sector simply by securing an all-round acceleration of economic growth. This solution was not attempted by the GDR economic authorities, presumably because of the high risks involved. Higher production targets would have boosted the need for imports, whereas export volumes depend on foreign demand rather than domestic planning.

The overall economic growth postulated by the plan for the period from 1976 to 1980 actually lies slightly below the figure for the preceding five-year period. Exports are to rise substantially, and investments, too, are to increase more rapidly than during the preceding quinquennium. These shifts in the use of resources are made at the expense of private consumption, which once again has been assigned bottom rank in the scale of priorities. At the same time consumption is still listed among the 'primary tasks', but now in a different context: under the heading of the 'unity of economic and social policy' it is pointed out that the boosting of consumption is merely one economic task among other, no less urgent ones.

Longer-term expectations At the ninth meeting of the SED Central Committee in May 1973, Erich Honecker announced tentative forecasts of economic development in the GDR, which had been elaborated for the period 1970 to 1990. This investigation envisages annual growth rates of the following orders of magnitude:

11

national income generated by the
productive sectors   5 per cent
output of industrial goods   7 per cent
labour productivity   6.5 per cent
consumption fund   4.5 per cent

These figures appear to represent extrapolated trends rather than the result of careful calculation taking account of the intricate pattern of interaction. The salient point which emerges is that in the long term the consumption ratio — the share of consumption in the domestic product — is expected to decline slightly. The plan for the years 1976 to 1980 fits in perfectly with this concept.

1.1.4 *Development and structure*

The economic plans of the GDR were not always fulfilled. Some of them were modified in mid-stream or even terminated prematurely. Nonetheless, the priorities laid down in those plans for structural development and economic growth proved decisive. The foremost economic policy aims envisaged changes in the economic structure and increases in productive capacities as a basis for rapid economic growth, greater efficiency and productivity, as well as the ultimate achievement of levels of consumption comparable to those in Western countries. The results will be set out in detail in the following, specialised chapters. Here it is proposed to give just a brief survey of basic trends.

It needs pointing out, however — and it will be pointed out again in the specialised chapters — that an analysis of the development of production in the GDR and its comparison with other countries is greatly hampered by the vagaries of statistics. Statistics released by the GDR are comparatively poor in quality and lacking in comprehensiveness. Frequently only index numbers or percentages are announced; the systems used for the preparation of data may be changed abruptly; price levels both before and after the introduction of relevant reform measures are unknown; in the GDR, as in all CMEA countries, the domestic product — a quantity indispensable for economic analyses and international comparisons — is computed by methods substantially different from those applied in the West. These deficiencies and discrepancies lead to many gaps in our knowledge, and must be filled by estimates.

One important aim of GDR economic policy, the transformation of the economic structure, has clearly been attained. It is reflected in the above-average growth of the industrial labour force in the 1950s. This was accompanied by marked changes in the relative shares of individual industries, resulting partly from general development trends, and partly from policy measures applied with a sense of purpose. Thus the share of the basic industries increased, above all as a result of the fostering of the metallurgical industry, especially at the beginning of the period of reconstruction, and of the chemical industry. In the metal-processing sector mechanical and electrical engineering increased their share, while that of the light industry declined markedly.

The development of capital assets shows a similar pattern: investments were channelled above all into industry, first the basic industries and subsequently the metal-processing industries.

The development can be divided into a series of characteristic phases.

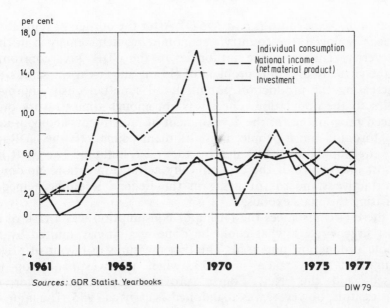

Sources: GDR Statist. Yearbooks

DIW 79

Figure 3   Development of the GDR economy since 1960 (at 1975 prices, growth rate in per cent)

The phase of reparations (1945-1953)   During this phase reconstruction was exposed to great strains. In the years 1946 to 1948, the proportion of the domestic product placed at the disposal of the Soviet Union (by way of occupation costs and deliveries from current production) reached about 25 per cent. The raising of this tribute required a supreme effort, straining all available resources to the utmost, while reducing the supply of all domestic needs to an absolute minimum. In 1946, private per capita consumption — 440 Marks at

13

1936 prices — had fallen to the subsistence minimum. It increased only slightly in the following years. It was then that the wide gap opened between the living standards of the population in the Soviet Zone and the Western Zones which was later to widen still further. The investments made during that period were insufficient to replace the losses; it was not possible to restore the industrial potential depleted by dismantlings. In 1950 the outstanding reparations obligations of the GDR were officially reduced by half; in August 1953 the remaining debt was remitted. From 1950 deliveries from current production declined year by year in absolute terms. The strain on the economy was reduced substantially. Only now was it possible to invest on any scale. Supplies to the population had the lowest priority during that phase.

The phase of the exodus (up to 1961)   After the burden of reparations had been removed, the country's economic problems emerged in their full severity. The economic authorities of the GDR were confronted with the virtually insoluble problem of closing all gaps at the same time, of increasing the production potential and simultaneously improving supplies to the population. There was not enough time to work out a balanced programme for the development of investments and consumption. More and more people, most of them young, left the GDR. By 1961, the population had fallen by about 2.6 millions. The GDR had thus lost one in five of the economically active population. No doubt, the attractive standards of living in the Federal Republic helped in stimulating this mass exodus.

In these circumstances the raising of consumption was a task of the utmost urgency; yet what could be done was strictly limited by the available production potential. The first measures in favour of private consumption were taken in 1953, when an investment stop was imposed, and the 'New Course' provided a changed pattern of priorities: this, however, was abandoned as early as 1955. The improvement of living standards was again proclaimed as the 'principal task' in the Seven-Year Plan. In the years 1957 to 1959 private consumption rose at an annual rate of about 8 per cent, and during that period the migration to West Germany actually registered a slight decline. But before long, in 1960, it turned out that the productive potential simply was not large enough to sustain expansion at such a rate. Moreover, the collectivisation of agriculture enforced in 1960 had an adverse effect on the production figures. The rate of growth of individual consumption declined considerably. Shortages reappeared and led to a renewed increase in the numbers of those leaving for the West. In August 1961 the exodus was halted by the erection of the Berlin Wall.

The phase of reforms (up to 1970) The economically most interesting phase in the development of the GDR opened at the beginning of the sixties when the growth crisis had been overcome. Methods of direction and planning were changed fundamentally by the introduction of the New Economic System; rigid planning was relaxed; numerous reforms were carried out. At the same time the conditions of growth had changed. With the manpower potential being utilised to the full, further growth was possible only on the basis of higher productivity and new technology. Extensive had to give way to intensive growth. Technological progress became the most important growth factor. Addressing the People's Chamber in 1963, Walter Ulbricht praised the significance of science for production in almost rhapsodic terms. From 1967 on, attempts were made to raise the efficiency of research and development by organisational measures. At the same time a policy of concentration was applied in industry by the formation of combines, which was expected to stimulate growth. The earlier aim of catching up with and overtaking the Federal Republic was superseded by the slogan of over-taking, without a thought of merely catching up.

Even though it was to be expected that the introduction of such far-reaching reforms could not be effected without some dislocations, overall economic development after 1963 was very favourable at first. Total production showed high as well as stable growth rates, and invest-ment increased by substantial amounts. The role of foreign trade as a growth factor was discovered. On the other hand, private consumption was again at the bottom of the list in terms of growth.

It was only towards the end of the sixties that difficulties emerged. The concept of 'structural key tasks' and the repeated intervention by the central authorities in important spheres — effected virtually without co-ordination, following no coherent pattern — had far-reaching conse-quences for the economic fabric as a whole. The expansion of selected industries, financed by the state, led to additional investments and made excessive demands on existing resources. The projected output failed to materialise, because the industries supplying raw materials and semi-manufactures had not been similarly expanded, and so could not meet the increased demand.

The years 1969 and 1970 had been supposed to prove the superiority of the New Economic System. Not only did this not happen, but that period was marked by a multitude of bottle-necks which wasted resources, though their effect on overall growth rates was slight. In addition, foreign indebtedness increased, posing new financial problems. The outcome was inevitable, both for the instruments and for the aims of economic policy. The first step was a revision of the targets of the 1970 Economic Plan. Immediately afterwards a re-examination of the entire system of planning, forecasting and management was taken in

15

hand. The phase of the New Economic System had come to an end.

The post-1970 phase Several shifts in economic policy aims and tasks have marked the period initiated by recentralisation. At the beginning of the seventies private consumption attracted the weightiest support, while only modest funds were allocated for investment. But the spectacular rise of raw material prices put an end to this approach. A rapid increase in exports became the overriding aim. To attain it, investment activity had to be reinforced once again, and consumption fell back to the bottom in the list of priorities.

In terms of the economy as a whole, the post-1970 phase has been distinguished by remarkably high and steady growth. The bottle-necks and disproportions of 1969 and 1970 were soon overcome. From 1972 on, the efforts to bring about a consolidation were clearly seen to bear fruit. Fluctuations of output were reduced, and the supply of materials and semi-manufactures improved. During the five-year period 1971 to 1975 the GDR was able to fulfil most of the quantitative targets set by the plan. In many spheres the development turned out to be even more favourable than the economic authorities could have expected during the drafting stage of the plan. The 'produced national income', i.e. the part of the national income supplied by the productive sectors, grew at an average annual rate of 5.5 per cent during the five-year period, while the standard of living of the population rose perceptibly, largely as a result of an increase in old age and disablement pensions, which had been wretchedly low.

A renewed change in the conditions of growth became apparent at the beginning of the five-year period 1976 to 1980. Plan targets have been set more cautiously, and these lower figures have barely been attained. Even so, with an industrial growth rate of 5 to 6 per cent, the economic development of the GDR, whether considered on its own or in the context of international comparisons, continues to be worthy of note.

Standards of living and levels of productivity in the GDR are still below those achieved in the Federal Republic. In fact, the gap in the material standard of living, which at the beginning of the sixties was about 25 to 30 per cent, has further widened in the meantime and is not likely to be reduced in the foreseeable future.

As regards labour productivity, too, the gap has widened since 1963, when Walter Ulbricht estimated that the GDR was lagging behind the Federal Republic by 25 per cent on average. Lack of efficiency in utilising the productive resources constitutes the most important problem facing the GDR economy:

1   In spite of the shortage of labour, the use of manpower is in

16

many cases inefficient. Subsidiary production processes suffer generally from poor organisation, and the process of production as a whole is subject to extreme discontinuity owing to frequent breakdowns and spells of waiting time.

2   A similar failure to enforce rationalisation applies to capital assets. Highly productive plants are not fully utilised, there is hesitation in scrapping obsolete plant, and the preparation and execution of investment projects proceeds at a very slow pace.

3   The consumption of raw materials and fuel is comparatively high. The enterprises are frequently given no incentives for thrift. Altogether, production in the GDR involves relatively high inputs of labour, capital and materials. This unsatisfactory state of affairs has for a long time been the chief concern of the economic policy makers, but has so far been tackled with limited success.

1.2   Factors of production

1.2.1   Territory and mineral wealth

With an area of 108,178 sq.km., the state territory of the GDR is less than half that of the Federal Republic (248,577 sq.km.). In 1952, the five states (*Länder*) of the SZ (Mecklenburg, Brandenburg, Thuringia, Sachsen-Anhalt and Saxony were newly divided into 14 areas (*Bezirke*), or 15 if (East) Berlin is included. This led to the merging of economic regions that were formerly under separate administrations. Thus the Lower Lusation brown coal region was now entirely within the Cottbus area. The number of rural districts (*Landkreise*) was increased, reducing the number of communes per rural district to an average figure of 50. In 1975 there were 7634 communes in 28 urban and 191 rural districts.

Moving from the southern to the northern areas, there is a marked decline in the rate of industrialisation, reflecting the traditionally dominant role of agriculture in the north and the concentration of mineral deposits in the south. Even though in the Neubrandenburg, Schwerin and Rostock areas new industries were started and old-established ones — notably fisheries and shipbuilding in the Rostock area, food processing, mechanical engineering and vehicle building in all three — were expanded, the three northern areas, covering 25 per cent of the territory of the GDR, still provide no more than 7 per cent of its industrial production. In contrast, the southern areas of Dresden, Halle,

Figure 4   Location of major raw material deposits in the GDR

18

Karl-Marx-Stadt and Leipzig, containing the greatest concentrations of industry, while equal in size to the three northern areas, supply half the country's gross industrial production.

The industrially less developed regions are also characterised by lower population densities, sparser settlements and weaker links of economic interdependence, both regional and sectoral. These regions comprise the three northern areas as well as the northern parts of the Magdeburg and Potsdam areas.

Viewed in terms of agricultural employment, three zones can be distinguished: the agricultural employment ratio, i.e. the percentage of the economically active population working in agriculture, is highest in the Neubrandenburg and Schwerin areas, with figures respectively of 29 and 23 per cent. Next come Frankfurt, Magdeburg, Potsdam and Rostock, with ratios varying between 15 and 17 per cent. Finally there are the strongly industrialised Saxon areas (Dresden, Karl-Marx-Stadt and Leipzig) as well as the Halle, Gera and Suhl areas, where the agricultural employment ratio is 10 per cent or less.

Among mineral deposits, brown coal is the most important, supplying as it does nearly the whole domestically produced power output (94 per cent in 1975). Total profitably workable deposits are estimated at 24,000 million tonnes. This is less than 2 per cent of the world reserves; nevertheless the GDR, with its output of 247 million tonnes in 1975 — 30 per cent of world production — is the world's leading brown coal mining country. Before the second world war, the chief brown coal regions were situated west of the Elbe. In the early 1950s production was launched east of the Elbe, centring on the Cottbus area.

No substantial increases in production are envisaged until 1980. To maintain the present production figures it is necessary to prepare or establish new open cast mines and to extend existing ones, affecting altogether 14 sites. One of them is the Jänschwalde deposit, north-west of Cottbus (commissioned in 1976), which is to be the country's biggest open cast brown coal mine. Less favourable conditions at the new sites (increased proportions of spoil, poorer quality of the mined coal) entail higher production costs.

The rapid increase in the production of natural gas (from 200 million cu.m. in 1969 to 8 billion cu.m. in 1974 and subsequent years) points to the success of the prospecting work carried out in co-operation with the USSR. The gas deposits are situated predominantly in the western border region near Salzwedel, Magdeburg area. The total reserves are estimated at 150 to 200 billion cu.m. about 10 per cent of them in the Federal Republic. With its calorific value of 3,000 to 3,500 Kcal/cu.m. this gas is far inferior to the North West European norm of 7,600 Kcal/cu.m.

Deposits of other mineral fuels are insignificant. Hard coal deposits have been estimated at 200 million tonnes. There are very few profitably workable seams; for some time, hard coal was mined only in the deposits of the Zwickau Depression, and output declined consistently from the 1960 figure of 2.7 million tonnes. In 1977 production was closed down altogether. Nor do the exiguous oil deposits enable domestic production to reach a significant level. It totals about 200,000 tonnes, so that the GDR is almost completely dependent on oil imports.

The GDR possesses substantial uranium deposits (ca. 60,000 tonnes confirmed reserves of U_3O_8). From 1947, prospecting and extraction was carried out by the Soviet Joint Stock Company (SAG) Wismut; since 1954 run as a Soviet-German Joint Stock Company of the same name. With an estimated annual output of 5,000 tonnes of U_3O_8, the GDR is one of the world's leading producers of uranium. But the output is claimed by the USSR.

Alkaline, especially potassium salts constitute the most important mineral deposits both for supplying the chemical industry and for export. As a producer of potash fertilisers, the GDR ranks fourth in the world (after the USSR, Canada and the Federal Republic), recording in 1975 an output of 3.0 million tonnes of K_2O. Just under half the output is exported to CMEA countries; total exports reached 2.3 million tonnes in 1975. Most of the potash is still mined in the Werra and Southern Harz regions. New deposits were recently opened up north of Magdeburg, where the largest potash enterprise of the GDR was established in 1973 at Zielitz.

Domestic iron ore deposits, concentrated in the Thuringian Forest and the Harz Massif, enable the GDR to cover no more than 0.3 per cent of its iron and steel requirements. In 1975, the output was 2.2 million tonnes. There is also a shortage of ores of metals used in the making of alloy steels, with the exception of nickel ore, which is mined in the region adjoining the Ore Mountains.

As regards non-ferrous metals, too, only a small proportion of the GDR's requirements can be met from domestic sources. The GDR has deposits of copper, lead, zinc and tin ores. The most important copper deposits, chiefly in the form of copper slate, are in the Mansfeld and Sangerhausen Depressions, south-east of the Harz, with ores containing up to 3 per cent of copper. In the last few years, the Mansfeld Depression was superseded as the main production centre by the Sangerhausen Depression. Profitably workable deposits of lead and zinc ores (with metal contents varying from 2 to 5 per cent) are found in the Freiberg region; minor quantities of the same ores accompany the Mansfeld copper slate. Annual output of these ores is about 300,000 tonnes, and there are no prospects of raising this figure in the near future. Tin ores are mined at Altenberg in the Eastern Ore Mountains; annual output is estimated at about 1,000 tonnes.

1.2.2   Population

In spite of heavy losses incurred during the war, the population of the central regions of Germany was higher in 1946 (18.1 million) than it had been in 1939 (16.7 million), owing to the influx of refugees expelled from the German Eastern territories. The population reached a peak in 1948, when the Soviet Zone, inclusive of East Berlin, numbered 19.1 million inhabitants. After that, the numbers were being constantly depleted to a low of 17.1 million in 1961. By that time 2.6 million persons, most of them young, had left the GDR. They and their children have left a gap in the population structure of the GDR. Up to the early seventies, the population figure remained virtually stationary; since then, there has been a further decline (to 16.8 million in 1975). The latter changes only reflected the natural population movement, dependent on age structure, expectation of life and reproductive behaviour.

1.2.2.1   Demographic development and age structure   Basically, the structure of the age pyramid is much alike in both parts of Germany. The *age structure* bears the marks of two world wars and the economic slump at the beginning of the 1930s. The two wars decimated a number of age groups, while the slump as well as the wars caused falls in the number of births. These troughs have reproduced themselves periodically in an attenuated form to this day. To some extent, the falling birth rate reflected also the general tendency towards small families which had first become noticeable in the inter-war period. This trend was reinforced after 1972 by improved methods of contraception, the legalisation of abortion and the issue of contraceptives free of charge. This development has led to anomalies in the age structure, such as the fact that in the GDR today the survivors of the age group born in 1905 are exactly equal in number to those born in 1975.

The *birth rate* (live births per 1,000 inhabitants) was 10.8 in 1975, like that of the Federal Republic (9.7) one of the lowest in the world. Thus, after a steep rise, with a peak of 17.6 in 1963, it reverted to the low of 1946. Social policy measures were taken to counter this trend: maternity leave was extended twice and is now 26 weeks, maternity allowances were increased, and after the birth of their second and any subsequent child, working mothers are granted paid leave for a year. These measures, and in particular the 'baby year' appear to have achieved their purpose as indicated by the recent rise of the birth rate (to 13.3 in 1977).

The dependence of fertility on age has changed. Since 1954, the age

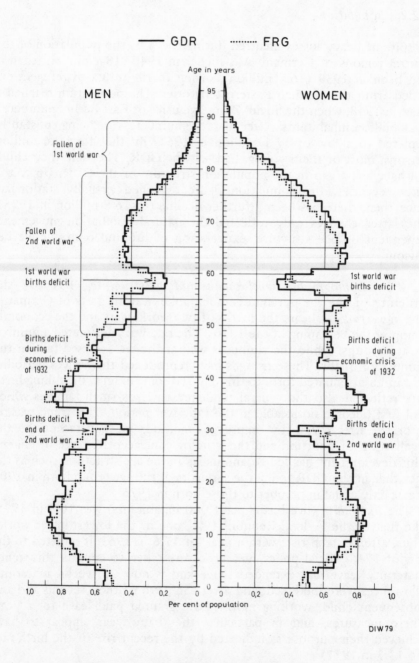

Figure 5 Age structure of the residential population on 31.12.1975

22

of women showing the highest fertility rate has dropped by two years, from 22 and 23 years to 20 and 21 years. This reflects the lower average age at first marriage, which has decreased since 1953 for women from 23.5 to 21.3, and for men from 25.2 to 23.1 years. The marriage rate (number of marriages per 1,000 inhabitants) has shown marked fluctuations. After a first peak of 11.7 in 1950 and a second peak of 9.9 in 1961, the number of marriages declined in keeping with the post-war fall in births and the smaller numbers reaching marriageable age. After 1967, the marriage rate began to pick up again. The number of divorces has increased in both parts of Germany, but the divorce rate (per 1,000 inhabitants) in the GDR is 50 per cent above that in the Federal Republic and is one of the highest in the world. Year by year more marriages are terminated in the GDR (by death or divorce) than are newly started.

By 1950 the high mortality of the first post-war years had reverted to the 1938 level of 11.5 per 1,000 inhabitants. Owing to the unfavourable age structure, the death rate is higher in the GDR than in the Federal Republic (14.2 as against 12.1). Infant mortality, on the other hand (number of deaths in the first year of life per 1,000 live births),

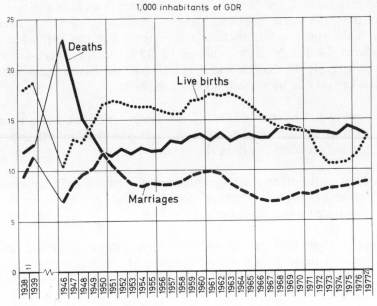

1) Without war deaths. – 2) Provisional data.
Sources: Statistisches Jahrbuch der DDR 1978

DIW79

Figure 6   Marriages, live births and deaths

23

has been reduced from 72 in 1950 to the present figure of 16, as compared with 20 in the Federal Republic. At the same time the *expectation of life* (average life span of those surviving the first year of life) has risen substantially. In the period 1952 to 1974, the figure rose for women from 71 to 74 years, for men from 67 to 69 years (as compared with 75 years for women, 69 years for men in the Federal Republic in 1972/74).

Allowing for emigration, the population is expected to decline by 1990 from the 1975 figure of 16.8 million to 16.0 million. The greatest declines are expected for children (by 675,000) and persons of pensionable age (by 900,000), while the population of working age is expected to increase (by 760,000), as numerically strong age groups move up and numerically weaker age groups retire from active life. The increase will be most pronounced up to 1980, then continue at a lower rate until 1985, when it is expected to stop. A similar development can be foreseen for the Federal Republic (cf. Appendix, table 2).

1.2.2.2 Distribution of population and structure of settlement The average *population density* (inhabitants per square kilometre) of the GDR was 155 in 1975, far below the figure of 249 recorded in the Federal Republic. The spatial distribution of the population is still largely determined by the pre-war structure: lower densities in the agricultural northern regions, higher densities in the industrialised south. Thus the population densities registered in the individual areas vary from 58 for Neubrandenburg to 329 for Karl-Marx-Stadt (cf. Appendix, table 5). Nevertheless, the disparities have been somewhat reduced since 1939 by certain population shifts:

— Owing to the availability of accommodation, and as a result of official measures, the incoming refugees and expelled persons settled predominantly in the north.[1]

— The establishment of new industrial centres counteracted the tendency towards further concentration in the most densely populated southern regions.

The reconstruction period in the 1950s witnessed sizable *internal migrations* accompanying the establishment of important new industrial capacities (Eisenhüttenstadt, Hoyerswerda, Schwedt, Halle-Neustadt)

---

1 From 1939 to 1946, the population increased in the territory of the Schwerin area by 60 per cent, in the Rostock and Neubrandenburg areas by 42 per cent, as compared with the GDR average of 7.8 per cent.

24

together with new housing. Later on these movements abated. Permanent population gains as a result of such migrations have been registered, apart from Berlin, only by the Cottbus and Frankfurt areas, owing to the establishment respectively of the 'Schwarze Pumpe' brown coal combine and the Eisenhüttenkombinat Ost.

Changes of domicile, across district boundaries, registered annually per 1,000 inhabitants dropped from 47 in 1953 to 17 in 1974. Compared with the Federal Republic, where the corresponding figure in 1974 was 53, regional mobility in the GDR is low at present. This is partly because the housing shortage makes it difficult for people to change their place of work.

Population trends in the areas are thus determined in the main by *natural demographic development*. Here, too, there are regional differences. Owing to lower birth rates and a relatively unfavourable age structure, a significant decline of the population is expected by 1990 in the Berlin, Dresden, Leipzig, Karl-Marx-Stadt and Gera areas. A smaller decline, possibly even a slight increase, is likely to result in the Neubrandenburg, Rostock, Schwerin, Frankfurt, Erfurt and Cottbus areas.

The settlement pattern in the GDR is severely fragmented. The process of urbanisation is slower than in the Federal Republic: in 1950, for example, communes with up to 2,000 inhabitants accounted, in both parts of Germany, for 29 per cent of the population. By 1975 this figure had dropped to 8.2 per cent in the Federal Republic, but only to 24.5 per cent in the GDR. Whereas in the Federal Republic a shift of population away from the large towns and into intermediate and local centres (with populations between 2,000 and 20,000) has been observed in recent years, in the GDR it is still the communes with populations in excess of 20,000 which attract internal migrants. Apart from the fragmentation into small units of settlement, the less industrialised regions are characterised by comparatively large distances between towns and the nearest villages and by the small number of major urban centres with supra-regional functions.

The present concept of settlement planning appears to be guided by the intention to

a) press on with the development of the large cities (in particular the area capitals) into supra-regional centres, and of the major medium-sized towns (with populations from 50,000 to 10,000) into regional centres, while at the same time improving the network of communications so as to give the surrounding territories better access to the material and cultural facilities offered by the towns;

25

b) to promote co-operation between small communes – predominantly in the shape of federations of communes fostering co-operation between the local administrations of communes in each district – especially with a view to the joint utilisation of various facilities (e.g. in the execution of repairs and provision of services).

1.2.3 Employment

In the SZ as in West Germany, war damage and dismantling brought unemployment in their wake. As reconstruction got into its stride and the drain of migrants to the West continued, the situation changed. Since the mid-fifties labour in the GDR has been in short supply. The number of gainfully employed persons[1] declined in step with the number of people of working age (which in the period 1955-60 dropped by 13 per cent). In 1961, the decline of the labour force was stopped by the erection of the Berlin Wall. In the following period the number of gainfully employed even showed a slight increase (cf. Appendix, table 6), even though the number of people of working age continued to decrease until the end of the sixties. From 1965 to 1975, the number of gainfully employed persons rose on average by 0.5 per cent annually,[2] reaching in 1975 the figure of 9 million or 53 per cent of the total population, one of the highest activity rates in the world (compared with 45 per cent in the Federal Republic).

This development is due above all to the growing number of women taking up employment. From 1965 to 1975, the number of gainfully employed women rose on average by 1 per cent annually, although during the same period the number of women of working age declined. In 1975, 79 per cent of all women of working age and women of retirement age still at work were gainfully employed (as compared with 64 per cent in 1960). This figure suggests that nearly all women in the relevant age groups are going out to work, with the exception of school pupils, students, mothers of small children and mothers with many children. As more women were taking up employment, the number of part-time workers increased. Today one working woman in three is in part-time employment.

1 For the sake of comparability with West Germany, we have included here groups of employed persons omitted in the official statistics of the GDR, i.e. members of the People's Army, the police and other paramilitary and social organisations, persons employed in arms factories and penal institutions as well as members of families helping on farms.
2 Since the number of women working part-time doubled from 1960 to 1970 and GDR statistics give no details about overtime working, no statement can be made about the labour volume, the total number of hours worked.

26

Chart 1
Percentage share of women in economically active population

Economic sector	1960	1975
Industry	38	42
Construction	9	14
Agriculture	47	41
Transport, posts, telecommunications	32	38
Trade	65	71
Services	56	62
Economy as a whole	43	47

Sources: Tables 6 and 7

Most of the working women in the GDR are employed in occupations in which women have traditionally played an important part, that is in health services, social welfare, education, administration and the distributive trade. These are the spheres that have benefited from the increase in female employment (cf. Appendix, table 7). The decline in agriculture is due to the fact that the help of relatives on the land is less important than in the past. The increase of female labour in the building industry seems to have been made possible by technological change; in this industry women account for 14 per cent of the labour force, an unusually high proportion (as compared with 7 per cent in the Federal Republic).

From 1965 to 1975, the number of employed women rose by 410,000, that of men only by 60,000. In the latter year, gainfully employed men represented over 89 per cent of all men of working age plus pensioners continuing to work. The figure was even higher a few years ago and will continue to fall owing to the progressive intensification of education and vocational training.

The labour situation is likely to remain tight, even though numerically strong age groups are due to attain working age in the next few years. The demand for labour is constantly growing. In addition, the number of people of pensionable age continuing to work will decline in step with the age groups concerned. At present over 650,000 old age pensioners are still working. Altogether, the number of gainfully employed persons is likely to rise from

1976 to 1980 by 285,000,
1981 to 1985 by 215,000,
1986 to 1990 by   40,000.

This expansion of employment will predominantly, in the eighties

27

even exclusively, affect the male population, thus reversing the previous trend.

It appears that there is no intention to increase the employment of foreign workers, believed to number currently about 50,000 (mostly Poles, Hungarians and Vietnamese). Many of them, however, are in the GDR only for purposes of training (cf. p.275).

The distribution of employment among the various branches of the economy generally follows the contribution made by each to the total effort of the economy. In 1975 industry, the largest employer, accounted for 41 per cent of the labour force, followed by the services sector with 24 per cent and agriculture with the comparatively high proportion of 11 per cent.

Since 1960, the *structure of the labour force* has undergone considerable changes. The number of persons employed in the primary sector (agriculture, mining) declined, while those in the secondary sector (processing industries, building industry) and above all in the tertiary sector (distribution, services) increased. These structural changes are in line with the typical tendencies of growing industrial societies. The decline of employment in agriculture is due to a number of reasons: advances in mechanisation and efficient large-scale production made it possible to release manpower. In addition the GDR had to cope with the problem of flight from the land. The industrial labour force increased only slightly. Growth of production was achieved mainly by improved productivity. In the service sector the scope for raising productivity is much narrower, hence its need for more manpower.

As in other countries, the number of self-employed persons and unpaid family workers has dropped, while employed persons increased

Chart 2

Economically active persons by economic sector

	1960	1975	1960	1975
	Mill. persons		%	
Industry	3.6	3.7	42	41
Construction	0.5	0.7	6	7
Agriculture	1.5	1.0	17	11
Transport, posts, telecommunications	0.6	0.6	6	7
Trade	0.9	0.9	11	10
Services	1.5	2.1	18	24
All sectors	8.6	9.0	100	100

Source: Table 6

Chart 3
Economically active persons by socio-economic group

	Percentage of economically active population			Numerical change in per cent
	1960	1965	1975	1965-1975
Employed persons	81	83	89	+ 13.1
Members of co-operatives	10	13	9	− 26.2
Self-employed	5	3	2	− 42.3
Unpaid family workers	4	1	*	− 54.5
Economically active population	100	100	100	+ 5.5

Source: Table 8   *No data available

their share of the economically active population. One special feature that is typical of the *socio-economic structure* of the GDR is the high proportion of members of co-operatives. Actually, co-operative employment has steadily declined since the mid-sixties owing to many members of agricultural producer co-operatives reaching pensionable age and to the conversion in 1972 of artisan producer co-operatives engaged in industrial production into publicly owned enterprises. The number of self-employed was also drastically reduced by measures of socialisation. At first they were subjected to stricter supervision by the conclusion of co-operation treaties with socialist enterprises or through direct partnership with the state. In 1972, this policy led to the final nationalisation of private industrial and building enterprises.

Levels of training of the labour force were consistently raised in the GDR. According to the 1971 census, half the population, that is to say two thirds of the economically active, had completed some vocational training. The proportion is even higher for the younger age groups. No less than 80 per cent of those aged between 25 and 30 had vocational training. For women these figures continue to be substantially below those for men, but in the younger age groups the differences are less marked. The number of graduates of institutions of higher education and of technical colleges registered a truly dramatic rise, trebling from 1960 to 1975. This increase was all the more necessary in order to compensate for the large numbers of academically trained personnel who had left the GDR up to 1961.

Working hours have been reduced in the GDR on several occasions since 1960. The 45-hour week, however, was not made law until 1966. In the same year the five-day week was introduced, to begin with for every second week, from 1967 permanently. At first, the loss of Saturday's work was made up by extra hours during the rest of the week. When that arrangement was cancelled, the working week came

29

Chart 4
Distribution of vocational qualifications among the
GDR population 1971 (in per cent)

	Population over 16 years of age	of which		
		25 to 29 years	55 to 59 years	women
Total	100	100	100	100
with vocational training	50.1	79.9	44.5	35.9
higher education	2.7	6.0	1.3	1.3
vocational college education	4.9	10.0	3.1	3.1
foremen	3.7	3.2	5.1	0.6
skilled worker's certificate	38.8	60.8	35.0	30.9
no vocational training	49.9	20.1	56.5	64.1

Source: Authors' collectise, 'Zur Reproduktion des Qualifikationsniveaus der Werktätigen und der Bildungsfonds', Forschungsberichte des Zentralinstituts für Wirtschaftswissenschaften der Akademie der Wissenschaften der DDR, nr.5, East Berlin, 1973, pp 21 ff.

down to 43¾ hours for all employed persons. Special arrangements were made for shift workers, who are to work 42 hours under the two-shift system, or 40 hours when working three or more shifts. Working mothers with two or more children are also to work a 40-hour week. These arrangements have been in force since 1 May 1977.

The gradual reduction of working hours was bound to aggravate the labour shortage. In these circumstances, an economic policy bent on rapid growth is compelled to accelerate the increase in labour productivity through the intensified use of capital resources, that is by modernising and expanding capital assets.

1.2.4 Capital assets

Where, as in the GDR, the economy is controlled and supervised by the state, in order to ensure optimum results an accurate knowledge of the size and efficiency of available productive capacities is vital for the process of decision making if optimum results are to be obtained. Up to the early 1960s a realistic assessment of the productive potential was made impossible by a lack of uniform yardsticks in evaluating capital assets.[1] In consequence, the planners held mistaken notions concerning

1 The term 'capital assets' here denotes the sum total of buildings and such equipment (machinery, laboratory installations, etc.) as has a useful life of over a year and a value, when new, of over 500 Marks.

At the end of the second world war, all existing machinery and equipment was entered in the books at the fixed prices of 1944, while all buildings were entered at 60 per cent above the 1913 value. Goods procured between 1948 and 1953 were entered at the prices ruling at the material time. The book value of assets established after 1953 corresponds to the fixed prices introduced at the time.

the profitability of production plants, and this led to wrong investment decisions.

In the course of the economic reforms a revaluation of the gross capital assets of publicly owned industrial enterprises, reflecting the state of assets on 30 June 1963, was carried out on the basis of 1962 replacement prices. (Private, semi-state and co-operative industrial enterprises were revalued some time later). The value resulting for the gross capital assets of GDR industry as a whole amounted to 104,000 million Marks, of which 47,000 million Marks was accounted for by buildings and 58,000 million Marks by plant and equipment. The capital assets of other branches of the economy were revalued in the subsequent years.

1.2.4.1 Capital assets of the various sectors The size of capital assets is established annually in the GDR by adding up the book values of all economic units. In 1975, the aggregate gross capital assets of the GDR totalled 577,000 million Marks at 1962 prices. The 'producing' sectors[1] accounted for 367,000 million Marks, or 64 per cent of the total. The share of the non-productive sectors — above all infrastructure (roads, housing, state administration, cultural and social institutions) — was about 36 per cent, substantially below the corresponding figure in the Federal Republic, where the non-productive sectors are represented by 58 per cent of the sum total of capital assets. Within the sphere of material production, the *processing industries* held the greatest share of capital assets with 231,000 million Marks, followed by *transport, posts and telecommunications* with 56,000 million Marks, *agriculture* 48,000 million Marks, *internal trade* 19,000 million Marks, *building industry* 11,000 million Marks, other branches of material production 2,000 million Marks.

Data specifying the relative shares of buildings and equipment in the total of capital assets are available only for the 'producing' sectors. The immovable assets of these sectors, totalling 176,000 million Marks in 1975, are concentrated in the main on the 'processing branches'[2] with 102,000 million Marks; agriculture — 33,000 million Marks; transport, posts and telecommunications — 24,000 million Marks. The share of buildings in the total of capital assets was highest for agriculture with 69, and internal trade with 62 per cent, as compared with the average

1 According to the 'Accounting System of Material Product Balances' used by the GDR as by all CMEA countries, the producing sectors (or sphere of material production) comprise industry, agriculture, construction, transport and trade.
2 The term 'Verarbeitendes Gewerbe' here and in table 9 includes mining and the power industry as well as the processing industries and trades to which the term is generally confined in GDR statistics (see for instance tables 12 and 13 and section 3.3, p.91).

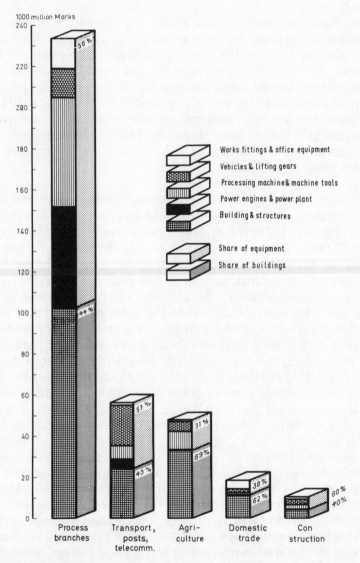

1000 million Marks

Legend:
- Works fittings & office equipment
- Vehicles & lifting gears
- Processing machine & machine tools
- Power engines & power plant
- Building & structures
- Share of equipment
- Share of buildings

Process branches: 56%, 44%
Transport, posts, telecomm.: 57%, 43%
Agriculture: 31%, 69%
Domestic trade: 38%, 62%
Construction: 60%, 40%

*Industry (including power and mining), other producing branches and productive artisan trades (without building trades).

DIW 79

Figure 7   Capital assets of the producing sectors by type of capital goods in 1974 (in bn. Marks and in per cent)

32

figure of 48 per cent. The share of equipment was highest in the building industry with 60 per cent, vehicles, lifting and haulage gear alone accounting for 25 per cent of total assets, a massive share surpassed only by the transport sector where this particular class of capital goods represents 35 per cent of total assets.

In industry, equipment made up 56 per cent of capital assets, with two major groups — processing machines, including machine tools, and power engines and power plant — each accounting for well over 20 per cent; vehicles plus lifting and haulage gear, and works fittings plus office equipment (including measuring and testing apparatus) contributed 6 per cent each.

In agriculture, with its high share of immovable assets, machines made up 19 per cent and vehicles 10 per cent of the total.

An analysis of the development of capital assets shows that the assets of the productive sectors more than doubled during the period 1960 to 1975 (cf. Appendix, table 9). Capital assets of the remaining sectors — in the main infrastructure (roads, waterways, state administration, hospitals, schools) as well as the housing stock — increased during the same period at a slower rate (by 29 per cent).

In terms of capital growth, the leading sectors were construction and the 'processing branches'. Within industry, the most striking increases were recorded by electrical engineering plus electronics plus instrument building (257 per cent), mechanical engineering plus vehicle construction (174 per cent), and the chemical industry (165 per cent) (cf. Appendix, table 11). The capital expansion of the industries closer to the consumer, on the other hand, was below average.

1.2.4.2 Comparison with the Federal Republic A comparison of capital assets between the two German states is difficult, because there is no simple common denominator for the differing price levels and price structures of the two states, and because the various sectors of the economy are defined and delimited in different ways. The calculation was made for the GDR at 1962 prices, for the Federal Republic at 1970 prices, in each case in the official currency of the state concerned.

Nearly two-thirds of the capital assets of the GDR, as recorded in 1975, belong to the 'producing sector', of which industry accounts for 40 per cent, transport, posts and telecommunications for 10 per cent, agriculture and forestry for 8 per cent, trade for 3 and the building industry for 2 per cent.

A comparison with the capital structure of the Federal Republic reveals marked divergencies: in West Germany the share of the producing sector accounted for only 42 per cent of total gross capital assets, which in 1975 at 1970 prices were recorded as 3,310,000 million DM. (It must be borne in mind, however, that a comparison with the GDR

Chart 5
Gross capital assets in the GDR and FRG
(structure by economic sector in per cent)

Sector	GDR[5]		FRG[6]	
	1965	1975	1965[7]	1975[8]
Producing sector[1]	55.4	63.6	43.1	42.1
Industry[2]	33.7	40.0	24.2	24.2
Construction	1.2	1.8	1.5	1.5
Agriculture	7.2	8.3	4.5	3.5
Transport, posts and tele-communications	10.2	9.8	7.9	7.4
Trade[3]	2.9	3.2	5.0	5.5
Services[4]	44.6	36.4	56.9	57.9
Total	100.0	100.0	100.0	100.0

1 GDR: including 'other producing branches', with shares of 0.2 and 0.5 per cent respectively in the two years.
2 Including power, mining and water resources, as well as in the GDR producing artisan trades (without building trades), and in the FRG processing trades.
3 GDR: domestic trade (including catering); FRG: including foreign trade enterprises, not including catering.
4 GDR: finance, banking, insurance; services; health and social affairs; education science and learning, art and culture; the state; social organisations; housing.
5 Average capital stock at 1962 prices.
6 At 1970 prices.
7 Year end data.
8 Beginning of year.

Sources: GDR: Statistiches Jahrbuch der DDR (henceforth cited as GDR Statistical Yearbook) 1976, p.44. FRG: Bernd Görzig and Wolfgang Kirner, 'Anlageinvestitionen und Anlagevermogen in den Wirtschaftsbereichen der Bundesrepublik Deutschland. Ergebnisse einer Neuberechnung', Beiträge zur Strukturforschung des DIW, no.41, West Berlin 1976.

equivalent can be no more than an approximation owing to different methods of computation). The assets of industry and agriculture represent far lower shares of the total of capital assets than they do in the GDR. This disparity reflects the investment policy of the GDR, which for a long time has been bent on speeding the expansion of industry, while at the same time granting a high degree of priority to agriculture so as to lessen dependence on imported foodstuffs. The share of domestic trade in the GDR is only half the corresponding figure in the Federal Republic, which goes some way to explain the frequent dislocations occurring in the GDR distribution system. On the other hand, as regards transport, posts and telecommunications[1] as well as the building industry, the capital assets of these sectors are much the same in relative terms in both states.

Conversely, the relative weight of the non-productive sectors is much greater in West Germany, with 58 per cent of the total of capital assets, including 30 per cent for housing alone. The relatively low shares of housing and other sectors (services, state administration, private households and non-profit-making organisations) in the GDR indicate a marked neglect of investments in the infrastructure.

1.2.5 Scientific-technical progress

In a planned economy, where the enterprises are not in a position to base their decisions on market data and where the spur of domestic competition is missing, it is difficult to ensure technological progress. As a result of the labour shortage, the problem became acute at the beginning of the 1960s. There was no option but to press on with the substitution of capital for labour. Thus the labour shortage led to the need for rationalisation, the introduction of modified or new processes. Additional pressure in favour of innovation emanated from the foreign trade sector. Technological progress necessitates imports, in particular imports of technologically sophisticated goods from Western industrial countries, which must be paid for by exports. Thus it is the task of research and development to enable the GDR to offer internationally marketable products.

The *organisation of research* in the GDR differs from that of the Federal Republic in that the links between research and production are much weaker. According to a rough estimate, about one-fifth of the GDR research effort (measured by the numbers of research personnel) is concentrated in institutions operating above enterprise level, whereas in the Federal Republic no more than 5 per cent of the research effort (measured in terms of expenditure) is carried out outside company premises. In the GDR, three types of research institutions operate above enterprise level: the Academy of Sciences; universities and other schools of higher education and finally the Central Institutes attached to various Ministries. Some of these institutes, such as the Research Institute of the Ministry for the Chemical Industry, serve only one single industry, others, like the Central Institute for Manufacturing

---

1 In these statistics, the transport sector includes all means of transport, as well as other equipment and buildings owned by transport enterprises, but excludes the public transport links (roads, waterways, etc.), which are assigned to the state. Accordingly, the sector of road construction (far more highly developed in West Germany) affects the assets of the state rather than of transport.

Techniques, deal with problems shared by a number of industries. At the intermediate level, there are research institutes attached either to the Associations of Publicly Owned Enterprises (*Vereinigungen Volkseigener Betriebe* — VVB) or to the major combines which are subordinated directly to the competent Ministry. The VVB institutions include project-planning enterprises, development and design bureaux, technical bureaux (*Ingenieurbüros*) for rationalisation, and above all scientific-technical centres (WTZ) and institutes serving specialised industries, e.g. the Institute for Electrical Plant. The activities of the central and specialised industrial institutes range from research proper to the building at their own experimental and design workshops of fully developed prototypes ready for production runs.

To raise *R & D efficiency*, the following methods have been used, especially since 1967:

1   Linking research with production by means of the commissioning of research projects. By tying the financing of research, including research carried out at the universities and the Academy of Sciences, to such projects, research and development are to be guided towards meeting economic needs, and the industrial sponsors, with their immediate interest in practically useful results, will check on progress and prevent a dissipation of effort.

2   Co-operation of research, to ensure the most effective allocation of resources (e.g. optimum utilisation of high-grade instruments and equipment).

3   Concentration of research facilities on projects accorded priority by the Economic Plan. In 1976 30 per cent of total research capacity served such projects.

In the period 1967 to 1971, *research policy*, dominated by the slogan of 'overtaking without catching up', endeavoured to accomplish within the briefest possible time span pioneering achievements that would place the GDR in a position of international leadership in important fields. After the Eighth SED Congress and the replacement of Ulbricht by Honecker in the leadership in 1971, the high flung expectations gave way to a more cautious approach. The large-scale research centres planned by Ulbricht were left in abeyance and the rigorous principle of commissioned research was moderated: by making state funds available for fundamental research, a healthy balance between fundamental and applied research was to be restored.[1] Moreover, the Academy of Sciences was in 1972 entrusted with wider functions of planning and co-ordination of fundamental research. But fundamental research, too, is to take account of economic requirements. This involves research into problems of power supplies and raw materials, development of new man made materials, etc.

Looking at the organisational structure of research as a whole, it appears that there are two problematical phases in the research process: the specific formulation of research tasks by the enterprises, and the transfer of research results to production. The research policy pursued since 1971 centres on the endeavour to bring about an efficient organisation of the latter process:

1 Owing to the separation of research from production, it is often difficult to integrate the results of outside research in the technology of an enterprise.

A number of 'Academy-Industry-Establishments' (*Akademie-Industrie-Komplexe*), combining industrial and research capacities, have been set up experimentally in the fields of pharmaceutical research, technical microbiology and organic polymers.

2 Application of research requires improved planning of the preparatory measures (availability of materials, project planning capacities, etc.) which must precede the introduction of an innovation. Planning directives have been issued to this effect.

The most crucial problem, however, seems to be presented by the reluctance of the enterprises to accept innovations: plan indices in their present form are not flexible enough to allow changes in technology to show unmistakable results in the production records. It may even happen that changes in technology lead to a drop in gross output; more often they leave output stationary, so that the enterprises have no incentive to reorganise production. (Cf. section 2.5.4, pp

The *research potential* is indicated by the size of research staffs, which in 1974 numbered 155,000. Of this potential, 70 per cent is deployed in the research institutes of industry, 20 per cent in other productive sectors and 10 per cent in the Academy of Sciences. About

---

1 Between 1972 and 1974, the volume of commissioned research carried out by the Academy dropped from 45 to 31 per cent of the total. Budgetary expenditure on science and technology increased from 22 per cent in 1971 to 29 per cent in 1974.

half the research staffs are graduates of universities or equivalent institutions, or of vocational colleges.

The Science and Technology Section of the Five-Year Plan for the period 1976 to 1980 specifies tasks for which a total of 35,000 million Marks — that is 4.2 per cent of the national income — is earmarked, an increase of 10,000 million Marks over the preceding quinquennium.

2 Economic organisation and planning system

In a planned economy, decisions on needs and production and on the use and distribution of goods are taken in principle by the central political authorities. To be able to plan and issue directives, the central authorities must first ascertain the degree to which the supply of goods required by the economy is inadequate, that is, they must compare and assign priorities. The more highly developed an economy is, the more complex becomes the task of aggregating groups of goods and establishing utility criteria. Quantities and prices enter into the plans for the production, use and distribution of goods. The individual economic units influence the content of the plans at least insofar as they contribute to the preliminary stage of data gathering.

Thus, the crucial condition for the operational viability of central planning is the establishment of a set of serviceable control instruments, that is to say of a system of planning and directing the economy in which the interests of individuals and individual enterprises are not only taken care of but stimulated and brought into harmony with those of the central authorities. In order to resolve the conflicts of aim which are bound to arise, the system needs an apparatus that must be as effective in gathering, processing and disseminating information as in monitoring performance and initiating corrective action.

2.1 The concept of the new economic system

During the first two decades planning was in the main confined to the setting of quantitative production targets for the enterprises, which were in growing numbers taken over by the state.

After the failure of the Seven-Year Plan in 1962, the economic authorities of the GDR realised that their methods of planning, their pricing system and their economic organisation were no longer adequate:

a) quantitative planning ('tonnage ideology') neglected important economic factors and led to erroneous investment decisions;

b) distortions of the price structure encouraged waste of raw materials and delayed technological progress;[1]
c) over-centralisation of decisions inhibited interest, initiative and readiness to accept responsibility in the enterprises.

To overcome these deficiencies and generally improve the planning system, the Sixth SED Congress, meeting in mid-January 1963, decided to introduce the *New Economic System of Planning and Direction*.

The foremost aim of the New Economic System was the optimum combination of central state planning with the indirect guidance of enterprises through monetary measures ('economic levers'). To this end, the structure of the system of economic direction was modified, with limited powers of decision being vested in the intermediate economic authorities and in the enterprises themselves. New incentives were provided by enabling enterprises to make profits and, within limits, decide what use to make of them. It was hoped that this would raise the economic efficiency of all factors of production and bring about an improvement in the economic structure.

To enable a system of 'monetary steering' to operate effectively, it was essential to establish economically warrantable criteria of valuation. Accordingly, the reforms started by carrying out a *revaluation of the gross capital stock of industry* in mid-1963 on the basis of replacement prices applying in 1962. On the basis of the revaluation results, the depreciation rates, which previously had been too low, were increased in 1964. During the period 1964 to 1967 a comprehensive *reform of industrial prices*, designed to introduce prices 'reflecting costs', was carried out in three stages. Even though this reform succeeded in eliminating many of the serious price distortions, the GDR pricing system continued to suffer from major shortcomings, in particular the inadequate allowances made for the cost of capital.[2] In addition, the new prices still failed to take the scarcity of the production factors adequately into account, and, as in the past, prices did not respond with sufficient flexibility to changes in demand.

These reform measures were followed up by further steps intended to encourage local initiative in the enterprises. Thus, the system governing contracts between enterprises was revised, the methods of cost accounting were improved, and the banks were reorganised. Next, the batch of measures designed to ensure the indirect guidance of the enterprises ('system of economic levers') was further developed.

---

1 Raw materials, such as coal, gas, electric power, timber, iron, bricks, building blocks, were priced at only 45 to 60 per cent of effective production costs, the difference being made up by state subsidies.
2 Allowance was made for depreciation, but not for interest on capital.

Basic features of this system were:

a) The *principle of the autonomous raising of funds*, according to which investments were no longer financed by grants from budgetary means, as had been the case in the past, but rather out of local profits and depreciation allowances, supplemented by credits;

b) the *production fund levy*, fixed in principle at 6 per cent of the gross value of the fixed capital assets plus the working capital of each enterprise, a form of interest on capital, payable out of profits;

c) the *'fund-related price'*, which allowed for up to 18 per cent of the capital expenditure of an enterprise for a product to be considered in the calculation of the price. The procedure laid down in this respect was based on the capital requirements of the most successful enterprises;

d) *'price dynamisation'*, i.e. downward flexibility of prices, stipulating automatic price reductions in the event of reduced costs;

e) the *unified record of enterprise results*, which provided for export yields to be included in the calculation of profits;[1]

f) the *net profit levy*, i.e. payment to the state budget of a certain proportion of the net profit achieved by an enterprise. By varying the rate of the levy, the state was in a position to be discriminating in its support of specific branches of production.

In addition, a number of *enterprise funds* was set up, most of them fed out of profits. They included notably a bonus fund, amortisation fund, fund for science and technology, and a cultural-social fund. The enterprises also contributed to the *funds of the Associations of Publicly Owned Enterprises*.

It was clear that the success of the New Economic System would ultimately depend on the extent to which it was possible to attain its basic aim of persuading enterprise managements through the incentive of profit retention to take autonomous investment decisions, thus bringing about a more efficient utilisation of the factors of production.

1 Cf. chapter 6, p. 233.

41

2.2 Towards the termination of the New Economic System

In theory, the concept of the New Economic System seemed to be workable, yet, in practice there were considerable obstacles: enterprise managers had to unlearn old habits and adjust themselves to 'entrepreneurial thinking'; bank staff had to be retrained; ambiguities concerning the respective authority and competencies of publicly owned enterprises and Associations of Publicly Owned Enterprises led to conflicts. Moreover, some discrepancies and frictions arose from the uneven pace at which the various stages of the reforms were introduced. Nor were the instruments of the new policy free from faults. Thus, price dynamisation resulted in price increases instead of price reductions, and this in turn hampered the introduction of the fund-related prices. Yet without that type of price capital-intensive industries were not able to pay the full amount of the production fund levy.

Apart from such difficulties, a serious problem was presented by the question of economic structure. On the one hand, structural changes appeared to be called for, in order to mobilise technological progress and ensure faster growth. On the other hand, events showed that with their autonomous investment decisions the enterprises deviated widely from the aims set by the policy makers. The economic authorities of the GDR recognised that monetary measures alone were insufficient to ensure the development of the desired economic structure. To meet this situation, they evolved as early as 1968 the concept of 'structural key tasks', that is a priority programme for growth industries, which involved a return to mandatory quantitative plan indices. Thus an important field of production was placed outside the New Economic System.

The targets to be attained by means of the new concept were presented to the public with the propaganda slogan 'overtaking without catching up'. The high risks inherent in this policy were not at first appreciated. The planners had foreseen neither the consequences of downgrading the sectors not accorded priority nor the inadequate flexibility of the New Economic System in the face of unexpected contingencies. It was only in the autumn of 1970, when a widespread crisis paralysed growth and necessitated a scaling down of plan targets, that the economic authorities of the GDR decided to take drastic action.

At the fourteenth session of the SED Central Committee in December 1970, the new concepts were subjected to vehement criticism, and instead of continuing to develop the reform model, the Central Committee decided to introduce significant changes in the methods of planning and direction, which marked a return to a measure of centralisation: the scope of the enterprises and the powers of the Associations of Publicly Owned Enterprises and other intermediate-level authorities were curtailed, direct guidance by the state was reinforced, the number of mandatory plan indices was increased, quantitative commodity planning was extended, while some of the instruments of indirect guidance were dismantled or modified.

The following reasons are likely to have prompted the discontinuation of the reforms:

1   In 1969 and 1970, the very years in which the concept of the reforms was to have proved itself, a crisis of growth developed. Unfavourable weather conditions led to bottlenecks in the use of power and to dislocations in a number of sectors (transport, building industry, agriculture), which were further aggravated by the preference accorded to 'structural key tasks'. In the end, even the most favoured branches suffered from the neglect of the remainder. Many investment projects in particular were delayed, and plan targets were not attained. As a result the targets for the 1970 plan had to be lowered, and this in turn affected the projections of the Perspective Plan 1971 to 1975.

2   Growing discrepancies emerged between micro-economic aims and the structural pattern envisaged by the state, since the enterprises had been encouraged by the incentives of the New Economic System to operate on their own initiative. Thus, production was concentrated on the goods with the highest profit margins, which led to a substantial shrinkage in the range of goods on offer.

In the event, the SED could not tolerate the widening gap between micro-economic and macro-economic trends. Moreover it found it impossible to guide the ever more complex economic processes as accurately through monetary instruments as through the methods of physical planning. Thus the phase of the New Economic System had come to an end.

2.3   System of economic planning and direction

The following description of the structure and mode of functioning of the system of planning and directing applied to GDR industry presents in essence the planners' model, since we have no complete picture of the extent to which reality deviates from the model. Some of the discrepancies are openly criticised by the Party leadership and the

43

economic authorities or discussed in the economic press, others can only be deduced by theoretical considerations. The potential influence of political bodies, primarily the SED, on economic decision-making must always be borne in mind. The institutionally buttressed dominance exercised by the Party determines the course of events in the economy as in society. Numerous organisational linkages make sure that all decisions comply with Party directives. At the very top there is the personal identity of the economic and Party leadership; the Politburo issues mandatory decisions on questions of principle; at the bottom, the local Party branches (basic organisations) exercise functions of mobilisation and supervision.

2.3.1 Organisation of the economy

Central economic planning serves to guide the production of the economic units in a direction concordant with centrally determined aims, while avoiding disproportions in the economic system as a whole. Supply and demand are to be matched, the various factors of production are to be balanced in the best possible manner. Each of the tasks emerging from these basic aims, depending on its significance for the economy as a whole, is assigned to the appropriate level of the economic hierarchy.

The *Council of Ministers*, as the highest governing and administrative authority, supervises and co-ordinates the activities of all other central authorities. The members include all the top-level administrators: heads both of the traditional economic government departments and of the Industry Ministries, as well as the chiefs of certain offices and organisations (currently the State Planning Commission, the Office for Prices, the State Bank, the Committee of the Worker-Peasant Inspectorate). Although its economic-policy-making prerogatives were increased in 1963, the Council of Ministers continued in the subsequent years to confine itself in the main to the laying down of objectives in general terms. It was only as a result of the recentralisation measures of December 1970 that its field of action was substantially enlarged. In particular, the Council of Ministers

a)   adopted more decisions on matters of detail within the framework of centralised planning of the production of goods, especially in the investment sector and in respect of balance projections and consumer goods planning (see pp 80 ff, section 2.3.2 below);

b)   issued precise instructions and intervened directly in economic processes with the intention of removing bottlenecks, for instance in the supply of materials.

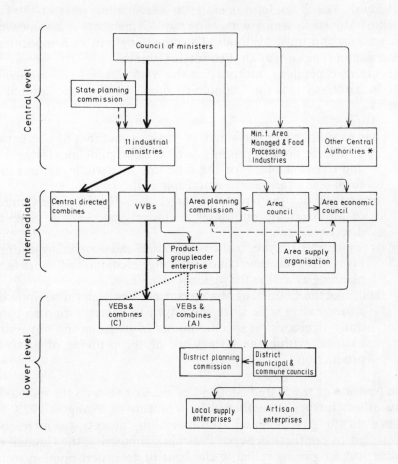

C = Centrally managed enterprises
A = Area-managed enterprises
——— Direct subordination
– – – Other relationships (cooperation, differentiation, coord.)
·········· Product group activities
  * Ministries for foreign trade; Trade and supply; Finance; Science and technologie;
   Management of materials; State secretariats for labour and wages; Vocational
   training; Offices for prices; Standardisation, weights and measures and commodity
   testing; Inventions and patents; Industrial design.

DIW 79

Figure 8   Schematic diagram of the structure of authority in industry

45

The real decision-making centre is the Praesidium of the Council of Ministers (currently numbering 16 members under the chairmanship of Willi Stoph). The Praesidium operates at a level above that of the full Council of Ministers, which with currently 42 members is a somewhat heterogeneous and unwieldy body. On the strength of its composition, the Praesidium functions as an 'Economic Cabinet'.

The supreme planning authority is the *State Planning Commission* which, in its capacity as the 'economic general staff' of the Council of Ministers,

a) has to submit to the Council of Ministers outlines of alternative structural policy options as well as basic guidelines for annual and five-year plans for the economy as a whole, set out in a form ready for governmental approval;

b) must flesh out the basic plan targets laid down by the Council of Ministers, by publishing tentative guide figures, planning directives, etc.;

c) is responsible for the final co-ordination and dovetailing of draft plans, for the dovetailing of long, medium and short-term planning as well as for regional planning;

d) and, like the Council of Ministers itself, has been called upon on an increasing scale since the return to centralisation to hand down decisions on specific points of planning and projecting balances within the framework of the planning of material production.

The position of the State Planning Commission vis-à-vis the industrial ministries was further strengthened by a Statute of 9 August 1973. Its influence on the governmental decision-making process was increased. In the event of conflicts between individual ministries, the Council of Ministers was to give its ruling in the light of an expert opinion to be submitted by the State Planning Commission; the Commission was to inform the Council of Ministers of any difficulties arising in the course of executing the plan. To some extent, the commission was vested with the power to issue direct instructions to ministries and other central state authorities.

Detailed direction of the development in the several industrial sectors is entrusted to 11 *Industrial Ministries* for

Coal and Power
Geology
Ore Mining, Metallurgy and Potash
Chemical Industry
Electrical Engineering and Electronics

Heavy Engineering and Plant Construction
General Mechanical Engineering, Agricultural Machinery and
   Vehicle Building
Machine Tool and Processing Machine Construction
Light Industry
Glass and Ceramics Industry
Area Managed Industries and Food Processing Industry.

The organisational structure of the industrial ministries follows both functional and sub-sectoral boundaries. Thus we find a Division for Supply and Co-operation and, at the Ministry for Light Industry, a Division for the Wood Processing Industry.

In each industrial sector it is incumbent on the responsible Ministry to support the State Planning Commission in the formulation of long-term structural projections. The return to centralisation has given the industrial ministries broad responsibilities:

1   Planning at the level of the industrial ministries has become more extensive and more detailed in respect of determining the production programme, allocating available resources and guiding scientific-technological development, even at the level of individual rationalisation projects.

2   The industrial ministries have been given a higher degree of direct responsibility for the efficient running of the economy according to plan. This has led to a plethora of directives and frequent interventions at operational level. Thus, the ministries may take action to regulate inter-enterprise co-operation in order to assure essential supplies from sub-contracting enterprises; they carry out plan checks (concerned, for instance, with quality control, or with the prompt application of research results in production); and they may take direct measures when acute problems arise.

Each industrial ministry is in charge of the specialised agencies (of the centrally managed sector) in its particular field of production, that is, the Associations of Publicly Owned Enterprises (VVBs) and the 'directly subordinated' major combines. The Ministry for the Chemical Industry, for instance, presides over the VVB Agrochemicals and Intermediate Products, VVB Plastics and Elastic Materials, VVB Pharmaceutical Industry, VVB Light Chemical Industry, VVB Chemical Plant and VVB Varnishes and Paints, as well as over the following 'directly subordinated' combines: Chemiefaserkombinat Schwarza 'Wilhelm Pieck', Chemiekombinat Bitterfeld, Petrolchemisches Kombinat Schwedt, Fotochemisches Kombinat Wolfen, Leuna Works, and Chemische Werke Buna.

The VVBs constitute the link between the central economic authorities and the production units. In dealing with the enterprises within their sphere of competence, the VVBs have the following functions:

a) co-ordinating efforts and projecting balances in the preparation of plans for the industrial sector concerned;
b) selective use of VVB funds in order to promote and guide processes of concentration and co-operation;
c) centralised management of tasks such as research and development (e.g. by means of technical bureaux for rationalisation), standardisation, specialisation, etc.

In 1963 the status of the VVBs was upgraded from that of purely administrative authorities to corporate bodies in their own right, subject to the 'principle of commercial accounting (*wirtschaftliche Rechnungsführing*)', which obliges them to account for their profits and losses. The functions discharged by the VVBs in dealing with their enterprises are comparable to those of the head offices of industrial corporations in the West. Yet, since the return to centralisation, their position within the structure of leadership has become once again that of executive organs of the industrial ministries.

A different form of economic direction is manifest in the *combines* (*Kombinate*), representing either horizontal or vertical amalgamations of enterprises. Combines are subordinated either directly to the industrial ministry concerned, or to a VVB or to an area authority. The combines subordinated directly to the ministries exercise functions similar to those of the VVBs (accountancy, pricing, etc.). Horizontal amalgamations are predominant in the food processing and consumer goods industries, in mechanical engineering and plant construction, and in the building industry. Vertical amalgamations (including associations for the utilisation of specific raw materials) predominate in the metallurgical and petrochemical industries.

The decisive advantage, which is likely to have prompted the establishment of combines, lies in the fact that through them an industry, especially one consisting of a small number of major enterprises, can be more firmly controlled than through the VVBs. In addition they promise the following advantages:

a) Lowering of costs through centralisation of certain tasks (e.g. procurement and marketing, sales organisation);

b) Lower investment cost per unit of output achieved by longer production runs at larger plants;

c) Acceleration of the pace of technological progress through the concentration of resources at the disposal of the combines.

As the establishment of combines continued to be promoted, the number of VVBs declined,[1] although there is no intention to replace them altogether. Indeed, the VVBs will continue to play a significant part in industries composed of large numbers of small or medium-sized enterprises, or enterprises under area management. Small and medium-sized enterprises are still considered to be most effective in coping with certain tasks. This applies to subcontracting enterprises supplying components and subassemblies, and to consumer goods enterprises producing small quantities of a narrow range of goods where standards of accuracy and quality are particularly exacting.

The 'production principle' of sectoral direction is supplemented by the 'territorial principle' of *regional direction*. Thus an area-managed sector co-exists with the centrally directed sector of industry. The area-managed publicly owned enterprises and combines are controlled by Area Economic Councils, which exercise functions similar to those of the VVBs, without however being subject to the principle of commercial accounting. They are responsible both to the Ministry for Area-managed Industries and the Food Industry[2] and to the Area Councils concerned.

Regional planning — or 'territorial planning' as it is called in the GDR — is carried out at area level. It involves:

a) optimum location of industry;

b) co-ordination of each enterprise's environmental requirements with regional resources. The requirements mostly concern technological infrastructure (communications, power, water supply, effluent disposal) as well as available manpower, and material supplies and social amenities for the labour force;

c) settlement planning.

The 'Act on Local Representative Assemblies and their Organs in the GDR', issued in July 1973, clarified the respective spheres of compe-

---

1 The number of VVBs dropped from about 85 at the end of 1967 to 52 in 1972. In 1974, the 40 combines directly subordinated to the industrial ministries employed more than one third of the industrial labour force.
2 About 20 per cent of the GDR's entire industrial production of finished goods and 60 per cent of all consumer goods are manufactured under the auspices of this Ministry.

tence of the *local authorities* (Area, District, Municipal and Commune Councils). *Supplies to the population* are to be improved through firmer economic planning and direction.

In addition to running the area-managed industrial enterprises, the *Area Council* is in charge of those supply enterprises (i.e. publicly owned and municipal enterprises, industrial enterprises making important contributions to local supplies) that operate across district boundaries, such as dairies, bakery combines, distributive trade enterprises. It is up to the area authorities to draw up detailed 'area supply plans', to formulate long-term planning concepts for the development of the services and repairs sector, and, in conjunction with the District Councils, to set in motion processes of concentration and specialisation.

The *District Council* is in charge of those industrial enterprises that are neither centrally- nor area-managed. They are enterprises of importance for local supplies as well as the Artisan Producer Co-operatives and private artisan enterprises concerned with services and repairs.

The *Municipal* and *Commune Councils* have little say in directing the economy. Their role is confined in the main to advising and supporting the District and Area authorities.

To assure the utilisation of all available resources in supplying the population, the responsible Councils are entitled to exact, within limits, compulsory deliveries from all centrally managed, private and co-operative enterprises within their territory, especially in matters concerning working and housing conditions, commuter traffic, further education and training, child welfare, school meals, health and social care, holiday and recuperation facilities, repairs and services.

The consistent direction of individual industries is promoted by *product groups*, which constitute a *lateral link* between *centrally-* and area-managed sectors. They are loose associations of enterprises producing similar goods or applying related technologies, no matter whether the enterprises are publicly owned or co-operative, centrally- or area-managed. The product groups are supervised by the relevant VVBs or combines of equivalent rank.[1] The VVBs select the enterprises to be included in a particular product group in co-operation with other VVBs and the Area Councils. Once a group has been established, the parent organisation picks a leader enterprise (*Leitbetrieb*), which it invests at its discretion with more or less far-reaching functions of planning and leadership. The product groups are active in the fields of specialisation,

---

1 Thus the Schmalkalden Tool Combine is in charge of nine product groups (e.g. product group for electrical tools), comprising the 370 tool-making enterprises of the GDR, distributed over nine different areas. Area-managed enterprises account for 43 per cent of the output.

standardisation, unification of product ranges as well as in the central-isation of tasks such as research and development, rationalisation, preparatory work for the introduction of electronic data processing, sales organisation and market research, planning and accounting at enterprise level. The product groups represent an instrument by means of which the parent organisation (VVB or combine) is in a position to influence the development also of area-managed enterprises.

2.3.2 Determination of plan targets

The plan targets for the economy as a whole are determined by means of a comprehensive forecasting system, combined with calculations of detailed interaction effects (input-output table). The structure of the plans and the legal force of the plan provisions vary according to the time scale, ranging from long-term to medium-term (five-year) and short-term (annual) periods.

Work on long-term planning (for the period 1975-1990) was started in 1972, apparently inspired by the 'Complex Programme' for the economic integration of the CMEA countries adopted the year before (see p. below). Until then, long-term planning had been confined to specialised spheres (e.g. generation and distribution of power, trans-port, erection of new housing). In contrast, the new long-term plan was more comprehensive and less authoritative:

1 The first stage (1976 to 1980) was to be equivalent to the Five-Year Plan in comprehensiveness, attention to detail, and binding character of the guide figures.

2 The second stage (1981 to 1985), however, is to be drafted on the basis of a simplified system of guide figures, which here point to broad trends rather than mandatory tasks.

3 The third stage (1986 to 1990) is to be confined to qualitative structural changes, guidelines for scientific-technical develop-ment and the broad aims of CMEA co-operation.

The chief responsibility for the elaboration of long-term plans rested with the State Planning Commission which, with the approval of the Council of Ministers formulated 'main trends and basic proportions of economic development', a document that determined the structural features of the plan. The first results were announced at the end of May 1973 at the ninth session of the SED Central Committee in the form of a list of growth rates envisaged up to 1990 for national income, goods production, labour productivity, monetary net proceeds and consumption fund. It was stated at the same time that rough guidelines had been established for a number of sectors, including that of investment policy, with due regard for specialisation and co-operation within the CMEA.

More recently, the CMEA countries decided to work out long-term demand forecasts (see p. 274).

In addition there is a large number of long-term programmes for particular spheres and different levels of authority in the GDR economy:

a) the housing construction programme up until 1990;
b) the long-term fuel and power programme;
c) the 'concept concerning the development of science and technology in the period up to 1990 for important sections of the economy, bearing in mind the demands on the development of the research and development potential', and the guidelines for the 'long-term development up to 1990 of fundamental scientific and mathematical research applicable to selected technological systems';
d) long-term concepts and programmes for various branches of the economy;
e) concepts of intensification and rationalisation formulated by the economic authorities at all levels.

With the exception of the housing programme (for which see page 129 below), no detailed information is available on the contents and timing of those plans.

As regards the medium-term (five-year) and annual plans, on the other hand, the timing of the various phases is laid down in detail. Two comprehensive new planning procedures were introduced to this end at the beginning of 1975. Earlier regulations were modified, so as to reduce the cost of planning and stabilise the methodology of planning. The new approach was formulated in the 'Order concerning the Code of Economic Planning 1976-1980' (Planning Code) and the 'Order concerning Outline Directives for the Annual Planning of Industrial and Building Enterprises and Combines' (Outline Directives). The Planning Code represents the first attempt to ensure continuity of planning methods over an entire quinquennium. Here the decisive aim is to raise the accuracy and uniformity of planning and accounting methods, and to treat each calendar year as a rigorously predetermined part of the five-year period.

The Outline Directives set out the procedures to be adopted in drawing up the yearly plan and arriving at precise definitions of annual targets. The continuity of planning methods throughout the five-year period is of great advantage, as it obviates the need for annual changes

52

in the accounting procedures of the enterprises and facilitates continuity of planning at enterprise level. In return, the enterprises must meet more exacting demands. They have to cope with an expanded system of index figures as well as with a multitude of separate computations, such as their figures on efficiency and labour productivity.

The following quantities relating to the economy as a whole provide the crucial data for a planning period:

a) rate of growth of the economy as a whole;
b) volume and structure of the total domestic product and its use for 'accumulation' (investment, both in new and existing projects, formation of stocks and reserves) and 'consumption' (individual and social);
c) the labour force and its distribution among the major economic sectors and individual branches of the economy and among the regions;
d) volume and structure of exports and imports (including major projects within the framework of CMEA co-operation).

As regards planning at enterprise level, the relevant index figures include the following:

total output
output of important products in terms of quantity and value
exports and imports
investment
labour productivity
size of work force
wages fund

The Five-Year Plan sets fewer index figures than the annual plan. In contrast to the plan for 1971-1975, the *Five-Year Plan 1976-1980* was elaborated in one single planning phase. The main effect of this change was to curtail the discussion phase and thus the opportunity of the individual enterprises to influence the final shape of the plan.

The planning procedure for the 1976-1980 Five-Year Plan began with the Council of Ministers issuing guide figures, which were incorporated in the Directive on the Five-Year Plan adopted at the Ninth SED Congress. On this basis the State Planning Commission produced a first draft, which was passed down successively for completion to the lower echelons. The completed draft plan made the same journey in reverse from level to level in the economic hierarchy until it reached the Council of Ministers for confirmation. The finalised plan then once again travelled down the various levels of authority, and the bulk target figures were broken down stage by stage, until the individual enterprises received their mandatory tasks. The Five-Year Plan, the Annual Economic Plan and the State Budget Plan, like all laws, acquire legal force with their enactment by the People's Chamber.

The 1976-1980 plan is the first five-year plan to have been rigorously divided into one-year periods, with all index figures broken down to enterprise level, excepting only minor enterprises integrated in the quinquennial planning of VVBs or territorial authorities.

In drafting the plan, account had to be taken of the results achieved during the various stages of CMEA planning co-ordination, which is concerned above all with the basic power and raw materials sector. A 'dovetailed plan for multilateral integration measures of the CMEA member states during the period 1976-1980' was adopted towards the end of June 1976, but has not been published. The measures envisaged include joint investments for the opening up of potential sources of raw materials, specialisation and project co-operation.

The formal *annual planning procedure* is illustrated in figure 9, where numbers indicate the following successive steps:

1   On the basis of the guidelines laid down by the Council of Ministers, the State Planning Commission determines the central propositions, the 'nucleus' of the plan, from which it derives the plan tasks to be assigned to the industrial ministries.[1]

2   The industrial ministries subdivide those tasks and allocate them to the various VVBs and combines.

3   On this basis the VVBs fix index figures for all enterprises within their sphere of competence.

4   After consultation and co-ordination with their contractual partners and local authorities (e.g. concerning power requirements), each publicly owned enterprise works out a draft plan for the year in accordance with the fixed index figures presented to them.

5-7 The enterprise draft plans are passed back stage by stage to the Council of Ministers. On the way, the VVBs co-ordinate and

1   The Ministry for Ore Mining, Metallurgy and Potash, for instance, is presented with bulk figures for (1) output of rolled steel products, including in particular transformer laminations, cold rolled strip steel and bright steel (in each case according to gauge, type and quality); (2) net profit levy payable to the state; (3) total investment funds.

54

balance the enterprise plans and harmonise them with the overall concept of the particular industry. The VVB plans are aggregated by the industrial ministries and theirs in turn by the State Planning Commission.

8-11 Having been confirmed by the Council of Ministers, the annual plan is again broken down successively, until it reaches the individual enterprise in the form of mandatory plan targets.

At each level, the superior authority must be kept informed of the progress of actual as compared with planned performance.

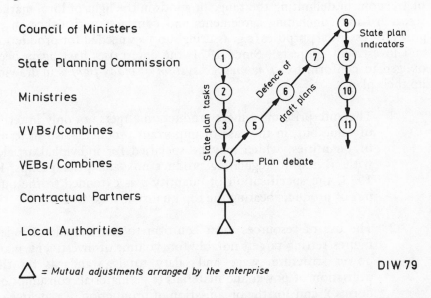

Figure 9   Schematic diagram of annual planning procedure

The setting of production targets is supplemented by '*balance determinations*'. 'Materials, equipment and consumer goods balance projections' set down supply and demand for those three categories. These balance projections account for a major proportion of domestic output and imported goods in terms of quantity and value at ex-factory prices (cf. pp 68 f. below), and thus provide binding decisions on production and marketing. The process of compiling such projections, 'balance determination' (*Bilanzierung*) in short, was decisively modified in 1971 with a view to turning it into a more effective instrument and corrective for planning decisions, under the heading 'balance determination as a major instrument of planning'. In keeping with the trend towards more direct controls in planning, the number of centrally balanced items has increased since 1971,[1] and the transfer of balance determination functions to intermediate-level authorities envisaged by the New Economic System has been reversed.

It is true that the planning process prescribed for the annual plans allows for repeated exchanges of information and corrective adjustments between planning authorities and economic units. It is supposed to be the function of the *publicly owned enterprise* to supplement central macro-planning by local micro-planning. Yet, according to current practice this amounts to no more than finding technological-economic solutions for the tasks handed down (with possibly a measure of freedom in delimiting the range of goods in the light of local market research) and concluding agreements and contracts with other enterprises for essential purposes (e.g. assuring supplies needed for production and investment projects). Since 1971, the enterprises have again been obliged to conform to a *fine-meshed system of index figures* in drawing up their plans:

1 The enterprise must meet production targets not only in terms of value but, in the case of important products, also in terms of quantities, which may be specified for individual articles with a view to regulating product mix and price groups. In 1973, the specification of quantity was extended to the output of products bearing the top quality marks 'Q' or '1'.

2 The use of resources must conform to a multitude of index figures setting targets notably for: volume of investment; manpower structure; wage and salary totals; standards for the utilisation of power and materials (e.g. 'materials consumption norms'), and for the organisation of production (e.g 'degree of mechanisation and automation').

Since central balance projections cannot cover all products important for supplies to the consumer, the economic authorities have since 1971 developed a *'Central Supply Plan'* which, as an integral part of the Annual Economic Plan, has legal force. In this plan, the goods covered by central balance projections are listed in quantities and units of value, and to some extent according to price groups; other products important for consumer supplies are included in the form of detailed 'product

1 At present 300 balance projections are determined at the level of the State Planning Commission, another 500 at the level of the industrial ministries. Taken together, they account for about 55 per cent of total industrial output.

56

catalogues', compiled by the competent VVBs and other balance-casting authorities in the administration of production and wholesale trade, and confirmed by the central authorities. The Central Supply Plan is the point of departure for the Area Supply Plans. Enterprise plans must give priority to all items listed in the Central Supply Plan.

Investments can only be launched after a protracted 'paper war':

1   For each proposed project the enterprise must submit comprehensive studies, on the basis of which the competent authority arrives at what is called the preliminary investment decision. Depending on the scale and importance of the project, the decision-making power may rest with authorities at any level: Council of Minister, State Planning Commission, industrial ministries, VVBs, Area Councils.

2   Together with its preliminary decision, the competent authority issues a large number of further index figures to which the enterprise must conform: technological-economic indices, 'cost-benefit norms', etc. Investments for the expansion of existing plant are sanctioned only if all existing facilities, especially highly productive plant, are used to full capacity by multi-shift working, and if all possibilities of rationalisation have been exhausted.

3   On the basis of these index figures, the enterprise then has to justify the proposed project by submitting a comprehensive 'documentation' to the competent authority, which files the application in its 'list of titles'.

The planned investment volume may not be exceeded, except when devices for rationalisation are made on the premises, or when the excess expenditure involves the purchase of used plant, the application of innovator suggestions or the installation of new equipment evolved by research and development.

In planning for the sector of consumer goods manufacture, a measure of flexibility was introduced in 1971. Deviations from the plan are permitted on a limited scale. Certain index figures (in particular value of output and net profit) are linked with margins of permissible deviation (*'tolerances in plan execution'*), thus enabling the enterprises to change product mix and price groups without being penalised. The use of these margins, however, is sanctioned only when there is a 'demonstrable improvement in meeting the needs of the population'. In addition, the new Decree on the Management of Publicly Owned Enterprises (*VEB-Verordnung*) authorises all enterprises to submit to the competent economic authorities proposals for modifications of enterprise plan targets in the event of changes in demand or in 'basic conditions'. This concession takes account of the fact that shifts in the demand for consumer goods are bound to affect the demand also for intermediate products and investment goods; at the same time it allows for the need — which may arise for many reasons, in particular as a result of changes in technology — to modify plans for the construction of capital goods.

A new instrument for the mobilisation of enterprise reserves has been devised in the form of the so-called *counter plan obligations* first introduced by law in 1973. Their purpose is to counteract the tendency to adopt 'soft' (i.e. easy) plans. A production effort exceeding the targets of the state plan on the basis of a counter-plan drawn up by the enterprise is valued more highly than unplanned overfulfilment of the plan. The counter plan is conceived on two occasions, first during the planning stage, when targets exceeding those of the draft plan are proposed, secondly during the first quarter of any year, when higher targets may be set than those laid down in the completed and enacted annual plan. The second occasion gives rise to additional planning problems, since increased production targets necessitate changes in the balance projections for materials.

In the course of the 'intensification' drive launched by the Eighth SED Congress — aiming at the intensive utilisation of available production capacities and manpower — much attention has been given to the activation of 'socialist emulation'. Many and varied methods, some based on Soviet models, are propagated to this end:

1 The 'Slobin method' (since the end of 1972). This involves the setting of clearly quantifiable tasks to the building brigades (building time, cost, use of materials, quality, labour productivity per production worker on site) and the granting of bonuses for fulfilment.

2 'Personal and collective creative plans'. These provide specific index figures covering notably output, working time per unit product, quality, cost of refinishing work, rejects, materials in relation to the effort of the individual worker or the brigade concerned.

3 'Notes on the plan' record machinery breakdown times and seek to ascertain the reasons, so as to improve plant utilisation.

4 The 'Bassow initiative' is to reduce accidents and damage to equipment.

5   The 'initiative shifts'. These are well prepared shifts during normal working hours, organised in order to ascertain optimum performance figures.

6   'Shift guarantee'. This is an effort to eliminate production losses and impairment of quality during shift change-overs.

2.4   Monetary devices for guiding the economy

The current system of 'economic levers' differs in several respects from that of the New Economic System. The only indirect devices retained without modification after the return to centralisation at the end of 1970 are the production fund levy and a portion of the funds to be established by publicly owned enterprises and VVBs. By far the greater part of the funds has been modified; one new fund, the performance fund, has been added to the list. Regulations governing the unified record of enterprise results have been altered. The net profit levy is now assessed as a fixed amount, payable even when the enterprise makes a loss. 'Price dynamisation' has been dropped altogether; no further steps were taken to introduce 'fund-related prices' (see p.41). On the other hand, the principle of the autonomous raising of funds has been fully preserved.

2.4.1   Cost consciousness before profit

In order to improve the convergence of micro- and macro-economic development trends and to harmonise financial with physical planning, while ensuring that the state's economic aims prevail, the economic authorities appeared to see no other way but to streamline decentralised decisions and assign a drastically reduced role to *profit*. In 1971-72 the profit to be earned by the enterprise was made a mandatory index figure (guide figure), and thus became an integral part of financial planning. Beginning in 1973, profit appeared as a derived index figure, a quantity computed indirectly from other, mandatory guide figures.

If an enterprise exceeds the planned profit, half of the surplus has to be paid to the state budget, and the use of the remainder is strictly limited.[1] Inadmissible profits made through price manipulations must

---

1   It may be used for payments into the bonus fund, the performance fund and the liquidity fund (set up to safeguard the tasks undertaken in the counter plan); for improving organisation of work (in particular looking after the needs of shift workers): and finally for financing out of enterprise reserves the 'in-house' production of aids to rationalisation (clearly not always with great efficiency).

be paid to the state in full. If an enterprise fails to achieve the plan figure for profits owing either to increased costs or underfulfilment of physical production tasks, it is faced with financial difficulties: it will not be able, then, to feed the funds envisaged in the plan or to finance all the planned investments, which however are vital for the profits of future years. Tide-over credits, apart from being expensive, are difficult to get, since one of the index figures relates to 'change in the credit volume for fixed capital'.

To meet such problems of financing, the net profit levy has been rendered more flexible in recent years. While in 1971 the levy was exacted in full, whether or not the planned profit had been attained, 30 per cent of the deficiency was remitted in 1972, and 50 per cent in 1973 and afterwards. If even the reduced quota still exceeds the actual profit, the levy will be further reduced to the level of the actual profit. A new regulation was issued in this context in 1976: increased costs due to higher prices of raw materials without compensatory rises in producer prices may be absorbed in part by reductions of the net profit levy. (Cf. pp 70 f.).

The main purpose of the monetary devices currently in use is to reinforce the effect of the multiplicity of physical production targets through financial planning, applied above all to profits, use of profits and credits, so as to ensure the firm grip of the central authorities on the performance and plan fulfilment of the enterprises. Squeezed between physical targets and financial barriers, the enterprise can ease the pressure only by reducing costs.

That is why great significance is attached to *cost planning* and *planned cost reduction*. The enterprises are to plan costs in advance, classified in detail in three ways: according to cost elements (types of costs), cost centres (organisational or functional units where costs are incurred) and cost objectives (final products or product groups to which costs are assigned), a procedure that involves precise forecasts of intermediate consumption, final proceeds and profit margin for each product. In addition, the costs notified by the enterprise each year for inclusion in the plan must be lower than the planned prime costs of the preceding year (base costs), and the savings by means of which such cost reductions are to be achieved have to be specified with reference to the relevant rationalisation measures and types of costs involved. In planning on these lines, the enterprises must keep to the prescribed norms for the use of materials, intermediate consumption and planned wage costs, as well as to the norms for overhead costs as authorised by the superior authorities. Extra costs incurred through the fault of the enterprise are called 'non-plannable' and cannot be covered by the plan. On the other hand, additional costs resulting from the introduction of new products or processes (e.g. starting costs of a production run, increased depreciation allowances, costs of authorised increases in reserves) may be included in the plan figures.

Apart from ensuring a more efficient use of resources and enabling the authorities to get relevant data for comparative assessments of different enterprises and different industries, these very comprehensive cost planning arrangements serve to keep the authorities informed in advance of intended or possible initiatives by individual enterprises that may run counter to official policy, well before any such move can get off the ground.

2.4.2   Current procedures for the formation of funds

The funds are instruments for tying parts of the financial resources of enterprises, combines and VVBs to particular uses, as laid down by law.

The VVBs (and equivalent group managements of combines) have at their disposal the *profit fund*, which receives the net profit levies paid in by the enterprises. Part of these sums is transferred to the state budget, the remainder is either redistributed within the VVB (or combine) or used for the financing of the *reserve fund*, the *publicity fund* or the *disposal fund*, the last named serving to stimulate outstanding production efforts by the award of bonuses.

Important funds at enterprise level are the *investment fund*, the *science and technology fund*, used for financing new developments, the *bonus fund* and the *performance fund*. The two last named provide incentives designed to spur the work force on to greater efforts. They have gained in importance in recent years, and shall therefore be considered more closely.

The precise amount of the *bonus fund* is laid down in the state plan as a mandatory index figure. The fund is fed by allocations from the part of the net profit retained by the enterprise. It is used for the payment of tax-free bonuses awarded for distinguished efforts (such as initiatives serving to promote rationalisation, improve work organisation, raise quality, or save materials) and for the payment of the year end bonus paid to the work force as a whole. The plan figure for the amount of the year-end bonus per employee must not be less than the corresponding figure for the preceding year.

In 1971, the size of the bonus fund depended on the net profit of the enterprise and on the fulfilment of at least two plan tasks, which the enterprise was allowed to select in advance. Since 1972 the bonus fund has been tied to the attainment of the state plan's index figures for goods production and net profit. If the bonus fund is to be increased above the level foreseen in the plan, any two of the following plan targets must be reached in addition: exports, production of goods for the population, labour productivity or manufacture of important

61

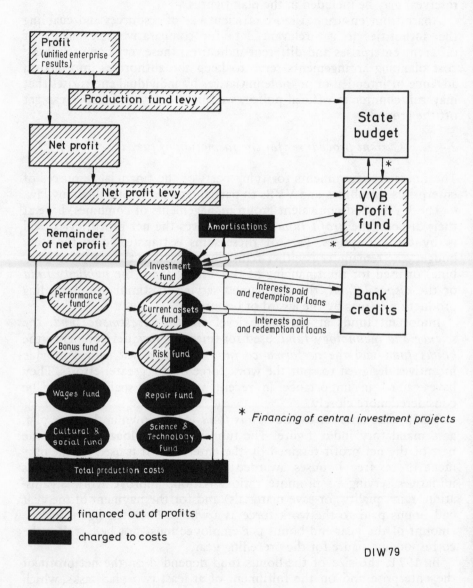

Figure 10   Use of profits and formation of funds
in the publicly owned enterprise

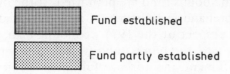

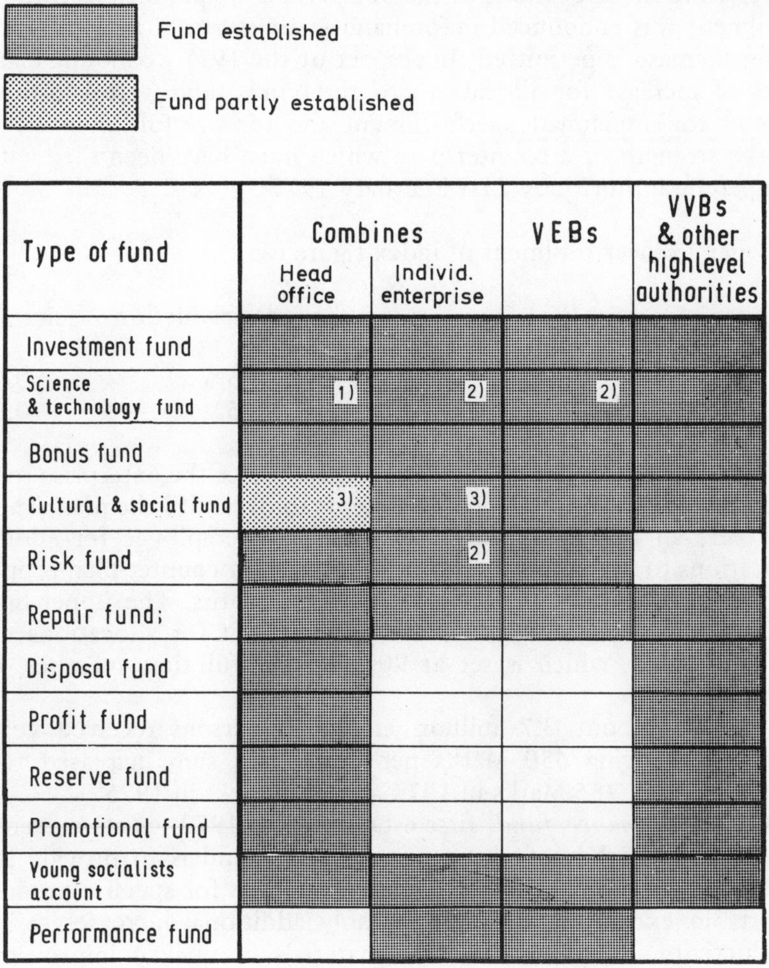

Fund established

Fund partly established

Type of fund	Combines		VEBs	VVBs & other highlevel authorities
	Head office	Individ. enterprise		
Investment fund				
Science & technology fund	1)	2)	2)	
Bonus fund				
Cultural & social fund	3)	3)		
Risk fund		2)		
Repair fund;				
Disposal fund				
Profit fund				
Reserve fund				
Promotional fund				
Young socialists account				
Performance fund				

1) *In some cases held entirely by the VVB. -* 2) *Unless centralised at combine head office or VVB. -* 3) *May be located at head office, subject to consent of Works Trade Union Committee.*

DIW 79

Figure 11   Funds in the publicly owned economy

63

products (e.g. spare parts, certain consumer goods). If the index figures for goods production and net profit are not attained, the allocations to the bonus fund must be reduced;[1] if the figures are exceeded, limited increases in the allocations to the bonus fund are permitted. If the over-fulfilment was announced beforehand in the form of a counter plan, a larger increase is permitted. In respect of the 1977 Economic Plan, the rates of increase for allocations to the bonus fund were laid down as follows for unplanned overfulfilment and for overfulfilment achieved on the strength of a counter plan which must have been filed with the competent authority by 21st February 1977:

per 1% overfulfilment of index figure for

	goods production	net profit
generally	1.5%	0.5%
based on counter-plan	2.5%	0.8%

The increased allocations are designed to induce the enterprise to enter in advance into voluntary commitments to overfulfil the plan. There is, however, an upper limit of 150 Marks per employee for additional allocations to the bonus fund on the strength of counter-plan proposals. The allocations are financed out of extra profits. The upper limit of 150 Marks may be added to the general limit for allocations to the premium fund, which is set at 900 DM per full-time member of the work force.

In 1972, about 3.7 million employed persons received year-end bonuses averaging 650 Marks per head. This sum increased to 725 Marks in 1973, 755 Marks in 1974 and 764 Marks in 1975.

The *performance fund*, first established in 1972, exists currently in nearly all branches of the economy. This fund is to provide labour collectives or entire enterprises with incentives for specific production efforts in excess of the plan, notably additional increases in labour productivity, economical use of materials or quality improvements.

Allocations to the performance fund are financed out of profits retained after payment of net profit levy, provided one of the following conditions is met:

a)   if labour productivity has been increased in excess of the plan

---

1   These cuts must not exceed 20 per cent of the planned bonus fund, so that the minimum bonus amounts to 80 per cent of the standard rate payable per full-time employee. If the enterprise, after payment of the net profit levy, cannot from its own resources allocate even 80 per cent of the planned amount to the bonus fund, the deficiency will be made up from the profit or reserve fund of the competent superior authority.

target; here, again, additional allocations are permissible if the overfulfilment was envisaged in advance in the enterprise plan or counter plan;

b) if consumption of materials has been reduced below the plan figure of the preceding year;

c) if quality has been improved and the reject rate reduced;

d) if additional profits have been made through the manufacture of new or improved products.[1]

Disbursements from the performance fund must be made by agreement with the trade union works executive and are intended to serve the general improvement of the 'working and living conditions of the working people',[2] including central measures by the FDGB (Trade Union Federation), such as the establishment of holiday villages and rest centres. The fund may also be used for the promotion of rationalisation measures out of the enterprise's own resources. At present the annual allocations to the performance fund are likely to be of the order of about 200 Marks per employee. In 1974, a total of over 500 million Marks was allocated to this fund in the enterprises of the centrally controlled industrial sector.

2.4.3 The banking and credit sector

The banks of the GDR are state institutions, and there is no competition between them. They are set apart according to their distinctive tasks and are subject to the 'principle of commercial accounting'. The GDR banking sector includes the State Bank, state and co-operative commercial banks and savings banks. The main difference from the banks in the Federal Republic is that they have a part to play in the planning and supervision of economic processes. There is, of course, no money or capital market in the GDR.

Over the years, the banking system has been modified on various occasions, in particular during the period of the New Economic System, when an attempt was made to adjust financial processes to the growing independence of the individual enterprises. Since then, the tendencies towards renewed centralisation have become dominant in the banking system as elsewhere.

---

1 Subject to the further condition that the plan figure for manufacture of goods bearing an official quality mark ('Q' or '1') or else the serviceability mark (Attestierungszeichen) has been reached.
2 E.g. improved amenities for shift workers, as well as general cultural and social tasks. The fund may also be used to assist members of the work force participating in self-help housing schemes, so that they can build new homes of their own or modify and extend existing accommodation.

65

The leading institution is the *State Bank*, which is responsible for issuing money, controlling foreign exchange transactions and keeping accounts for the state budget. In addition, the State Bank is entitled to play a prominent part in the preparation of planning decisions affecting the economy as a whole.

The *Bank for Industry and Commerce (Industrie- und Handelsbank)* is competent for financing investment and working assets of the enterprises. In 1974 it was incorporated in the State Bank. With its over 40 branches, the bank carries the accounts of the enterprises and economic organisations; it effects payments and settlements of accounts, and it supervises and monitors plan fulfilment, above all of the tasks laid down in the investment plan.

The *Bank for Agriculture and the Food Industry (Bank für die Landwirtschaft und Nahrungsgüterwirtschaft)* caters for the sector indicated in its title. The *Co-operative Banks for Crafts and Trade (Genossenschaftsbanken für Handwerk und Gewerbe)* are the commercial banks serving the distributive and artisan trades.

The *German Foreign Trade Bank (Deutsche Aussenhandelsbank AG)* and the *German Co-operative Bank (Deutsche Handelsbank AG)* transact payments and settlements of accounts in connection with foreign trade.

The banks are in a position to check all financial transactions of the enterprises and organisations, which are under an obligation to bank with the nearest branch of the competent bank and to transact business with other enterprises by cashless transfers. This means, for instance, that funds must be deposited with the competent bank, and that all cash receipts must be paid into the bank without delay. As a rule, cash withdrawals are effected only for the payment of wages.

Since on principle only production according to plan may be supported by credits, the granting of credits is made conditional on the fulfilment of certain stipulations on the basis of the Credit Plan adopted by the Council of Ministers. Even so the possibility cannot be excluded that enterprises may go in for projects which, though highly efficient, run counter to the plan. That is why in recent years the banks have been given far stronger powers of supervision over processes taking place within enterprises, irrespective of the source of finance. It is the duty of the banks to support production projects which conform to the plan and meet demand, while bringing their influence to bear to prevent violations of the plan. This is achieved by

a)   commenting on draft plans and taking part in the intermediate-level review of enterprise plans (when the enterprise is called upon to defend its proposals);

b)   co-operating with the chief accountant of the enterprise, who in

1971 was invested with important control functions, and other control bodies;[1]

c) keeping the relevant managerial and consultative bodies at enterprise level as well as the superior authorities informed about the results of their performance checks;

d) imposing penal interest payments in the event of violations of the credit agreement, or when the conditions for granting credit cease to apply; furthermore, the bank may curtail credits or even refuse credit altogether for specific periods. In very grave cases of failure to meet plan targets, the bank may declare an enterprise to be not credit-worthy.

Credits are usually granted for a five-year term at an interest rate of 5 per cent. The enterprise contracting a credit must fulfil a great many conditions:

1 To be eligible for *investment credits*, a project must have been prepared in detail and included in the plan; in addition several effectiveness criteria (relating to return on capital, technical performance, repayment period, etc.) must be met; finally, it is incumbent on the banks to see to it that plant is expanded only when existing capacities are used to the full and sufficient labour is available to man any additional plant.

2 *Credits for working assets* are made conditional on the attainment of index figures and fulfilment of norms governing the use of materials and stock management, and on the ability of the enterprise to repay the loan within a reasonable period. The banks are expected to encourage the enterprises to keep to specific price groups in the manufacture of consumer goods, to produce sufficient spares and to accelerate their stock turnover. Excessive working assets are to be penalised by interest surcharges, whereas increases in working assets for the purpose of plan overfulfilment are to be facilitated by reduced rates of interest.

The rate of interest can be reduced to as little as 1.8 per cent, when credits are granted for the financing of rationalisation measures; conversely it can be increased to 8 per cent when credits are needed outside the plan to bridge a temporary liquidity difficulty, and to as much as

---

1 These include next to the 'Worker-Peasant Inspectorates', which have relatively wide powers, the 'Central Permanent Production Consultation' and the 'Permanent Production Consultations' attached respectively to the works and departmental trade union committees.

10 per cent in the event of violations of the credit agreement.

Foreign exchange credits envisaged in the plan may be granted to foreign trade enterprises. Further credits may be extended by the banks for additional imports liable to stimulate highly profitable export production in excess of the plan within a short period.

2.4.4 Price formation and price problems

In the GDR, the formation of prices follows principles different from those prevailing in market economies. In a market economy with effective competition, prices are the instruments co-ordinating the multitude of individual decisions on the markets. The price mechanism tends to balance supply and demand; it tells the market parties which lines of production are profitable, in other words, which goods are useful. In the GDR, on the other hand − as in the other states of the Eastern bloc − price formation is a function of the state and serves above all to attain goals set by the state. Prices, then, are fixed by the state and remain as a rule constant over lengthy periods. A number of important principles governing price formation especially in the industrial sector (for special problems concerning agriculture, see section 4.3) will be discussed below.

Until well into the 1960s the prices of important basic materials were supported by subsidies in order to help the investment goods sector. But this price system clearly ran counter to the principle of covering production costs, considered a desirable aim by the East European regimes as elsewhere. In the GDR, it was only the industrial price reform of 1964 to 1967 which asserted this principle to any significant extent.

At the same time, the New Economic System introduced price dynamisation, intended to bring about automatic price reductions when costs went down, and 'fund-related prices' taking account of capital costs. Prices thus came closer to reflecting costs.

Recentralisation introduced towards the end of 1970 dealt a serious blow to the GDR price system: price dynamisation was abolished; the formation of 'fund-related prices' was halted after having been established for only one third of industrial output; a general price stop was imposed, in the first place until 1975, since extended until 1980, though excepting products for which price corrections are provided for in the plan (e.g. power) as well as new or substantially improved products for which a complex costing and confirmation procedure has been laid down (see below).

Prices are calculated according to the scheme illustrated in figure 12.

For *investment goods* and *goods entering into the production process* (raw materials, other materials, semi-manufactures), so-called *industrial*

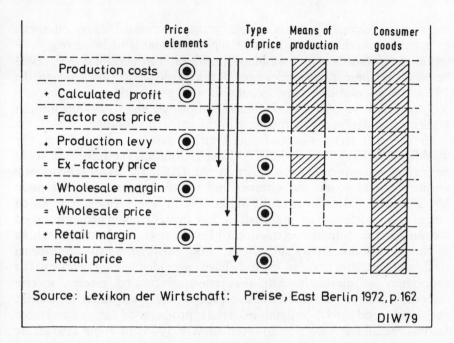

Price elements	Type of price	Means of production	Consumer goods
Production costs ⊙		▨	▨
+ Calculated profit ⊙		▨	▨
= Factor cost price	⊙	▨	▨
+ Production levy ⊙			▨
= Ex -factory price	⊙	▨	▨
+ Wholesale margin ⊙			▨
= Wholesale price	⊙		▨
+ Retail margin ⊙			▨
= Retail price	⊙		▨

Source: Lexikon der Wirtschaft: Preise, East Berlin 1972, p.162

DIW 79

Figure 12   Price structure of capital goods and consumer goods

prices apply in transactions between enterprises and with the capital goods trade. There are two types of industrial price, the *net producer price* or factor cost price (*Betriebspreis* = calculated cost + permitted profit) and the *ex-factory price* (*Industrieabgabepreis* = net producer price + production levy). For many investment goods, which are exempted from the production levy, the two prices are identical.

For consumer goods, the industrial prices are supplemented by the *wholesale price* (= ex-factory price plus wholesale margin) and the *retail price* (= wholesale price plus retail margin). Many retail prices, however, are kept low for political reasons, and these cannot be derived from the net producer prices. In such cases the gap between the relatively high net producer price and the ex-factory price (established by deducting the trade margins from the fixed retail price) is closed by subsidies or tax remissions to the enterprises. This category of low prices is distinct from prices fixed for seasonal goods (fruit and vegetables) or for clearance sales. Conversely, retail prices of some other goods are kept deliberately high, and on these the production levy can be increased substantially.

Prices are subsidised for a number of staple foods (e.g. bread, potatoes, fish, meat, cakes and pastries), for children's clothing and for some services (e.g. rents, public transport fares, laundry charges). In contrast, products significant of higher standards of living (e.g. television sets, motor cars, washing machines, refrigerators) are taxed heavily. In these cases prices are meant to influence distribution. In 1975, the population's total expenditure on goods and services amounted to about 90,000 million Marks, of which about 14,000 million Marks was contributed by the state in the form of subsidies.

In 1975 the GDR was confronted with a new external problem: the worldwide energy price rises. Although domestic and foreign trade prices are on principle kept apart in the GDR, the central economic authorities had to decide whether and to what extent domestic price levels should take account of dearer — in some cases very much dearer — imports of raw materials and of the worsening geological conditions for the domestic extraction of brown coal. To absorb the whole of the increased costs by subsidies without raising prices was not practical politics, because it would have provided no incentives for economies in materials. For that reason increased prices for raw materials and raw-material-intensive products (e.g. oil, electrical power, gas, heat, solid fuels, building materials, products of ferrous and nonferrous metallurgy) were announced in May 1975, to come into effect on 1 January 1976. In January 1977 increased prices were introduced for semi-manufactures, spare parts and a number of finished goods (e.g. metallurgical and chemical products, timber, glass, building materials, mechanical engineering products). In view of the policy of keeping consumer prices constant, however, the price changes affected only industrial users. Increased costs were absorbed by means of price subsidies, tax changes (notably reduction of the net profit levy) as well as by productivity drives on the part of the enterprises.

Planned periodic price revisions of this kind will have to be applied in the future, too, partly in order to adjust the prices of processed goods, partly because import prices of oil and other energy sources have changed again in the meantime.

In spite of the increased prices, no major reduction in the consumption of raw materials was recorded. In view of the problems presented by stringent consumption norms, enterprises which did not manage to save materials would often find it more advantageous to barter their surplus rather than report their economies. Moreover, enterprises continued to prefer to go on with the manufacture of obsolete products instead of embarking on costly new developments, because it is easier to raise profits by lowering costs through rationalisation at the old production lines turning out goods sold at fixed prices. New developments involving economies in the use of materials were particularly unfavourable, since the decrease in the material content would lead in some cases to a lower price for the finished article, despite the price

70

increases for materials. In that event, the enterprise was penalised for its efficiency, because it was obliged then to produce larger quantities to meet its production target in terms of value.

To provide effective incentives for economies in the use of raw materials as well as for the improvement of products, the central economic authorities of the GDR introduced in July 1976 new regulations designed for short-term effect:

1 Enterprises lowering production costs through economies in materials may charge the old producer price until 1980 and thus will benefit by an increase in their profits.

2 Prices for new or improved products are fixed in accordance with the so-called *price-performance ratio*, a quantity indicating the gain in utility in relation to comparative products. This represents a modification of the former price policy governed by cost alone. According to the new guidelines for price calculation, the producer is entitled to 70 per cent of the increment in utility value, the remainder going to the consumer, who thus in terms of utility gets a cheaper product. The additional profit granted to the manufacturer in full for two years and to a lesser extent for another three is designed to provide an incentive for improvements in quality.

In actual fact, these regulations constitute only a small step towards the desired improvements. There are three reasons for this:

1 The incentive for the development of new products and economies in materials is still not high enough, since the current regulations for the use of profits oblige the enterprises to pay a proportion of any extra profits to the state and to use the remainder for limited and precisely specified purposes (notably formation of enterprise funds).

2 There are in many cases no objective yardsticks by which to measure the utility of new products, so that unsatisfactory methods of measuring the cost involved have been replaced in effect by unsatisfactory methods of measuring and assessing utility.

3 The determination of the prices of new products according to the price-performance ratio has not eliminated the existing price distortions, but only made sure that new products are slotted more effectively into the existing product ranges.

71

Furthermore, the new procedure has failed to solve a problem that had arisen before: there are hidden price increases, when goods in the lower price groups disappear from the market, to be replaced by supposedly improved products offered at higher prices.

Leaving apart the special prices introduced for consumer goods on the grounds of economic and social policy, there are today in principle the following — mutually incompatible — price groups:

a) Prices laid down in 1967 in the course of the industrial price reform on the basis of costs prevailing at the time;
b) 'fund-related' prices which, in contrast to the methods of the industrial price reform, take account also of capital costs;
c) prices of new or improved products determined on the basis of cost according to the regulations in force until the middle of 1976;
d) prices of new or improved products determined according to the price-performance ratio.

All in all, the *weaknesses of the price system*, which were mitigated by the industrial price reform, have again become more acute for the following reasons:

a) The prices fixed at the time of the reform no longer reflect costs.
b) The prices of 1962 used in the revaluation of capital assets do no longer correspond to the actual replacement costs of today.
c) Prices in many sectors still fail to take account of the economically necessary capital expenditure involved.
d) The current price system fails to stimulate effective competition so as to get costs and prices down.
e) The new methods for determining prices still do not offer sufficient incentives for innovation.
f) The Office for Prices, which issues guidelines for price calculation and, acting in conjunction with the State Planning Commission and the Ministry of Finance, lays down the profit norms allowed for in the announced prices, is over-extended and cannot cope with all the demands made on it.

2.5 Functional deficiencies of the current planning system

The functional deficiencies of the planning system, already present in the New Economic System, were markedly aggravated as a result of halting the reforms in 1970: inadequate co-ordination and information, lack of flexibility, limited incentives for improved performance, and above all a reluctant attitude to innovation. All this was reflected in poor efficiency. More recent regulations – the 'Planning Code and Outline Directive' issued at the end of 1974 – managed only to improve rationalisation and unify procedures in the preparatory stages of planning. On the other hand, the introduction of a host of new details in planning procedures in some sectors has burdened the planning system as a whole.

Thus, the growing number of norms and index figures and processes for the harmonisation of developments, together with the cumbersome procedures for making and processing applications, tend to clog the administrative apparatus both in the enterprises and in the central and intermediate authorities. At the higher administrative levels so much time is taken up by the correlation and evaluation of the immense volume of data that the consideration and analysis of viable alternatives does not receive the attention it deserves. In addition the system of direction suffers from ambiguously defined and overlapping competencies. The system is too rigid to permit of speedy adaptation to unforeseen changes in supply or demand. Reserve stocks have been kept so low that external fluctuations lead immediately to delays in production which have to be made up later amid considerable strain. Finally, one decisive problem remains unsolved: how can technological progress be effectively promoted?

2.5.1   Setting of aims

Decisions on structural development are the prerogative of the central economic authorities, which are here confronted with the task of squaring the politically desirable and economically necessary with the practically attainable. The planners must assess macro-economic quantities, allow for their interaction, take note of important structural developments affecting particular industries or regions, reckon with the effects of imponderable influences on the world markets, and recognise in advance the future trend of scientific-technological development. Often enough, this process is further complicated by the need for co-ordination of plans – frequently in great detail – with the CMEA partners whose aims may at times diverge from those of the GDR.

The political leadership as a rule confines itself to the formulation of global aims or of partial aspects of the goals they visualise. The leadership bodies have not been able to present a catalogue of aims, listing the various objectives in order of priority according to their urgency and their importance in the context of the economy as a whole, while taking account both of the interdependence of various individual

73

objectives and of the constantly changing conditions for their attainment. There is always more than one possible solution by which a desired development can be brought about, and this presents the decision-makers with problems of choice, and each choice carries with it its own limitations. Each choice commits resources, which then are no longer available for other tasks; each change in the distribution of resources as between consumption and investment touches on the alternative of promoting today's living standards or tomorrow's growth prospects. Nor is it possible, in the light of existing resources, to plan private consumption independently of money incomes, capital formation and exports. Then, it must be borne in mind that every demand for a final product entails demands successively on the preceding stages of production. Thus any decision involves many parallel model computations. A further difficulty arises from the still very imperfect state of market research.[1] So long as the planning authorities have no clear idea of future demand, there can be no planning that will meet the needs of the population.

Optimisation calculations are made harder by the fact — admitted by the exponents of economic theory — that no way has yet been found of listing the various objectives according to criteria of economic benefit, since the formulation of such criteria is itself very problematic. Thus it happens frequently that the utility criteria accepted by the political leadership do not tally with the preferences shown by society as a whole. It is scarcely possible to translate political preferences into precise economic quantities. For these reasons, optimisation calculations in the GDR are still at an early stage.

At present the development of suitable forecasting and co-ordinating procedures is considered the only practicable way by which the problems of selecting objectives can be brought closer to a solution:

1   *Forecasting procedures* are beset with grave problems despite the introduction of refinements, because

   a) they often contain straightforward extrapolations of past developments;

   b) it is difficult to combine the heterogeneous partial forecasts compiled by different bodies for different fields;

   c) owing to the deficiencies of the price system, there is an absence of meaningful economic yardsticks; thus the parameters of the models used may be based on dis-

---

1 An example are the difficulties encountered in the elaboration of long-term consumption norms for the period up to 1990. Cf. Wirtschaftswissenschaft, no.2/1976, p.200.

torted prices, and thus on incorrect notions of structure.

2 The available *system of information* is inadequate to the needs
   of the central planning authorities for the purpose of extensive physical planning, even though a vast volume of data is
   regularly collected and further supplemented by separate
   investigations into specific sectors. The more details are to be
   covered by the plan, the less is the chance of reducing the
   volume of information step by step as it is passed on to the
   higher levels of the planning apparatus. Thus the central
   economic authorities have a vast mass of data at their command, but are unable either to evaluate or to use them
   adequately. On the other hand, it happens time after time that
   important specific data are not available, so that the planners
   must resort to estimates, which of course introduce more
   sources of error.

3 Finally, the pinpointing of objectives is rendered yet more
   difficult by the lack of information on economic *scarcity
   relations*, which impedes the costing of alternative projects
   and, even more important, calls in question the relevance of all
   available criteria of efficiency.

On these grounds it would appear that an economically meaningful
listing of objectives in order of their urgency is almost impossible.

2.5.2   *Balance projection for the economy as a whole*

Long-term planning starts with the selection of one of a number of
alternatives in the light of given political aims and immutable basic
factors. The planners working out a long-term projection for the
economy endeavour by means of rough balance determinations to find
a state of equilibrium between availability of materials, commitment of
resources needed for production, and use of the resulting product,
always bearing in mind the interlocking relationships between different
stages and fields of production. By comparison with annual draft plans,
such long-range projections are far less subject to the corrective of feed-
back from the lower echelons. Thus any errors made by the central
authorities are bound to have far-reaching consequences, since correction by the intermediate and lower planning authorities is at best an
exceedingly protracted and cumbersome process.

The starting point for the computation of important basic proportions is a model of interlocking relations within the economy with the
help of which certain macro-economic quantities are to be derived from

a number of preselected parameters. But the input-output tables used in this calculation are not satisfactory:

1 Planners engaged in determining balance projections must needs make use of highly aggregated models with a correspondingly sparse network of data. Even so, such a projection cannot be completed in less than two or three years, which means that it can do justice no more to short-term changes than to intricate patterns of interaction. Attempts to use more differentiated models were not pursued further in view of the additional labour involved.[1]

2 Successful use of input-output tables for forecasting presupposes a long-term foreknowledge of input-output ratios (e.g. consumption of power and raw materials per unit product). But these vary in consequence of scientific-technological developments, which can hardly be forecast.

2.5.3 Co-ordination

Inadequate co-ordination techniques are among the important functional weaknesses of the planning system: as a result of the growing number of products subject to central planning, combined with an increasingly stringent control of quantities and prices and with the profusion of mandatory index figures governing the organisation of production and cost accounting, it is becoming more and more difficult to take in all relevant factors. Although it is explicitly stated in the regulations that an enterprise is entitled to get *mutually adjusted index figures*, the growing number of norms entails the danger of contradictory instructions. Discrepancies arise over and over again between production targets and resources (e.g. goods production and exports on the one hand, manpower and available production capacities on the other) and between physical and monetary projections. Thus, in the case of technological innovations it is hardly possible to determine increases in utility and reductions in cost with any accuracy. This leads to difficulties of financing when the forecast cost reductions fail to materialise.

At one and the same time more than 350 bodies operating at different levels determine some 5,000 *individual balance projections*, thus making decisions about a multitude of economic quantities: material balance projections settle output and requirements in respect of raw

---

1 The table for 1959 covered 27 product groups. In 1972 it was as many as 164. But the balance projection for 1977 envisaged only 118 (cf. Statistische Praxis, no.1/1977, pp 12 ff.).

materials and semi-manufactures, corresponding projections for finished goods determine supply and demand in respect of investment and consumer goods. Relations between enterprises regulating production and the flow of materials and components are presented in specific input-output projections (*Teilverflechtungsbilanzen*). The individual balance projections are highly aggregated. Yet, without considering the fine structure of the various ranges of products, it is impossible to assess the requirements for materials, the demand on processing technologies and many other factors. Detailed models for such ranges of assorted products have actually been elaborated in individual cases, but they have not so far been adequately integrated into the system of planning and balance projections.

The immense labours involved in the balance projections for the flow of materials and semi-manufactures throughout industry can be gauged from a critical comment made by Honecker in March 1977, when he pointed out that in the centrally directed industry about 600,000 material consumption norms had not been reviewed for over two years.[1]

Many *timing difficulties of co-ordination* arise from the fact that basic data which form a point of departure for the processes of planning and balance determination are not ready on time. Projected demand figures are on the whole not available before the beginning of the year for which the plan is to be drawn up. Yet, preparations for production and the technological measures entailed by it, such as the drawing up of projects, and ordering of equipment and materials must be taken in hand long before that. Serious difficulties are encountered particularly in assuring the timely supply of equipment for plant construction projects. The producers of equipment are supposed to have placed firm orders for necessary machinery, semi-finished parts and materials, and to have passed the relevant data to the competent balance-determining authority before being told whether or not their project has been sanctioned and will be included in the economic plan.

Investment decisions, crucial for the transition to the industrial structure of the future, are made almost exclusively by the central economic authorities. Restoration of central control in this field was one of the results of the return to centralisation initiated in 1970. To ensure more effective control of *investment preparation* for important projects, a 'Plan for the Preparation of Selected Investment Projects' was first introduced in 1974. This plan features in the first place important automation and rationalisation projects, selected from the State Plan for Science and Technology. The aim is to ensure more effective

1 Cf. Neues Deutschland, 18.3.1977, p.4.

examination and more thorough preparation of investment projects. [1] Project planning in particular is to be speeded up, and the co-ordination of the various efforts involved is to be improved. At the same time preliminary decisions on investments and balance projections are to be produced more promptly and efficiently. In addition, attempts have been in progress since the beginning of the latest Five-Year Plan period to improve all aspects of the use of capital. The aim is to subdivide the investment volume for the entire five-year period neatly according to years, industries, enterprises and regions, while at the same time projecting manpower needs and laying down mandatory index figures (success indicators) for technological and economic performance.

In spite of all these efforts, the planning processes are still unsatisfactory, as witnessed by recurring criticisms of projects being finished after long delays and costs exceeding estimates by wide margins. Critics have also drawn attention to the fact that highly productive plants are often working only single shifts, whereas some obsolete plants operate multi-shift systems.

2.5.4   Incentives

One of the important functional deficiencies of the current planning system lies in the severe curtailment of the *entrepreneurial initiative* which the manager of an enterprise is able to exercise. Since the return to centralisation, there is hardly any incentive left that would prompt him to take risks or to think constructively in terms of 'new factor combinations'. The enterprises were deprived almost entirely of their former freedom, limited as it was, to decide themselves on the use of profits, including extra profits resulting from overfulfilment of the plan. Thus profit has largely lost its function as an incentive. It is true that even during the phase of the New Economic System managerial personnel did not benefit directly from improvements in performance, with their relatively low salaries and the modest bonus payments. Nevertheless, other than material motives should prevail among the leading cadres: a striving for self-realisation, recognition, prestige,

---

1 Commenting on this subject, an official of the Ministry for the Chemical Industry wrote: 'International comparisons show that new chemical plants are built abroad in a period varying from one to three years, whereas in the GDR it often takes over three years. The reasons lie not so much in the construction process itself as in the relative time scales of the phases of preparation and execution. Abroad, the phase of executing an investment project is much shorter than the phase of preparation. In the GDR this proportion is often reversed. In other countries, technological documentations must be compiled, the basic projects completed, contracts for the delivery of equipment concluded, before construction begins. In the GDR, these jobs are often left for the implementation phase. This mode of working also entails the need for extensive operational activities on the part of the authorities up to the level of the central state authorities.' Cf. Die Wirtschaft, no.11/1974, p.11.

power, as well as the consciousness of participating in the shaping of new, 'socialist' forms of society. In an environment in which the liberties of the individual and his scope for development are generally restricted, such idealistic motives can provide a sufficient incentive for those capable of adjusting to the political facts of life in the GDR.

The profit incentive was removed as a deliberate act of policy, but no other instrument calculated to stimulate innovation has taken its place. In any case, prospects of innovation are seriously prejudiced by the existing price distortions. There is no way of comparing capital productivity and profitability for different investment projects, because the prices on which such calculations are based differ from case to case. The prospect of raising profits by introducing new or improved products, held out by the new price regulations (cf. pp 71 f. above), is no more likely to boost innovations, since part of any extra profits has to be paid to the state budget and the permissible uses of the remainder are not particularly attractive. The enterprises, then, continue to have few inducements to venture on genuine innovations which always involve the risk of unforeseen technical and organisational difficulties and incidental losses.

Since the enterprises are set plan targets for profit, which must be attained, they will be tempted, when financial difficulties arise, to go in for the soft option of profitable lines, while dropping or curtailing the production of goods that may be needed to meet demand, but are less profitable. Frequently old products are disguised as new at higher prices. In many cases, the state authorities are unable to distinguish genuine innovations from insignificant improvements, nor can they enforce an adequate examination of cost and utility of goods. That is why the current regulations concerning profit are to some extent counterproductive, in that they tend to conserve old technologies instead of promoting technological progress.

Labour, one of the basic factors of production, is to be induced to improve performance by a combined system of material and moral incentives. In the GDR, as elsewhere, the material incentives have proved to be more effective, in particular wages and premiums as well as non-monetary benefits (housing, holiday travel). Moral incentives include public commendation, awards and titles, which however are often supplemented by money premiums. Yet, all these measures combined have proved insufficient to raise labour productivity to Western levels. The reason appears to be that the incentives are in part too low, in part too little differentiated:

1   The growth of wages (at an average annual rate of 3.5 per cent during the last ten years) is felt to be inadequate.

2   The *'extra-performance wage'* (*Mehrleistungslohn*, cf. pp 199 f below) has in practice become a regular part of the worker's income, and rarely reflects genuine extra production efforts.

3   Income differentials are inadequate: more highly qualified personnel, such as foremen, are paid flat wage rates laid down in the collective agreements, and are thus at a disadvantage by comparison with the shopfloor workers. Improved qualifications are frequently not reflected in higher pay.

4   Allocations from the bonus fund are made only to a minor extent (about one fifth of the total) for outstanding contributions. The bulk of the fund is paid out for normal working performance in the form of the year-end bonus, which has come in effect to play the role of a thirteenth monthly salary. It is scarcely a spur to better performance, with more and more enterprises reaching the legal upper limit of 900 Marks per head.

5   The performance fund fails to act as an incentive, because its benefits do not accrue to the individual worker, but to social amenities and even to the enterprise as a whole for the manufacture of rationalisation devices (cf. p.65 above).

6   Enterprises and their work forces tend to keep some performance potential in reserve, for it is on the cards that today's overfulfilment becomes tomorrow's mandatory target. For the same reason the institution of the 'counter-plan' has had little success.

2.5.5   Efficiency

The unsolved problems of the setting of aims of co-ordination and of incentives have all contributed to the relatively low efficiency of the GDR economy. But there are many more contributory factors:

a)   the extremely unfavourable starting position as a result of war damage and dismantling, and the lopsided economic structure consequent upon the partition of Germany;

b)   the economy's prolonged isolation from the world market and thus from competition with more advanced industrial countries. Integration within the CMEA region in partnership with less developed countries was hardly conducive to endeavours to raise efficiency.

We may add that the forces that can be mobilised within the system are not strong enough to promote technological progress sufficiently. This is manifest in the partly obsolete capital equipment and in the low technological standards of many products. Thus Honecker told the Fifth Session of the SED Central Committee in March 1977: 'Currently only about 10 per cent of our scientific-technological results play a part in setting international standards. In important industries, such as office machines, air conditioning equipment or medical and laboratory instruments, the proportion is even smaller.'

One crucial deficiency inherent in the system is the lack of sound criteria for measuring performance. Thus the maintenance of economically incorrect prices militates against the optimum utilisation of the factors of production: it may even prevent loss-making productions from being recognised, and conversely may lead to the neglect, obstruction or distortion of economically necessary innovation processes.

When the economic authorities had to face the fact that owing to price distortion, profit had ceased to be a reliable yardstick for the success of an individual enterprise, new methods were introduced for the measurement of efficiency, operating with a plurality of indicators instead of with a single one, e.g. labour productivity (in terms of value added); output/capital ratio; export profitability; intensiveness of material costs; cost per 100 Marks goods production; industrial goods production in respect of new and improved products and of products bearing a quality mark. This procedure is based on the notion that a number of different indicators will mutually complement each other and project in combination a better picture.

The price distortions are reflected in all index figures relating to value. But these are by no means the only deficiencies. Thus, labour productivity is measured by the relevant index figure on the basis of the gross output of goods, without deducting the value of intermediate consumption. This makes it attractive to concentrate on the production of goods with a high material content, contrary to the dire need for minimising the consumption of materials. Other index figures fail to give sufficient consideration to varying conditions of production (size of enterprise, technological equipment, manufacturing processes, levels of qualification among work force).

All in all, the system is characterised by excessive bureaucratisation and lack of flexibility. There are neither effective incentives nor a genuine readiness for innovation. Centralisation of decision-making has heightened the danger of grave negative consequences. These typical features of a planned economy cannot be eliminated by piecemeal reforms.

All these shortcomings tend to depress in the first place the level of *efficiency* of the economy: considering the volume of resources, labour, capital and raw materials, employed, the productivity attained by the GDR is relatively low. Economic *growth*, on the other hand, is less impaired, as can be seen from the impressive and consistent growth rates of recent years.

3 National accounts

Productive performance and wealth of a nation are usually gauged by the size and composition of the gross national product, computed by a national accounting system. Such a system on principle takes account of all results of economic activity and records their distribution and use. The accounting system provides the basis for an analysis of the economy as a whole, for all economic policy decisions with more than short-term implications, as well as for forecasts of likely economic trends. The system also serves as a basis for international comparisons of living standards and development.

Since national accounting systems deal with quantities relating to the economy as a whole (macro-economic aggregates), they can present at best a summary view of individual behaviour. In any case, it is a moot point to what extent such behaviour can be a fit subject for statistical investigation. This limitation must be borne in mind in any international comparison of macro-economic entities. Similarly, such international comparisons are often unable to take account of the quality of comparable goods.

3.1 Methods of assessing the domestic product in East and West

Foremost among the difficulties besetting comparisons of Eastern and Western economies are the diverging methodological concepts underlying the computations and the absence of realistic conversion rates for the national currencies concerned.

In the West, the *gross national product* (GNP) is the most important indicator of the national accounting system, whereas in the socialist countries it is the *'national income'*. The differences between these two statistical entities are illustrated in figure 13 and chart 6 (cf. also tables 12 to 16 in the Appendix).

The national income is computed according to principles going back to the labour theory of value as formulated by Karl Marx. It differs fundamentally from the System of National Accounts (SNA) recommended by the United Nations and adopted by the Western countries in that only economic activities concerned with the production or distri-

83

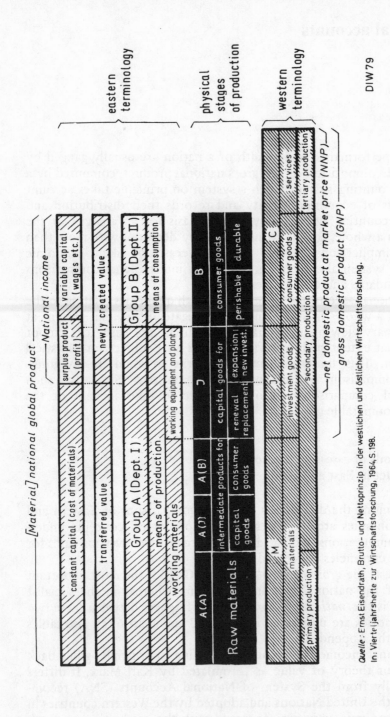

Figure 13 Content and mutual relations of Eastern and Western macro-economic concepts in the sphere of production

Quelle: Ernst Eisendrath, Brutto- und Nettoprinzip in der westlichen und östlichen Wirtschaftsforschung. In: Vierteljahrshefte zur Wirtschaftsforschung, 1964, S. 198.

Chart 6
Components of 'national income' in the Eastern sense as percentages of the sectoral contributions to the FRG's gross domestic product (Western definition)

Economic sectors classified according to the West German System of National Accounts	Percentage counting towards 'national income'		
	direct	indirect	total
Industry, construction, agriculture, transport	100	0	100
Trade	96	0	96
Catering and hotels	90	0	90
Science and learning, education, art, media	50	38	88
Other services	29	32	61
Credit and insurance institutions	0	49	49
State, health, private households and private non-profit-making organisations	0	9	9
All sectors	79	4	83

Calculated on the basis of 1966 input-output tables and national accounts computation of DIW.

bution (trade) of material goods are credited with the creation of values. The large sector of services[1] is left out of this side of the account. The turnover and incomes recorded in this sector are rated not as 'production' but as 'redistribution' of incomes originating in the material sphere. An exception is made, however, for services used by the 'producing' sectors; these are included in the gross production values attributed to the sectors concerned, and thus enter indirectly into the national income. The orders of magnitude are illustrated in chart 6: rents for homes and services supplied by the state are almost totally absent in the Eastern system of national accounting (System of Material Product Balances, MPS), whereas at least half of the remaining services are included. Moreover, there are signs indicating that a certain part of total production — relating above all to military products — is not featured in GDR official statistics.

The socialist countries also diverge from the UN recommendation in their methods of recording the *use of the GNP*. In the Western countries the dividing line between private and public consumption is drawn in accordance with the status of the purchaser of the goods in

---

1 This applies to credit institutions and insurance, residential lettings, the state, private households, private non-profit-making organisations, foreign trade, other services. However, the accounting system of the GDR does include the following 'other services': catering; publishing, literature and the press; architectual and engineering bureaux, laboratories and similar institutions; laundries and dry cleaning establishments.

Chart 7
Relation of gross national product (Western style) to national income (Eastern style)

	FRG				GDR	
	at current prices		at 1967 prices			
	Bn. DM	%	Bn. DM	%	Bn.M	%
‑Gross national product	1043.6	100	663.2	100		
‑Balance of foreign transactions	1.9	0	1.1	0		
= Gross domestic product[1]	1045.5	100	664.3	100	177.7	100
‑Services[2]	281.4	27	146.3	22	19.3	11
+Services to producing sector (Intermediate consumption)	53.5	5	28.7	4	7.7	4
= Gross material domestic product	817.6	78	546.7	82	166.1	93
‑Depreciation[3]	92.6	9	64.1	10	18.0	10
= National income (comparable)	725.0	69	428.6	73	148.1	83
‑Corrective items[4]	–	–	–		6.4	4
= National income (official)	–	–	–	–	141.7	80

1 Including general overhauls less special subsidies.
2 Excluding 'material contributions'.
3 In the producing sector.
4 Contributions of economically active persons not included in official statistics; general overhauls.
Differences due to rounding.

Source: DIW calculations.

question, whereas in the socialist countries it is the status of the final consumer that matters.[1] Private consumption does not include rents and services. Investment data in East and West are readily comparable on the whole, with the exceptions of durable military installations, which according to the Western system are counted as consumption by the state, but classified as investments in the East.

In the following sections, the GDR economy is described in terms of the *GNP computed by Western methods*. The relevant calculations were recently made at the German Institute for Economic Research (DIW). The main discrepancies between the two methods were eliminated so that the East and West German data can be confronted subsection by subsection. Although comparability has thus been established in principle, some problems as yet unsolved remain:

1 Thus, medical appliances and drugs paid for by social insurance, held in the West to form part of public consumption, are in the socialist countries bracketed with 'individual consumption', since the patients are the ultimate consumers.

86

1   A computation of the GNP of the GDR at current prices is impossible, because macro-economic data are published in the GDR almost exclusively at *1967 or 1975 prices*. For the same reason it is impossible to correlate current nominal income data with production data given at constant prices. Moreover, there is reason to suspect that owing to methodical shortcomings some price increases are erroneously represented in GDR statistics as genuine increases in economic performance.

2   Both indirect taxes and subsidies are included in the valuation of products. This introduces *distortions* of uncertain extent into the statistical picture of the structure of production, since in the GDR indirect taxation affects by and large only consumer goods significant of higher living standards, while investment goods and consumer goods classed as necessities are barely touched. This makes consumer goods production appear larger than it actually is in relation to total production. In addition, certain subsidies referring to intermediate consumption, i.e. to materials and semi-manufactures, are given in global figures and cannot be assigned to individual industries.

3   One fundamental and vital shortcoming of GDR statistics is the incompleteness of the definitions used. The official key is not made available to the public, so that the precise significance of many statistics remains unclear.

Apart from these reservations on methodological grounds, it has been argued that data issued by official authorities in the GDR cannot be taken at their face value irrespective of the method used, since they serve the SED leadership as an instrument of propaganda. As far as the presentation of short-term results is concerned, for instance the annual reports on plan fulfilment, there is substance in this objection, as can be shown by a number of examples. Yet, the genuine character of the statistics in general appears to be borne out by the fact that basic guides to decision-making, models and forecasts in the GDR have been elaborated on the basis of the published data. The use of GDR official statistics thus seems justified.

3.2   Composition of the gross national product

From 1960 to 1977, the GDR registered a steady growth of its GNP at an average annual rate of close on 5 per cent (cf. Appendix, table 12).

Comparison with the Federal Republic shows that the GDR succeeded in avoiding major fluctuations.

In the GDR, as in other industrial countries, the economy underwent a marked *structural change*: whereas the volume of agricultural production — as distinct from the monetary value which follows price movements — rose only at a slow rate, the output of the manufacturing and building industries increased at a faster-than-average rate. From 1965 to 1975, the fastest growth was registered by the electrical engineering/electronics/instrument building industries with an average annual growth rate of 8.6 per cent and the chemical industry with 7.6 per cent, as against 5.2 per cent for the domestic product as a whole.

The relative contribution of industry and the building trade as a proportion of the entire GNP is correspondingly high. In West Germany, too, the share of these sectors in the domestic product is very high by international standards at over 50 per cent.[1] Yet, in the GDR that proportion is higher still, by a full 10 per cent. On the other hand the share of the services sector at constant prices declined slightly, in contrast to the development in the Federal Republic.

To some extent, these apparent differences of macro-economic structure reflect different *price relations* in the two German states. Wages are relatively low in the GDR; wage-intensive sectors, notably services, are therefore undervalued by comparison with West Germany.

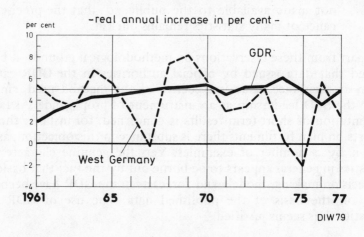

Figure 14   Growth of gross domestic product in
the GDR and the Federal Republic

1   Medium-term average at 1967 prices.

88

Chart 8
Contributions to gross national product of GDR and FRG

	GDR Bn. M at 1967 prices		FRG Bn. DM at 1967 prices	
	1960	1976[3]	1960	1976
Agriculture and forestry	11.9	14.0	18.2	22.5
Commodity producing trades	51.3	121.3	176.1	343.2
Trade and transport	13.9	29.5	65.0	110.6
Services[1]	13.4	22.3	69.4	132.7
Gross national product[2]	90.4	184.3	328.6	609.0

1 Non-producing sector and 'other producing branches'.
2 Differences due to global subsidies, general overhauls and rounding.
3 Provisional data.

Sources: DIW calculations; Federal Office of Statistics

Conversely, agricultural producer prices, fixed with a view to safeguarding peasant incomes, are much higher than in the Federal Republic, not to speak of world market prices. Thus the share of agriculture in the GNP of the GDR is much higher in monetary than in real terms. Chart 9 shows the extent of the resulting distortions.

Chart 9
Structure of gross national product in GDR and FRG 1976
By originating sector (in per cent)

	GDR		FRG
Originating sector	GDR 1967 prices	Current FRG prices	
Agriculture and forestry	7	4	3
Commodity producing trades	65	54	49
Trade and transport	16	17	18
Services	12	25	30
Gross domestic product	100	100	100

Source: DIW calculations

Restating the quantities making up the GNP of the GDR in terms of West German prices (cf. Appendix, table 16), we are able not only to compare the structure of the two economic systems, but also to gauge the true *gap separating the Federal Republic from the GDR*. The results are shown in chart 10. It must be borne in mind, however, that the picture is blurred by substantial methodological uncertainties. In many cases, for instance, it is not possible to allow adequately for differences in quality between Eastern and Western products. In estimating true price levels we are reduced to educated guesses. Furthermore, the comparison is affected by the fluctuating levels of economic activity in the Federal Republic during the period in question.

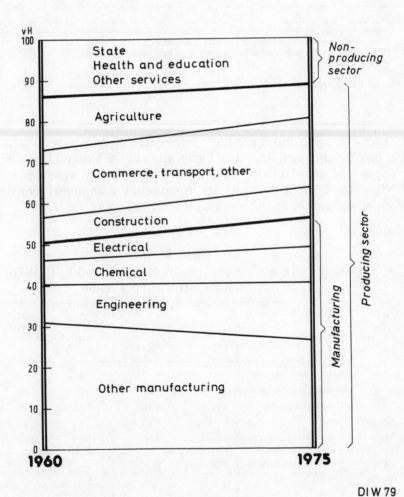

DIW 79

Figure 15   Contributions of individual sectors to the GDR's gross domestic product, 1960 and 1975

90

Chart 10
Comparison of gross national product in GDR and FRG
(FRG = 100)

	absolute			per inhabitant			per economically active person		
	1967	1973	1976	1967	1973	1976	1967	1973	1976
Gross national product (total) contributed by	22	21	22	78	78	83	67	64	63
Agriculture and forestry	41	37	34	141	135	124	92	76	61
Commodity producing trades	24	23	25	84	83	91	72	67	65
Trade and transport	19	20	21	65	75	78	59	65	62
Services	19	18	18	67	67	68	66	62	64

Source: DIW calculations; cf. table 16.

Nevertheless, the resulting picture presents clear outlines: the GDR attains about four fifths of the West German per-capita performance. However, in terms of productivity — GNP per economically active person — the discrepancy is greater. Here the GDR is lagging behind by roughly one third. The effect of the productivity gap is mitigated by the fact that a larger proportion of the population is economically active in the GDR than in the Federal Republic (53 as against 41 per cent). Hence the more favourable results for the per-capita figures.

3.3 Productivity of labour and capital

In most economic sectors of the GDR growth of production was achieved with only minor increases in the labour force, and was therefore due almost entirely to the raising of labour productivity.[1] This, in turn, was accomplished above all through the expanded and improved use of capital. The ratio of capital equipment per work place (capital intensity) was rapidly increased throughout the period in question, and as production plant was progressively modernised, so labour became steadily more efficient.

Yet, an expansion of productive capacity does not always lead to

1 Labour productivity here defined as GNP per employed person (including those not officially classified as employed, notably those engaged in arms production). Productivity per unit of working time cannot be considered here, since the number of hours worked — a function of the size of the labour force, the average working week and the extent of part-time and overtime working — is unknown.

91

Chart 11
Production and factors of production in the sectors of the GDR economy. Average real annual growth rate for the period 1965 to 1975 (in per cent)

	Economically active persons	Gross capital assets	Contribution to gross domestic product
Commodity producing trades	0.7	5.6	6.0
Power, mining, water resources	−0.7	4.4	4.6
Processing trades	0.5	6.1	6.0
basic materials	0.3	6.5	6.9
capital goods	1.5	6.6	7.5
consumer goods	−0.5	4.9	4.2
Construction	2.1	8.7	6.4
Agriculture and forestry	−2.5	5.3	2.5
Trade and transport	0.2	3.8	5.6
Services	1.1	0.7	2.4
Health, education, State housing	2.3	2.4	3.7
Housing	*	1.6	*
All sectors	0.5	3.9	5.2

*No data available

Source: DIW calculations

commensurate improvements in labour productivity. In the GDR this was the case particularly in two sectors: the building trade and agriculture. Even after the economic crisis of 1961 to 1963 had been overcome, and after the introduction of the economic reforms, the development of labour productivity showed marked fluctuations, though, it may be noted, not nearly as wide as cyclical fluctuations in Western countries.

In the period 1965 to 1970, following the introduction of the economic reforms, capital productivity[1] was raised at an average annual rate of 0.5 per cent, with the processing branches (here defined as industry, including the productive artisan trades, but excluding power generation, mining and water resources) in the lead. During the same period, capital productivity in the Federal Republic declined on average by 1.3 per cent a year. The development in the GDR indicates improved utilisation of production capacities. Since 1970 the increase in production in the GDR has again fallen back slightly behind the growth of capital assets. In the commodity-producing industries capital productivity has declined since 1970 at an average annual rate of 0.4 per cent (as compared

1 GNP per unit of gross capital assets.

92

with a decline of 0.9 per cent per year — adjusted for capacity utilisation — in the Federal Republic). Drastic drops in capital productivity from 1960 to 1975 were recorded in agriculture and the building trade with respectively 44 and 36 per cent.

It emerges from these figures that the central economic authorities in the GDR will have to assess their prospects for the foreseeable future in a much more sober light than only ten years ago. To ensure rapid advances in production and thus in national welfare, substantial *investment efforts and additional manpower* will be required. Thus the 1971-75 Five-Year Plan was designed to attain rapid growth of production primarily through an increased contribution from technological progress. This objective was not attained. Instead it was necessary — as

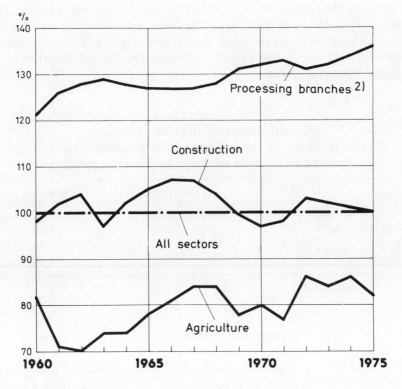

1) *Gross domestic product per economically active person*

2) *Including power, mining and water resources*

DIW 79

Figure 16 Labour   productivity[1]   in   the
GDR economy (all sectors = 100)

93

in other industrial countries — to achieve the scheduled growth rates by substantially expanding the use of capital. The substitution component of growth increased, while the contribution from technological progress even registered a slight decline.

The GDR economy as organised at present — with all the short-comings of planning and direction discussed above — is clearly not in a position to close the *productivity gap* in relation to other industrial countries and the Federal Republic in particular. On the face of it, it should be possible, through the imitation of advanced products and production methods, to ensure rapid improvements in economic per-formance without vast increases in the employment of labour and capital. But that is an aim which GDR economic policy after the halting of the reforms can approach only slowly, with tentative steps. Rapid progress in this direction is impeded by ideological reservations. Thus contacts of GDR specialists with Western colleagues are restricted in volume and subject to detailed regulations. Here as in other spheres, reduced efficiency is the price to be paid for the stabilisation of the politico-economic system.

Chart 12
Growth-factors in the GDR economy
Percentage shares in the increase of the commodity producing
trades contribution to the gross domestic product

Period	Increase in employment	Substitution of capital for labour	Remainder: techno-logical progress
1960-1975	6	36	58
1965-1970	16	26	58
1970-1975	7	40	53

Source: DIW calculations

3.4 Use of the gross national product

Since rapid economic growth is one of the priority aims of policy in the GDR, a constantly growing proportion of the GNP has been allocated for *investment*, in particular since the overcoming of the crisis of the early sixties and the beginning of the economic reforms. From its low of 19 per cent in 1962, the investment rate rose steadily to 26 per cent in 1970 and has now settled at about 25 per cent. Thus the investment rate of the GDR since 1970 is equivalent to the long-term average of the Federal Republic since the middle fifties.

The share of *private consumption* presents a different picture. Since

94

the beginning of the 1960s the consumption ratio in the GDR has fallen by 10 percentage points, whereas in the Federal Republic an average share of about 55 per cent has been maintained consistently, apart from cyclical fluctuations. The continual shift in the use of GNP at the expense of private consumption in the GDR was halted only during the years from 1971 to 1974, when the policy of raising the standard of living — proclaimed as the 'principal task' by the political and economic leadership — managed temporarily to neutralise the trend, without being able to reverse it in the long run. Indeed, it is likely to be reinforced in the coming years with their high demand on investment activity and exports.

The share of *consumption by the state* is larger in the GDR than in the Federal Republic. This item can be assessed only approximately, because in GDR official statistics it is lumped together with the 'external contribution', i.e. net exports (valued in the domestic currency). In contrast to the Federal Republic, where the export surplus amounts on average to about 2 per cent of GNP (rising to as much

Chart 13
Use of national product in the GDR and FRG 1976

| | GDR | | FRG |
	Bn. M[1]	%	%
Gross national product	184.3	100	100
Private consumption	98.0	53	58
Investment	50.0	27	23
gross capital investment[2]	45.7	25	22
investment in stocks	4.3	2	1
State consumption plus net exports	36.3	20	18

1 At 1967 prices.
2 Including general overhauls and investments not officially recorded.

Source: DIW calculations

as 4 per cent in 1974), it is likely to lie near zero in the GDR, or the current balance may even be negative. Thus the share of state consumption proper in the GDR exceeds that of the Federal Republic by 4 to 5 percentage points. The difference is probably due to relatively higher expenditure for internal and external security, combined with a larger administrative apparatus.

A comparative analysis of the use of GNP in the two German states is again rendered more difficult by the *different price relations* in the

95

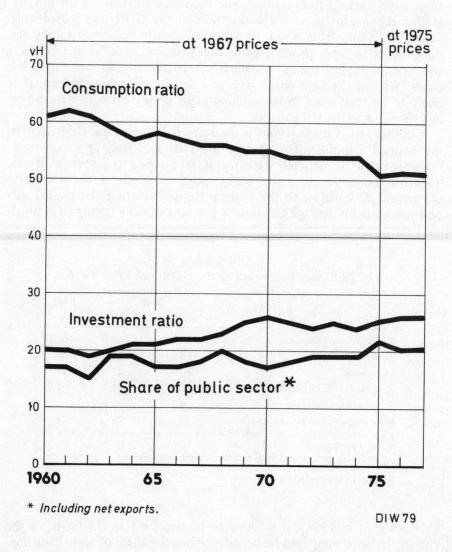

vH

├─────────at 1967 prices─────────→ at 1975 prices

Consumption ratio

Investment ratio

Share of public sector *

1960   65   70   75

* Including net exports.

DIW 79

Figure 17   GDR's gross national product by
type of expenditure at constant prices

96

Chart 14
Use of national product in the GDR and FRG 1976
assessed at GDR and FRG prices (in per cent)

	GDR		FRG
	GDR 1967 prices	FRG 1974 prices	
Gross national product	100	100	100
Private consumption	53	45	55
Investment	27	25	22
State consumption plus net exports	20	29	23

Source: DIW calculations

two territories. An approximate calculation shows, however, that the main features described in the foregoing emerge yet more clearly when the GDR items are valued according to West German prices.

3.5 Distribution of gross national product

The most recent data concerning the apportionment of the GNP among the various types of income and the redistribution of those incomes by the state (including social insurance) refer to 1975, the new base year for the price system used in official statistics.

The fundamentally different economic systems prevailing in the two parts of Germany have led to conspicuous differences in the distribution of the national income among households, enterprises and the state, as illustrated in charts 15 and 15a and table 41. Private industrial enterprises have virtually ceased to exist in the GDR. There, the notion of an entrepreneurial sector separate from the state is methodologically dubious in view of the structure of society, as well as empirically untestable owing to the lack of data.

Even so, the computation of GDR incomes carried out by the DIW has elicited figures for household incomes, including in particular the profits accruing to the self-employed and members of co-operatives. Retained profits of the entrepreneurial sector are treated as belonging to the state sector.

Another aspect of the special role played by the state in the GDR economy is the magnitude of its share in primary income distribution. The vast bulk of state revenue is derived from indirect taxation and from levies on the profits of enterprises. Accordingly chart 15 presents

Chart 15
Distribution of national product 1975

	GDR Bn. M	FRG Bn. DM[4]	GDR Percentages	FRG Percentages
Gross national product	180.9	1,030.3	107	113
Depreciation allowances	11.2	117.0	7	13
Net national product at market prices	169.7	913.3	100	100
Share of the state and of enterprises[1]	69.9	127.4	41	14
Share of private households (gross incomes)[2]	99.8	785.9	59	86
Income from employment	80.7	583.9	48	64
Income from co-operative and own-account activity and from capital assets[3].	19.1	202.0	11	22

1 Incl. retained profits.
2 Incl. payments in kind.
3 Without retained profits
4 Provisional data.

Sources: DIW calculations; Federal Office of Statistics, Fachserie 18, Reihe S 2 (Revidierte Ergebnisse 1960 bis 1976).

Chart 15a
Redistribution and use of household incomes 1975

	GDR Bn. M	FRG Bn. DM[2]	GDR Percentages	FRG Percentages
Net national product	169.7	913.3	–	–
Incomes from economic activity and from capital (gross)[1]	99.8	785.9	100	100
+ social insurance and social welfare benefits received	16.6	179.1	17	23
+ other income transfers to households	3.3	22.6	3	3
Total receipts of private households	119.7	987.5	120	126
– direct taxation	6.6	109.4	7	14
– social insurance contributions[1]	11.5	173.5	12	22
– other income transfers from households	3.6	37.1	4	5
Disposable income	98.0	667.6	98	85
– savings	6.1	93.0	6	12
= private consumption	91.9	574.6	92	73

1 Including social insurance contributions paid by enterprises (employers).
2 Provisional data.

Sources: DIW calculations; Federal Office of Statistics, Fachserie 18, Reihe S 2 (Revidierte Ergebnisse 1960 bis 1976).

incomes in relation to net national product at market prices (rather than at factor cost).

Conversely, chart 15 shows that in the GDR incomes from employment (totalling 80,700 million Marks in 1975) represent a substantially smaller share of the net national product than they do in the Federal Republic. The difference of 16 percentage points, already enormous, rises to about 25 percentage points if the labour effort of the self-employed and members of co-operatives is taken into account by assigning a putative entrepreneurial wage to individuals in these categories. The amplified wage ratio computed in this way was 55 per cent in the GDR, 80 per cent in the Federal Republic in 1975. But the indicator most revealing of the contrast between the two systems is the share in the current net national product claimed by the state and enterprise sector, mainly in the form of indirect taxes and retained profits. It amounts in the Federal Republic to 14 per cent, in the GDR to no less than 41 per cent!

These differences are balanced, though only to some extent, by the redistribution of incomes, which, as illustrated in chart 15a, exhibits striking contrasts, now in the opposite direction. In the Federal Republic, private households have to bear a substantial burden of direct taxes and social insurance contributions. The stark picture of exploited working people presented by the primary income distribution in the GDR by comparison with West Germany is thus mitigated when the effects of redistribution are considered. The final figures, obtained in this way for the share of private consumption in the net national product reduce the gap between the two states to under 9 percentage points (54.2 per cent in the GDR, as compared with 62.9 per cent in the Federal Republic).

4 Production in the individual economic sectors

4.1 Industry

Industry (including the productive artisan enterprises) contributes 56 per cent of the gross national product of the GDR, as calculated by the Western accounting system. On this showing, the GDR would seem to have a better claim to the title of an 'industrial state' than has the Federal Republic, where this sector accounts for less than half − 46 per cent − of the GNP.

Measured in terms of the Eastern concept of national income, industry's share is no less than 62 per cent; furthermore it accounts for about 40 per cent of the economically active population and an equal proportion of gross capital assets, and thus surpasses all other sectors by far.

4.1.1 Enterprises and production

The industrial sector in the narrow sense, i.e. without the productive artisan trades, [1] comprised in 1977 some 6,500 enterprises, with an industrial gross production of 230,000 million Marks. There has been a consistent and marked trend towards concentration, which apparently has not yet run its course. Since 1960, the number of enterprises has shrunk to less than half, while the number of employees rose by 6 per cent and production increased almost threefold.

This *process of concentration* went hand in hand with nationalisation. In 1971, publicly owned enterprises accounted for 88 per cent of industrial production, semi-state enterprises for about one tenth of the total, and small private enterprises for 1.5 per cent. The socialisation campaign which started in 1971 and was concluded in mid-1972 resulted in the transfer of nearly all semi-state and private enterprises and all industrially productive artisan enterprises to public ownership. Thus industrial output is now in its entirety produced in publicly owned enterprises.

---

1 Industrial enterprises which do not figure in GDR statistics (e.g. SDAG Wismut) are not considered in the investigations of the present chapter, in contrast to the analysis of the GNP in chapter 3, which dealt with the economy as a whole.

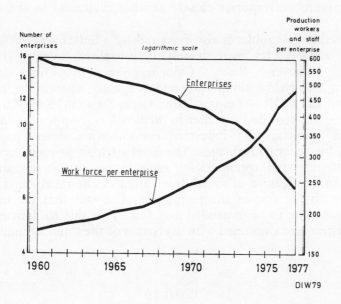

Figure 18   Concentration of production units in GDR industry

Especially towards the end of the 1960s the change in the relations of ownership was supplemented by the concentration of managerial powers in combines, VVBs and other co-ordinating bodies. At the same time a *concentration of production* through the amalgamation of production units led to the emergence of many large enterprises operating under a unified management.

The crucial consideration in promoting this trend towards concentration appears to have been the fact that it seemed to offer better opportunities for econòmic planning and direction. Labour productivity is not invariably best in mammoth enterprises. It is true that the statistical figures for labour productivity (gross production per employee) in the GDR show a slight superiority in enterprises with a labour force of over 1,000. The picture, however, becomes less clear when the situation is reviewed in greater detail, considering individual industries and using a more differentiated classification of enterprises according to size.

The trend in the *Federal Republic* was only superficially similar. Here the process of concentration during the last decade consisted almost exclusively in the *amalgamation of firms*, that is to say, in the concentration of ownership, whereas the structural distribution of production units according to size has remained virtually unchanged.

This structure corresponds closely to that evidenced in the GDR in 1960.

The Federal Republic is also favoured by a better *regional distribution of industry*. Its most densely industrialised areas — Hamburg, Bremen, Hanover, Ruhr, Cologne/Bonn, Frankfurt/Mannheim, Stuttgart, Munich/Augsburg — are widely spaced, whereas the industrial centres of the GDR — Leipzig/Halle, Gera, Zwickau, Karl-Marx-Stadt, Dresden — are crowded together in the South (cf. Appendix, table 10). Here the advantages of industrial concentration appear to be outweighed by the disadvantages. The asset of high productivity in the region of industrial agglomeration must be set against environmental damage and a measure of social deprivation of the inhabitants in comparison with the rest of the population. The fact that the industrial centres continue to be expanded may largely be due to deficiencies of the infrastructure combined with overstrain of the building industry.

Chart 16
Concentration of industrial production in the GDR and FRG

Size of enterprise by size of workforce	GDR				FRG	
	1960	1965	1970	1974	1965	1974
Percentage of total industrial labour force[1]						
under 100	14	13	10	8	15	14
100-1000	35	34	27	25	34	34
over 1000	51	53	63	67	51	52
Labour productivity[2] (all industry = 100)						
under 100	85	86	83	86	94	84
100-1000	102	103	105	99	95	92
over 1000	102	101	100	102	105	110

1 GDR: employees (wage and salary earners); FRG: all economically active persons.
2 GDR: gross output per employee; FRG: turnover per economically active person.

Source: DIW calculations

Gross industrial production has registered a *steady growth* since the mid-sixties. During the ten years up to 1975 the average annual growth rate was 6.5 per cent, declining to 5.9 per cent in 1976 and 4.9 per cent in 1977. Naturally, the development was uneven in the various industries. During the ten-year period up to 1975, the fastest growth was registered by the electrical engineering/electronics/instrument building

Chart 17
GDR growth industries
(average annual growth rate in per cent)

Industry	1966/1970	1971/1975
Electronics	9.6	13.5
Manmade fibres	14.4	13.2
Plastics	12.9	11.6
Office machines, EDP	22.7	11.2
Machine tools	8.0	9.3
Agricultural machines	11.2	9.0
Control technology	8.9	8.6
Pharmaceuticals	7.2	8.6
Oil, gas, coal derivatives	8.5	7.7
Steel construction	9.4	7.5
All industry	6.5	6.3

Calculated from data of the GDR Statistical Yearbooks

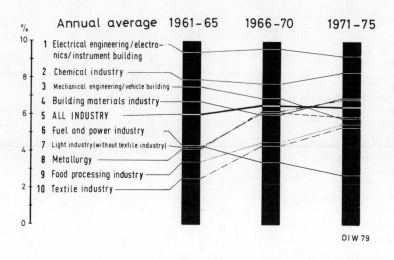

Figure 19 Development of industrial gross production
(average annual growth rates in per cent)

sector with an average annual growth rate of 9.4 per cent, followed by the chemical industry with 8.0 per cent. The fuel and power industry brought up the rear with an average growth rate of only 3.0 per cent, which must be rated low even by international standards; moreover, this average covers a declining trend, which continued during the 1970s. The shifting growth relations are illustrated in figure 19.

Above-average growth was recorded in the GDR as elsewhere in the industries most affected by worldwide technological changes. The ranking of the growth industries in the GDR is little different from that in other advanced industrial countries.

4.1.2 Factors of production and productivity

From 1960 to 1975, the number of wage and salary earners working in industry,[1] increased at an average annual rate of only 0.7 per cent. Accordingly, the rapid increase in production was largely due to higher *labour productivity*, all the more so since the average number of working hours declined slightly during the period in question.

The *development* of the numerical strength *of the labour force* and of labour productivity varied considerably from industry to industry. In particular, the sectors electrical engineering/electronics/instrument building and mechanical engineering/vehicle building augmented their

Chart 18
The GDR industrial labour force 1975

Industry	1000 employees	All industry = 100	Percentage change since 1960
Water resources, fuel and power industries	215	7	+ 0
Chemical industry	335	11	+ 7
Metallurgy	127	4	+ 7
Building materials	94	3	+ 0
Mechanical engineering and vehicle building	872	28	+ 28
Electrical engineering/electronics/ instrument building	429	14	+ 41
Light industry	505	17	- 0
Textile industry	244	8	- 26
Food processing industry	242	8	+ 15
All industry	3064	100	+ 12

Sources: GDR Statistical Yearbook and DIW calculations

1 Including water resources and fuel and power industry. A detailed long-term analysis of industrial development faces great difficulties owing to frequent changes in statistical procedures. Here it has been attempted to establish comparability for data covering long periods.

Chart 19
Capital assets of GDR industry 1975

Industrial sector	Gross capital assets			Capital intensity[2]	
	Bn. M	Structure	Growth rate[1] 1961/75	Relations	Growth rate[1] 1961/75
		%			%
Water resources, fuel and power industries	69.7	30	5.7	435	5.7
Chemical industry	45.6	20	6.7	183	6.0
Metallurgy	13.2	6	6.3	139	5.4
Building materials	8.4	4	6.3	121	6.4
Mechanical engineering and vehicle building	35.5	15	7.0	54	5.2
Electrical engineering/ electronics/instrument building	13.2	6	8.7	41	5.9
Light industry	16.8	7	5.4	45	5.3
Textile industry	10.7	5	3.4	59	5.8
Food processing industry	16.1	7	4.9	89	4.0
All industry	229.2	100	6.1	100	5.3

1 Average annual growth rate.
2 Gross capital assets per employed person.

Source: DIW calculations

Chart 20
Development of productivity in GDR industry
(average annual change in per cent)

Industrial sector	Labour productivity[1]		Capital productivity[2]	
	1961/1975	1971/1975	1961/1975	1971/1975
Water resources, fuel and power industries	3.9[3]	1.5[3]	− 2.0	− 2.6
Chemical industry	7.1	7.0	1.2	0.8
Metallurgy	4.9	6.0	− 0.5	1.4
Building materials	6.3	5.8	0.2	0.3
Mechanical engineering/vehicle building	5.6	4.7	− 0.2	− 1.0
Electrical engineering/electronics/ instrument building	6.9	6.6	0.6	0.3
Light industry	5.9	5.1	0.0	0.9
Textile industry	6.4	6.5	0.4	0.3
Food processing industry	3.7	3.7	− 0.4	− 0.5
All industry	5.8[3]	5.3[3]	− 0.0	− 0.1

1 Industrial gross production per employee.
2 Industrial gross production per unit of gross capital assets.
3 Not including water industry

Sources: GDR Statistical Yearbooks and DIW calculations

105

labour force respectively by 41 and 28 per cent, whereas at the other extreme the textile industry registered a 26 per cent drop in employment.

The most substantial advances in *labour productivity* were recorded in the 'classical' growth industries, chemicals and electrical engineering/ electronics/instrument building, as well as in the production of building materials. In recent years major productivity increases occurred also in sectors where labour had been made redundant by *rationalisation*, above all in the textile industry, which incidentally was leading the field also in the Federal Republic with an average annual productivity increase of 5.7 per cent during the period 1970 to 1975.

Capital productivity, i.e. production per unit of gross capital assets, declined almost imperceptibly over the last five years, at an average annual rate of 0.1 per cent. With this showing the GDR comes off well in an international comparison, for in other industrial countries, including the Federal Republic, the required rate of increase of capital assets is clearly higher than the corresponding growth of production.

Any assessment of the development of productivity in the GDR suffers from the uncertainties due to the *distortion* of production statistics by *price effects*. As pointed out before (see chapter 3 above), the real increases in production are exaggerated in the official statistics of the GDR, because at least some of the price increases introduced in the GDR were not taken into account. Assuming that such unacknowledged price increases amount to 1.5 per cent annually, the decline of capital productivity from 1970 to 1975 now comes out as just over 1.0 per cent on average per year, an order of magnitude very close to the corresponding West German figure. On the same assumption, the average annual growth of labour productivity would be reduced from 5.3 to very nearly 4 per cent, which again looks a reasonable figure. Even so, chart 20 illustrates the different levels and trends of productivity in the various industries of the GDR.

The productivity of GDR industry constantly lies about one third below that of the Federal Republic. Similar estimates have been made from time to time by GDR quarters.

4.1.3   The main branches of industrial production

The structure of GDR industrial production is presented here in terms of gross production at 1967 prices. These prices were fixed in the course of the industrial price reform, and they were intended to be more in line with production costs than the earlier fixed prices. As pointed out before (p.40 above), the new prices still suffered from grave shortcomings, notably the insufficient consideration of capital costs. Moreover, the statistical figures for gross production give no

106

indication of the varying levels of intermediate consumption. These reservations must be borne in mind when attempting to interpret the picture of the GDR's industrial structure.

To be able to compare the industrial structure of the GDR with the pre-war state, the 1936 figures of industrial production for the territory of the present GDR had to be broken down according to the classification currently in use. The same had to be done for the GDR data covering the years 1950 and 1955 in order to present a coherent picture of industrial development since 1950.

In 1936 about 30 per cent of industrial production in the areas now occupied by the two German states came from GDR territory. The main industries in that territory were brown coal mining, textile machines, printing, precision engineering, optical instrument building, light industries (knitwear, yarns, rayon, staple fibre) and the food processing industry. It was a lop-sided industrial structure, with the food processing and light industries (including textiles) accounting for more than half the total industrial output of the region, while the chemical industry contributed no more than 6 per cent and the engineering and vehicle building industries only 16 per cent of the total output (cf. Appendix, table 18).

About 45 per cent of the productive capacities were destroyed as a result of hostilities during the war or dismantled after the war by the Soviet Occupying Power. Thus economic reconstruction had to start from a very unfavourable position. Without iron ore or hard coal, the region had no facilities for the production of pig iron, crude steel or rolling mill products. In addition, the Soviet Zone was virtually devoid of capacities in the heavy engineering and power plant building sectors. Since at that time the gap could not be closed by means of foreign trade, an all-out effort was made to overcome the disproportion between on the one hand the underdeveloped metallurgical and capital goods industries and on the other hand the light industries and the remainder of the manufacturing industry.

The sectoral structure of GDR industry was decisively altered by the development of a heavy engineering industry and the expansion of the metallurgical and chemical industries. As early as 1955 notable changes were registered, when the metallurgical industry had increased its share of total industrial output to 9 per cent, and the mechanical engineering and vehicle building industry its respective share to 19 per cent. Further improvements were achieved especially in the 1960s by means of structural policy measures. The industries producing important investment goods, modern basic materials and intermediate goods were foremost among the sectors that increased their share in total output.

In the following we propose to give a clearer picture of the current situation of the most important industries, although a detailed sectoral

107

analysis cannot be presented within the scope of this broad survey. Specialised studies on this subject have been published by the DIW and other institutions.

The *fuel and power industry* (including water resources) has recorded the slowest growth of all industries in the GDR. From 1960 to 1975, its gross output rose on average by only 3.5 per cent annually, as against 6.2 per cent for industry as a whole. This appears to have been due largely to the high degree of capital intensity of the fuel and power sector, which accounts for only 5 per cent of industrial gross production but no less than 24 per cent of the gross capital assets of industry. The slow rate of growth was not sufficient to close the energy gap; there were recurring power cuts and interruptions of gas supply especially in the 1960s.

The supply of raw materials for the fuel and power industry is characterised by the following features:

1   Just under three quarters of the requirements of primary energy in the GDR are supplied by solid fuels (as compared with barely one third in the Federal Republic). Brown coal alone supplied nearly 66 per cent of the total in 1975 (as against 10 per cent in the Federal Republic).

2   The intensive utilisation of the domestic brown coal deposits substantially reduces the economy's dependence on imported energy sources and the need for foreign exchange. In 1975 the GDR was able to cover 70 per cent of its energy requirements from domestic production (as against 50 per cent in the Federal Republic).

3   As the expansion of brown coal production had been postponed until after 1980, the increased consumption of primary energy will have to be met to begin with by the use of oil and natural gas. But this is bound to increase the dependence of the energy sector on imports. By far the most important supplier is the Soviet Union, which in 1975 accounted for very nearly 80 per cent of GDR energy imports, thereby covering over 25 per cent of the country's requirements of primary energy.

The *generation of electric power* presented for many years a major bottleneck in the energy sector. Over the ten-year period 1965 to 1975 the power output increased at an average annual rate of only 4.7 per cent (as compared with the West German figure of 5.8 per cent for the same period and as much as 6.8 per cent for the years 1965 to 1974).

Although the target set by the last Five-Year Plan (1971-75) for the construction of new power stations was not met,[1] the power supply situation has eased during the last few years. In 1975 the power supply to industry functioned for the first time smoothly and without interruption.

Close on 85 per cent of the total power output of the GDR is generated in brown-coal fired power stations. Nuclear power stations are playing a growing part. Under the 1976-80 plan the existing generating capacities totalling 17,000 MW are to be supplemented by an additional 5,000 MW, and one quarter of the new capacities is to be provided by nuclear power stations. At present the GDR has two nuclear power stations, at Rheinsberg and at Lubmin (Greifswald District) with capacities respectively of 75 and 880 MW. In 1975 these two power stations accounted for only 3 per cent of the total power output, while in the Federal Republic 7 per cent of the power output was generated by nuclear plants. Both the Lubmin power station (*Kernkraftwerk Nord*) and the projected third nuclear power station at Stendal near Magdeburg are to reach final capacities of 3,520 MW. The 440 MW reactors and the enriched uranium are supplied by the Soviet Union.

Gas supplies have also improved since the beginning of the seventies. The output of natural gas rose from 200 million cu.m. in 1969 to 8,000 million cu.m. in 1975. However, the calorific value of the gas is rather low (about 3,000 Kcal per cu.m.). Thanks to the simultaneous increase in the output of town gas by the leading producer, the Schwarze Pumpe Combine — which from its brown coal coking plant supplied in 1975 about half the total GDR output of 5,100 million cu.m. — GDR industry in 1972 for the first time received all the gas it needed.

The *consumption of mineral oil products* is low by comparison with western industrial countries.[2] As a result, the GDR has been hit less hard than other countries by the oil price explosion. The requirements of mineral oil products are wholly supplied by the domestic refineries at Schwedt, Böhlen, Zeitz and Leuna, which between them produced about 17 million tonnes in 1975. Owing to the steep rise in the price of crude, refinery output is scheduled to increase at a slower rate than in recent years. The target for 1980 is a total consumption of 23 million tonnes.

Parallel with the increase in output, efforts are being made to reduce

---

1 The plan provided for additional capacities totalling 6,000 MW. The increase actually achieved was only 4,300 MW.
2 Per capita consumption in 1975 was 1.2 tonnes in the GDR, as against 2.6 tonnes in the EEC countries.

Chart 21
Sources of primary energy consumed in the GDR 1960 and 1975

	Brown coal	Hard coal	Coke	Mineral oil	Oil products	Natural gas	Primary electric power	Total consumption	
			Mill. t			Bn. N m^3	Bn. kWh.	Mill. t HCE^2	%
1960									
Production	225.5	2.7	–	0.0	–	0.0	0.6	68.02	89.2
Import	5.5	8.1	2.5	1.9	0.4	–	0.1	13.75	18.0
Export	6.3	–	–	–	0.7	–	0.5	5.47	7.2
Domestic consumption of primary energy	224.7	10.8	2.5	1.9	- 0.3	0.0	0.2	76.30	100.0
1975									
Production	246.6	0.5	–	0.2	–	8.0	4.7	78.88	70.5
Import	–	6.4	3.0	17.0	0.1	3.2	1.4	37.98	34.0
Export	2.3	–	–	–	2.8	0.0	0.7	5.05	4.5
Domestic consumption of primary energy	244.3	6.9	3.0	17.2	- 2.7	11.2	5.4	111.81	100.0
Percentage shares of domestic consumption of primary energy^3									
1960	83.1	11.0	2.9	3.4	- 0.5	0.0	0.1	100.0	–
1975	65.5	4.8	2.5	22.0	- 3.4	6.9	1.7	100.0	–

1 From hydroelectric and nuclear power stations plus net imports.
2 Hard coal equivalent.
3 In HCE.

Sources: GDR Statistical Yearbooks; CMEA Statistical Yearbook; DIW calculations

demand. They may well succeed up to a point, since the figures for specific energy consumption, i.e. consumption of primary energy per unit product, are relatively high. It has been stated by GDR sources that for similar production processes energy consumption in the GDR is about 20 per cent above that in other industrial countries;[1] wasteful use of energy is likely to be part of the reason for the discrepancy. Accordingly, efforts to ensure the economical use of energy are being

1 This is borne out by the figures for per capita consumption of primary energy, which in 1975 was 5.6 tonnes of hard coal equivalent in the Federal Republic, as against 6.6 tonnes in the GDR.

intensified:[1] thus energy consumption norms are being set, with material rewards in store for enterprises observing them and fines for those exceeding them.

The *management of water resources* is a sector of constantly growing importance in the GDR. From 1960 to 1975, the amount of water actually supplied to consumers rose at an average annual rate of 3.5 per cent; taking the last five years alone, the average was 4.5 per cent. Supplies to industry and transport increased more rapidly at a rate of 5.4 per cent. The water resources of the GDR are under considerable strain. The annual supply fluctuates between 6,000 and 30,000 million cu.m., with an average of 15,000 million cu.m. Current demand has already reached 8,000 million cu.m. a year and is expected to rise to about 14,000 million cu.m. by 1980. The demand varies considerably from region to region. In the southern industrial centres shortage of water has been in evidence for years. Great efforts are being made, therefore, to improve the situation by the building of river barrages, reservoirs and purification plants. At present and for the foreseeable future, the water authorities in the GDR do not appear to be in a position to prevent major environmental pollution, especially in regions where the chemical industry is concentrated. This affects chiefly the Mulde, Saale and Werra rivers and their tributaries.

For the purpose of GDR statistics, the *chemical industry* in the wider sense includes extraction of petroleum and natural gas, petroleum processing, potassium and rock-salt mining, and the processing of rubber, asbestos and plastics. The rapid expansion of this sector is due above all to the advance of the plastics industry, which increased its gross production during the period from 1960 to 1975 at an average annual rate of 11.5 per cent.

A comparison with the chemical industry in the Federal Republic shows that in terms of per capita output the GDR industry has considerable leeway to make up, especially in the manufacture of modern products, and in particular of those requiring substantial expenditure on development, e.g. synthetic fibres, plastics and dyes. A comparison would be even more unfavourable for the GDR in respect of paints and varnishes as well as pharmaceuticals, but for these sectors accurate statistics are not available.

The GDR chemical industry has been much slower than its West German counterpart in switching from coal as its foremost raw material to the technologically more advantageous oil and natural gas. Oil and gas account at present for about 60 per cent of the industry's raw

---

1 Energy savings equivalent to 40 million tonnes of brown coal are to be made in the 1976-80 period by reducing the product-specific consumption of brown coal in industry by 5 per cent and that of electric power by 3 per cent a year.

Chart 22
Output of the branches of the GDR chemical industry
Average annual growth rates in per cent

Industrial branch	1960/65	1965/70	1970/75	Plan[2] 1975/80
Oil, natural gas, coal derivatives	8.6	8.5	7.7	6.0
Basic chemicals (inorganic and organic)	5.2	2.2	7.4	9.5
Pharmaceuticals	11.8	7.2	8.6	10.5
Plastics[1]	10.0	12.9	11.6	9.0
Rubber and asbestos	8.9	7.2	6.7	7.0
Manmade fibres	8.7	14.4	13.2	4.5
Chemical and chemotechnical special products	6.0	6.3	7.5	6.5
All branches	7.9	7.7	8.3	7.6-7.9

1 Production and processing.
2 Data for the various branches relate to representative product groups; partly estimated.

Sources: GDR Statistical Yearbook 1976; Directive for the 1976/80 Five-Year Plan; DIW calculations

Chart 23
Output of selected chemical products

Products	Multiples of	1960	1975		
			Absolute	Index 1965 = 100	FRG = 100
Petrol	1000 t	1,080	2,933	183	17
Diesel fuel	1000 t	1,289	4,853	215	50
Fuel oils	1000 t	393	8,102	470	16
Rock salt	1000 t	1,785	2,380	141	1,266
Sulphuric acid	1000 t H_2SO_4	730	1,002	102	24
Hydrochloric acid	1000 t HCl	75	100	151	14
Calcium carbide	1000 t	923	1,291	108	265
Ammonia	1000 t NH_3	477	1,117	210	46
Methanol	1000 t	73	240	210	31
Potash fertilisers	1000 t K_2O	1,666	3,019	157	136
Nitrogenous fertilisers	1000 t N	334	539	155	37
Organic dyes	t	8,423	16,272	114	19
Plastics	1000 t	115	605	277	12
Synthetic fibres	1000 t	8	113	594	18
Tyres	1000 units	2,714	6,272	167	13

Sources: GDR Statistical Yearbook; Federal Office of Statistics, Fachserie D, Reihe 3

materials, a proportion that was reached in the Federal Republic as long ago as 1963. However, the gap is now being diminished as a result of the construction of new petrochemical capacities which came on stream in recent years, notably the plants for the production of ethylene and propylene at Böhlen, polyurethane at Schwarzheide, and nitrate fertilisers at Piesteritz.

The development plans up to 1980 envisage continuing high growth rates for the chemical industry. Such efforts are indeed necessary, considering the extent to which the industry is still outstripped by the West German chemical industry. If the planned increase in output, at an average annual rate of close on 8 per cent is attained, the gap between the two German states is likely to be reduced in the medium term, as there are signs of the upward trend in the West German chemical industry levelling off.

Chart 24
Production of selected metallurgical products (in 1,000 tonnes)

Products	1960	1975		
		Absolute	1965 = 100	FRG = 100
Pig iron	1,995	2,456	105	8
Crude steel	3,750	6,472	150	16
Hot rolled steel	2,613	4,281	143	15
Products of second processing stage	498	2,793	382	*

Sources: Statistical Yearbook of the GDR; Federal Statistical Office, Fachserie D, Reihe 3
*No data available.

The output of the *metallurgical industry* has increased roughly seven-fold since 1950. This was necessary in order to lessen the disproportion between the low domestic output of iron and steel and the demand of the metal processing industry. Since 1960, however, metallurgical production has achieved an annual growth rate of only 5.7 per cent, which is less than the growth rate for industrial output as a whole. Following an initial period characterised by the building of new and the expansion of existing plants for the production of pig iron and steel, a new direction was imparted to the industry's structural development in the mid-sixties, with the accent on products of the second processing stage:[1] the GDR steel industry now concentrates on the production of

---

1 The second processing stage is concerned with the treatment of hot-rolled products which, after cooling below the temperature of recrystallisation, are reprocessed into products of different shapes and qualities (e.g. cold-rolled strip and plate, drawn and pressed structural shapes, tubes, extruded products).

high-grade and special steels, while requirements of lower grades of steel are met chiefly through imports. This trend towards higher quality products and a relatively lower output of the first processing stage has affected the quantitative performance of the metallurgical industry whose share in the country's industrial output, rising steeply from 1950 to the early sixties, has shown a slight decline since then.

The development of the *building materials industry* of the GDR reflects a particularly rapid transition to the use of prefabricated components. Conspicuous progress in productivity was recorded with a labour force that remained virtually constant. After the development and testing of standardised systems of residential housing construction, several works for the manufacture of prefabricated slabs are coming on stream in the GDR. Their output will play a vital part in attaining the ambitious targets of the long-term housing programme.

Chart 25
Production of selected building materials

Products	In	1960	1975		
			Absolute	1965 = 100	FRG = 100
Industrial quick-lime	1000 t	2,116	3,030	127	49
Plaster of Paris	1000 t	217	306	141	23
Chippings and ballast	1000 t	7,670	20,908	181	35
Standard bricks	mill. units	2,272	1,351	96	*
Roof tiles	mill. units	359	80	24	131
Concrete products	1000 t	6,973	23,503	220	*
Cement	1000 t	5,032	10,653	175	30

Sources: GDR Statistical Yearbook; Federal Office of Statistics, Fachserie D, Reihe 3
*No data available.

The price to be paid for this restructuring of the building materials industry is the continuation of the permanent shortages of traditional building materials, affecting supplies not only to the public but often to the building enterprises also. Time after time work is held up because bricks, or plaster, or roofing felt are not available. Even cement supplies were occasionally still erratic in recent years, in spite of the commissioning of new plants.

Mechanical engineering and vehicle building accounts for one quarter of the GDR's industrial output. This is the largest industrial sector, and its importance has constantly increased. Apart from the classical branches of mechanical engineering, the sector comprises steel constructions, the building of road and rail vehicles, shipbuilding, foundries,

114

Chart 26
Output of selected branches of the GDR
mechanical engineering and vehicle building industry
(average annual growth rate in per cent)

Engineering branch	1960/65	1965/70	1970/75
Chemical industry equipment	6.3	19.8	2.8
Equipment for the refrigeration engineering industry	14.6	11.0	6.2
Machine tools	5.7	8.0	9.3
Rail vehicles	4.9	3.4	0.9
Road vehicles and tractors	8.3	8.1	5.5
Shipbuilding	5.4	6.1	5.0
Agricultural machinery	6.5	11.2	10.0
Metal goods	8.6	7.8	6.5
All branches mechanical engineering/ vehicle building	7.4	7.0	5.8

Source: GDR Statistical Yearbook

manufacture of metal utensils and of some electrical household appliances (e.g. washing machines, refrigerators), while the manufacture of office machines belongs to the electrical engineering/electronics/ instrument building sector. Although detailed information on the relative weight of these individual branches is not available, the structure of the sector appears to be fairly similar to that of its West German counterpart, apart from the GDR's very much lower output of motor vehicles and the absence of an aircraft industry.

The mechanical engineering sector is of decisive importance for economic policy on a number of counts:

a) This sector assures the reproduction of the domestic industry by manufacturing production plants;

b) it assures technological progress by introducing new plants;

c) it constitutes the most important source of GDR exports;

d) it provides a large part of the supplies needed by other industries for their processes of production, ranging from screws and nuts, tubes and valves to pumps and gearboxes.

The rapid expansion of the industry was in response to these manifold demands. From 1960 to 1975 the labour force increased by 190,000 (28 per cent), capital assets rose by no less than 174 per cent and gross output by 166 per cent.

115

Chart 27
Output of selected products of the
mechanical engineering and vehicle building industry

Products	In multiples of	1960	1975 absolute	1975 1965 = 100	1975 FRG = 100
Equipment for					
– metallurgy	Mill. Marks	135	353	157	–
– chemical engineering	Mill. Marks	349	836	198	–
– refrigeration technology	Mill. Marks	338	1,569	213	–
– processing of plastics	Mill. Marks	–	298	–	–
– manufacture of manmade fibres	Mill. Marks	14	51	925	–
– printing	Mill. Marks	114	392	249	–
– textile, clothing and leather industry	Mill. Marks	294	857	220	–
– food processing industry	Mill. Marks	267	632	200	–
– agriculture	Mill. Marks	601	2,844	366	–
Cast iron and steel, malleable cast iron	1000 t	1,142	1,288	112	33
Metal-cutting machine tools	Mill. Marks	344	1,089	248	–
Cold forming machine tools	Mill. Marks	201	352	156	–
Automatic lathes	Units	521	577	178	16
Milling machines	Units	2,694	2,970	125	32
Grinding machines	Units	4,812	4,553	70	14
Hydraulic presses	Units	–	1,302	107	36
Railway coaches	Units	4,085	6,675	205	207
Passenger motorcars	1000 units	64	159	155	6
Lorries	1000 units	13	36	236	15
Domestic electric cookers	1000 units	59	115	210	10
Domestic washing machines	1000 units	132	374	129	25

Sources: GDR Statistical Yearbook; Federal Office of Statistics, Fachserie D, Reihe 3

In this way, the GDR has succeeded in maintaining, and partly con-solidating, its position as the technologically leading supplier of investment goods within the CMEA. Nor has it lost ground by compari-son with the Western industrial countries. It achieved this objective by following the worldwide trends, though usually with some delay, and in particular by updating the range of goods produced in line with modern technological developments. Thus, in the GDR as in other modern industrial countries the production, say, of machine tools, of plastics, processing machines or electronic and optical devices has expanded at a rate considerably above the average for industry as a whole. New pro-duction lines were developed, e.g. for chemical plants, open cast mining equipment and textile machinery.

116

The continual extension of the range of goods, which continued unchecked until very recently, brought in its train all the disadvantages of a fragmentation of production. Research and development, spread over so many fields could only rarely maintain a leading position in any one. On the other hand, the multiplicity of goods made it almost impossible to arrange for optimum production runs. The competitiveness of the GDR engineering industry is therefore endangered, especially on the Western industrial markets. Efforts are being made to remedy the situation by organising specialisation and co-operation within the socialist economic bloc.

Division of labour among the CMEA countries is relatively well advanced in the mechanical engineering sector, with over fifty co-operation agreements at state level, followed up by hundreds of specific arrangements between individual enterprises. The GDR plays a part especially in the sectors of metallurgical and chemical plant, agricultural machinery, haulage equipment, printing and textile machinery, shipbuilding and railway waggon construction. In addition, the GDR is pursuing independently the development of a number of technologically advanced products (e.g. numerically controlled machine tools, specialised production equipment), which presumably are to be turned over to the CMEA for collective utilisation at a later stage.

The *electrical engineering/electronics/instrument building* sector, which today contributes one eighth of industrial output, holds a key position as the producer of rationalisation, control and automation equipment as well as of electronic products serving communications and entertainment. It is especially the electronics and data-processing industries which are responsible for the above-average growth of this sector. Nevertheless, in technological terms the GDR is still lagging behind such countries as Japan or the Federal Republic, mostly by substantial margins (e.g. in the manufacture of micro-electronic components and all instruments based on them, including data-processing equipment).

The problems faced by this sector are similar to those of the mechanical engineering/vehicle building industry: the need to meet high volumes of domestic and export demand; fragmentation induced by over widening product ranges; shortcomings in research and development; a trend towards specialisation and co-operation within the CMEA. This co-operation is particularly marked in the fields of communications and data-processing technology, generating plant construction, scientific instruments, process control and medical technology.

East Berlin is the foremost centre of this sector, which contributes one third of the city's industrial output. Most of the other enterprises of the electrical engineering/electronics/instrument building sector are

117

Chart 28
Output of branches of the
electrical engineering/electronics/instrument building sector
(average annual growth rate in per cent)

Branch	1961/65	1966/70	1971/75
Electrical engineering	9.4	7.3	6.5
Electronics	10.3	9.6	13.5
Measuring and control engineering	15.6	8.9	8.9
EDP and office machines	10.0	22.7	11.2
Precision engineering/optical industry	4.7	11.9	6.2
All branches	9.4	9.6	9.3

Source: GDR Statistical Yearbook

Chart 29
Output of selected products of the
electrical, electronic and precision engineering industries
and of optical instruments

Products	Multiples of	1960	1975		
			absolute	1965 = 100	FRG = 100
Power transformers	Unit	12,770	10,047	89	*
High and low voltage switch gear and accessories	Mill. M.	556	2,105	255	—
Cables and wires	Mill. M.	624	1,770	183	—
Radio receivers	1000 units	810	1,068	132	95
TV receivers	1000 units	416	509	95	20
Electronic components	Mill. M.	133	2,235	1,001	—
Monitoring and control equipment	Mill. M.	105	1,028	361	—
Office machines and EDP equipment	Mill. M.	189	2,264	646	—
Typewriters	1000 units	244	407	201	32
Electrical measuring and testing apparatus	Mill. M.	57	277	247	—
Field glasses	1000 units	114	176	217	117
Cameras	1000 units	530	806	156	20
Wrist watches	1000 units	2,748	3,789	171	56
Medical apparatus	Mill. M.	71	234	241	—
Laboratory equipment	Mill. M.	39	120	220	—

Sources: GDR Statistical Yearbook; Federal Office of Statistics, Fachserie D, Reihe 3

*No data available.

118

located in the southern areas (Erfurt, Gera, Karl-Marx-Stadt, Dresden). The *consumer industries* comprise the food processing industry, accounting for 16 per cent of industrial gross production, light industry with 11 per cent, and the textile industry with 7 per cent. These figures, recorded in 1975, add up to 34 per cent for the entire sector, a drop of nearly 3 percentage points since 1970, and that in spite of the fact that the improvement of the people's living standards had been declared the principal task of the 1971-1975 Five-Year Plan. Nevertheless, the output of a number of products rose considerably after 1970.

Chart 30
Output of consumption-oriented industries
(average annual growth rate in per cent)

Industry	1961/65	1966/70	1971/75
Light industry	4.2	6.1	5.8
cellulose and paper	4.2	5.5	5.0
musical instruments, toys, sport equipment, etc.	7.3	8.4	7.3
clothing	3.2	4.7	4.4
leather, footwear and furs	4.6	6.2	6.1
Textile industry	2.5	4.3	5.3
Food processing industry	3.4	4.5	5.5

Source: GDR Statistical Yearbook

Despite the efforts to offer a greater variety of goods, better adapted to consumer demand, a great many consumer wishes continue to be ignored, as far as the domestic consumer is concerned, all the more so since a large proportion of the highest quality goods is exported.

Light industry manufactures a multitude of consumer goods as well as products such as window glass, ceramic sanitary fittings, hardboard and chipboard and packaging materials. Within the industry, the greatest increases in production from 1971 to 1975 were recorded for wallpaper (108 per cent), furniture (57 per cent), leather goods (44 per cent), and china (36 per cent).

In the *textile industry* notable increases in output from 1971 to 1975 were registered for carpets and runners (65 per cent), tulles and curtains (53 per cent) and hosiery (38 per cent). The sewing-knitting technology for the stitch-bonding of fabrics, developed in the GDR and introduced at considerable expense, has not so far scored a signal success internationally in spite of its undoubted advantages in production technology over the customary weaving technique.

In the *food industry* the development from 1971 to 1975 centred on

119

Chart 31
Output of selected light industry products

Products	In	1960	1975 absolute	1965 = 100	FRG = 100
Furniture (non-metal)	Mill. Marks	1,173	3,765	255	—
Paper	1000 t	542	796	124	22
Wallpaper	t	10,213	32,461	270	22
Musical instruments	Mill. Marks	112	203	149	—
Gymnastic and sport apparatus	Mill. Marks	48	152	254	—
Toys	Mill. Marks	207	799	218	—
Protective, working and service clothing	Mill. Marks	311	436	131	—
Outer garments for					
men	1000 units	8,861	14,492	138	*
women	1000 units	14,812	21,327	91	*
children	1000 units	*	19,555	99	*
Household linen	Mill. Marks	306	514	168	—
Footwear	1000 pairs	57,405	79,014	122	70
Leather goods	Mill. Marks	328	956	238	—
Window glass (stand. thickness)	1000 sq.m.	16,090	23,381	110	*
Fibre glass	t	12,209	7,720	58	5
Household and hotel china	t	22,151	38,358	148	*
Sanitary ceramics	t	13,313	16,365	128	*

Sources: GDR Statistical Yearbook; Federal Office of Statistics, Fachserie D, Reihe 3
*No data available.

non-alcoholic beverages, processed meat and sausages, vegetable and fruit preserves, and processed poultry meat. Sugar, butter and beer continue to figure prominently among the industry's range of goods. There was a marked increase also in the manufacture of feeding stuffs. In response to shifts in demand, production of cigarettes increased, while that of cigars and cigarillos declined.

4.1.4 Basic features of GDR industrial policy

Every economic policy measure affects industry, as the largest sector of the GDR economy, directly or indirectly, but there are specific measures concerned with industry in particular, so that there is justification in speaking of an autonomous industrial policy. The people's economic wellbeing is underpinned by industry in two ways: by meeting domestic needs directly and by exporting so as to open the way for imports. It is therefore vital for GDR industry to ensure its *competitiveness* in the medium and long term. In this effort, the decisive factors are:

a)   the structure of production;
b)   the technological standard of the products; and
c)   the level of costs, judged by international standards.

As regards *production costs*, it would seem that GDR industry should have no difficulty in being competitive on account of the relatively low real wages. Part of this advantage, however, is wiped out by the industry's lower efficiency. That is one of the main reasons why GDR industrial policy is geared to a drive for productivity gains. The utilisation of all factors of production, manpower, potential skills, capital assets, supply of materials and intermediate products, is to be intensified. Since the pressure of market forces is limited, unceasing efforts are made to improve the mechanism of economic planning and directing. To do this effectively, however, it would be necessary to bring the state-controlled prices into line with the actual conditions of production and demand, for in a planned economy, too, prices play a crucial part by largely determining planning decisions on subcontracting links, on production and marketing, and on structural development. It would further be necessary for the enterprises to act in an economically constructive way. Yet, to attain these aims in the GDR, immense obstacles have to be overcome (as pointed out in section 2.5 above): in many cases both the material prerequisites and the motivation needed for the fulfilment of the ambitious economic tasks set by the leadership are missing.

To be able to meet future demand and to take its place in the international division of labour, GDR industry must carry out adjustments which, in the given circumstances, present an exceedingly complex task. The *structure of production* ought to be centred on relatively sophisticated goods in the manufacture of which the qualities of a highly skilled labour force are utilised to the full. Thus, the GDR should not, in the long run, try to offer products which can be supplied just as well by low-wage countries (such as uncomplicated machines, most textiles, footwear, simple articles of clothing). That such an exercise in self-denial can be successful in the GDR, has been shown by the example of the shift in metallurgical production. While there is full employment, the sacrifice of some traditional lines of manufacture will make it possible to shift resources to more rewarding activities, thus increasing national wealth. The order of priorities is clearly apparent in the 1976-80 Five-Year Plan.

While industrial output as a whole is scheduled to go up on average by 6 per cent a year, the corresponding growth rate for the manufacture of machine tools and processing machines is 9.3 per cent, and for electrical engineering with electronics 7.7 per cent. It may be noted, however, that the need to adjust to worldwide economic trends is still to some extent obscured in the GDR by the fact that co-operation with the CMEA partners assures GDR industry of a stable market for products lagging behind the latest advances in modern technology.

Priority in technologically advanced products cannot be achieved without a great *research and development* effort. When the available research capacities are insufficient to keep all lines of production technologically up to date, the sensible response is courageously to shed some of the load and specialise. The risks of inadequate diversification are undoubtedly less than the risks involved in a dissipation of energy. Moreover, international co-operation can improve the prospects of specialisation, especially when there is collaboration between technologically strong partners.

4.2 The building sector

In 1975, the building sector's share in the gross domestic product, calculated according to the Western concept, amounted to 7 per cent. Similarly, the sector's labour force accounted for 7 per cent of the economically active population. The building industry contributed 67 per cent of the total building output, another 11 per cent came from the building trades, about 8 per cent from agricultural building enterprises, and 14 per cent from other enterprises outside the building sector.

4.2.1 Building output

The development of building output in real terms in the GDR has been rather uneven, following a pattern not dissimilar to the growth of capital investments. It is a pattern reflecting the growth crisis of the early sixties, the slight decline of investments in 1966, and the reduced average growth rates of capital investments in the seventies by comparison with the period from 1964 to 1969. A noteworthy feature, clearly manifest in the graphs of figure 20, is the fact that there is a wider divergence between the two curves after 1969 than before. In the later period investment activity was subject to major fluctuations, whereas the building output maintained almost constant growth rates. This relative stability is due to the overcoming of some structural weaknesses of the building sector (e.g. shortages of building materials, fragmentation of effort among too many sites, inadequate planning and project preparation), combined with the growing weight of housing construction.

122

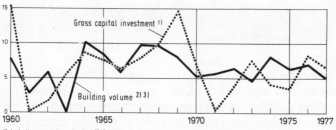

1) Including general overhauls.-'2) Building output of all sectors, including building repairs.- 3) The
result of 1969 has been corrected for items which in GDR statistics were not listed under the heading
of building output until 1969 (steel constructions, light-weight metal constructions, building work
executed abroad under export agreements, own-account project preparation by building enterprises).
This correction reduces the growth rate for 1969 from 10.6 to 8.0 per cent.

DIW79

Figure 20   Development of building volume and gross
investment 1960 to 1977 at 1967 prices.
Annual growth rates in per cent.

A comparison of the building output of the two German states (see
Appendix, table 20) shows that the output of the GDR, taken as a percentage of that of the Federal Republic, rose from 16 per cent in 1960
to 20 per cent in 1970 and 29 per cent in 1975 (assessed in each
territory at 1967 prices). In terms of *per capita output* the GDR
gradually caught up, reducing a lag of 50 per cent in 1960 to 30 per
cent in 1970 and 20 per cent in 1973. In 1975 the GDR's per capita
building output was actually slightly higher than that of the Federal
Republic, a result due in part to the recession in the West German
building industry.

The above comparison is scarcely distorted by the use of 1967 prices
in the two territories. In that year, general price levels for building work
diverged only to a minimal extent in the two states, so that the comparative figures should present a good approximation to the relative
performance of the industry in the two parts of Germany.

The building output is an aggregate composed of repairs, other building output and new constructions (building investments). The share of
repairs (including general overhauls) has varied since 1960 between 22
and 28 per cent. About one third of the repairs serves the maintenance
of the over-aged housing stock.

The share of the category of *other building output*, comprising
demolition and rubble clearance, architects' services as well as outlays
for site preparation, land use charges, etc., have shown a steep rise in
recent years in line with the intensification of preparatory work that is

123

indispensable for the complex large-scale projects now being taken in hand.

4.2.2 Building investment

Up to 1966, the growth rates of building investments (i.e. building output minus repairs and 'other building work') were slightly below those of investment activity as a whole; after that the trend was reversed and building investments increased at a slightly faster rate, except in the years 1969, 1970 and 1973.

Building investments, like general investments, are largely concentrated on the 'productive' sectors, whose share in the total volume of building investments rose from 58 per cent in 1960 to 66 per cent in 1975 (cf. Appendix, table 35). This is more than twice the corresponding percentage in the Federal Republic. *Industry* alone accounted for 40 per cent of all building investments in the mid-sixties and early seventies, registering a steep increase since 1960, when its share was only 30 per cent. *Agriculture and forestry* ranks second among the investors of the productive sectors, with a share of between 16 and 21 per cent of all new buildings. This is a reflection of the transition to 'industrial production methods' in agriculture, which is accompanied by building activity on a major scale. The two sectors, *transport, posts and telecommunications* and *trade*, each accounted for 5 per cent of new buildings. In the sectors 'outside material production', the erection of new buildings is dominated by the sector of *housing construction*. In spite of the large-scale housing programme of the 1970s, the share of residential building in the total volume of new buildings actually declined from 28 per cent in 1960 to 22 per cent at present. The bottom rung of the scale of priorities is occupied by the *remaining nonproductive sectors*, comprising state administration, culture, social institutions, banking and insurance, and services. Their share in building investments dropped from close on 11 per cent in 1960 to a mere 4 per cent in 1975. This curtailment involved the neglect of important sections of the infrastructure.

4.2.3 Housing construction

4.2.3.1 Volume of housing construction In purely quantitative terms the post-war housing situation was better at first in the territory of the

GDR than in West Germany.[1] This was a consequence of less extensive war damage and a stagnant population. In 1950 the housing density (number of persons per dwelling) was 3.6 in the GDR, as against 4.9 in the Federal Republic.

That is why housing construction went ahead full tilt in the Federal Republic during the last two decades, whereas there was no need for such intense activities in the GDR, where the share of housing construction in the total building output is correspondingly much lower than in the Federal Republic (cf. Appendix, table 21): in the 1950s the relevant figures were over 50 per cent in the West, as against 35 to 40 per cent in the GDR, and that at a time when the GDR's per capita building output was low. The contrast is thrown into relief even more vividly when per capita housing construction is made the basis of comparison. In this sector, the per capita building output of the GDR was no more than one third of the West German figure in 1960, rising to about 40 per cent at the beginning of the seventies and to 64 per cent in 1975.

In the extensive housing programme of the 1971-75 Five-Year Plan great prominence was given to new housing construction and the modernisation of the old housing stock. In effect, the volume of housing construction increased on average by 9 per cent a year. GDR housing expenditure in 1975 amounted to 6,000 million Marks at 1967 prices, of which 3,800 million Marks for new constructions and 2,200 million Marks for repairs. Thus housing investment had risen nearly twofold since 1960, and the expenditure on housing repair — badly neglected up to the early 1960s — even by a factor of two-and-a-half.

During the period from 1961 to 1975 1.2 million dwellings were built, 470,000 of them in the last five-year period. In the Federal Republic the comparative figure for the 15 years was about 8.4 million dwellings. The volume of housing construction in the GDR varied from year to year; the annual output declined from 80,000 dwellings in the early sixties to 65,000 in 1966, then rose again to as much as 111,000 in 1975.

Of the dwellings made available since 1961, 14 per cent were the result of extensions or conversions,[2] which leaves a figure of about 1.1 million dwellings newly built. Of these, nearly 80 per cent (850,000 dwellings) were built by the assembly method. This average percentage

1 Even before the war the territory of the present GDR was better off in this respect than the West German regions, with a density in 1939 of 3.35 persons per dwelling in the East as against 3.7 in the West. Cf. Klaus Dieter Arndt, Wohnverhältnisse und Wohnungsbedarf in der sowjetischen Besatzungszone, Sonderheft des DIW, no.50, Berlin 1960, p.36.
2 Examples are the conversion of attics, basements and shop premises.

conceals a noteworthy development: the proportion of new residential buildings completed by the assembly of prefabricated components increased from 48 per cent in 1961 to 93 per cent in 1966, after which it fell back slightly to 80 per cent in 1975.

The rationalisation of housing construction techniques, manifested in the high proportion of buildings completed by the assembly method, is well ahead of the building industry in the Federal Republic. This circumstance, together with improvements in the planning of building operations, has had a markedly favourable effect on the speed and cost of building work. Over the fifteen-year period the average construction time was reduced by half to nine months. The price advantage of the assembly method by comparison with the traditional building processes was in 1965 on average 13 per cent, rising in the case of the most favourable projects to as much as 20 per cent. Today the price difference is likely to be very much higher.

Apart from adding to the housing stock by building and conversions, work on the modernisation of existing dwellings has been undertaken on a substantially increased scale since 1971.[1] In the five-year period to 1975 a total of 136,000 dwellings were modernised.

The amenities of new dwellings were greatly improved. Nearly all the dwellings built in 1975 have bath or shower rooms, constant hot water supply (as against 17 per cent in 1960) and fitted kitchens (26 per cent in 1960), while 90 per cent have central heating (9 per cent in 1960) and 72 per cent a balcony or loggia (37 per cent in 1960). The improvement of amenities affected the cost of construction per unit area of floor space. Expenditure per square metre increased from 494 Marks in 1960 to 574 Marks in 1973, followed by a slight decline to 555 Marks in 1975. Another factor which led to higher unit costs in the 1960s was the reduction in the average size of dwellings from 56 sq.m. in 1962 to 51 sq.m. in 1967. After that, the average size of dwellings was again increased, reaching 59 sq.m. in 1975, with a beneficial effect on costs.

A comparison with unit costs in the Federal Republic shows that in 1967 cost per square metre in the GDR was 544 Marks, in West Germany, with larger dwellings, 601 DM. The difference of about 10 per cent was probably offset by superior quality and amenities. Since 1967, however, building prices in the Federal Republic have risen sharply, while those in the GDR have remained constant, so that the gap has widened to around 35 per cent.

1 Modernisation is to bring amenities up to modern standards. Modernisation measures include notably connection to mains water supply, installation of hot water supply systems, indoor lavatories, showers and bathrooms and the building of central heating systems. Old housing stock is eligible for modernisation, provided the cost does not exceed 70 per cent of the outlays for comparable new dwellings, and provided the remaining useful life of the old stock is extended by not less than thirty years.

If economic rents were charged, the *level of rents* in the two states would accurately reflect the disparity in costs. But that is not the case: in the GDR the monthly rent for new dwellings ranged from 0.80 to 1.25 Marks per square metre in 1975, as compared with 6.20 DM for non-subsidised housing in the Federal Republic. The discrepancy arises from the fact that the fixing of rents in the GDR is a political decision. Rents as currently charged are not sufficient to finance repairs, depreciation and interest on capital. Rents are kept low on the grounds of social policy by means of substantial subsidies out of the state budget.

4.2.3.2 The current housing stock   According to the housing census, there were about 6 million dwellings in the GDR on 1 January 1971; by the end of 1975, the figure had risen to about 6.45 million. As the residential population numbers about 17 million, 383 dwellings were available in the mid-seventies per 1,000 inhabitants, as compared with 327 in 1961. In the Federal Republic the corresponding figures were 382 in 1975 and 292 in 1961. It must be borne in mind, however, that dwellings in the Federal Republic are larger, by 30 per cent on average, than those in the GDR (75 as against 58 sq.m.). In terms of floor space per inhabitant, then, the Federal Republic is better off, showing an increase from close on 20 sq.m. in 1961 to 29 sq.m. in 1975, compared with the corresponding rise from 17 to 22 sq.m. in the GDR.

Comparative figures for the number of rooms per dwelling give similar results. In West Germany 36 per cent of all dwellings have one or two rooms (not counting kitchens), as against 47 per cent in the GDR, where two-room flats alone account for 36 per cent of all dwellings. In the Federal Republic, the three-room flat, with 31 per cent of the total, is the dominant unit. The average room size was 15 sq.m. in the GDR, 20 sq.m. in the Federal Republic.

A picture of the current age structure of the housing stock can be obtained on the basis of the 1971 housing census supplemented by recent figures of housing construction and modernisation. Over half the dwellings in the Federal Republic have been built since the second world war, but in the GDR the proportion was only just over one quarter at the end of 1975. More than half the GDR housing stock (52 per cent) dates back to before 1919, another 21 per cent of all dwellings was built between 1919 and 1945.

According to the housing census of 1971, no less than 62 per cent of all dwellings were located in privately owned tenement houses. As the house building programme progresses, this ratio will be gradually reduced, for although building for owner occupation has lately been supported, fewer than 10 per cent of the dwellings built between 1971 and 1975 are privately owned.

Housing standards depend largely on the amenities with which a

Chart 32
Housing stock by number of rooms per dwelling
(all dwellings = 100)

Number of rooms	GDR	FRG[1]
1	11	11
2	36	25
3	34	31
4	13	17
5 and more	6	16

1 Since the FRG housing census, unlike that of the GDR, counts kitchens as dwelling rooms, the West German data have been brought into line.

Sources: GDR Statistical Yearbook; Federal Office of Statistics, Fachserie E, Reihe 6.

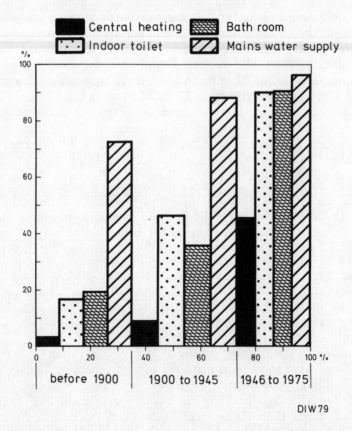

Figure 21   Age structure and equipment of housing stock 1975

128

dwelling is equipped. These in turn depend predominantly on the age of the housing stock, and thus leave much to be desired in the GDR. Substantial improvements have been introduced since the 1960s. Whereas in 1961 fewer than 3 per cent of all dwellings had central heating, and only 33 per cent had indoor lavatories, by the beginning of 1976 these figures had risen to 17 and 48 per cent respectively. During the same period, the proportion of dwellings with bathrooms rose from 22 to 45 per cent, and of those with mains water supply from 66 to 86 per cent. As pointed out before, the oldest houses have the poorest amenities. Of the dwellings built before 1900 — they still represent 35 per cent of the current housing stock — only one in thirty had central heating, one in six an indoor lavatory, one in five a bathroom.

The picture is further complicated by regional distortions and the uneven utilisation of dwelling space. The GDR has 990 dwelling rooms per 1,000 inhabitants (as compared with 1,200 in the Federal Republic), but this average is not evenly spread, under-occupation of large dwellings being balanced by the crowding of small ones.

4.2.3.3 Housing construction targets up to 1990 The 1966-70 Perspective Plan envisaged the construction of 400,000 dwellings. The number actually completed was 364,000, including conversions. Modernisation did not come into the picture at that time. The 1971-75 Five-Year Plan set a target of 500,000 dwellings, of which 383,500 were to be newly built, the remainder to be improved by general overhauls. These targets were exceeded, with 400,000 new constructions and 209,000 completed modernisations. The current Five-Year Plan provides for the years 1976 to 1980 a target of 750,000 dwellings, including 550,000 new constructions (including those for owner occupation). This programme has since been extended by the voluntary commitment of the FDGB to modernise an additional 100,000 dwellings. New constructions are being concentrated in the areas with a high proportion of old housing stock, so that it should be possible in the early eighties to begin with the demolition of old dwelling houses which are beyond repair. The remainder of the old housing stock is to be brought up to today's standards by modernisation. Another important aim of the housing construction programme is the provision of housing for the labour force in new industrial centres, notably in the Frankfurt, Cottbus and Rostock areas.

One tenth of the new constructions is to be erected in East Berlin, including the creation of an entirely new Borough — Biesdorf/Marzahn, ninth Borough of the City of Berlin — with 20,000 dwellings to be completed by 1980, rising by 1985 to a total of 35,000 dwellings due to accommodate a population of 10,000. High plan targets have been set also for the Halle, Karl-Marx-Stadt and Dresden areas (upwards of

55,000 dwellings) and the Leipzig and Magdeburg areas (40,000 dwellings each). Here too, the development of new residential districts is planned, such as, for instance, Leipzig-Grünau[1] and Magdeburg-Nord.[2]

Housing construction for owner occupation has been supported since 1971. In the 1976-80 period 55,000 dwellings are to be built for owner occupation, the maximum outlay per dwelling varying from 65,000 to 80,000 Marks. These dwellings are intended chiefly for workers and co-operative peasants and generally for large families. So far 85 per cent of the occupiers of such dwellings belong to one of these categories. The building of homes for owner occupation is supported by various concessions from the state,[3] but shortages of materials still constitute a limiting factor.

The 1976-80 Five-Year Plan provides for an expenditure of 60,000 million Marks for the housing construction programme, inclusive of site preparation work. Out of this total, 5,000 million Marks is earmarked for investments in the building materials industry. The plan envisages a net building cost per dwelling averaging 58,000 Marks, an increase of 6 per cent over the preceding five-year period. The increased expenditure allows for improved amenities as well as for a larger proportion of three and four-roomed dwellings. The average expenditure on modernisation has been raised from 14,000 to 18,000 Marks. The modernisation drive is one of the reasons for the trebling of the sum set aside for building repairs from about 5,000 million Marks in the 1971-75 period to close on 15,000 million Marks in the current Five-Year Plan.

Since even this ambitious programme cannot improve the housing situation sufficiently by 1980, housing construction has been declared the most crucial investment sector for the period up to 1990. For the ten years from 1981 to 1990 an expenditure of 140,000 million Marks on housing construction is to be used for the construction or modernisation of another 2.0 to 2.2 million dwellings. These projections, however, were made at a time when general conditions of growth seemed more favourable than they look at present.

1 A new residential district, comprising 20,000 dwellings, is to be established at Leipzig-Grünau by 1980.
2 Work is already in progress on the establishment of this new residential district, which is to comprise eventually 10,500 dwellings.
3 E.g. loans, waiving of ground rent for publicly owned land, exemption from land tax, state aid for repayment of loans (10 per cent of the amount repaid by the owner-occupier).

4.3 Agriculture

4.3.1 Structure of production units, modes of production

The GDR's agrarian policy is dominated by the concept of the 'socialised large-scale enterprise'. This objective was pursued consistently, and it may be said, relentlessly. Agriculture has been subjected to fundamental changes in the conditions of living and production, changes without parallel in any other sector of society. In 1955 there were 800,000 agricultural enterprises with holdings averaging 8 hectares. By the spring of 1960 collectivisation was accomplished in respect of over 90 per cent of the agricultural land, which was now farmed by agricultural producer co-operatives (LPGs) and publicly owned estates (VEGs) of an average size of 300 hectares of agricultural land.

Yet, the indicator of 'agricultural land per enterprise' still understates the extent of the process of concentration in crop production in view of the schemes of inter-enterprise co-operation and the establishment of specialised crop-farming producer co-operatives. At present, arable farming is carried out predominantly by 'Co-operative Plant Production Departments' (Kooperative Abteilungen der Pflanzenproduktion – KAPs), each of which farmed on average more than 4,000 hectares in 1975.[1]

The model of two forms of socialist ownership, state and co-operative, was taken over from the Soviet Union, where it exists in the shape of state-managed Sovkhozes and co-operatively run kolkhozes, except that in the Soviet Union the ownership of Kolkhoz land, too, is vested in the state. Also the Soviet state farms play a far more important part than those of the GDR. The Sovkhozes, engaged in a process of expansion, are currently farming about half the agricultural land in the Soviet Union. In the GDR the agricultural producer co-operatives constitute by far the larger sector.

The *publicly owned estates* were set up in the course of the land reform immediately after the war.[2] The VEGs are either centrally or area-managed. They are farmed by a labour force of wage and salary earners paid according to rates laid down in collective agreements. Many VEGs specialise in large-scale crop production, especially of seed

---

1 In the Federal Republic the average holding of agricultural enterprises was only just over 12 hectares in 1975. Out of 1.04 million enterprises, only 3,900, farming between them only 5 per cent of the agricultural land, exceeded 100 hectares of agricultural land.
2 The land reform covered 3.3 million hectares, 30 per cent of the farmland and woodlands of the Soviet Zone. Measured in terms of area, 80 per cent of the properties transferred to the land fund had been privately owned, and most of them exceeded 100 hectares; the remainder had been owned by the state. One third of the distributed land was given to the VEGs, two thirds to landless or land-starved peasants, agricultural workers or resettlers, who became private owners. Over 210,000 new peasant farms were thus created and more than 120,000 existing holdings were enlarged.

crops, or in the breeding of pedigree stock.

The *agricultural producer co-operatives* are characterised by mixed co-operative and private ownership. In particular the land brought into the co-operative by each member remains his private property.[1] The establishment of agricultural producer co-operatives started in 1952 when the Second SED Conference proclaimed the construction of socialism, and was virtually completed in the spring of 1960, when nearly all the remaining independent peasants were forced to join LPGs. The proportion of agricultural land farmed by the producer co-operatives rose from 20 per cent in 1955 to 45 per cent at the end of 1959 and to 85 per cent at the beginning of June 1960. Although GDR agrarian policy is based on Lenin's principles of co-operative farming, one of those principles, that of voluntariness, was frequently disregarded, in particular during the final phase of collectivisation, portrayed by the GDR information media as the 'socialist spring in the country-side'.

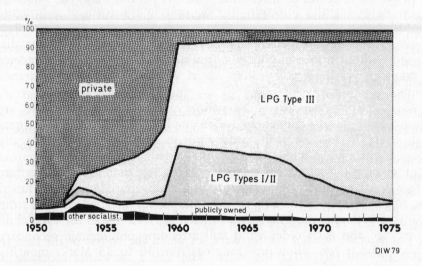

Figure 22   Structure of agricultural land in the
            GDR by type of ownership

1 This is not, as has frequently been claimed, an empty legal title, but a tangible asset. It is true that income distribution within the LPG is in current practice not greatly influenced by the amount of land contributed by each member (see pp 133f below). On the other hand, when land forming part of an LPG is converted to industrial use, indemnification is paid to the individual members and not to the co-operative.

The structure of agriculture in the GDR continued to undergo marked changes even after 1960. Thus the average size of agricultural producer co-operatives rose from 280 hectares of agricultural land in 1960 to nearly 1,200 hectares in 1975. This development reflected the advance of Type III agricultural producer co-operatives, whose share in the agricultural land farmed by the producer co-operatives increased from barely two thirds in 1960 to 93 per cent in 1975.

According to the model statutes, the three types of agricultural producer co-operatives are distinguished by the degree of socialisation of the means of production — that is to say, the degree of the collective utilisation of land, livestock, machines and farm buildings — and by the distribution of revenue. In the Type III co-operative all means of production are used collectively. In the other two types this applies to only some of the means of production, in the case of Type I in particular only to the utilisation of arable land. Types I and II thus can be regarded as stages of transition.

In the two 'lower' co-operative forms stock farming, with the exception of breeding stock, is carried on by the individual members on their own account, without co-operative supervision or distribution of individual incomes achieved in this way. The membership of these types of co-operatives has shrunk to about 10,000, representing hardly more than a footnote to the history of GDR agriculture.

In all three types, the land brought into the co-operative and the individually used means of production remain the private property of the members concerned, while the right to utilise the land is vested in the co-operative, with the exception of the private plots. Members of Type III co-operatives have an additional obligation: they must on entry make a stock contribution (buildings, livestock), which becomes co-operative property.

The revenue accruing from co-operative work is distributed in the main according to the work put in, measured in work units. The value of a work unit depends on the effective performance, the grading factor (reflecting the degree of difficulty and responsibility of each job) and the daily work norm. Since the final value of the work unit can be determined only by the year-end accounts, the precise level of personal incomes remains uncertain until that stage. Accordingly, the members of the co-operative receive advances assessed in the light of the plans, which in turn are based on the preceding year's results. Co-operative incomes, then, are not wages, in the sense of fixed payments (determined by agreed rates) for specified quantities of labour: they are residual proceeds arising, like profits, from the balance of revenue and costs. The co-operative peasant's income thus has an element of risk attached to it.

The income from work may be supplemented by payments in compensation for the use of the land which each member of the co-operative has contributed to the common pool. According to the model statute for the Type III co-operatives, such payments may reach up to 20 per cent of total incomes in money and in kind, but in practice the amounts paid for land use are negligible. Finally, the members of Type III co-operatives are entitled to private household plots of up to 0.5 hectare with limited numbers of livestock. Thus, the co-operative peasant has, in principle, three sources of income: work units, land use compensation and the proceeds of the private household plot.

The first of those three sources is by far the most important. The share of income from work has been constantly on the increase and is currently likely to make up roughly four fifths of the total. The value of the work unit varies substantially from one co-operative to another. There are considerable differentials concerning rates of pay for different jobs; thus, in terms of work units, the job of a cowman rates twice as high as that of a member engaged in crop farming. In many Type III co-operatives the household plot has had a balancing function: when the business outlook for the co-operative seemed poor, there was a strong incentive to concentrate more energy on the household plot. But with the increasing consolidation of the co-operatives, this motive lost in importance.

The highest authority of an agricultural producer co-operative is the general meeting of all the members, which decides on all questions of importance, in particular:

election, confirmation and recall of the Executive, the chairman and holders of leading positions (e.g. brigade leaders)

admission and expulsion of members

formulation of operating and working regulations

decisions on co-operation at inter-enterprise level

formulation of plans (for production, investment, utilisation of productive forces, etc.)

fixing of norms and principles of remuneration

distribution and use of revenue.

This far-reaching formal sovereignty of the general meeting is much curtailed in practice by generally applicable rules and regulations — such as the provisions of the model statute or the requirements of the economic plan — and by the influence brought to bear by outside bodies which usually take a guiding hand in the preparation of the resolutions to be submitted to the meeting.

Land reform and collectivisation were followed at the end of the sixties by the third phase of the agrarian policy of the SED: transition to industrial methods of production. This made a great difference to the shape of the 'traditional' agricultural producer co-operative. Relieved of responsibility for certain branches of production — chiefly crop farming, but also various stages of animal production — the co-operatives are losing more and more of their functions. New kinds of agricultural producer co-operatives are now being formed on the basis of inter-enterprise co-operation; they are the so-called specialised crop cultivation and animal production LPGs.

4.3.2 Utilisation of the factors of production

The supply to agriculture of means of production made by industry, chiefly fertilisers and machines, has greatly improved as a whole.

Thus, during the period 1959-60 to 1974-75 (reckoned in harvest years, 1 July to 30 June) the supply of nitrogen almost trebled, that of phosphate more than doubled (see Appendix, table 24). The following quantities of commerical fertilisers (pure nutrients) were applied in the GDR in 1974-75 per hectare of agricultural land: nitrogen 104 Kg, phosphate 72 Kg, potash 113 Kg, lime 199 Kg. Nitrogen and phosphate were in short supply in the 1950s; the pre-war levels were attained in 1956-57. The use of potash and lime was always higher in the GDR than in the Federal Republic; the use of nitrogen surpassed the West German level in 1964-65; as regards phosphate, the West German level was reached in 1967-68.

The rapid rise in the stock of machines is instanced by the availability of tractors. There were about 140,000 tractors in 1975, twice the number available in 1960. Actually the tractor fleet declined in numbers to a slight extent after 1970, but the numerical loss was more than made up for by the increase in engine power. Measured in terms of horse power, the strength of the GDR tractor fleet increased more than threefold from 1960 to 1975. Marked increases were also recorded for other types of agricultural machines and equipment, notably for lorries and for potato and beet combines. The number of combine harvesters was going down in recent years, but here, too, more modern and efficient machines replaced the older models. According to GDR statistics all grain crops have been harvested with large-type combines since 1970.[1] As for potatoes, 95 per cent of the crop was lifted by fully

---

1 Here, the increasing use of the combine harvester Type E 512 (first introduced in 1968) is noteworthy. In 1970 it had accounted for half the fully mechanised grain harvest; by 1975, this figure had risen to 98 per cent.

mechanised harvesting were 100 per cent in 1975, as against 75 per cent in 1965.

Comparing the GDR tractor figures for 1975 with those of the Federal Republic, it emerges that the GDR reached 22 per cent of the West German level in terms of tractor numbers per unit area of agricultural land, and 36 per cent in terms of tractor horse power per unit area. The average engine power of agricultural tractors was 54 hp in the GDR, 33 hp in West Germany. In a comparison of the number of combine harvesters per unit area of cereal cropland, the GDR attained 14 per cent of the West German figure. But the significance of such comparisons with the notoriously overcapitalised Federal Republic must not be overrated. To complete the picture, it is necessary to consider two important factors:

1 the degree of utilisation of the machines: it has been established for instance, that in the Federal Republic in 1967, tractors and combine harvesters were used to less than 50 per cent of capacity; again, in 1968, the average operating hours per tractor in the GDR were three times the West German figure. This was due in part to the larger average acreage of the agricultural enterprises and to the effect of shift-work by the tractor crews.

2 the superior performance of the large machines used in the GDR, which however is difficult to quantify for statistical purposes.[1]

The agriculture of the GDR is conspicuous for the large size of its labour force, which in 1975 numbered some 900,000 persons, 11 per cent of the economically active population. Considering the predominance of large production units, this share seems unduly high. The number of full-time workers[2] per 100 hectares of agricultural land was 12.0 in 1975, as compared with 9.0 in the Federal Republic, with its numerous small farms (even though smallholdings of 2 hectares or less were not counted in arriving at the West German figure). If the comparison is made, more relevantly, with West German production units exceeding 50 hectares of agricultural land, the deployment of man-

1 The E 512 cuts a swathe 4.2 or 5.7 m wide, and at an average working speed of 3-5 Km/hr harvests about 1.5 hectares per hour. Its superiority over the compact West German combine is such that comparisons in terms of numbers or even horse power per unit area are pointless.
2 'Full-time worker' here represents a notional statistical unit (whole time equivalent), with seasonal and part-time workers reckoned as fractional units.

power in the GDR comes out as three times the West German figure.[1]

The high ratio of agricultural employment in the GDR is doubly surprising, because, apart from the favourable size distribution of production units, agriculture (inclusive of forestry) received no less than 13 per cent of total investments during the period from 1960 to 1975, which should have afforded ample opportunity to substitute capital for labour.[2]

One reason for this discrepancy appears to lie in the social circumstances of the restructuring of the industry. The merger of formerly independent peasant farms into agricultural producer co-operatives did not release agricultural manpower, since the peasants, as members of their co-operatives, continued to be active in agriculture, in contrast to corresponding structural changes in Western countries, where farmers giving up their holdings usually leave the land. Later on it was the lack of mobility — that is to say, of the readiness or ability to seek work elsewhere — that prevented manpower from flowing out of agriculture into other sectors of the economy. In some regions there were not enough vacancies in industry. The age structure of the agricultural labour force, with the older age groups represented disproportionately, was another important factor inhibiting mobility. Deficiencies in the organisation of work also play their part. With regard to most recent developments, it must be borne in mind that, once concentration exceeds a certain level, the advantages of large production units, among which the rational use of labour is to the fore, can easily be lost. Long-distance transport, long journeys to and from the place of work increase costs.

In the mid-sixties statistical projections predicted on the basis of the given age structure that by 1980, 40 to 50 per cent of the labour force would have retired from economic activity on the grounds of age, leaving in 1980 an agricultural labour force of under 700,000.

The agricultural labour situation is much alike in the GDR and the Federal Republic in one important respect, yet fundamentally different in others. The similarity is in the age structure, the difference lies in the relative size of the labour force and, it may be presumed, in the future outlook. Whereas in the GDR the decline of the labour force due to natural wastage will reduce the current over-employment, in the Federal Republic the shrinkage of the overaged agricultural labour force

---

1 Such comparisons, however, exaggerate the difference between the two countries, since in the GDR categories of personnel entrusted with certain services (e.g. maintenance of agricultural machinery) are counted as part of the agricultural labour force, whereas in the Federal Republic they are classified differently, for example as artisans.
2 In the Federal Republic, the share of agricultural investments was about one third of the total. This comparison, too, must be considered with some reservations in view of the different price structures involved. Similar caution is called for in comparing the structure of agricultural investments.

may lead eventually to an acute shortage of labour in this sector.

The use of *capital* as a factor of production in the GDR's agriculture is largely conditioned by the fact that the radical agrarian structural transformation entailed a vast demand for investments, concentrated at first in the building sector.[1] Although large means have been allocated for agricultural buildings over the years – a higher proportion of gross investments was used for buildings than in any other sector of the economy – the need for new buildings is by no means exhausted. This applies in particular to stock farming; it has been calculated that currently only about half the pigs and about two thirds of the cattle population can be accommodated in the newly constructed large animal houses.

As regards the extent of capital equipment, the structure of the capital employed and the degree of mechanisation in stock farming, available data are inadequate. To judge from known individual cases, however, it would appear that the degree of mechanisation in livestock keeping is far below that in arable farming. As for the large machines used in crop farming, it must be realised that numbers alone do not give a complete picture, since the availability of such machines varies from region to region and from enterprise to enterprise. The utilisation of agricultural machinery is also limited by bottlenecks in the supply of spares and the execution of repairs, deficiencies which even in most recent years have been the subject of frequent complaints. The appalling condition of some of the agricultural machinery in the GDR is due in part to negligent handling and maintenance and in part to the absence of facilities for keeping machines under cover when not in use.

4.3.3   Production and productivity

On the whole, the development of agricultural output in the GDR during the period under review was positive. If we measure agricultural performance by the yardstick of market production[2] – the quantity recorded most exhaustively by GDR statistics – we arrive for the period from 1960 to 1975 at an average annual growth rate of 3.4 per cent.

The upward trend, however, was on several occasions interrupted by

1 The share of building, i.e. outhouses and land improvement, in gross agricultural investment is smaller in West Germany, where on the other hand investment in machines is proportionately higher than in the GDR. But the amount of capital sunk into agricultural machinery in West Germany is generally held to be excessive.
2 The quantity shown in the statistics is 'deliveries to the state'. Market production, strictly speaking, also includes some marginal items, such as direct ex-farm sales, which however are of little importance. Output of all products is measured in tonnes of grain equivalent (GE). The conversion key depends for vegetable products on their starch content, for animal products on the starch content of the input of feeding stuffs.

setbacks. Both in the early and in the late sixties marked drops in production were registered. Poor weather was a contributory factor on both occasions, aggravated in the earlier period by the difficulties of adjusting to the structural transformation initiated in 1960. In the years 1969 to 1971, the impact of the crop deficiencies was lessened by additional imports of animal feeds, so that the setback was confined to crop production. Considering crop farming alone, major shortfalls were recorded also in 1975 and 1976. In the latter year — due again to the weather — gross crop yield (total crop production in grain equivalent per unit area of agricultural land) dropped back to the level of 1964 (31 q/ha).[1] The total production of foodstuffs in the GDR attained the pre-war level of the corresponding territory for the first time in 1957 and has exceeded it consistently since 1963.

The GDR's agricultural output is dominated by animal products,

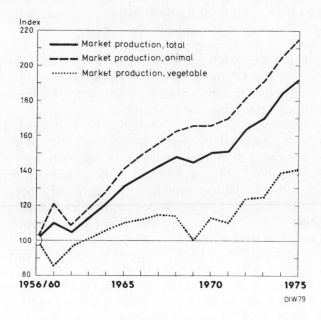

Figure 23 Development of agricultural market production in the GDR (1956-60 average = 100)

1 On methodological grounds, these figures cannot be compared with the data given in the West German literature. They were calculated on the basis of the conversion keys used in the GDR, in particular the GE-key.

which, measured again by conversion into grain equivalent, account for about three quarters of market production, much as in the Federal Republic. As regards the quantity of production, the two most important items are milk and pigmeat. If market production is assessed in terms of sales proceeds the share of animal products is greater still. This is due to the fact that, while agricultural producer prices in the GDR are generally high, those for animal products are exceptionally advantageous (see Appendix, table 27).

The predominance of animal production has been further reinforced in recent years, owing to above-average increases in the production of poultry and, above all, of beef. Even so, the current percentage share of beef is still considered to be too small. Earlier forecasts of future consumer demand and required product ranges assumed that beef would account for 40 per cent of total meat consumption and foresaw a per capita consumption of 80 Kg of meat. But this target is likely to be substantially exceeded. If the development continues along the lines it has followed since the mid-sixties, per capita meat consumption must be expected to rise to about 90 Kg by 1980, as compared with 78 Kg in 1975 (83 Kg in the Federal Republic in the same year).

Acreage yields — production per unit area — also have improved in the long term. Pre-war production figures were overtaken for grain in the second half of the 1950s, for potatoes and sugar beet only towards the end of the 1960s. Hectare yields, however, are below those of the Federal Republic, in particular for root crops.[1]

Labour productivity — net production per notional full-time worker — is still depressed by overmanning, even though the labour force declined from 1.3 million in 1960 to 900,000 in 1975. The shrinkage of the labour force went hand in hand with an increase in output. Since 1961-62 labour productivity has clearly been on the increase. It must be remembered, of course, that in dealing with agriculture, changes in the weather must be taken into account, as they affect crops and thus productivity.

Productivity comparisons with the Federal Republic are not straightforward. As regards labour productivity, the scope of a comparison is limited on statistical grounds; as regards productivity of capital, comparison is altogether impossible on methodological grounds. As regards acreage yields and stock farming productivity, it is estimated that the GDR is lagging behind the Federal Republic by about one fifth in each of the two sectors.[2]

1 Pre-war hectare yields in the territory of the GDR were about 10 per cent below the West German figure for sugar beet; they were slightly lower for rye and slightly higher than West German yields for potatoes and cereals as a whole.
2 This refers to gross production per unit area, and to total animal production in relation to the livestock population. Labour productivity in GDR agriculture has been assessed by K. Merkel (of the Berlin Technical University) at one third below the West German figure.

In other words: for the production of one unit of agricultural produce more labour, more land and more livestock had to be used in the GDR than in West Germany.

Milk yields provide an example of the productivity gap in stock farming. In 1975 the yield per cow (in standardised units of 3.5 per cent fat content) was 3,600 Kg in the GDR, 4,300 Kg in the Federal Republic. In the case of fat stock, the gap is manifested in higher feed consumption, less efficient feed utilisation, or longer fattening periods. Thus, for pigs the slaughter turnover (number of pigs slaughtered in a year as a percentage of the mean pig population) in the GDR is about one third below the West German figure, that is to say, while it takes about a year to fatten a pig until it is ready for slaughter in the GDR, the fattening period in the Federal Republic is not much more than eight months. The reason lies partly in inadequate feed supplies (shortage of highly concentrated commercial feeds).

Owing to its lower population density — the number of inhabitants per 100 hectares of agricultural land in 1975 was 268 for the GDR, 465 for the Federal Republic — domestic food production per capita is about one fifth above that in West Germany. Except for beef and fruit, GDR per capita production is higher for all agricultural products, the difference being most marked for potatoes, sugar beet and grain. This is due in part to the different proportion of arable to pasture land in the two parts of Germany. In the GDR arable makes up about three quarters of agricultural land, while in West Germany the proportion is

Chart 33
Production of important agricultural products
(Kg per inhabitant, annual average)

Products	Actual figures				FRG^1 = 100
	1956-1960	1961-1965	1966-1970	1971-1975	1971-1974
Grain (total)	347	342	404	511	147
Potatoes	767	707	719	637	288
Fat stock[2]	73	83	103	125	123
including: pigs	49	50	62	74	131
poultry	3	5	6	9	160
Eggs[3]	170	206	241	276	108
Milk	315	334	412	455	129

1 GDR: calender year; FRG: harvest year.
2 Live weight.
3 Pieces

Source: table 26

141

only somewhat more than half.[1]

At the end of the 1960s the degree of self-sufficiency, i.e. domestic production as a proportion of consumption, was around 85 per cent in the GDR and less than that in the Federal Republic. Domestic needs are covered completely, or almost completely, for some of the most important staple foods — potatoes, butter, eggs, milk, meat — though for others, notably grain and fresh fruit, imports are still needed.

4.3.4   Agrarian policy, development trends

The aim of raising production was from the outset at the centre of agrarian policy considerations in the GDR, and it continues to be of primary importance. The problem was urgent indeed during the initial years when agricultural production was in disarray and vast numbers of refugees had to be fed. Later the basic strategy, clearly geared to the goal of complete self-sufficiency, became questionable on several grounds, above all in view of labour productivity which, according to official data from GDR sources, is considerably lower in agriculture than in industry. Since a high degree of self-sufficiency has been attained already, any further expansion of production is likely to saddle the GDR with the problem of surplus production. More importantly still, the policy of maximising production, pursued hitherto with manifest unconcern, must raise the question as to whether it would not make more economic sense to use scarce resources of labour and capital for the production of other goods, that is to say, to abandon the production of high-cost agricultural goods and turn instead to the manufacture of internationally competitive industrial products, which would readily finance the additionally needed agricultural imports. But an abandonment of the policy of autarky would, of course, affect the GDR's foreign economic relations. The socialist countries, where the GDR has good prospects of marketing its industrial products, do not have the agricultural surpluses required, at least not on a regular basis, while the agricultural surpluses available in some Western countries are virtually out of reach, since the export opportunities to Western markets for GDR industrial products are very limited, so that the GDR could not obtain enough foreign exchange to pay for food imports.

Pricing policy is an important instrument of agrarian policy. The setting of producer prices has a long tradition as a device for the regulation of incomes. In the GDR it has been applied simultaneously

---

1   Generally, the share of pastures as well as of individual crops in the total area of agricultural land has remained remarkably constant (see Appendix, table 25). Notable changes have occurred only within the grain sector, where the cultivation of wheat and barley was substantially increased at the expense of rye, which lost its previously dominant position.

as a device for the selective stimulation of production. Apart from the economic impact, pricing was also used to promote social policy objectives, offering incentives at first for the formation of producer co-operatives, currently for the introduction of industrial methods of production, in accordance with the maxim that 'pricing policy is class struggle'. There is wide scope for a price policy, since the GDR has instituted four separate price systems, respectively for agriculture, industry, the retail trade and foreign trade. Thanks to this compartmentalisation of prices, producer prices can be raised without being passed on to the consumer.

The development of agricultural producer prices in both parts of Germany started from the common baseline of the pegged prices of 1944. By 1955 the price level in the GDR had run ahead of that in the Federal Republic by 20 per cent (on the basis of Mark = DM). After that, the GDR producer prices continued to rise at an average rate of about 3 per cent p.a.; by 1971 they exceeded the West German level by 80 per cent.[1] Since then, agricultural producer prices have not risen further in the GDR, during the very years in which the Federal Republic experienced substantial price increases, so that the gap has narrowed. But the GDR still remains a country of high agricultural producer prices, in particular for animal products. Since consumer prices, in spite of great variations in detail, are on average much the same in the two territories, it is clear that the subsidies paid out of the state budget must be enormous.

Since the mid-fifties, the raising of producer prices has accounted for two fifths of the increase in the agricultural sales proceeds. High producer prices thus assumed growing importance as an instrument of support for agriculture. They made it possible to withdraw direct subsidies that had been granted in the form of concessionary prices for the means of production.[2] This was in keeping with the endeavour of the New Economic System to establish realistic interdependent prices. Accordingly, prices for means of production were raised as follows:

1966 and again in 1971 for feeding stuffs

1967 for agricultural machinery and commercial fertilisers

1971 for building materials, building work, electric power and diesel fuel

1975 again for diesel fuel, bringing agriculture into line with other consumers

1 The West German level, as, indeed, that of the EEC countries in general, in turn exceeds the world market price levels by a considerable margin.
2 Support for agriculture has taken, and continues to take, many forms, including for instance direct transfers of income (state contribution to the payment of work units, tax exemption for co-operative incomes).

143

The modification of the earlier farm support policy was begun in 1963, when the stock of the machine-and-tractor-stations (MTSs) was transferred to the agricultural producer co-operatives, free of charge to Type III co-operatives and by way of sales to those of Types I and II. This move relieved the state budget of annual subsidies for the upkeep of the stock of machines.

While obviating the need to subsidise agricultural means of production, the policy of raising producer prices did not, of course, do away with subsidies, but merely shifted them from one sector to another, since consumer prices were kept constant. The official designation of 'consumer price subsidies', however, tends to obscure the fact that these subsidies actually support high agricultural producer prices and a high-cost agriculture.

Bridging the gap between consumer and producer prices has required very large subsidies. In the five-year period 1966 to 1970 food subsidies amounted to 22,000 million Marks, and during the subsequent five-year period to as much as 32,000 million Marks, of which 7,200 million Marks was in 1975 alone, an expenditure of the same order of magnitude as the state budget for health and social welfare or for education. About one tenth of the revenues accruing from the publicly owned economy is used to pay for food subsidies.

The methods of guiding agricultural production were modified at the beginning of the 1960s. The phase of predominantly administrative direction gave way to the maximum use of economic policy devices intended to set the course for agricultural development. During the e earlier stage, livestock and cropping plans (up to 1956-57), compulsory delivery quotas and price differentials — bonus prices for surplus deliveries — were among the salient features of agrarian policy. After the initiation of the New Economic System they were replaced by uniform producer prices (introduced in 1964 for vegetable products, in 1969 for animal products), supplemented by bonus payments for increased production, while deliveries were assured through contractual relations (annual contracts between producers and purchasing agencies to regulate market production). At the same time, compulsory plan targets were retained for some products, including grain and potatoes.

As regards production techniques, the agrarian policy of the GDR is bent on the introduction of industrial methods in order to bring the efficiency of agricultural production up to the level of other sectors of the economy. Measures taken to this effect include notably the mechanisation of the various production processes, the establishment of large specialised production units — that is to say, not the mere amalgamation of a number of producer co-operatives without changing their production programmes — and, as a temporary expedient at least, inter-enterprise co-operation. This policy is based on Marxist theory, which

144

holds that large-scale production is invariably superior in all economic sectors, hence also in agriculture.

Some years ago, the economic authorities decided to construct cattle breeding units for up to 6,000 head of cattle, dairy cattle units for up to 2,000 head and pig fattening units for up to 40,000 animals.

At an early stage a drive was launched to encourage both horizontal and vertical co-operation, which took the form of 'co-operation communities' (Kooperationsgemeinschaften, KOGs) and 'co-operation federations' (Kooperationsverbände, KOVs).[1] These were later superseded by the 'co-operative institutions of agricultural producer co-operatives, publicly owned estates and market gardening co-operatives, as well as of the socialist enterprises in the food industry and the distributive trade'. It is these institutions which are to provide the framework for co-operation above enterprise level, according to model statutes passed by the Council of Ministers in 1973. In these statutes the 'co-operative institutions' are described as 'specialised production units, operating increasingly with industrial methods, having their own managements, operating plans and funds'. The statutes provide for the formation of 'permanent labour collectives', working teams composed of workers delegated for that purpose and of members of the co-operatives involved. The position of the team members is determined in the case of members of co-operatives by a 'delegation agreement' and in the case of manual and clerical workers by the conclusion of a special labour contract. The decision-making bodies are the manager, nominated by the District Council, and the Council of the co-operative institution, on which sit representatives delegated by the participating co-operatives and enterprises as well as representatives of the staff of the institution itself.

The co-operative institution has the legal status of a body corporate. The remuneration of the workers and salaried employees is determined by the rates laid down in collective agreements. The members of co-operatives, it appears, will eventually be remunerated in the same way. The model statutes speak of transitional arrangements 'pending the introduction of uniform rates of remuneration'.

Co-operation between agricultural enterprises can take many forms, ranging from the common utilisation of machines and equipment (with or without transition to common ownership) to the establishment of common facilities, such as drying plant, large-scale stock farming units

1 These were the instruments of vertical co-operation, connecting enterprises involved in the successive stages of production of certain products. Partners in such federations were enterprises from the sectors of agriculture, industry and the distributive trade. The co-operating enterprises retained their legal independence, while the co-operation federations did not attain autonomous legal status.

or mixed fodder production units, and to the setting up of separate units specialised in the discharge of certain functions. The Agro-chemical Centres are a case in point. They look after fertilising and pest control, and have lately extended their activities to seed cultivation and transport tasks. The establishment of a network of Agrochemical Centres was completed at the end of 1976, when there were 266 such centres with an average labour force of 100 persons. Each Centre serves more than 20,000 hectares.

Specialised production, i.e. the isolation of one or several branches of production, constitutes the highest form of co-operation. This leads to large-scale production, tillage operations in crop farming extending over vast areas unencumbered by boundaries, while animal production is transferred to large units. Thus agriculture, too, is to benefit from the advantages of mass production.

Specialised large-scale animal production enterprises have been set up either as 'inter-co-operative' or 'inter-enterprise institutions' or as 'industrial fattening combines'. The first two types are co-operatively owned, the last-named are publicly owned enterprises managed by the area administration. They are specialised in a single production stage or in several consecutive stages.[1]

Of the 390 large-scale stock farming units existing in 1976, 360 belonged to the first two types, the remaining 30 were industrial fattening combines. The percentage share of the output of the indus-trial production units in agriculture is still low, covering less than 4 per cent of dairy cattle, under 20 per cent of sows and about one third of the number of laying hens.

Industrial production methods are far more advanced in the crop farming sector, where at the end of 1975 1,200 'co-operative depart-ments for plant production' were farming 4,100 hectares of agricultural land each on average, or a total of 80 per cent of the GDR's cropland.

The most recent form of large-scale agricultural production is centred in the 'special agricultural producer co-operatives for plant and animal production', which are still in their early stages. New model statutes, designed to adapt organisation and administration of the enterprises to vastly enlarged scale of operations, were submitted for discussion at the end of 1976.

Whether these 'special LPGs' constitute the final stage in the develop-ment of agrarian policy in the GDR, remains an open question. It is

---

1 Some of these combines are well known model enterprises, such as the cattle fattening com-bine Ferdinandshof, handling 24,000 bullocks; or the Eberswalde pig breeding and fattening combine with an annual turnover of 15,000 porkers; the Spreenhagen breeding centre for hybrid laying hens which in 1974 supplied 8.75 million chicks; or the VEB KIM Königswuster-hausen, which covers 45 per cent of East Berlin's requirement of eggs, and 80 per cent of its consumption of poultry meat.

worthy of attention, however, that in May 1976, an 'Agrarian-Industrial Association' (Agrar-Industrie-Vereinigung, AIV) farming 32,000 hectares of cropland under a single management was presented to the Ninth SED Congress.

Summing up, there is no doubt that working and living conditions have been transformed more drastically in agriculture than in any other sector of life in the GDR. Thoroughgoing structural change led to new forms of production. The socialised large-scale production unit predominates today, nevertheless the fulfilment of the declared aim of managing agricultural production entirely by industrial methods is still a long way off.

The new forms of agricultural units and the level of production appear to indicate that the GDR's agrarian policy has been highly successful. But such an assessment cannot be accepted without some reservations: the economic costs of agricultural production are very high, as witnessed by the vast input of production factors, by the high producer prices and the food subsidies.

The superiority claimed by the GDR for its mode of production will only be established if and when major advances in productivity have been achieved. Only then will it be possible to combine high investments with high incomes without the need for heavy subsidies.

4.4 Transport

4.4.1 Infrastructure

The *structure and capacity of the communications network* is still governed largely by the starting position at the time of the partition of Germany. Owing to the dearth of resources it has not so far been possible to adjust especially the road system to the increased traffic volume.

To begin with, the extension of the communications infrastructure was dominated by political motives, in particular the need to bypass West Berlin. This was at the root of the construction of the Havel Canal and the outer ring railway circling Berlin. The Rostock port extension, enabling the port to handle ocean-going vessels, was motivated not only by economic considerations — the desire to be independent of both Hamburg and Szczecin for seaborne trade and the need to save foreign exchange — but also by a striving for national prestige.

The pre-war *railway network* of 18,500 Km was much reduced as a result of war damage and dismantling. To this day, the dual task of restoration and expansion, to cope with the constantly growing transport

147

needs, has not been solved satisfactorily. Currently, the network totals 14,300 Km. Its density of 13.2 Km per 100 sq.Km does not differ much from that of the Federal Republic, but the quality is hardly comparable. In the Federal Republic, lines with two or more tracks make up two fifths of the total, in the GDR only one fifth.

The conversion to *modern modes of traction* (electrical and diesel traction) is well advanced but not yet complete. Over four fifths of the railways' haulage effort is accomplished by electric or diesel locomotives. The last steam locomotives are to be withdrawn in the 1980s.

Electrification of the main lines is not undertaken systematically in the GDR, as has been the case in the Federal Republic, where electrification extends over 10,000 Km, nearly one third of the entire network. In the GDR only 1,454 Km of railway line, or 10 per cent of the total, had been electrified by 1975, and those 10 per cent are almost exclusively in the Saxon industrial region.[1] Apart from an extension of the networks of the municipal railways of the large cities, the current Five-Year Plan provides for the completion of the electrification of the Dresden-Schöna line (49 Km), which is of importance for North-South transit traffic, and for the electrification of the Muldenstein-Berlin and Dresden-Berlin lines and of the southern section of the Berlin outer ring railway.

Chart 34
Transport routes (Km)

	1960	1965	1970	1973	1974	1975
Railways	16,174	15,930	14,658	14,317	14,252	14,298
main lines	7,362	7,436	7,365	7,491	7,494	7,577
electrified	708	1,057	1,357	1,383	1,406	1,454
Inland waterways	2,644	2,519	2,519	2,546	2,546	2,538
main waterways[1]	1,812	1,853	1,853	1,502	1,502	1,577
Motorways	1,378	1,390	1,413	1,495	1,531	1,561
Trunk roads	10,957	10,992	11,003	10,892	11,396	11,417
Highways (1st & 2nd class)	33,144	33,338	33,313	33,258	34,676	34,595
Local roads	*	*	74,202	*	*	*
Long-distance pipelines	—	27	681	710	766	951

1 Chief navigable reaches of rivers and most important canals.

Source: GDR Statistical Yearbooks.

*No data available.

1 The Leipzig-Riesa-Dresden line has been electrified for a number of years. This fact is by mistake not shown in figure 24 (The Main Railway Lines).

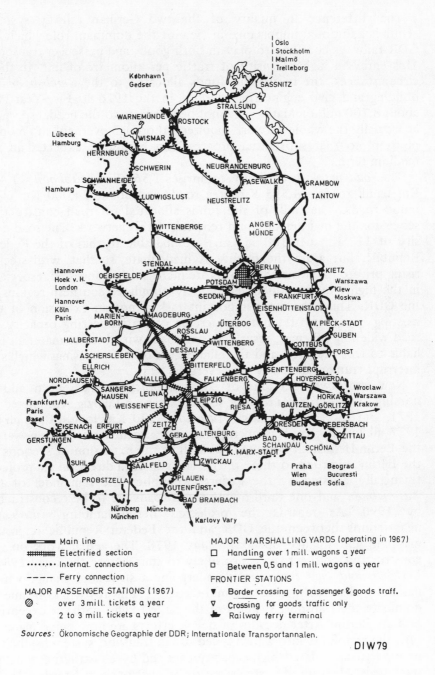

Main line
Electrified section
Internat. connections
Ferry connection

MAJOR PASSENGER STATIONS (1967)
⊘ over 3 mill. tickets a year
⊘ 2 to 3 mill. tickets a year

MAJOR MARSHALLING YARDS (operating in 1967)
□ Handling over 1 mill. wagons a year
▫ Between 0,5 and 1 mill. wagons a year

FRONTIER STATIONS
▼ Border crossing for passenger & goods traff.
▽ Crossing for goods traffic only
⚓ Railway ferry terminal

Sources: Ökonomische Geographie der DDR; Internationale Transportannalen.

DIW 79

Figure 24   Main railway lines

149

The difference in quality of the two German railway systems acquires additional importance in view of the dominant role which the GDR railways continue to play in both goods and passenger transport. This entails a higher density of traffic per kilometre of line. In these circumstances, the investment funds allocated to the *Reichsbahn* for building and civil engineering work — in the 1976-80 Five-Year Plan about 8,700 million Marks — cannot be adequate to the need, especially as virtually the whole network requires a thorough overhaul and modernisation, so that substantial progress can hardly be expected in the medium term.

The *road network* currently comprises 1,561 Km *Autobahn*, 11,417 Km trunk roads, 34,595 Km area roads and about 74,000 Km commune roads. The bulk of the funds allocated for road construction serves for the maintenance and renewal of this network. The road density of 112 Km per 100 sq.Km is comparable to that of the Federal Republic, but again the quality is inadequate, so that, with steeply rising private car ownership, roads are increasingly congested, especially in the highly industrialised and densely populated southern regions of the GDR. Thus, the most important task is not an extension of the existing road network, but an increase of traffic-bearing capacity by road widening schemes, resurfacing of roads with heavier materials less liable to frost damage, and the elimination of level crossings which still interrupt trunk roads on average every 18 Km.

New motorway sections of some importance have been added, notably the 74 Km *Autobahn* section Dresden-Leipzig, completed in 1971, and the Berlin-Rostock *Autobahn*, 270 Km long, of which by 1977 all but 60 Km was operational. The urgently needed renewal of the Berlin-Helmstedt *Autobahn* as well as the extension of sections of the Berlin ring road to three traffic lanes in each direction are projects financially assisted by the Federal Republic. The remainder of the *Autobahnen* and one third of the trunk roads are to be reconstructed by 1990. As regards the projected Berlin-Hamburg *Autobahn*, negotiations between the GDR and the Federal Republic on route mapping and finance opened in May 1978. The actual work on the construction of the road is not likely to start before the early 1980s.

Urban and city transport is undergoing a structural change which has been observable since the mid-sixties. Tramways will continue to dominate the transport systems of the large towns, with the exception of East Berlin. After decades of delay, efforts are now being made to turn the tramways into a high-speed urban transport system by the use of modern articulated high-capacity cars and by constructing separate track-beds. High-speed systems are to be developed in Dresden, Halle, Leipzig, Magdeburg and Rostock. In Berlin urban passenger transport is dominated by the S-Bahn and U-Bahn, the elevated and underground

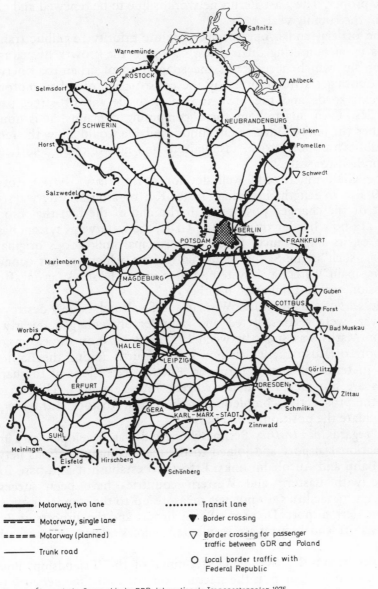

Saßnitz
Warnemünde
ROSTOCK
Selmsdorf
Ahlbeck
SCHWERIN
NEUBRANDENBURG
Linken
Horst
Pomellen
Schwedt
Salzwedel
BERLIN
POTSDAM
FRANKFURT
Marienborn
MAGDEBURG
Guben
COTTBUS
Forst
Worbis
Bad Muskau
HALLE
LEIPZIG
Görlitz
ERFURT
DRESDEN
Zittau
GERA
KARL–MARX–STADT
Schmilka
SUHL
Zinnwald
Meiningen
Eisfeld Hirschberg
Schönberg

▬▬▬ Motorway, two lane	••••••• Transit lane
═══ Motorway, single lane	▼ Border crossing
==== Motorway (planned)	▽ Border crossing for passenger traffic between GDR and Poland
——— Trunk road	○ Local border traffic with Federal Republic

Sources : Ökonomische Geographie der DDR; Internationale Transportannalen 1976.

DIW79

Figure 25   Trunk roads

151

electric railways. There is, incidentally, no underground railway in the GDR proper. The East Berlin network is due to be renewed and expanded in the coming years.

The official endeavour to give absolute priority to public transport needs is encountering difficulties, owing to the growth of private car ownership, which necessitates the adaptation of urban road networks to mounting traffic volumes by the construction of urban motorways and exit roads and the provision of kerbside and off-street parking facilities. Even apart from these competing demands, it is doubtful whether the limited investment funds available would allow the renewal of public transport stock, installations and networks on a sufficiently comprehensive scale.

The GDR inherited a well developed *waterways system* totalling 2,550 Km in length, including 1,600 Km of arterial waterways. As a result of the changed position of Berlin and of the fact that Elbe and Oder are now border rivers of the GDR, the waterways system has lost some of its importance. Since the principal bulk goods originate in regions, such as the Saxon industrial regions, which are not connected to the main waterways system, the port of Rostock, even after its extension, was not linked to it either.

The *seaports* of Rostock, Wismar and Stralsund, largely destroyed in the war, were reconstructed and considerably enlarged. Nearly 700 million Marks was spent between 1957 and 1970 on the extension of the port of Rostock, which now ranks fourth among the Baltic seaports in terms of annual turnover. Further extensions of the harbour basins are provided for in the current Five-Year Plan. This, together with the prospective completion of the Berlin-Rostock *Autobahn*, will consolidate the position of the port.

As regards *air traffic*, Berlin-Schonefeld was developed as a major international airport and joined to the main communications network by S-Bahn and Autobahn links. Efforts to establish it as a base for air traffic with Eastern and Western countries have been successful, although its facilities do not yet measure up to the standards expected of a modern airport. Dresden's Barth airport and the airports of Erfurt, Heringsdorf and Leipzig are to play an increasing part in international air traffic.

Schwedt, on the river Oder, terminus of the 'Friendship' Pipeline from the Soviet Union, is the starting point of a *pipeline network* totalling 1,000 Km (as compared with 1,600 Km in the Federal Republic) for conveying mineral oil and oil products as well as natural gas. Its most important components are the Schwedt-Leuna and Schwedt-Rostock (oil harbour) oil pipelines and the pipeline to Berlin, carrying oil products.

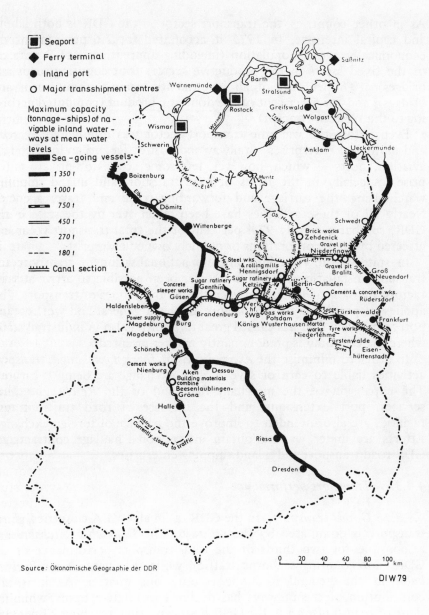

Figure 26   Seaports, inland ports, inland waterways

153

4.4.2   The position of transport within the national economy

As in other countries, the transport sector in the GDR is both labour and capital intensive. In 1975 it accounted for 7.6 per cent of the economically active population (including apprentices); 15.3 per cent of the fixed assets in the productive sectors (not counting roads and bridges); 10.8 per cent of all investments (again without roads and bridges); and for 5 per cent of the domestic product (computed according to the Western concept).

Even before the war, the transport sector was dominated by state and municipal enterprises — railway and post office, urban local traffic, aviation, ports — which, however, left some scope for private enterprise, especially in the fields of road transport and inland shipping, warehousing, the carriage and forwarding trade and travel agencies. Nearly all of these activities have been taken over by the state in the GDR, so that currently 97.4 per cent of the total transport volume is effected by state corporations or publicly owned enterprises.

In spite of the virtually complete nationalisation of transport and transport installations, it has not so far been possible to arrive at satisfactory division of labour between the various modes of transport. This applies in particular to the balance between general and works transport; a problem that has caused great difficulties also in industrial states where the economy is predominantly market-oriented.

In order to minimise the *expenditure of foreign exchange*, transport activities liable to earn or save foreign exchange are being cultivated. The expansion of the merchant fleet and of the *Reichsbahn* ferry services, port extensions, and the increase of road traffic transit facilities are also intended to improve the balance of foreign exchange. Efforts are under way to obtain international haulage contracts for GDR road transport and inland shipping enterprises.

4.4.3   Transport performance

4.4.3.1 Goods transport   In the GDR, as in all CMEA countries, goods transport is dominated by the *railways*. The *Deutsche Reichsbahn* is responsible for two thirds of the total transport performance of the GDR (not counting seaborne traffic), while the share of the *Bundesbahn* in the Federal Republic is only one quarter. As it is, the contribution of the railways has declined in relative terms, while the share of *road transport* in the GDR has been rising, reaching 23 per cent in 1975 (as compared with 44 per cent in the Federal Republic). *Inland shipping* accounted for 3 per cent of the transport volume. Three fifths of this modest share was contributed by local traffic, the remaining two fifths by long-distance traffic, which requires a special licence. (In the

154

Federal Republic inland shipping handles no less than 23 per cent of the total transport volume, a full two thirds of it on long-distance trips). The volume of transport contributed by *maritime shipping* has greatly increased since the commissioning of the Rostock port extension in 1960. Mineral oil has increasingly been transported by means of *pipelines* in recent years.

The development of the various forms of transport clearly points to *structural changes in goods transport.*

As regards long-distance goods transport, the railways have so far been protected from the competition of road transport. Apart from narrowly defined exceptions, haulage of goods over distances of more than 50 Km as the crow flies is reserved for the railways and inland shipping; but the latter, owing to the location and capacity of the inland waterways, offers no serious competition. Goods haulage within a radius of 50 Km is considered to be carried out most efficiently by road, and is accordingly assigned to road transport.

In 1975 the railways carried 289 million tonnes of goods and registered a transport performance of 50,000 million tkm, only 9 per cent below the performance of the West German railways with twice the length of track. Bearing in mind the quality and state of repair of railway lines in the GDR, one can hardly be surprised at the annually recurring bottlenecks.

Brown coal, though its role is gradually declining, is still the most important single item, making up one third of the volume of *railway goods transport.* The remainder is made up largely of building materials, manufactures and piece goods which in Western countries are carried mostly by lorry or inland shipping.

Inland shipping continues to be of slight importance, in spite of the increasing use of push tugs, which have been developed specifically for canal navigation and have proved to be very efficient. Two thirds of the volume of waterborne inland transport is now being effected by push tows. The most important single items carried by inland shipping were building materials and, again, brown coal, the latter, again, tending to decline.

In the GDR as in the Federal Republic, the volume of *road goods transport* has risen steeply in recent years, but its structure is completely different in the two parts of Germany. As a result of legal restrictions, the share of *long-distance lorry traffic* in the total *goods transport volume* (exclusive of short-distance road transport) is only 9 per cent, as compared with 27 per cent in the Federal Republic. *Works transport* increased its share in the volume of road transport from about half in 1960 to nearly three quarters in 1975 (Federal Republic: ca. 60 per cent). To establish proper co-ordination between public and works transport is an urgent problem. The works vehicle fleets add up to roughly 70 per cent of the entire road transport capacity of the GDR. Their vehicles, it is true, are used less intensively — both in terms of operating hours and loading to capacity — than the lorries of the publicly owned road transport enterprises; yet, the constant availability and greater flexibility in use of the works-owned lorries are important advantages, so that they are increasingly employed for transport tasks also above enterprise level. Even so, it has not yet been possible to get rid of transport bottlenecks, especially in the building sector.

Road transport will continue to grow. As uneconomic branch lines of the railways are being closed down, it will have to play a growing part in the distribution of goods over shorter distances. Whether road transport can cope with the increased demand will largely depend on the extent to which the lorry stock of currently about 240,000 vehicles (as compared with 1.1 million in the Federal Republic) can be augmented and technically adapted to the needs of staged haulage.

In the *maritime shipping* sector, a merchant fleet totalling 1.2 million grt was built up, partly for reasons of prestige. It ranks third among the CMEA countries, after the Soviet Union and Poland. At the same time work was carried out on the extension of the overseas facilities of the port of Rostock, which now handles 80 per cent of the GDR's seaborne goods turnover, followed by Wismar with 15 per cent and Stralsund with 5 per cent of the total. Successful efforts were made to channel part of the transit traffic of other states, especially Czechoslovakia, Hungary and Rumania, via Rostock. This is all the more remarkable, as Rostock lacks inland shipping links — no less than 95 per cent of incoming and outgoing dry goods are carried to and from the port by rail — and is thus at a clear disadvantage vis-à-vis Hamburg and Szczecin. Up to 1971 the goods turnover of the port increased at an annual rate of roughly 1 million tonnes, reaching in that year 11.8 million t. After that the figure changed very slowly; in 1975, 12.3 million t was recorded. This may well be due to the neighbourhood of Szczecin, the largest Baltic port. Co-ordination of the cargo-handling capacities of the GDR and Polish ports, bearing in mind in particular the transit requirements of other CMEA countries, is the official task of the GDR-Polish economic organisation *Interport* which started its activities on 1 April 1974, with its seat in Szczecin. It appears, however, that the foundation of this body was largely motivated by a desire, especially on the part of the GDR, to check on the shipping and port policy of the treaty partner.

The GDR has embarked on a drive for the advance of *container transport*, which establishes an unbroken chain from loader to recipient and thus entails great advantages: lower packaging costs, avoidance of transport and transhipment damage, better co-ordination of transport

156

and storage, higher labour productivity — all of which adds up to a reduction in total transport costs. Nearly all types of transport must adjust to the container traffic. The *Deutsche Reichsbahn* has already established a system of 20 container depots. Regular container train services are linking the GDR with the capitals of all CMEA countries. The growing importance of international container traffic has found expression in the foundation of *DDR-Cont*, an agency charged with the co-ordination of the GDR's bilateral and transit container traffic, especially with CMEA partners.

4.4.3.2 Passenger traffic   Rising living standards and the consequent increase in private motorised transport have initiated changes in the structure of passenger transport. The volume of *private transport* is going up, while public transport stagnates. It may be estimated that in 1975 private motor transport accounted for about half the total volume of passenger transport (as compared with four fifths in the Federal Republic). But in the GDR private motor transport is still dominated by motorcycles and mopeds, which constitute about two thirds of the entire stock of motor vehicles. The number of motorcars (including those used partly for business purposes) was 112 per 1,000 inhabitants in 1975, as compared with 290 in the Federal Republic. More than one GDR household in every four thus had a motorcar. If motorcycles and mopeds are included, the number of motor vehicles per 1,000 inhabitants comes out as 315, very close to the Federal Republic's figure of 325.

Owing to the high level of prime cost and maintenance costs of motorcars, combined with substantially subsidised public transport fares, especially for commuter traffic and school children's journeys to and from school, private cars have so far been used predominantly for *leisure transport* (excursions, weekends, holidays), although the traffic congestion at peak hours in the GDR towns indicates the growing use of private cars by commuters.

The popular Trabant costs, according to the level of equipment, from 8,000 to 10,000 Marks, the Wartburg from 17,000 to 18,000 Marks, imported cars up to 24,000 Marks. The price of petrol, at about 1.50 Marks per litre (1.65 Marks for super), is considerably higher than in Western countries. Waiting times for the delivery of new cars are long. As a result, vehicles are kept on the roads much longer than in Western countries, and the need for repairs is correspondingly greater. Thus the production of spare parts in the GDR amounts to more than a quarter of new production, as compared with barely 10 per cent in the Federal Republic. Even so, there is an acute shortage of spares. There is no system of regular official vehicle tests in the GDR, whereas in the Federal Republic such tests are compulsory at two-year intervals. Tests

Chart 35
Motor vehicle density[1] in the GDR and FRG 1960-1975

	GDR			FRG		
	Motor vehicles per 1000 inhabitants		Percentage share of passenger cars	Motor vehicles per 1000 inhabitants		Percentage share of passenger cars
Year	All vehicles[2]	Passenger cars[3]		All vehicles[2]	Passenger cars[3]	
1960	94	17	18	156	81	52
1961	118	22	19	163	95	58
1962	136	26	19	166	111	67
1963	150	30	20	175	127	73
1964	164	34	21	182	143	78
1965	176	39	22	191	158	83
1966	186	42	23	202	174	86
1967	199	48	24	210	186	88
1968	210	54	26	218	196	90
1969	224	61	27	231	210	91
1970	239	68	28	251	230	92
1971	249	74	30	268	247	92
1972	262	82	31	283	260	92
1973	278	91	33	300	274	91
1974	296	101	34	309	279	90
1975	316	112	35	325	290	89

1 Not including commercial vehicles.
2 Passenger and estate cars, motorcycles, scooters and mopeds.
3 Passenger and estate cars.

Sources: GDR Statistical Yearbooks; FRG Statistical Yearbooks.

of the operating and traffic safety of all vehicles were, however, prescribed in 1975 by an executory order to the road licensing regulations, and vehicles passing the test were issued with a green disc, but that was a single, non-recurring measure. The large proportion of overaged cars, shortage of spares and inadequate repair shop capacity no doubt contribute to the constantly rising number of road accidents.

In the sector of private passenger transport the number of journeys increased threefold and the transport performance (passenger kilometres) as much as fourfold from 1960 to 1975. This development reflects not only the rapid increase in the number of vehicles, but also the more intensive use of vehicles that goes hand in hand with rising living standards.

In the GDR as in the Federal Republic the increase in mobility (number of journeys per inhabitant per year) is due almost entirely to the development of private motoring, but the share of public transport in the total number of journeys is still twice as high in the GDR as in the Federal Republic.

The share of the railways in *public passenger transport* continues to decline gradually, while that of buses and coaches is going up. In 1975 the railways carried one in six of the passengers using public transport. Structural changes in urban and suburban transport appear to be in the offing as a result of the expansion of private motor transport. Whereas in West German towns municipal transport services — buses, trams, underground and elevated railways — have registered a slight decline, in the GDR their performance has continued to go up, though only by small amounts. The number of passengers carried by the tramways has changed little in recent years, but in 1975 they still transported more than two thirds of all passengers on local journeys. Buses, on the other hand, increased both their transport volume and transport performance by more than half from 1970 to 1975. The transport tasks arising from the closing down of uneconomic suburban *Reichsbahn* lines and from the development of new residential districts on the outskirts of towns are mostly assigned to buses. The level of public transport fares is determined by political considerations, they fall far short of the operating costs of the transport enterprises. The fare for single journeys on municipal transport services has been pegged for many years at 0.20 Marks. According to GDR sources, receipts from fares cover less than half the operating costs, with a ratio of receipts to subsidies of 1:1.37. Yet, even these extremely low fares — almost equivalent to a zero rating — cannot in the long run stop the expansion of private motor transport.

In the most densely populated urban regions of the GDR the growing use of private motorcars has not yet led to traffic congestion on a scale comparable to that of some West German towns. In the big West German cities the private car carries more passengers than the public transport services, even during the rush hour dominated by commuter traffic. In the GDR the ratio of private to public transport volume is still as low as 1:4, which is not surprising, with a rate of car ownership per thousand inhabitants hardly more than one third of the West German figure. Yet, considering the obsolete street systems in the GDR towns, it is on the cards that with progressing motorisation, GDR traffic snarl-ups in the foreseeable future will be even worse than the West German ones.

In the field of *civil aviation*, the *Interflug* corporation operates air routes totalling 85,000 Km with a fleet of about 30 aircraft, compared with the Lufthansa's 90 aircraft and a route network of 422,000 Km. Since Interflug is not a member if IATA, it is able to offer competitive fares and attract some of the traffic also to and from non-socialist countries. Thus Interflug handles 90 per cent of the international air traffic of the GDR as well as an increasing share of international transit traffic. West Berlin in particular feels the competition of the Schönefeld airport, where a new passenger terminal for international flights was opened in 1976.

4.4.3.3 Postal and telecommunication services Per capita performance of postal and telecommunication services is relatively low. As regards *telephones*, the number of subscribers per 1,000 inhabitants is only about half that of the Federal Republic. About 10 per cent of long-distance calls are still operator-connected. Lines and equipment are overaged and overloaded, so that over 50 per cent of attempted calls do not get through.

The volume of *postal traffic* is relatively low because of the absence of the business mail and circulars which figure so prominently in Western countries.

In the field of *sound broadcasting and television*, the development of services and level of licence fees are comparable in the two German states. Almost every household in the GDR has a radio and television licence. There are five sound broadcasting programmes and two television channels. For television transmissions in colour the French Secam system is used.

The current Five-Year Plan envisages a 20 per cent increase in the performance of the postal and telecommunications services, the main effort bing devoted to improvements in the quality of the telephone service and in the reception of radio and television broadcasts, and to speeding up mail deliveries.

4.4.4 Planning and development trends

To cope with changing transport needs and shifts in traffic flows as well as with structural changes affecting transport volume and the division of labour between various types of transport, long-term planning is essential, bearing in mind the long life of transport routes and means of transport. Only in this way is it possible to apportion available resources rationally and effectively to future needs.

To meet these demands, *General Transport Plans* have been drafted for a number of years for the areas and for 25 towns. These plans are to be dovetailed with the regional General Building Plans. Moreover, since the regional transport systems are to an increasing extent interlocking, a unified *General Transport Scheme* was drawn up on the basis of the regional plans and in the light of the long-term trends of the economy as a whole. This scheme has the same function as the integrated Federal traffic routes plan, the infra-structure plan covering all forms of transport in the Federal Republic.

In practice, however, there is no sign yet of an integrated transport policy that would co-ordinate the separate measures listed in the Five-Year Plans according to a comprehensive concept. The plans for the various forms of transport and the corresponding investments continue to build on the established division of labour in goods and passenger transport and are concerned only with short-term increases in demand. Future targets for the period after 1980 are not specified as a rule, but only qualitatively adumbrated. And those concepts that are stated in quantitative terms are liable to continual revision, as is the case, for instance, with projections of the future transport tasks of the railways, which will continue to be the dominating form of transport but are beset by operational difficulties.

In the GDR the traffic problems caused by the private car in Western countries are often cited as a warning example, and the authorities make every effort to ensure the continuing dominance of public transport in the field of passenger transport; yet, in spite of all that, the GDR, too, is surrendering to the motorcar. Thus, traffic plans foresee that motorisation will reach a saturation point at a ratio of about 300 cars per 1,000 inhabitants, which clearly contradicts the planning guidelines, which postulate a ratio of 7:3 in the division of labour between public and private passenger transport in towns. Since traffic will be concentrated in the towns and industrial centres, the GDR must expect to be confronted with the same problems of transport policy that have dogged other countries.

4.5   Artisan trades

The position of the artisan trades and their importance for the national economy were from the outset controversial subjects in the GDR. Ideological and economic considerations frequently pointed in opposite directions. The history of the artisan trades is characterised accordingly by alternating phases of encouragement, toleration and restriction.

The year 1976 could well be the starting point for a new period of expansion. A Council of Ministers decision of 12 February 1976 on the encouragement of the artisan trades has not so far been published, but is frequently mentioned in the GDR press. This decision comprises a number of measures providing improved working conditions above all for private artisans, and to a lesser extent for the artisan producer co-operatives. A more liberal attitude is to be shown in the grating of business licences; credits are to be extended on favourable terms for the preservation and expansion of existing, and the establishment of new, artisan enterprises; the training of apprentices is to be encouraged; finally, certain groups of artisans are to benefit from tax concessions. Following the announcement of these measures, the number of applications for artisan business licences was substantially higher than in the preceding years. In Berlin alone, 273 new private artisan enterprises were licensed and five new artisan producer co-operatives were founded

161

in the course of 1976,[1] and in the GDR as a whole some thousands of artisan enterprises were newly established or reopened. It must be added, however, that in the same year many private artisans closed down their businesses, mostly on the grounds of age. It is an open question, therefore, whether the current policy of encouragement for artisans will actually lead to an increase in the number of artisan enterprises — which would answer an urgent public need for goods and services — or whether the new measures will merely check the process of shrinkage of the artisan trades, which has been going on for many years.

Thus, on the one hand the contribution of the artisan trades to the supplies of the population and their role as subcontractors to industry, important in dealing with unexpected bottlenecks, are welcomed, yet, on the other hand the independent artisans at any rate are looked upon askance as private owners of means of production, and thus as alien bodies in the socialist economy of the GDR. This attitude led as early as the 1950s to pressure being brought to bear on artisans, who were enjoined to form co-operatives. There was no forcible socialisation, as in agriculture, but the state held out special inducements, in particular tax concessions, as a means to encourage co-operative mergers. Owing to the advantages of larger production units, the artisan producer co-operatives achieved a substantially higher labour productivity than did the independent artisan enterprises.

The number of independent artisans has been steadily declining (see Appendix, table 30), while the artisan producer co-operatives markedly expanded up to 1971, when they produced 51 per cent of the total output (in terms of value) of the artisan trades, as compared with 2 per cent in 1957. This development, however, was halted by a Decree of July 1972 on the 'restructuring' of the artisan trades. A large proportion of the then existing artisan producer co-operatives, in particular those engaged in industrial production or in the building and building assembly trades, were transformed into publicly owned enterprises. As a result the number of artisan producer co-operatives, their working personnel and their turnover dropped to about half of their previous levels, and the share of the co-operatives in the total artisan output fell back to one third, then recovered slightly, reaching 38 per cent in 1975. Thus, in the artisan trades, alone among all branches of the GDR economy, the private sector continues to dominate, accounting for 62 per cent of the output.

Independently of their status, the material position of private as well as co-operative artisans was relatively favourable. Thanks to their flexibility in attending to gaps in market supplies and their ability to respond immediately to public needs in respect of goods and services,

1 According to Berliner Zeitung (East Berlin) of 23 December 1976.

artisans both in the private and co-operative sectors have been assured of good incomes. This prompted numbers of skilled workers to leave industry for work in co-operative or private artisan enterprises. In view of the acute shortage of labour, the authorities saw themselves compelled to take counter-measures, which took the form of increased taxation for industrially producing independent and co-operative artisan enterprises. In introducing the measure, which came into force on 1 January 1971, it was stated openly that it had to be taken because the enterprises concerned had netted unwarrantably high incomes. The higher rate of taxation did not apply to artisan enterprises carrying out repairs or supplying other services to the public, nor to any artisan enterprises not engaged in industrial production.

The restraints imposed on the industrially producing artisan co-operatives through the tax legislation of 1971 and their nationalisation in 1972 suggest that the continued existence of those producer co-operatives, which presumably had achieved a productivity well above average, was no longer considered an economic necessity, and that their absorption into the publicly owned industry appeared to make better economic sense. It is different with the private and co-operative artisan enterprises working on traditional lines, and above all those carrying out repairs and supplying services. These enterprises are still essential to the economy, in view of the vast gap between supply and demand in this field. Moreover, with rising affluence and living standards, demand in this sector is bound to increase more rapidly than the general level of production.

The results of the restructuring measures so far taken, can already be noted in a survey of trends in the various artisan trades (cf. Appendix, table 31). The commodity producing trades – in the main the building trades, meat processing, mechanical engineering and vehicle construction, electrical engineering and the wood working trades – continue to be dominant, although their share in the total turnover of artisan enterprises declined from 75 per cent in 1970 to 63 per cent in 1975. The share of repair work in the gross output value of artisan enterprises increased during the same period from 21 per cent to 30 per cent. The distribution of the enterprises engaged in repair work among the various trades reflects the constantly increasing dissemination of consumer durables, from clocks and watches to cars. So far, repairs to radio and television receivers and sound recording equipment have ranked first in terms of value of output, followed by motor car repairs and maintenance. The latter item is likely to move closer to the top in future, considering the rapid increase in the number of private motor vehicles in the GDR.

The service trades proper (hairdressing, laundries) increased their share in the total performance of the artisan trades from 4 per cent in

163

1970 to 7 per cent in 1975. Both the repair and service trades can be expected to expand further in the coming years. Here, in the official GDR view, in the specific tasks, lies the specific mission of the artisan trades in the socialist economy. In 1972, the powers of the state planning authorities were extended to cover the regulation of co-operative and private artisan enterprises. The central authorities are thus in a position to require artisan enterprises to undertake any specific services or repairs that may be deemed necessary for the fulfilment of the economic plan.

4.6 Distributive trade

The development of domestic trade, like that of other sectors of the GDR economy, is characterised by a succession of socialisation measures. By means of taxation measures shopkeepers were induced, and in some cases forced, to give up their businesses or carry on under a changed legal status. Further pressure was exerted by giving the consumer co-operatives preference in the allocation of goods. The leading part in the socialisation of the retail trade, however, was played by the State Trading Organisation (*Handelsorganisation*, HO) with its shops, stores and restaurants. Founded in 1948, they have since then consistently enlarged their range of goods. To begin with, they had a monopoly in the sale of high-quality products and goods subject to central controls. Private as well as co-operative retail shops wishing to sell rationed goods had first to conclude commodity allocation contracts with the HO, whose dominant position was thus consolidated. The 'socialist transformation' of retail trade was speeded up by temporary measures such as curtailment of deliveries and withdrawal of food ration cards from shopkeepers. In 1956 a different method came to the fore: it was the conclusion of *commission trading contracts*, which debarred the retailer from effecting any business on his own account; he was assured of deliveries on a par with the state-owned retail outlets, but became in effect an employee of the state-owned or co-operative trading organisations.

The structural transformation is clearly reflected in the changing shares of the various forms of retail trade in the total turnover, as set out in chart 36.

The state takeover of the *wholesale trade* proceeded much more rapidly. The 'Industrial and Trade Offices' (*Industrie- und Handelskontore*), founded in 1946, were succeeded two years later by the German Trading Association (*Deutsche Handelsgesellschaft*, DHG), which operated as the roof organisation of the entire wholesale trade in the Soviet Zone. This in turn was superseded between 1949 and 1951

164

Chart 36
Retail turnover by form of ownership (in per cent)

	1946	1950	1960	1965	1970	1975
Private retail trade[1]	86	53	16	13	10	7
Commission trade[2]	–	–	7	9	9	7
Consumer co-operatives	14	17	33	34	81	86
Publicly owned trade[3]	–	30	44	44		
All retail trade	100	100	100	100	100	100

1 Including retailing by artisans and catering establishments.
2 Including businesses with State participation.
3 HO, Mitropa, works canteens of publicly owned enterprises, State pharmacies, etc., department stores, mail order trade.

Sources: GDR Statistical Yearbooks.

by the German Central Boards for Trade (*Deutsche Handelszentralen*, DHZ). Several more changes in the organisation of wholesale trade followed in the subsequent years.

The most important agencies concerned with the *trade in means of production* are

the state offices (*Kontore*) subordinated to the appropriate industrial ministries (e.g. metal office, timber office, textile office)

the trade or marketing departments of some Associations of Publicly Owned Enterprises

within the sphere of competence of the Council for Agricultural Production and Foodstuffs, the appropriate trade offices and publicly owned enterprises for the purchase and processing of agricultural products

within the sphere of competence of the Area Economic Councils, the appropriate publicly owned enterprises (e.g. for the scrap and waste materials trade, dairy equipment, etc.)

the Peasant Trading Co-operatives of the Peasant Mutual Aid Association.

4.6.1 Organisation of trade

The difficulties in the supply of consumer goods in the GDR, which continue to this day, are due only in part to inadequacies of planning and production. Another important cause must be sought in short-comings in the sphere of distributive trade. To improve the efficiency of distribution, numerous organisational measures were introduced in the course of the economic reform launched in 1963-64. It was hoped that more effective rationalisation of retail shops, specialisation, establishment of department stores and regional goods depots, introduction of self-service, intensified co-operation and the foundation of special organisations to promote it would lead to the development of 'rational marketing systems' in wholesale and retail trade, which in turn would contribute to improved and regionally balanced supplies of consumer goods to the public and of means of production to the factories.

These endeavours crystallised in the form of numerous organisational changes, some of which were merely tentative. Taken together, both in the consumer goods and producer goods sectors, these measures add up to a very complex and somewhat diffuse picture.

Private trade in consumer goods (private wholesale and retail traders, retail traders operating on the basis of a commission contract or with state participation, purchasing co-operatives with commission contract or state participation, independent purchasing co-operatives, and catering establishments) is guided by the Chambers of Industry and Commerce, while the trading institutions of the artisan trades (bakers, butchers, etc., purchasing and supply co-operatives) are supervised by the Craft Chambers.

4.6.2   Retail trade performance

The State Trading Organisation (HO) and the consumer co-operatives constitute the two components of 'socialist retail trade'. Their share in the total retail turnover rose from 81 per cent in 1971 to 86 per cent in 1975, with the HO generally dominating the urban centres and the consumer co-operatives the rural trade. Private retailers, mostly artisans with retail shops, such as butchers or bakers, handled 7 per cent of the turnover, and the remaining 7 per cent passed through the shops of the commission traders, who run their formerly independent businesses still in their own name but on state account.

According to the most recent census, there were about 128,000 retail establishments in the GDR in 1971[1] (as compared with 196,000 in 1962), including about 97,000 shops and 29,000 catering establishments.[2] Thus the number of retail establishments fell by one third in the course of nine years. The trend appears to have continued in the subsequent years. GDR sources have given the number of retail shops and catering establishments in 1975 as respectively 90,000 and 25,000,

---

1 For the purpose of the industrial censuses carried out at irregular intervals, retail establishments include only shops with a fixed sales area, catering establishments and certain artisan enterprises.
2 According to Presse-Informationen, published by the Press Office of the Chairman of the GDR Council of Ministers, 25 August 1972.

166

in addition to 39,000 other retail outlets, such as kiosks or mobile shops.[1] It should be noted, however, that while the number of retail outlets is declining, the total sales area has remained virtually constant. The process of concentration was manifest in all areas of the GDR, most markedly so in (East) Berlin and still above average in the heavily industrialised southern areas.

In 1975, there were 26 department stores (*Warenhäuser*) in the GDR, half of them run by the HO under the name of 'Centrum', the other half by the consumer co-operatives under the name of 'Konsument'.[2] These are the largest retail units, which must have a sales area of at least 2,500 sq.m and must offer a comprehensive range of goods. In practice, the latter stipulation is not always met. Next in size are the *Kaufhäuser*, minor department stores, with sales areas of at least 1,000 sq.m; *Kaufhallen*, 'shopping halls', with at least 180 sq.m; and rural shopping centres with at least 200 sq.m.[3] *Kaufhäuser* as a rule offer the complete range of goods in one branch of commerce; there are 274 of them. *Kaufhallen* sell foodstuffs, drinks and tobacco goods as well as popular industrial goods. Their number is increasing rapidly. Nearly half the 800 *Kaufhallen* recorded in Spring 1976 had been opened in the previous five years.[4] Most of them are situated in the cities. Their share in the total retail turnover of the GDR rose from 11 per cent in 1970 to 20 per cent in 1975, but to no less than 35 per cent in East Berlin.[5] Rural shopping centres, as their name implies, cater specifically for the needs of the rural population. There are 300 of them.

In spite of the rapid advance of *Kaufhallen* and other large-scale units, small and medium-sized shops still outnumber them by far. In 1974 70 per cent of all retail units had a sales area of less than 50 sq.m, and 40 per cent even less than 25 sq.m.[6]

The labour force of the entire domestic trade of the GDR was stated to number 892,000 in 1975, including over 100,000 persons employed in the wholesale trade and about 150,000 in the catering and hotel trades.[7] Women play a leading part in the GDR's domestic trade; they make up about three quarters of the total labour force.

4.7   Remaining sectors

These sectors comprise all economic activities that may be classified as

1 Presse-Informationen, 1 July 1975.
2 Die Wirtschaft, 5 March 1975.
3 Definitionen für Planung, Rechnungsführung und Statistik, Part 5, East Berlin 1973, pp 86f.
4 Die Wirtschaft, 11 March 1976.
5 Der Handel, no.7/1976, p.270.
6 Berlin Radio, 17 June 1974, programme 'Meeting Place Alexandeplatz'.
7 Statistisches Jahrbuch der DDR 1975, p.248, and Presse-Informationen, 6 February 1976.

services in the widest sense. They include the fields of culture, health, social welfare, economic and state administration, banking and insurance as well as all services supplied to individuals and households. The number of persons employed in these sectors has grown steadily over the years (see section 1.2.3 above and Appendix, table 6). In 1975, the figure reached 2.1 million (including personnel left out of the GDR statistics), or nearly 24 per cent of all economically active persons. The official figures give only rough indications as to the distribution of employment within the services sector. Filling the gaps by estimates, we arrive at the following distribution of the labour force of 2.1 million (in units of 1,000 persons):

State (administration, police, armed services)	630
Education	470
Health care and social welfare	420
Artisan services (hairdressers, watchmakers, etc.)	70
Other services (including banking, insurance and 'other productive branches of the economy')	530

The proportion of women in the services sector is higher than the average for the economy as a whole. It exceeds 60 per cent, and the rising trend appears to be continuing. The share of women in the labour force is highest in the sectors of social welfare, with 94 per cent; health, 83 per cent; and education, 71 per cent, that is to say, in the spheres of work where in the Western economies, too, the proportion of female labour is traditionally high.

As regards the level of performance, there is a conspicuous gap between health and education on the one hand and services to individuals and households on the other.

In the fields of health care and education, as a result of far-reaching state support, concentration of resources on selected key projects, and streamlining of systems, a level of performance has been attained that is in no way inferior to that of the Federal Republic. The number of doctors and of hospital beds per 1,000 inhabitants is roughly the same in both parts of Germany. As regards some indices, the GDR is actually ahead of the Federal Republic, thanks presumably to a more elaborate system of communication and supervision: infant mortality is lower in the GDR than in the Federal Republic, probably in the first place because the staggered payment of the generous maternity grant is made conditional on the expectant mother, and subsequently mother and baby, undergoing regular medical examinations (see section 5.2.2.1 below).

In the field of education, performance and successes are difficult to quantify, but here, too, some evidence indicates that in some respects GDR standards are higher than those in the Federal Republic.[1]

Thus, the services supplied by the state for the benefit of the population as a whole present a bright picture, highlighted by satisfactory levels of national health and education. In stark contrast, the predominantly private services sector constitutes one of the weakest links in the GDR economy. Enterprises supplying services to individuals or households — laundries, clothes pressing establishments, dry-cleaners, hairdressers, etc. — though regarded as socially necessary, since they contribute to raising the population's standard of living, are still underdeveloped, both in terms of numbers and capacity. In this field, too, the capacity of the enterprises is to be increased by the introduction of modern forms of organisation. In recent years, so-called service combines have been established, primarily in the large towns. In these combines, different services can be supplied at the same time. Establishments of this type are to cater in particular for the population of new residential developments. The concentration of administrative work should enable those centres to provide more rapid and cheaper services.

1 For details, see Materialien zum Bericht zur Lage der Nation 1974, Paper VII/2423 of the West German Lower House, dated 29 July 1974, pp 111 and 147 ff., and Vergleichende Darstellung des Bildungswesens im geteilten Deutschland, Lower House Paper V/4609.

5 Use and distribution of product and incomes

5.1 Investment

Investments comprise purchases and construction or production on own account of buildings, machines and installations serving to replace obsolete plant and equipment or to augment the economy's capital assets. In Western economies dominated by market forces investments represent the chief indicators of cyclical development: poor profit prospects depress the entrepreneurs' propensity to invest and demand declines; good prospects heighten the propensity to invest and economic activity gathers momentum.

But in the planned economy of the GDR investment decisions are not made by the enterprises. It might be expected, then, that the central authorities would steer a course of steady investment growth. Yet, observation of investment activity in the GDR reveals considerable changes of speed, both overall and in individual sectors. These fluctuations reflect in the first place the dilemma of planners forced to set scales of priority for the allocation of limited resources: thus, as soon as priority is accorded to consumption, the sum total available for investments is reduced; similarly, if more funds are assigned to the housing programme, there remains that much less for other investment projects.

The 1971-75 Five-Year Plan declared the 'further increase of the population's material and cultural living standards' the principal economic task. Accordingly investments, with the exception of housing construction, were downgraded in the scale of priorities, while more attention was focused on the consumer goods industry and on the infrastructure in connection with the housing programme. But in the current 1976-80 Five-Year Plan this policy was again modified in view of the urgency of other tasks, notably the export drive, the opening up of domestic sources of energy, and co-operation within the framework of the CMEA.

For the five-year period from 1976 to 1980, the plan provides a cumulative investment volume of 242,000 million Marks (not including general overhauls), of which 8,000 million Marks is set aside for participation in CMEA investment projects and 116,000 million Marks for domestic machinery and equipment. The plan target for domestic investments corresponds to an average annual growth rate of 5.3 per cent, as compared with 4.1 per cent in the preceding five-year period

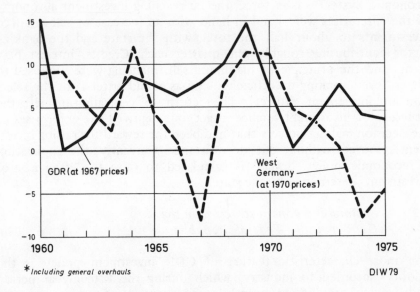

* Including general overhauls

DIW 79

Figure 27   Growth (in real terms) of gross capital
investment* in the GDR and the
Federal Republic (1960 to 1975)

1971-75. Investment in CMEA projects is expected to rise much more
steeply, as the total in the preceding five-year period was only 3,200
million Marks. This item includes deliveries of investment goods, secon-
ding of skilled labour and the granting of foreign exchange credits for
special projects (cf. pp 274 f. below), most of them involving the Soviet
Union.

From 1960 to 1975 the amount of investment (without general overhauls) increased by a factor of two-and-a-half, while the gross domestic
product (produced national income) doubled. Thus the investment
ratio went up, though at a very uneven rate.

The investment structure did not change significantly over the
fifteen-year period (cf. Appendix, table 33). Roughly half of all investment funds is spent on machinery and equipment, 42 per cent on
construction work and the remainder for sundry investment expen-
ditures (project planning, feasibility studies, etc.).

The ·mode of financing investments, on the other hand, underwent
substantial changes. Before the introduction of the New Economic
System almost two thirds of all investments were financed free of
interest out of the state budget, about one quarter was self-financed,
the remaining 10 to 15 per cent came from bank credits. While the New

171

Economic System was in force, the far-reaching investment autonomy of the enterprises went hand in hand with an increase of self-financed investments to about half the total, with the state and the banking sector contributing roughly one quarter each. Credits, interest payments and the principle of maximum self-financing were supposed to act as 'levers' jacking up efficiency and as sound criteria for the selection of investment projects. The return to centralisation left the structure of investment finance intact, but deprived the enterprises of the decision-making powers that had been the reward for raising investment resources without outside assistance. Currently, the application of economic policy 'levers' is calculated to raise the efficiency of investments determined by the state.

5.1.1   Sectoral investment structure in the GDR and the Federal Republic

The most characteristic feature of GDR investment policy is the priority accorded to industry, which during the fifteen-year period under review took up consistently over 50 per cent of total investments (cf. Appendix, table 34). The sectoral distribution of capital assets shows a similar relationship (cf. section 1.2.4 above). Industry's share in total investments is nearly twice the West German figure. Conversely, the share of important sectors forming part of the infrastructure, such as housing construction, amounts to barely half the West German figure, while the activities here classified as 'remaining sectors' — services, the state, private households and non-profit making organisations — attract only one quarter to one third of the West German percentage shares. The comparison reveals a considerable neglect of infrastructure investment in the GDR.

In contrast, the share of agriculture and forestry, with 12 to 13 per cent, exceeds the West German figure by a factor of three to four. The exceptionally high investment effort for agriculture forms part of the drive for the maximum attainable degree of self-sufficiency. The transition to large-scale agricultural production units with accommodation for large numbers of livestock and other new buildings required for the introduction of 'industrial production methods' called for very substantial investments.

A break-down of the figures according to type of investments — equipment, buildings, remainder — reveals that the sector transport,[1] posts and telecommunications recorded the highest equipment ratio, 76 per cent of total investments in that sector in 1975. This appears to be

---

1 Not including roads, which come under the state sector.

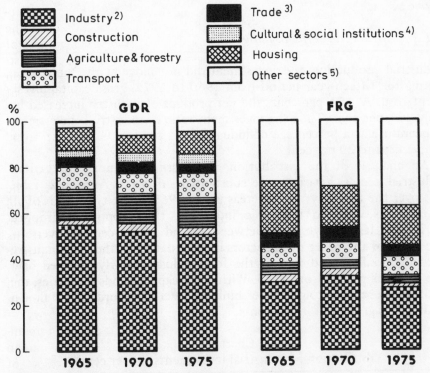

1) In the GDR without general overhauls.— 2) Including power, mining and water resources, and in West Germany also productive artisan enterprises (without building trades).— 3)GDR: Including state collecting and purchasing agencies as well as catering establishments. Federal Republic: including foreign trade enterprises, but excluding catering establishments.— 4) Education, culture and art, health and social services, sport and tourist amenities.— 5) GDR: Other "producing" branches (e.g. project planning and computing enterprises, publishing houses, repair combines), as well as services, state administration, state organs and social organisations. Federal Republic: State, private households, non-profit-making organisations, services (except residential lettings).   DIW 79

Figure 28   Gross capital investment[1] by sector

173

due partly to the expansion of the vehicle stock of the transport branches, especially shipping, and partly to the extension of the telecommunications equipment of the postal services and television. Industry, construction and the remaining productive branches of the economy all show equipment ratios of about 60 per cent, which is also above average.

5.1.2   Structural shifts in industry

Industrial production and investment did not move at the same pace: during the fifteen-year period from 1960 to 1975, gross capital investment rose by 153 per cent, the net product of industry increased by only 121 per cent. Thus the investment ratio of industry — investment expenditure as a percentage of industrial net product — went up from 18 per cent to 20 per cent.

An analysis of the distribution of investments among the various industrial sectors reveals some substantial shifts (cf. Appendix, table 37) over the fifteen years. Whereas up to 1965 about two thirds of all investments went to the basic industries, this proportion dropped during the last ten years to between 50 and 55 per cent. Conversely, the share of the other main sectors increased, that of the light industry actually doubled and that of the food industry nearly doubled over the ten-year period from 1965. Within the capital goods industries, the mechanical engineering/vehicle building sector recorded an almost continuous growth of investments.

Chart 37
Distribution of industrial investments (in per cent)

	Actual			Plan
	1960-1965	1966-1970	1971-1975	1976-1980[1]
Production of basic materials	66	52.9	55.0	60
Water industry	6	5.9	4.8	4
Capital goods industries	16	24.8	22.3	19
Consumer goods industry	12	16.4	17.9	17

1 Official figures supplemented by estimates

The overall level of investment activity can be gauged by the fact that in the course of five years, from 1971 to 1975, 40 per cent of the equipment assets of industry were newly supplied or modernised.

The current Five-Year Plan provides for a slowing down of the development of the *capital goods industry*, whose share in the total industrial investment is to go down. On the other hand, special urgency

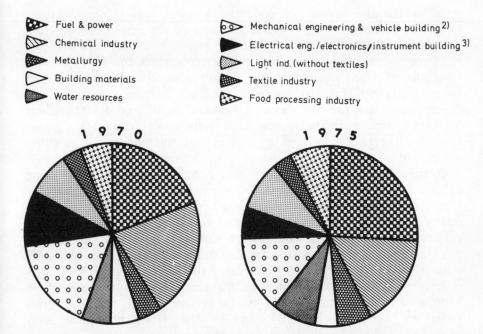

Fuel & power
Chemical industry
Metallurgy
Building materials
Water resources

Mechanical engineering & vehicle building [2]
Electrical eng./electronics/instrument building [3]
Light ind.(without textiles)
Textile industry
Food processing industry

1 9 7 0

1 9 7 5

[1])*Without general overhauls.* – [2])*Including foundries, forging shops, shipbuilding and hardware manufacture.* – [3])*Including precision engineering/optical industry, electronic data processing and construction of office machines.*

DIW 79

Figure 29   Industrial investment[1] by sector
(shares of total industrial investment)

is attached to the expansion of the *fuel and power industry*, which during the current five-year period is to absorb investments totalling between 31,000 and 33,000 million Marks, more than any other individual industry.

For the *chemical industry*, the second largest industrial investor, the plan envisages substantial increases in capacity for the production of plastics, manmade fibres, fertilisers and other basic chemicals, as well as of pharmaceuticals. Marked increases are also envisaged for petrochemical output and the utilisation of natural gas.[1] The plan

1   The largest investment project of the chemical industry in the period from 1971 to 1975 was the new nitrogen works at Piesteritz, completed at a cost of 2,400 million Marks. The Schwarzheide polyurethane plants and the Böhlen-Zaluzi olefine complex, a joint GDR-Czechoslovak project, also came on stream during the same five-year period.

provides for the import of modern chemical plants from Western industrial countries, and at the same time for increased bilateral co-operation under CMEA auspices.[1]

In the *metallurgical industry*, the plan provides for an expansion especially of rolled steel capacities. Finally a marked increase in investment is planned for the *building materials industry*, with a total expenditure over the five years of between 5,000 and 5,500 million Marks, earmarked largely for new plant in the concrete and brick industries, for the production of aggregates and for mechanical handling equipment.

In the *water industry*, on the other hand, the planned investment volume of up to 5,000 million Marks will hardly suffice to ease the supply situation, which has been strained for a considerable period owing to the steep rise in the demand for water from industry, agriculture and domestic consumers. During the last five-year period, storage capacity was increased by 230 million cu.m, and another 180 million is to be added by 1980, bringing the aggregate capacity of the reservoirs up to 1,400 million cu.m. But this will still not be enough to cope with the problems caused by the extremely high degree of utilisation of water in the GDR and by the, lately not infrequent, exceptionally low water levels in years of low rainfall.

5.1.3 Development trends

For a number of years the crucial problem of the productive sectors in the GDR has been the need to expand the economy by intensive rather than extensive means. In view of the very limited growth of the labour force in the productive sectors, with an increasing proportion of that limited force absorbed year after year by plant maintenance and by training for higher skills, there is very little prospect of raising output by creating new work places. It can only be done on any significant scale by providing existing work places with more and better equipment.

In order to solve these problems, intensification has for some time received priority. Now, while it is possible as a rule, on the occasion of plant renewals, to install modern equipment economical of manpower, the full utilisation of existing plant requires both rationalisation and shift-work, which again means additional manpower. That is why the GDR economic authorities have been only partially successful in their

---

1 An example is the 'Polymir 50' process for the manufacture of high-pressure polyethylene, developed jointly by GDR and Soviet chemists; the construction of a plant with an annual capacity of 50,000 tonnes at Novopolotsk is to be followed by a similar one at Leuna. A licence for the application of this process has been sold already to the Federal Republic.

176

endeavour to make sure that their investments should on balance reduce rather than increase the demand for labour. So far, the release of manpower actually achieved is far below the plan targets, and in some cases — which attracted sharp official criticism — new investment schemes resulted in a demand for additional labour.

Continuing the programme for the urgently required renewal of the country's capital assets, the 1976-80 Five-Year Plan allocates more than half of the total of industrial investments for rationalisation and modernisation. Plant extensions are sanctioned only provided the existing capacities are operated on a shift system; provided there is little scope for further rationalisation; and provided the proposed new plant is to be operated at least on a two-shift system. In addition, the efficiency of the investment process is to be raised by firmer planning. The Five-Year Plan must show the projected development of investment expenditure year by year, specifying the important projects to be undertaken by sectors, industries and enterprises and setting index figures for the progress of the work. Under a recent regulation, area investment plans must be drawn up in conjunction with the manpower balance projection, to make sure that planning conforms to the aim of minimising the demand for labour. The implementation of investment projects is to be subjected to closer supervision. Efforts have been revived of late to encourage the 'in-house' production of rationalisation devices with supplies drawn as much as possible from enterprise reserves and financed from the performance fund of the enterprise.

Yet, innovations that make for greater efficiency cannot be decreed from above. What is required to attain them is on the one hand a rapid development of improved technologies, and on the other hand the introduction of effective incentives encouraging improved performance by the enterprises. The plan allocation for new processes has been increased, but the current regulations on the use of profits make it scarcely worth while for enterprises to embark on new developments.

If living standards are to continue to rise in future and if the capital goods industries are to be strengthened — as a vital basis for pressing on with the domestic rationalisation drive and extended integration with other CMEA countries — it appears that investment must actually be increased in all sectors. This confronts the authorities responsible for arriving at an optimum balance in the structure of production and the use of resources with ever growing difficulties.

5.2 The state

5.2.1 *The state budget*

The state budget has a crucial function in the economic system of the GDR. It is the foremost instrument of guidance and supervision of the financial system, and thus forms an integral part of general economic planning. Outwardly, this close connection is reflected in the fact that the state budget and the economic plan for the corresponding period are adopted and enacted simultaneously.

The state budget, however, does not cover the entire revenue and expenditure of the state, which includes in addition the accounts of a number of special funds formed out of profits by publicly owned enterprises, associations of publicly owned enterprises and publicly owned combines, to be used, according to specific rules, for investments, bonus payments and other purposes. In 1975, these funds totalled 12,000 million Marks.

The state budget in the narrow sense comprises the budget of the Republic and the budgets of all territorial units of local government as well as of social insurance. Three quarters of revenue and expenditure relate to the central budget (including social insurance), the remaining quarter features the area budgets, which also include the entire revenue and expenditure of the lower-grade local authorities (districts, towns, communes). The West German equivalent of the GDR state budget is the consolidated budget of Federal Government, the individual States (Länder), communes and social insurance organisations. But there is no parallel in the West German, or any Western, budget to the appearance of parts of the profits achieved by the publicly owned economy on the credit side of the state ledger. For a long time no details of the state budget were published; later on the definitions of the various items were repeatedly modified, so that a detailed picture of the budget emerges only for the last few years.

5.2.1.1 Revenue Contributions from the publicly owned economy constitute by far the most important source of revenue for the state budget. Their share in the total revenue rose from 54 per cent in 1970 to 62 per cent in 1975 (cf. Appendix, table 38). The contributions of the publicly owned economy take three forms:

a) product-related levy (production levy, cf. p. 69 above),
b) production fund and trading fund levy,
c) net profit levy.

In 1970 half the total of the contributions came from the product-

178

related levy.[1] Since then its share has declined. This levy, which the producer recoups through price mark-ups, has the character of a differentiated tax on consumption. Today the vast majority of industrial consumer goods as well as drinks and tobacco goods are subject to this indirect tax, which on average for these classes of goods accounted for 56 per cent of the retail price in 1975, as compared with 49 per cent in 1970.[2]

The production fund and trading fund levy is in essence a tax on the capital (fixed and current assets) of publicly owned enterprises in industry, construction and distributive trade. It was introduced towards the end of the 1960s. It is comparable to a payment of interest on capital. Unlike the product-related levy, it must not be added to production cost, but has to be defrayed out of profits. It is intended to encourage a more efficient use of capital. Its share in the total contributions from the publicly owned economy is under 20 per cent.

The state's participation in the net profits of the publicly owned economy is a flexible instrument, liable to be adjusted from year to year — for example, on the grounds of structural policy — overall or for selected enterprises. In 1975, the publicly owned economy paid 68 per cent of its net profits to the state. The state's share in net profits has shown a clearly rising trend in recent years.

Contributions from the banks and *dues from agriculture* — amounting to 3,400 million Marks and 1,300 million Marks respectively in 1975 — are further sources of state budget revenue. The dues from agriculture are levied on gross income of crop farming enterprises; and on consumption (farm incomes, cultural and social funds, etc.) of all production units not already taxed on their profits. The dues are levied only on the agricultural enterprises; the individual members of agricultural producer co-operatives pay no tax.

On the other hand, *members of artisan producer co-operatives*, as well as the *self-employed* and *employed persons*, are taxed on their earned incomes (by way of wages tax, income tax, see section 5.3.1.3 below). In addition, the enterprises themselves — producer co-operatives as well as private artisan enterprises and shops — are liable to

---

1 The term (in German, produktgebundene Abgabe) was first used in 1972 to cover a series of levies — on production, services, consumption, and for price equalisation — that had been introduced in the publicly owned economy in the 1950s, by and large as replacements for corporation tax, trades tax, turnover tax and taxes on specific consumer goods.
2 These averages are taken over the entire range of goods in question, a small proportion of which actually carries a subsidy, equivalent to a 'negative tax'. If the subsidised goods were left out of account, the above percentages would be higher still. In the foregoing, net taxation was considered in relation to the prices actually paid by the consumer. Alternatively the tax load can be measured in terms of economic (non-intervention) prices, i.e. by expressing net taxation (product-related levy minus subsidies) as a percentage of global factor cost plus trade margins. On this basis the corresponding figures for 1975 and 1970 are 122 and 93 per cent respectively.

pay production fund tax or turnover tax (in some cases also trades tax) and, if their annual wages bill exceeds a certain amount, a pay-roll tax. Economically active individuals and their co-operative and private enterprises contributed 10,300 million Marks to the state budget in 1975.

A number of further taxes is levied irrespective of economic-social status. Of these only the yield of *local taxes* — comprising land tax, dog tax and entertainment tax — is known: it remained unchanged at 500 million Marks from 1970 to 1975. The yield of wealth tax, death duties, , gift tax, betting and lotteries tax and motorcar tax is likely to be included, together with the proceeds from customs duties, in the residual item, *other revenues*, which in 1975 contributed 10,200 million Marks to the state budget.

In addition to the contributions from the publicly owned economy and the various taxes, *proceeds of the state institutions* and *social insurance* constitute the third major source of state budget revenue. The institutions of education, health, social welfare and culture and the state administration contributed a revenue of 6,700 million Marks in 1975. In the same year social insurance contributions totalled 11,800 million Marks. These contributions, of course, are tied by law to a specific purpose.

5.2.1.2 Expenditure   State budget expenditure is dominated by spending on social and cultural objectives, which, together with the subsidies for consumer goods, public transport fares and rents, make up about half the total budget expenditure, about 55,000 million Marks in 1975.

This category of expenditure includes contrasting items. The largest of these, accounting for 21,000 million Marks in 1975, is *social insurance*. Social insurance pensions totalled over 12,000 million Marks in 1975. Over 6,000 million Marks was spent in the same year on the health services, especially for the maintenance of hospitals, policlinics and outpatient departments. The remaining 2,500 million Marks was made up of cash benefits, chiefly sickness and maternity benefits.

Health and social welfare outside social insurance, e.g. the maintenance of old age homes, nursing homes and children's homes, and the care of young mothers and infants, absorbed 7,800 million Marks in 1975. *Education* from play school to university, and *culture and sport* cost the state 10,500 million Marks.

Consumer price subsidies are to protect consumers from the consequences of high producer prices in agriculture and industry as well as rising import prices. The selection of items singled out for subsidies is guided by various considerations. Most importantly, price support pursues social policy aims in subsidising essential goods and services, such as bread, potatoes, homes, heating, transport. In addition, price support for children's clothing has a bearing on population policy, while subsidised book prices serve political-educational purposes. So far, price subsidies have risen year after year. Although no figures have been released concerning the rate of subsidy on individual items, it can be said that the price support ratio, i.e. the subsidy as a percentage of the unsubsidised price, ranges generally from 5 to 50 per cent, though in exceptional cases it may be as high as 80 per cent. For the main areas of subsidised goods and services, the following average price support ratios have been calculated:

foodstuffs	20 per cent
passenger transport	45 per cent
(including in particular	
local traffic	60 per cent)
rents	60 per cent

Official data on the *financing of investments* is very patchy. This item is subdivided into expenditure on specific investment projects of the publicly owned economy sanctioned by the Council of Ministers and expenditure on investments of state organisations and institutions. In 1974 the two items added up to 7,700 million Marks (in 1975 no figure was given for expenditure on specific investment projects). In addition, the state participates in the investments of the other sectors of the economy. Agriculture, for instance, received 2,000 million Marks in 1974, of which a part was used for land improvement and for construction of installations suitable for the application of industrial methods of production. Investment throughout the economy totalled 41,000 million Marks in that year (see Appendix, table 34).

Strong support is currently extended to *housing and housing construction* with a budget expenditure of 4,300 million Marks. According to the official elucidations, this item includes 1,300 million Marks for construction and modernisation and 3,000 million Marks for rent subsidies, with an additional 4,100 million Marks raised partly from private resources, partly through credits for construction and modernisation. Thus, a total of 8,400 million Marks was spent on housing and housing construction in 1975.

Expenditure on *administrative tasks* was about 3,500 million Marks, of which the bulk paid the wages and salaries of employees of the state apparatus and the economic authorities.

Defence expenditure, according to the official data, believed by Western experts to be of the right order of magnitude, amounted in recent years to between 8 and 9 per cent of total budget expenditure; for 1975 an expenditure of 9,600 million Marks was stated.

181

Although more information has been given in recent years on the structure of budget expenditure, no detailed data is available for about one fifth of total expenditure, which had to be listed as *'other expenditure'*. This residual item could include export subsidies, development aid and participation in CMEA investment projects. But the possibility cannot be excluded that part of this item may conceal discrepancies that could have arisen from unannounced changes in the budget system and the lines of demarcation between different items.

5.2.2   Social security[1]

The social security system of the GDR is remarkably similar to the traditional German system of social insurance in respect of entitlement to benefit on the grounds of (temporary) incapacity for work, (permanent) incapacity for gainful employment, maternity, old age, death of the breadwinner, neediness. Much else, however, has changed: this applies to the conditions and extent of benefits, the methods of finance, the target groups and the mode of administering the benefits.

The *organisation* of the system takes the form of a unified insurance scheme that still retains the traditional title of Social Insurance (*Sozialversicherung*, SV), which is divided into two major sections, the Social Insurance of Workers and Salaried Employees attached to the FDGB, and the Social Insurance of the GDR State Insurance Institution. The SV is also responsible for the care of incapacitated war victims, of former officials and, after their death, of members of their families unfit for work, as well as of other groups not engaged in economic activity (severely disabled, victims of Nazi persecution, etc.).

The *Social Insurance of Workers and Salaried Employees* operates through social insurance administrations attached to the Central Executive and to the Area, District and Urban Executives of the Trade Union Federation. But it is the responsibility of the Works Trade Union Committees to deal directly with the insured and the members of their families, and to grant the relevant benefits, with the exception of supplementary pensions. The Works Trade Union Committees are assisted in their task by Social Insurance Councils and Social Insurance Delegates.

For those members of the workers' and salaried employees' insurance scheme not working in publicly owned enterprises, doctors, students, pensioners, etc., and members of their families, the scheme is

---

1 A batch of new social security regulations came into force on 1 January 1978, too late for the German edition of this Handbook. Only the most important of these are considered in the present English version.

administered directly by the social insurance administrations attached to the District and Urban FDGB Executives. These bodies also exercise supervision over the running of the social insurance institutions in the enterprises.

The *Social Insurance of the State Insurance Institution* (*Sozialversicherung bei der Staatlichen Versicherung*) covers members of co-operatives and the self-employed. Again, as in the case of the FDGB Social Insurance Councils, there are Social Insurance Boards (*Beirate*) at central, area and district level, each insurance group having its own tier of boards. The benefits, including those accruing under the Voluntary Supplementary Pension Insurance, are granted directly by co-operatives with thirty members or more, and in all other cases by the District Insurance Boards.

There is no parallel to the *self-government* of social insurance bodies instituted in the Federal Republic. In the enterprises, the bodies in charge of social insurance are elected from among trade union members, while the Social Insurance Boards of the state scheme are not elected, though their members must themselves belong to the scheme. Disputes are handled in the first place by special commissions at enterprise level, but Arbitration Commissions have also been set up at district, area and central levels.

Other social insurance benefits (supplementary pensions, etc.) are granted predominantly by the State Insurance or the financial institutions, and for the rest by the local communes.

Compulsory insurance is almost universal. Over 85 per cent of the population are insured under the FDGB scheme and over 14 per cent under the state scheme. Exemption is confined basically to casual workers, to those earning less than 75 Marks monthly (unless they are apprentices), to clergymen, etc., as well as to foreign nationals employed for training purposes and in receipt of only a maintenance allowance.

Social insurance benefits are *financed* through social insurance contributions and out of the state budget. Actually, the accounts of the social insurance institutions form part of the state budget, but the social insurance funds of the two major institutions may be used only for their statutory purposes. This restriction is of no practical importance, since the insurance schemes are not self-financing and the institutions are increasingly dependent on grants from the state budget. The actuarial principle of fixing contributions commensurate with expenditure is not applied in the social insurance schemes of the GDR. Up to 1977 the contributions fixed at the outset were not raised or revised in spite of increasing expenditure.

The uniform contribution payable by wage and salary earners and covering all social insurance benefits with the exception of industrial

183

accidents and diseases amounts to 10 per cent of earnings liable to deduction, up to a limit of 600 Marks monthly. To this is added the contribution of the enterprise, which on 1 January 1978 was increased from 10 to 12.5 per cent (in the mining industry from 20 to 22.5 per cent) of relevant earnings. In return, the enterprises were relieved of the payment of a wage equalisation supplement to sick employees. This is now incorporated in the consolidated sickness benefit paid entirely by the Social Insurance.

Contributions under the state scheme vary for different groups. For members of producer co-operatives the rate was increased on 1 January 1978 from 20 to 22.5 per cent of income liable to deduction. Of this total, however, the co-operatives concerned contribute 12.5 per cent of relevant income, leaving their members to pay like employees at the rate of 10 per cent. As for all other groups insured under the state scheme — members of law practices, independent artisans, proprietors of small businesses, freelance professionals and other self-employed persons, as well as spouses working with them — their sickness benefit and contributions remained unaltered respectively at 50 per cent and 20 per cent of average relevant income.

Chart 38
Revenue and expenditure of GDR Social Insurance[1]

Year	Revenue	Expenditure	State subsidy	
	Mill. M			% of the expenditure
A. Social insurance with the FDGB				
1960	6,737	8,034	1,297	16.1
1965	7,015	9,547	2,532	26.5
1970	7,950	12,187	4,237	34.8
1975	10,148	17,617	7,469	42.4
B. Social insurance with the GDR State Insurance Scheme[2]				
1960	592	1,177	585	49.7
1965	764	1,648	884	53.6
1970	897	2,078	1,181	56.8
1975	1,371	2,760	1,389	50.3
C. Total				
1960	7,329	9,211	1,882	20.4
1965	7,779	11,195	3,416	30.5
1970	8,847	14,265	5,418	38.0
1975	11,519	20,377	8,858	43.5

1 Including Voluntary Supplementary Pension Insurance.
2 Up to 1968 Deutsche Versicherungsanstalt, including Vereinigte Gross-Berliner Versicherungsanstalt.

Sources: GDR Statistical Yearbooks; Statistische Praxis 5/1961, p.129; Neue Deutsche Bauernzeitung 3/1977, p.12.

In addition to the social insurance contributions proper, the enterprises have to pay an *accident premium* at a rate depending on the wage bill and the accident risks of each enterprise. Generally it amounts to 0.3 per cent of the earnings on which contributions are paid.

Finally, the social insurance funds are fed to an increasing degree by contributions to the *Voluntary Supplementary Pension Insurance*, for which workers and employees earning more than 600 Marks monthly are eligible. It appears that by the end of 1976 70 per cent of those eligible were covered by this scheme, towards which both the insured and the enterprise pay 10 per cent each of the amount by which the monthly earnings exceed 600 Marks. Freelance professional workers, the self-employed and members of co-operatives are liable to pay 20 per cent of the amount by which their annual income exceeds 7,200 Marks. Up to the end of 1976, there was a universal upper limit, with earnings in excess of 1,200 Marks monthly or 14,400 Marks annually not qualifying for the scheme. In 1977, wage and salary earners and members of co-operatives were freed from this restriction. After contributing to the supplementary scheme for 25 years, employees and members of co-operatives are exempted from the payment of further contributions, while the enterprise continues to pay its contribution of 10 per cent. For the group of self-employed, etc., who pay the 20 per cent contribution under the supplementary pension scheme, the payment is reduced to 10 per cent after 25 years.

By 1975, the contributions paid under the supplementary pension scheme had risen to about 10 per cent of the total yield of social insurance contributions, and this share is likely to continue to rise. Since the supplementary pension scheme is certain to show a surplus of revenue over expenditure for many years to come — in 1975 a surplus of 1,000 million Marks was recorded — it will reduce the deficit of the social insurance institutions as a whole and thus ease the strain on the state budget.

Foremost among the *social security benefits* are the payments and benefits in kind granted by the social insurance institutions, including the Voluntary Supplementary Pension Insurance. Benefits in kind are granted for the preservation and restoration of health and fitness for work, and for maternity. Monetary benefits are payable in the main in cases of temporarily reduced or absent fitness for work or capacity for gainful occupation resulting from illness (including illness of children in need of parental care), quarantine, accidents or maternity, and in cases of insured persons reaching pensionable age.

Other social benefits, accruing outside the social insurance schemes, comprise the following (apart from the wage equalisation supplement that used to be paid to sick employees by the enterprises before the introduction of the consolidated sickness benefit at the beginning of

185

1978):

    special emoluments, supplementary and honorary pensions for groups singled out for special treatment

    maternity grants, children's allowances, allowances for spouses, support for large families, etc.

    social welfare benefits

    study and training grants

The benefits are granted on presentation of the *Work and Social Insurance Registration Document* (*Ausweis für Arbeit und Sozialversicherung*), which certifies the insured status of the bearer and records data concerning vocational training, beginning and end of periods of employment, all earnings on which contributions are due as well as membership of the Voluntary Supplementary Pension Insurance. Thus the document serves as a basis for calculating the future pension, including the supplementary pension. Pensioners, persons receiving social welfare assistance and members of families of insured persons[1] have to produce an Insurance Registration Document (*Versicherungsausweis*) when claiming benefits. The insured's medical history is also recorded on those documents, which facilitates diagnosis in case of illness, though unavoidably at the expense of the confidential doctor-patient relationship.

5.2.2.1 Sickness, maternity, accidents   The main services and benefits in kind provided free of charge for the insured and their families in the event of sickness, accident or maternity comprise *medical* and *dental treatment* (no fee payable for medical certificates), *medicines* and *medical aids* (such as spectacles, artificial limbs, massage, remedial baths, etc.), confinement in hospital, *in-patient treatment in hospitals* without time limit.

Instead of hospital treatment, patients receive *medical and nursing care at home*, when necessary. To promote preservation, improvement and restoration of health and fitness, the social insurance provides stays at *health resorts* for preventive and remedial treatment and for convalescence.

Compensation for loss of income through sickness, accident or maternity is assured in principle, though at different levels, by short-term monetary allowances from the social insurance.

---

1 For children born after 28 February 1975 a Social Insurance and Vaccination Registration Document is issued.

In cases of unfitness for work owing to sickness, accident at work or an industrial disease, *sickness benefit* is paid for a period of up to 78 weeks (18 months) if in the doctors' view the patient is likely to be restored to fitness by that time.

Until 1977, the social insurance institutions paid sickness benefit at the rate of 50 per cent of average earnings on which insurance contributions had been paid, but not more than 300 Marks monthly. For up to six weeks in any calendar year, this benefit was topped up to 90 per cent of normal earnings by the enterprise in the form of wage equalisation payments. Under the new regulation which came into force on 1 January 1978, the full rate of 90 per cent is to be paid by the social insurance, while the enterprises are relieved of the obligation to pay wage equalisation.[1]

From the seventh week on, the rate of sickness benefit depends on need. Wage and salary earners with monthly incomes under 600 Marks as well as subscribers to the voluntary supplementary pension scheme (who, of course, earn more than 600 Marks) — and this applies also to the self-employed and members of co-operatives — get between 70 and 90 per cent of average net income according to the number of dependent relatives. Those earning more than 600 Marks but not insured under the supplementary pension scheme get 50 per cent of average net income plus additional allowances if they have two or more children, but generally at a lower rate than the rest.

Sickness benefit is paid indefinitely at the rate of 100 per cent of average net earnings in cases of temporary unfitness for work owing to industrial accidents or disease and at the rate of 90 per cent in cases of quarantine.

Trade union members who after six weeks of illness are no longer paid at the full rate of 100 or 90 per cent of normal net earnings receive from the FDGB additional sickness benefit at the rate of a weekly union subscription per day for a period with an upper limit ranging from six to nine weeks. In addition, there are some privileged groups (e.g. victims of Nazi persecution, fighters against fascism, members of the intelligentsia with individual contracts, members of the armed forces and the police) who are entitled to receive high rates of compensation, in some cases full pay, for prolonged periods or even indefinitely.

For the duration of *in-patient treatment* at a hospital or a course of treatment at a health resort, the insured received up to the end of 1977 a *household allowance* which generally amounted to 80 per cent of the (higher-rate) sickness benefit. As from 1 January 1978, the new regu-

---

1 See the Draft Code of Labour Legislation for the GDR, published in the supplement to Tribüne, East Berlin, no.15/1977, p.43.

lations for the payment of sickness benefit apply equally for the duration of hospitalisation or treatment at a health resort. Accordingly, the household allowance has been abolished.

Maternity benefits are more generous than in the Federal Republic. Expectant mothers get six weeks prenatal leave, followed by 20 weeks maternity leave, which in cases of medical complications or when more than one child is born is extended to 22 weeks. During that entire period the insured receives first a pregnancy allowance, then a maternity allowance equal to her average net earnings before leaving work. Under the state insurance scheme, these allowances, except for members of co-operatives, are subject to an upper limit of 14,400 Marks annually or 1,200 Marks monthly.

Further types of benefit have been added to this 'traditional' system. Mothers, whether insured in their own right or as family members, receive *maternity grants* of 1,000 Marks for each child, paid in instalments, provided they attend twice at a prenatal clinic, and after that four times at a babies' clinic.[1]

A remarkable additional benefit was introduced in May 1976: after the end of their maternity leave, insured working mothers may apply to be released from work for a full year after the birth of her second and any subsequent child, in order to personally look after the baby. During that period, mothers receive a *monthly maternity allowance* at a rate equal to the sickness benefit due after six weeks of unfitness for work, but, in the case of full-time workers, not less than 300 Marks monthly for a second child or 350 Marks for a third or subsequent child.

Another benefit enjoyed in the main by mothers is for *single parents*, who are *released from work* for two days to *look after sick children*. For those two days they receive sickness benefit, that is 90 per cent of their average net income. If the child's sickness necessitates a longer absence from work, single parents are entitled to sickness benefit at the rate which they, if sick themselves, would draw from the seventh week, payable for periods totalling between four and thirteen weeks depending on the number of children. The same arrangement applies to working spouses who must stay away from work to look after a sick child.

Under a measure introduced in 1972 the same benefit is paid to single working mothers compelled to interrupt work because there is no crèche where they can leave their child. If working full-time these mothers get a minimum of 250 Marks monthly for a first child, 300 Marks for two children, 350 Marks if they have three or more children.

On the death of the insured, a *burial grant* of between 160 and 400

---

1 Until 1 July 1972 the maternity grant was 500 Marks for a first child, rising in steps of 100 Marks to 800 Marks for the fourth child. Only the fifth and each subsequent child qualified for a grant of 1,000 Marks.

Marks, depending on average earnings, is paid. If death results from an accident at work or an industrial disease, the top rate is applicable. Miners get higher benefits.

5.2.2.2 Old age, disablement, death of breadwinner Since the pensions reform of 1968, the basis on which pensions are calculated has been similar to the practice prevailing in the Federal Republic. The main difference is the absence in the GDR of periodical 'dynamic adjustments' to the general trend of incomes.

Entitlement to the social insurance *old-age pension* arises after at least 15 years of activity subject to compulsory insurance, and on reaching retirement age (65 years for men, 60 years for women). For mothers of two or more children, as well as women who have brought up more than two children, the statutory minimum of 15 years is reduced by one year for each child after the second, provided they have been in insurable employment for at least five years. A further concession introduced on 1 July 1973 grants old-age or disablement pensions to mothers of five or more children even without any period of insurable employment in her own right. Since 1 December 1976, this pension has amounted to 230 Marks monthly.

Similar concessions, intended to compensate for the burdens of motherhood and bringing up children, are extended to women in the computation of the total *period of pensionable service*. For each child born before the pension is due, women are credited with an additional year. After 20 years of insurable activity, another additional year is credited to working women, and thereafter a further year for each successive five-year period of insurable activity (up to a maximum of five).

Additional periods of pensionable service are credited to men and women for other reasons. Up to one year of unemployment prior to 1946 is credited, and so are seven tenths of any period during which an insured person incapacitated to the extent of at least two thirds was in receipt of an invalidity or disablement pension. However, the reckonable period of insurance cannot exceed 50 years.

The amount of the monthly old-age pension is composed of a fixed sum of 110 Marks, plus the sum of 1 per cent of average net earnings for each year of pensionable service, including the credited periods.

Average net earnings for the purpose of this calculation are the average of monthly net earnings over the twenty calendar years preceding the termination of the last pensionable activity, with a lower limit of 150 Marks and an upper limit, consequential upon the earnings limit applied in the assessment of insurance contributions, of 600 Marks.

The methods of calculating pensions in the two German states are fairly similar, but the levels of pensions are much lower in the GDR. The social insurance old-age pension payable in the GDR in 1977 to a single person without dependent relatives and not insured under the voluntary supplementary scheme could not exceed 410 Marks monthly, even if he was credited with the statutory maximum of 50 pensionable years. This is due to the low upper limit in the assessment of contributions under the compulsory scheme. In the Federal Republic, where contributions and the upper earnings limit for the assessment of contributions are higher, a similarly placed pensioner may receive up to about 2,500 DM monthly.

In the GDR, but not in the Federal Republic, a lower limit has also been laid down. *Minimum pensions* for old-age pensioners range from 230 to 300 Marks monthly, according to the number of working years.

As in the Federal Republic, increased pensions are paid to insured persons with dependent relatives. The supplement payable for a spouse who is either invalid or of pensionable age and not insured in her or his own right is 100 Marks monthly,[1] while 45 Marks is paid for each dependent child up to the age of 18 or, if at that age engaged in a training scheme, until the completion of that scheme.

Invalidity pensions are calculated on the same basis as old-age pensions. Again, additional periods are credited to the insured, apart from the years of actual pensionable service, up to a combined maximum covering the entire period from the age of 16 to the incidence of the invalidity, and thereafter 70 per cent of the period until the attainment of retirement age. Minimum pensions are paid in the same way as for old-age pensions, also for disablement through accidents.

Since September 1972 persons receiving invalidity pensions have been allowed to take up employment with earnings up to the current monthly gross minimum wage (400 Marks since 1 October 1976), without any reduction in their pension.

An *accident pension* can be claimed by insured persons who as a result of an accident at work have suffered physical disablement to the extent of at least 20 per cent. In the event of 100 per cent disablement, the pension equals two thirds of the last monthly wage or salary on which a social insurance contribution was paid. In view of the upper earnings limit of 600 Marks for the assessment of contributions, the accident pension cannot exceed 400 Marks. In cases of partial disablement, the maximum pension is reduced pro rata. In the Federal Republic the maximum accident pension payable varies from 2,000 DM to 2,666 DM, the latter figure applying to the majority of occupational groups.

---

1 This also applies to dependent wives with one child under three, or two children under eight years of age.

Chart 39
Average monthly social insurance pensions
in the GDR (M) and FRG (DM)

Type of pension	1960	1965	1970	1975
		GDR[1]		
Old age pensions[3] [4]	146	163	188	248
Invalidity pensions[4]	142	154	207	264
Widows' pensions	120	131	157	210
Orphans' pensions	56	66	75	108
		FRG[2]		
Old age pensions[3] [4]	218	303	433	720
Invalidity pensions[4]	165	220	297	422
Widows' pensions	138	197	295	503
Orphans' pensions	60	82	119	200

1 Social Insurance of Wage and Salary Earners (FDGB) and GDR State Insurance, excluding voluntary supplementary pensions, up to 1970 excluding also old age pensions of Reich Railway and Post Office employees; state at year end.
2 Wage and Salary Earners' Pension Insurance and Mineworkers' Pension Insurance; in 1960, 1965 and 1970 after the pension adjustment of the current year; in 1975, wage and salary earners' insurance after, mineworkers' insurance before pension adjustment.
3 GDR: old age and old age invalidity pensions (including mineworkers); FRG: old age and mineworkers' retirement benefits (Ruhegelder).
4 GDR: invalidity pensions; FRG: incapacity pensions.

Sources: GDR: GDR Statistical Yearbooks; FRG: DIW calculations based on Federal Government reports on pension adjustments.

If the disablement is at least two thirds, the minimum accident pension is 300 Marks monthly, including a supplementary benefit of 80 Marks. For pensioners whose disablement ranges from 50 per cent to two thirds, a supplementary benefit of 20 Marks is payable.

As in the Federal Republic, there are separate arrangements for *miners*. In determining their old-age and invalidity pensions, the variable component is twice as high as for other workers, i.e. 2 per cent (instead of 1 per cent) of average monthly net earnings for each reckonable year. In addition a so-called full-rate invalidity pension is payable to miners who have reached the age of 50, have been in the miners' insurance scheme for at least 25 years and during that time worked at least 15 years underground. Another special pension is due to miners with at least five years in the miners' insurance scheme, and who have become unfit for further employment in the mines.

The GDR also pays *war disablement pensions*. Their level was increased on 1 December 1976 from 240 to 300 Marks monthly plus family supplements for dependent relatives. If the pensioner receives earnings from employment, the disablement pension is reduced, but a minimum of 30 per cent of the full rate (plus family supplements) will be paid in any case. After the pensioner has reached retirement age, the full pension is paid irrespective of additional earnings.

In the Federal Republic a basic war disablement pension is payable when earning capacity is impaired by 25 per cent or more.

Widows' and orphans' pensions (applying also to widowers) are paid if the deceased breadwinner would have been entitled to a pension in his or her own right, or if death occurred as the result of an accident at work or an industrial disease. At first, widows' (widowers') pensions were paid only when the surviving spouse had reached retirement age or if he or she was an invalid or in charge of one child under three or two children under eight years of age. These conditions were amended in July 1973, and since then surviving spouses below retirement age (currently about 30,000) receive a transitional bereavement benefit at the rate of the minimum pension for the duration of two years if the deceased was the main breadwinner.

A widow's pension is based on the entitlement of the deceased. The rate is 60 per cent of the pension due to the deceased, without supplements, but not less than 230 Marks monthly. Orphans who have lost one parent are entitled to 30 per cent of the deceased's notional pension, with a minimum of 100 Marks; those who have lost both parents get 40 per cent of the notional pension, with a minimum of 150 Marks monthly. However, the combined widow's and orphan's pensions must not exceed the full notional pension of the insured.

Divorced spouses of deceased insured persons, who were entitled to maintenance receive a *maintenance pension* at the rate of the alimony fixed by a court of law, up to a maximum of 230 Marks monthly, provided they meet the entitlement conditions for widows' pensions and draw no pension of their own.

Chart 40
Annual expenditure on old age, invalidity, accident, and
widows' and orphans' benefits and pensions
(per person of pensionable age[1])

Year	GDR (M)	FRG (DM)
1960	1740	3192
1965	2109	4424
1970	2625	6244
1971	2818	6692
1972	3093	7467
1973	3516	8276
1974	3616	9360
1975	3670	10472

1 Men over 65, women over 60.

Sources: As table 40.

192

Under a provision introduced on 1 October 1974, members of the *Combat Groups of the Working Class* in the factories — a voluntary organisation of the Home Guard type — of at least 25 years' standing have their old-age, invalidity and accident pensions (if the accident resulted in a disablement of at least two thirds) topped up by 100 Marks monthly. Their widows are entitled to an extra 60 Marks and orphaned children to 30 Marks or, if both parents are dead, to 40 Marks monthly.

Extra pensions are also paid under the auspices of the so-called *Special and Incremental Support Institutions (Sonder- und Zusatzversorgungseinrichtungen)*. Thus, members of the 'armed organs' of the state, i.e. police and armed forces, as well as employees of the customs administration, the Reich Railways and the Post Office receive pensions at a higher rate than is generally paid under the social insurance schemes, although the contributions of employees and employer are the same as for the rest of the working population. But no detailed information is available about these arrangements anymore than about similar arrangements introduced in the late 1960s for employees of other administrations, government departments and social organisations.

What is known is that railway and post office employees are entitled to old-age or invalidity pensions after ten years of continuous employment. Their pensions are determined as percentages of average earnings over the last five years of service. Post office employees reach their maximum entitlement of 65 per cent after 40 years, railway employees theirs of 70 per cent after 45 years of pensionable service. In both cases the maximum pension is 800 Marks monthly.

Another group entitled to higher old-age, invalidity and widows' and orphans' pensions is the 'intelligentsia'. Such *intelligentsia pensions* are paid to the 'technical intelligentsia', i.e. leading cadres in the factories, and to senior employees in scientific, artistic, educational and medical institutions at the rate of 60 to 80 per cent of their last salary, with no upper limit for the technical intelligentsia, but a maximum of 800 Marks monthly for the rest. In addition, the recipients of these pensions get the regular social insurance pension as well, minus the fixed component of 110 Marks. However, the two pensions combined must not exceed 90 per cent of the last salary.

Similar arrangements were introduced on 1 September 1976 for teachers and educationalists. Their supplementary pension is determined as 60 per cent of the average monthly gross earnings of the most favourable ten-year period of unbroken pensionable service, but as before, the aggregate pension must not exceed 90 per cent of average net earnings.

The supplementary pensions of the technical intelligentsia are financed by the enterprises, those of the rest of the intelligentsia and of the teachers by the state. Widows generally receive 50 per cent of the supplementary pensions.

Another type of supplementary pensions, designated as *Honour Pensions* (*Ehrenpensionen*) are paid by the state at the rate of 600 Marks for victims of fascism and 800 Marks for fighters against fascism in the event of invalidity or on attainment of retirement age which, for these categories, is reduced by five years. These pensions are paid in addition to a social insurance pension of 350 Marks monthly. Naturally, the group entitled to such pensions is rapidly diminishing as time goes on. There were 26,000 recipients (including widows) at the beginning of 1976. Other 'honour pensions' of between 600 and 1,500 Marks monthly are paid to citizens of exceptional merit.

Attendance allowance is paid to social insurance pensioners and other recipients of social benefits and their widows or orphans at a rate of between 20 and 80 Marks monthly, depending on the degree of care needed. Blind persons and the severely visually handicapped receive a *blind person's allowance* of between 30 and 240 Marks, and those most severely disabled (loss of more than one limb) get a *special attendance allowance* ranging from 120 to 180 Marks monthly, depending on the degree of disablement.

Generally it can be said that the conditions of entitlement to a pension are more stringent in the GDR than in the Federal Republic. No severance pensions are paid to those incapacitated from continuing to work in their trade or profession; widows fit for work are not eligible for a long-term pension. Indemnification and maintenance of war victims are on a minor scale. No one may draw more than one pension in full.

To lessen the impact of the sudden drop in income on reaching retirement age, the *Voluntary Supplementary Pension Insurance Branch of the Social Insurance* was set up in 1968, which offers higher sickness benefit and supplementary pensions in return for voluntary extra contributions (see p.185 above). Supplementary pensions are paid together with the general social insurance pensions.

The level of the *supplementary old-age pensions* is based on the amount by which average monthly earnings exceeded 600 Marks, and on the reckonable period, i.e. the years during which voluntary contributions were paid, plus additional years credited to those reaching retirement age within a comparatively short period after the inception of the scheme. The pension is then worked out as 2.5 per cent of the average monthly excess earnings for each reckonable year. (By way of example: if voluntary contributions have been paid for 20 years on average monthly earnings of 1,300 Marks, the monthly supplementary pension comes out as 20 x 0.025 x 700 Marks = 350 Marks).

The *supplementary invalidity pension* is calculated on the same basis of 2.5 per cent of average monthly excess earnings.

5.2.2.3 Other contingencies   Up to the end of 1977, *unemployment benefit* was paid in the GDR by the Social Insurance. It was officially described as 'assistance granted during a period of temporary unemployment to persons who lost their job through no fault of their own'. The rates of benefit, however, were so low that from 1954 they were supplemented out of social welfare funds to bring the total up to the level of social welfare benefit. But on 1 January 1978 the Decrees which provided the legal basis for unemployment insurance were superseded by the new Code of Labour Law. Under the new Code, enterprises which reduce their labour force in the course of rationalisation, restructuring, etc. are obliged to continue to pay their redundant personnel. The employment relationship is maintained by means of Amending Contracts, Transitional Contracts and similar devices. Retraining schemes are carried out at the expense of the enterprises, and if a new job involves a drop in earnings, the difference is made up for the duration of one year in the form of a *bridging supplement*.

Under the new dispensation, only employees who have been dismissed without notice and cannot find alternative employment receive assistance, which is paid out of social welfare rather than insurance funds.

Social welfare benefits are generally payable to persons who are incapable of earning enough to live on and have neither sufficient financial assets or income from other sources nor relatives both legally obliged and able to maintain them at an adequate level. In this context net income is considered adequate if it is not less than the social welfare rate. On 1 December 1976, the rate of social welfare benefit was raised for single persons from 175 to 200 Marks, for married couples from 250 to 300 Marks monthly, plus (unchanged) 45 Marks for each child under age and each older child still attending polytechnic secondary school, and a rent allowance ranging from 30 to 35 Marks monthly according to size of family.

Large families (four or more children) and single parents with three or more children now get rent allowances, provided the monthly gross income does not exceed 1,500 Marks (plus 100 Marks for the fifth and each subsequent child), or 1,000 Marks in the case of single-parent families. Special allowances are also granted for children's clothing.

Children's allowances financed by the state[1] are paid free of tax to GDR citizens for all children up to the completion of secondary education and for those who attend a vocational college without receiving a study grant up to the age of 18. The allowances are paid at the rate of 20 Marks monthly for the first and second child, 50 Marks for the third, 60 Marks for the fourth, and 70 Marks for the fifth and each subsequent child.

Another benefit, introduced in 1958 in compensation for the increase in food prices following the abolition of rationing, is the *married person's supplement*, payable on application at the rate of 5 Marks monthly to workers, salaried employees and members of co-operatives with monthly gross earnings of under 800 Marks, and at the rate of 9 Marks to students and recipients of social security benefits of under 600 Marks, provided their spouses have no income of their own. These supplements, however, are falling into disuse, as they are increasingly incorporated in the wage rates laid down by collective agreements.

The state also spends substantial sums on *study grants* and other training allowances directly out of the state budget, without involving the social security institutions.

About 90 per cent of the students attending courses at universities, other institutions of higher education and technical colleges in the GDR receive grants at rates depending on the social position of the student and his or her spouse or parents, on his progress in his studies and on his political activity. Beginning with the second year of study, the basic grants, ranging from 80 to 190 Marks monthly, may be supplemented by merit grants of between 40 and 80 Marks. Students of exceptional merit, assessed equally on scholarly and political criteria, are eligible for special grants. Their number was increased in 1977, but is still limited.

Special training grants ranging from 500 to 900 Marks monthly are paid to male students seconded by the National People's Army and to women students seconded by their enterprises. Finally, GDR students studying abroad receive foreign currency grants at rates laid down in international treaties.

As regards the relative numbers of students benefiting from grants, the arrangements in the GDR are clearly superior to those of the Federal Republic, where regulations for the support of undergraduate and post-graduate students under several Acts of educational and social welfare legislation provided in 1975 grants for about 60 per cent of all

---

1 Under the 'Decree on the Granting of State-financed Children's Allowances and Special Support for Large Families as well as Single Parent Families with Three Children' of 4 December 1975 sundry child benefits were consolidated into the 'state-financed children's allowances'.

students. On the other hand, GDR students must meet certain political conditions if they are to qualify for any except the very low basic grants.

5.2.2.4 Health services Outpatient *medical care* has greatly improved. At the end of 1975 15,300 doctors were available (in whole time equivalents), about twice the number recorded in 1965, including 9,646 doctors working in polyclinics, 2,791 in separate outpatient stations, 172 in hospital outpatient departments, 856 in first-aid posts, as well as 1,800 general practitioners employed by the state and 1,308 independent general practitioners. Together with those employed in hospitals, enterprises, etc. the total number of doctors in the GDR in 1975 was 31,300, one doctor per 540 inhabitants.[1] (Exactly the same ratio was recorded in the Federal Republic in 1974). The regional distribution of medical facilities, however, is very uneven. In the agrarian areas, such as Neubrandenburg, the number of doctors is proportionately much lower. The availability of specialists is similarly uneven. Thus, the 550,000 inhabitants of the Suhl area could call on only two urologists practising outside hospitals, and one attached to a hospital, and on two radiologists, both working outside hospitals. The Neubrandenburg area, with its 626,000 inhabitants, was also served by only two radiologists, whereas in the same year 1975, the 1.1 million people of East Berlin were looked after by 29 urologists and 45 radiologists.

It is such disproportions, in addition to shortages of medical auxiliaries and nursing staff, frequent instances of poor organisation and inadequate performance of medical equipment, which continue to impair the efficiency of the health services in the GDR. As a result of such shortcomings, the undoubted advantages of the comprehensive medical care offered at the numerous polyclinics and outpatient departments, where specialists in different branches of medicine can co-operate in the treatment of a patient, cannot become fully effective. Nor has the GDR come nearer than other countries to solving the problem of long waiting lists and waiting times.

Nonetheless, a great deal has been achieved in recent years. The *prevention of disease* has been improved through measures of preventive health care and a well organised system of industrial safety.[2] Measures of after-care and rehabilitation and the far-reaching endeavours in the field of social hygiene are commendable.

Thus, the preventive examinations carried out as part of prenatal and

---

1   Leaving aside the doctors engaged in in-patient treatment, there was one doctor per 1,018 inhabitants in the GDR in 1975.
2   The rate of industrial accidents in the GDR in recent years has been about half that of the Federal Republic.

postnatal care, and which mothers must regularly attend before and after their confinement, in order to qualify for social insurance benefits (see p.188 above), have clearly proved their worth: in 1974 infant mortality (deaths of babies during first year of life per 1,000 live births) was 15.9 in the GDR, as compared with 21.1 in the Federal Republic. The maternity death rate was about the same in both states.

In general, mortality trends in the GDR have been the same as in other industrial countries: a marked decline of deaths from certain diseases, notably tuberculosis, contrasting with an equally marked increase in deaths from tumors, diabetes and above all from cardiovascular disorders, which alone accounted for 60 per cent of all deaths in the GDR in 1974. It appears that in this respect the GDR has probably the worst record of any industrial country.

5.3 Private households

Income distribution in all countries is to some extent influenced by the state, more so in a planned than in a market economy. To the state planning authorities, incomes represent the 'purchasing fund', which they have to match with a 'commodity fund' of domestically produced and imported goods. The firm guidance by the state starts in the GDR with the formation of primary incomes: thus it is the central authorities which lay down the figure for the wages fund, whereas in the Federal Republic the development of wage levels depends largely on agreements concluded between representatives of workers and employers. As regards the redistribution of incomes, the state plays a dominant part in both parts of Germany. Social insurance contributions and taxes are levied on incomes, while conversely various benefits are dispensed to those not yet, or no more, or only partially engaged in work (e.g. students, the sick and the old). It is the task of an incomes policy to square the formation and distribution of incomes with the aims of social policy and economic growth.

5.3.1 Incomes

5.3.1.1 Wages policy and formation of incomes Like their Western counterparts, the GDR trade unions (FDGB) play a part in determining wages; yet, their function is fundamentally different from that of, for example, the West German trade unions. In the Federal Republic, trade unions may resort to the strike weapon in an attempt to enforce wage demands, but that is impossible in the GDR, where, in the official view, class conflicts and struggles for the distribution of incomes were done away with when the private ownership of the means of production was

198

abolished. The framework for the development of incomes is determined in accordance with the priorities set by the economic plans for the economy as a whole. The guidelines for wages and incomes policy are formulated by the Council of Ministers in co-operation with the FDGB Central Executive.

The crucial issues affecting the system of wage agreements are similarly settled by the Council of Ministers by agreement with the FDGB. Wage rates in publicly owned enterprises are fixed by outline collective agreements between the authorities in charge of an economic sector and the trade unions concerned. Wage rates in private enterprises are agreed in the same way between the trade union and the Chamber of Industry and Trade. All wage agreements are scrutinised and registered by the State Secretariat for Labour and Wages.

The *system of wages* in the GDR is designed to

a)   apply in practice the principle of payment by results;
b)   assure the right balance between various economic sectors and various sections of the population in accordance with the structural policy concepts of the state;
c)   encourage a readiness to accept responsibility and the acquisition of higher skills and qualifications.

Many discussions conducted in the GDR have revealed that the wages system does not in practice live up to these aspirations.

In principle the GDR wages system is determined by the contractually agreed pay scales; in actual fact it is characterised by the widespread use of the so-called extra-performance wage (*Mehrleistungslohn*). Currently only about half of the wage packets of most workers in the productive sectors is made up of payments regulated by the wage scales of the collective agreements.[1] Thus the efficacy of the agreements as an instrument of economic control is reduced to insignificance. This deficiency is compounded by the loss of function of the nominally performance-related wage component in the form of extra-performance wages and bonuses. These are paid if the official production norms are met, with only minor upward and downward adjustments for over or under-fulfilment.

Three major drawbacks of the extra-performance wage have become manifest:

1   It runs counter to the principle of payment by results whenever increases in labour productivity occur as a consequence of technological and organisational improvements. As technology

1   Wages are also augmented by special bonuses to compensate for unusual working conditions.

advances, managements find themselves continually in the invidious position of having to raise production norms, and often they prefer to leave well alone.

2   For a long time effective wage increases have been carried out by raising the extra-performance wage, while wage rates governed by the collective agreements have remained sub-substantially unchanged. This system discriminates against those sections of the labour force whose remuneration is more dependent on the fixed rates and less on the extra-performance component. Since this applies largely to more highly qualified personnel — salaried employees, foremen, technicians — the tendency towards increasing the relative weight of the extra-performance component acts as a dis-incentive against training for higher qualifications.

3   In a number of economic sectors (distributive trade, services) earnings are based predominantly on the fixed rates. This has led to an unwelcome exodus from those sectors into sectors with a high extra-performance component. In an endeavour to counteract this tendency, earnings in the affected sectors have been increased.

The shortcomings of the wages system were criticised at the Eighth FDGB Congress at the end of June 1972. In the meantime decisions on a modification of the wages system have been adopted. In the course of the 1976-1980 Five-Year Plan new basic wages are to be introduced for 1.5 million production workers. By the end of 1976 this was accomplished for 250,000 workers. The new basic wages are made up of the fixed-rates component plus substantial parts of what used to be the extra-performance component, adding up to between 70 and 90 per cent of total earnings.

Wage rates in the GDR are underpinned by a statutory minimum wage, currently, since 1 October 1976, of 400 Marks monthly.

Apart from the wages paid out of the 'wages fund', workers in the productive sectors receive additional *bonuses* financed through the enterprise bonus fund (see pp 61 f. above). Originally this fund, amounting to about 4 per cent of the wage bill, was used to reward production efforts of special merit. In 1965-66 this practice was superseded by the introduction of the *year-end bonus*, to which in principle every member of the labour force is entitled after one year's employment with the enterprise. The amount of the bonus depends on the enterprise's success in fulfilling the production and profits plans and meeting other index figures, but it must not be less than one third of monthly earnings nor more than 900 Marks. On average it ranges between 750 and 800 Marks.[1]

Christmas bonuses are only of minor importance in the GDR. They are paid only to workers earning less than 500 Marks monthly at the rate of 35 Marks for married persons, 25 Marks for single persons and 10 Marks for apprentices.

The incomes of *members of co-operatives* are in essence residual quantities, computed as shares in the collectively earned profits. But here, too, the state exercises considerable influence, since the economic results of a co-operative are largely determined by official price policy, by grants and credits, subsidies and taxation.

Members of agricultural producer co-operatives receive the bulk of their incomes through the number of work units to their credit at the end of the year. The work units express both the quantity of labour and qualitative demands (see pp 133 f. above). The value of the work unit is computed at the end of the year when the annual accounts have been completed. Where appropriate, the final results are brought into line with official policy, as the case may be, by special subsidies or by taxation. Members of artisan producer co-operatives receive regular payments equivalent to wages, supplemented by participation in profits.

The *self-employed* and independent professional people constitute the one group of the economically active population whose incomes are largely outside the influence of state planning measures.

At the other end of the scale all public *transfers of income* are subject to detailed planning.

5.3.1.2 Personal incomes   The gross income of all socio-economic groups rose from 68,000 million Marks in 1960 to 114,000 million Marks in 1975 (cf. Appendix, table 42). That corresponds to an average annual growth rate of 3.6 per cent; but the growth was uneven, gradually accelerating over the years. The average annual increase over the three five-year periods was

1961 to 1965	2.5 per cent
1966 to 1970	3.9 per cent
1971 to 1975	4.2 per cent

The lower growth rates in the early sixties reflect the growth crisis of that period; the higher rates of the last five years show the effects of

---

1 The bonus system was not spared by critics of counter-productive trends in the field of wages. Thus the Eighth FDGB Congress called for the elimination of 'differentials of unwarranted magnitude in the development of bonus payments in various enterprises and industries'.

Chart 41
Personal distribution of gross incomes in the GDR

	1965	1975	1965	1975
	Bn. M		%	
Employees[1]	53.0	84.8	69	74
Members of co-operatives and self-employed	17.9	19.1	23	17
Pensioners[2]	5.8	10.2	8	9
Total	76.7	114.1	100	100

1 Including apprentices and working pensioners.
2 Excluding recipients of orphans' pensions, including recipients of social welfare benefits.

Source: table 42.

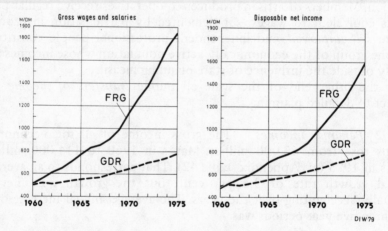

Figure 30 Development of monthly employee income
in the GDR and the Federal Republic

the higher priority accorded to consumption after the Eighth SED Congress.

The increase in incomes was not uniform for the various groups.[1] The gross incomes of *wage and salary earners* rose over the fifteen-year period at a rate of 4.0 per cent a year, with variations similar to those of the general trend. Their share in the total income of the population rose from 69 per cent in 1965 to 74 per cent in 1975. In those years both the average income of wage and salary earners and their numbers increased.

Incomes of *members of co-operatives* and the *self-employed* declined from 23 per cent of the total in 1965 to 17 per cent in 1975. This was due to the numerical decline of this group, while average personal incomes increased in most sectors.

Incomes of *pensioners* rose more rapidly during the ten-year period 1965 to 1975 than those of any other group, at an average annual rate of 5.8 per cent. In the GDR pensions were not tied automatically to the general trend of incomes, but were raised successively in 1968, 1971, 1972 and 1976. Yet, as can be seen from chart 41, pensions are so low in relation to other incomes that the above-average rise over the decade increased their share in the total income of the population by only one percentage point, from 8 to 9 per cent.

The ranking of the various groups of the population in respect of average net incomes had not changed since 1960. The self-employed and members of co-operatives remained at the top of the list, followed at some distance by the wage and salary earners, with the pensioners bringing up the rear.

In a *comparison with the Federal Republic*, where the ranking of the socio-economic groups is similar, it is striking that the gap in monetary incomes (disregarding differences in purchasing power) appears to be constantly widening. In 1960 the income of a GDR pensioner corresponded to 50 per cent of a West German one; by 1975 that proportion had shrunk to 26 per cent. The self-employed and members of co-operatives in the GDR — though for this category a comparison with the Federal Republic is of limited relevance — had incomes 22 per cent below those of the self-employed in West Germany in 1960, but by 1975 the gap had widened to 70 per cent. Average net incomes of wage and salary earners (as shown in tables 43 and 44) were much the same in the two states in 1960; yet, only five years later a gap of well over 20 per cent had appeared, which increased to more than 50 per cent by 1975. But for the higher deductions from earnings in the Federal

---

1 This analysis deals with personal incomes of all socio-economic groups. As far as wage and salary earners are concerned, their incomes are made up of earnings, social security benefits (e.g. sickness benefit), income from capital assets, etc.

Chart 42
Average monthly net incomes[1] per recipient in the GDR and FRG

	1960	1965	1970	1975
	GDR in M			
Employees[2]	494	556	653	780
Members of co-operatives and self-employed	901	940	1086	1489
Pensioners	163	186	219	283
	FRG in DM			
Employees[2]	476	710	974	1514
Self-employed	1154	1661	1968	4861
Pensioners	324	474	687	1109

1 Incomes from economic activity, social insurance and welfare benefits, investment income, other incomes.
2 Including apprentices and working pensioners. FRG: including unemployed.

Source: DIW calculations

Chart 43
Average monthly gross incomes[1] of working employees in the GDR and FRG in selected sectors of the economy 1975

	GDR	FRG	GDR	FRG
	M	DM	%	%
All employees	775	1866	100	100
of whom in				
Industry	785	1997	101	107
Construction	860	1930	111	103
Agriculture and forestry	633	1153	82	62
Transport	874	1947	113	104
Trade	663	1467	86	79

1 Gross wages and salaries.

Source: DIW calculations and estimates.

Republic by way of taxation and social insurance contributions, the GDR income lag would be even larger (cf. table 45).

Among wage and salary earners, there were structurally similar *sectoral income differentials* in the two parts of Germany, but they varied in extent.

Earnings in agriculture and the distributive trade are substantially below those in the productive sectors. Within industry the general pattern of income distribution is again similar in both states, with the metallurgical and power industries leading, and the food-processing, light and textile industries on the bottom rung.

Earnings of the *peasants* in the GDR vary according to the type of co-operative. In 1970, members of agricultural producer co-operatives of Types I and II earned on average nearly 30 per cent more than their colleagues in Type III co-operatives. Comparing the average net incomes of all farmers with those of the employees of the publicly owned economy, the difference is no longer significant, due partly to the tax exemption of co-operative incomes. In the early 1960s average peasant incomes were significantly below those of wage and salary earners.

5.3.1.3 Legal deductions from earnings   As pointed out before, *wage and salary earners* in the GDR are less burdened by taxation and social insurance contributions than those in the Federal Republic. This is surprising inasmuch as the *rate of taxation* for incomes up to 2,300 Marks/ DM monthly for single persons is higher in the GDR. According to the income tax scales (set out in table 46), taxation begins at a monthly income as low as 190 Marks with a rate of 10 per cent. As earnings increase, the tax rate, tax as a proportion of earnings, rises fairly rapidly, and finally remains constant at 20 per cent above 1,260 Marks.

On the strength of the stiff contributions exacted from the publicly owned economy, the state can afford to keep the wages tax at a low level. The average effective tax rate for wages and salaries as a whole is as low as 7.2 per cent, less than half the corresponding West German figure (15.2 per cent in 1975). Some components of employee incomes are altogether exempted from tax in the GDR or taxed at very low rates. This applies in particular to extra pay for overtime, to bonuses, and to a lesser extent to extra pay for work on Sundays and public holidays. Extra earnings derived from plan overfulfilment are taxed at the low rate of 5 per cent.

Members of *artisan producer co-operatives* are taxed in three ways: their basic pay is subject to the tax rates of the wages tax; earnings from output in excess of plan targets are taxed at rates varying from 5 to 20 per cent according to the degree of norm fulfilment; income from profits distribution is taxed at 10 per cent. By contrast, the earnings of members of *agricultural producer co-operatives* are tax-free (cf. p.179).

205

Taxation of the *self-employed* is not uniform.

Independent professional people are divided into two groups. The fiscally more favoured group, including, for instance, writers, doctors and architects, was up to 1970 taxed for low and medium incomes at the rates of the wages tax, with a higher marginal rate of 30 per cent for incomes of over 3,000 Marks monthly. In 1971, this groups was further subdivided, and increased rates were imposed on a number of professions, e.g. press photographers, commercial artists, advertising experts, architects, up to a top rate of 60 per cent for incomes exceeding 20,000 Marks monthly.

The less favoured professional group, lawyers, tax accountants, etc., is subject to income tax, with the entry point at an annual income of 1,200 Marks and an initial rate of 15 per cent, rising in a very steep progression to a marginal rate of 90 per cent for annual incomes of over 500,000 Marks. The income tax rate is higher than that of the wages tax even for relatively low incomes.

Self-employed tradesmen are also taxed in different ways. Independent artisans pay a profits tax which for annual incomes of up to 11,000 Marks is roughly equivalent to the wages tax, but rises after that progressively to a marginal rate of over 50 per cent for incomes of over 60,000 Marks. Shopkeepers on state commission contracts pay a single tax, the Commission Trade Tax, at rates generally above those of the wages tax, especially for higher incomes. Private shopkeepers are liable to income tax.

Whereas the various taxes on incomes are generally progressive, with higher rates for higher incomes, this is not the case in respect of the burden imposed by *social insurance contributions*. Up to the ceiling of 600 Marks covered by the compulsory insurance scheme, the employee's contribution is 10 per cent of monthly gross earnings. No further compulsory contributions are levied on incomes above 600 Marks, so that the proportion of gross earnings deducted for the compulsory social insurance scheme falls off for higher incomes. The contribution thus has the character of a regressive tax, absorbing in the GDR in 1975 6.6 per cent of gross earnings on average, as compared with 12.3 per cent in the Federal Republic, where the ceiling for contributions is flexible, while the rate of contributions has gone up over the years.

The picture changes, however, when the Voluntary Supplementary Insurance Scheme, introduced in 1968 and modified in 1971 (cf. pp 185 f.), is taken into account. There are strong incentives to join the scheme, and by the end of 1976 70 per cent of those eligible with monthly incomes over 600 Marks had done so, contributing 10 per cent of their gross earnings in excess of that sum, since 1 January 1977 without any upper limit. It can be expected, therefore, that the relative weight of the burden imposed by social insurance contributions will remain roughly constant in the foreseeable future.

The combined effect of wages tax and social insurance contributions on gross wages and salaries in the GDR changed very little over the fifteen-year period from 1960 to 1975, and was 13.8 per cent in the latter year. In the Federal Republic the figure rose during the same period from 15.8 to 27.4 per cent (as shown in table 45).

5.3.1.4 Incomes of private households   As a rule, more than one member of the household contributes to the household income. Comparing the average net household incomes of the various *socio-economic groups* over the fifteen-year period, it appears that household incomes of members of Type III agricultural producer co-operatives[1] were 10 to 15 per cent above those of employees (wage and salary earners), while the average pensioner's household had to make do with about 30 per cent of the wage and salary earners' income.

However, the average household size varies considerably from group to group, with an average of 3.5 persons per household for members of Type III co-operatives, 3.0 for wage and salary earners and 1.6 for pensioners. Thus income per household member, in other words, per capita income of the respective groups, was highest for the employee households, with a lead of initially 20 per cent, later reduced to 10 per cent, over members of Type III co-operatives, and of 50 per cent over pensioners.

As with personal incomes, the *gap between the Federal Republic and the GDR* has widened in respect of the household incomes of employees and pensioners. In 1960, the average wage or salary earner's household income in the GDR was only 10 per cent below that of his West German counterpart, and the per capita income of this group was actually the same in both states; but by 1975 employee incomes in the GDR, both per household and per capita, were lagging behind the West Germans by nearly 50 per cent.

During the same period the household incomes of GDR pensioners dropped from 44 to 28 per cent, and their per capita income from 55 to 31 per cent of the corresponding West German figures.

The income position of pensioners relative to other social groups is markedly different in the two states. In the Federal Republic in 1975 the same average income was recorded for each member of a pensioner's and an employee household, in other words, the per capita income of pensioners as a group was the same as that of wage and salary

---

1 According to a random test in 1965, the household income of members of Type I and Type II agricultural producer co-operatives exceeded the average employee household income by about 50 per cent.

207

Chart 44
Average monthly household net incomes in the GDR and FRG

	1960	1964	1970	1975
	GDR in M			
Employee household	758	807	1031	1307
LPG III household	864	885	1124	*
Pensioner's household[1]	220	249	316	427
	FRG in DM			
Employee household	856	1126	1589	2448
Pensioner's household[1]	504	651	957	1520

1 Household without income from economic activity

Source: DIW calculations.

*No data available.

Chart 45
Average monthly net income per household member
in the GDR and FRG

	1960	1964	1970	1975
	GDR in M			
Employee household	267	284	347	433
LPG III household	216	229	317	*
Pensioner's household[1]	133	151	192	259
	FRG in DM			
Employee household	272	362	532	831
Pensioner's household[1]	247	329	512	826

1 Households without income from economic activity.

Source: DIW calculations.

*No data available.

earners: the two groups have reached financial parity. In the GDR, on the other hand, the per capita income of pensioners was only 60 per cent of that of wage and salary earners, in spite of the successive pension increases of 1964, 1968, 1971 and 1972. They are still the 'stepchildren' of society. The latest pension increase of 1976 has made no substantial difference.

In view of the diverging levels and trends of purchasing power of the two currencies, a nominal comparison of monetary incomes cannot adequately reveal the differences in standards of living, or rather in those components of the standards of living that are determined by private consumption. For that reason, section 5.3.2.3 will present a comparison of real incomes.

Over half the private households in both parts of Germany are employee households. The *differentiation of employee households according to income* (as presented in table 47) shows that in 1960 the

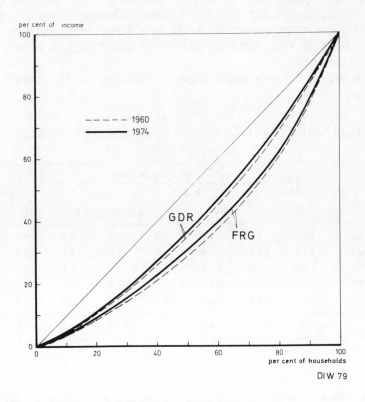

Figure 31   Distribution of disposable net incomes
of employee households in the GDR
and the Federal Republic

209

distribution of net incomes in the lower and medium brackets was similar in the two parts of Germany. Only for incomes exceeding 1,200 Marks/DM monthly was there a marked difference, with 19 per cent of West German households recorded in this category, as compared with 8 per cent in the GDR. During the following years, the pattern shifted in both states towards higher incomes, but much more so in the Federal Republic. Only 6 per cent of employee households in the GDR had monthly incomes of more than 2,000 Marks, as compared with 46 per cent in the Federal Republic.

The importance of income differentials, in statistical terms the dispersion of income distribution, is illustrated by the Lorenz curve (shown in figure 31): the more egalitarian the income distribution, i.e. the more the percentage of households corresponds to the percentage of total income, the closer the curve approaches the diagonal in the figure. A comparison of the distribution of the aggregate net incomes of wage and salary earners among five sub-groups[1] and the Lorenz curve show clearly that the distribution of income among employee households is more uneven in the Federal Republic than in the GDR, chiefly because West German salaries are much higher, with a wider range of variation.

Even so, a tendency towards greater equality can be noted in both territories.

Chart 46

Distribution of net disposable employee household incomes by quintiles

Proportion of households	Share in net income							
	1960		1964		1970		1974	
	GDR	FRG	GDR	FRG	GDR	FRG	GDR	FRG
1. Quintile	10.4	8.4	10.6	8.6	10.4	8.3	10.9	9.3
2. Quintile	15.3	12.6	15.6	12.9	15.8	12.7	16.2	13.3
3. Quintile	19.2	16.4	19.6	17.0	19.8	16.8	19.8	17.0
4. Quintile	23.4	22.8	23.3	22.9	23.3	22.3	23.2	22.1
5. Quintile	31.7	39.8	30.9	38.6	30.7	39.9	29.9	38.3
Total	100.0	100.0	100.0	100.0	100.0	100.0	100.0	100.0

Source: DIW calculations

1 Each of these consecutive 'quintiles' contains 20 per cent of the households of the group, arranged according to income in ascending order. Each quintile is characterised by its percentage of the aggregate group income. The lowest quintile, though comprising 20 per cent of households, will be found as a rule to command a substantially lower proportion of group income (e.g. 10.9 per cent in the GDR in 1974, as shown in chart 46).

5.3.2 Prices, purchasing power, real incomes

5.3.2.1 Prices The purchasing power of a currency is determined by the prices of goods and services. In the GDR, consumer prices are laid down by administrative order, often irrespective of production costs. As a result, some goods, especially industrial products, are heavily taxed, others, in particular agricultural products, heavily subsidised. Notwithstanding rising costs, the principle of constant consumer prices has been reaffirmed in the current Five-Year Plan.

The price structure of the GDR is characterised by generally low prices for the necessities of life, whether goods or services, combined with wide price differentials for the rest of consumer goods. Comparison with corresponding prices in the Federal Republic is beset by difficulties because of decisive differences in the quality, size, form and style as well as the availability of similar goods and services. Moreover, the range of goods on offer in the GDR is subject to fluctuations in time and from region to region. Such factors cannot be quantified, and cannot therefore be adequately taken into account in price comparisons and calculations of purchasing power. Accordingly it is necessary in some cases to depart from the principle of rigorous price comparisons by giving priority to the criterion of equivalence of use, or else altogether to give up the attempt at a comparison. This dilemma is present, for example, in considering holiday trips or a number of services, such as education or health care.

Nevertheless such an investigation gives a good picture of the most material orders of magnitude and the main trends:

Among *foodstuffs*, the prices of the simple staple foods, such as potatoes, vegetables (especially carrots and cabbage) and bread have been exceptionally low in the GDR for many years; at the beginning of 1977 their prices ranged from one to two fifths of comparable DM prices in the Federal Republic. Following substantial price increases in West Germany in recent years, meat and processed meat products, milk and some cereal products are now also cheaper in the GDR, at 60 to 80 per cent of West German prices. Other foodstuffs are dearer in the GDR, notably flour, eggs, butter, dairy products, preserves, fruit (especially imported fruit), cacao and confectionery, at prices varying from 110 to 370 per cent of those charged in the Federal Republic, where a very much wider range of goods is on offer. The same applies to *drinks and tobacco goods*. With the exception of beer, aerated fruit drinks and tea, goods in this category cost more, with some prices over twice or, as for coffee, even three times the West German level (see table 48).

Restaurant meals are very cheap, though, as in the Federal Republic, there are wide price differentials between establishments of different categories. On average, prices are 50 to 60 per cent of the West German ones.

As with foodstuffs and drinks, the relative purchasing power of the GDR currency varies widely for *other consumer goods*. GDR prices are mostly higher than West German ones, though the gap has narrowed for a number of goods as a result of price increases in the Federal Republic.

Generally, it can be said that goods satisfying needs arising from higher living standards, and largely also those made of newly developed materials are more costly in the GDR. Prices there are over twice the West German level, for example, for high-quality television sets and audio equipment, large electrical household appliances, higher-grade textiles made of manmade fibres or new wool, motorcars of medium engine capacity and accessories. On the other hand, GDR prices are particularly favourable for goods satisfying basic short-term needs and made in plain finish or subsidised on social policy grounds, such as children's clothing, books and newspapers and domestic fuel. Brown coal is exceptionally cheap, at under one sixth of the West German price for the amounts allocated by voucher, and under one third for free sales (see tables 49 and 50).

The third group of consumer prices, i.e. *prices of services*, are generally lower in the GDR than in the Federal Republic. Housing rents are fixed at rates which are strictly observed. Thus, rents for accommodation in pre-war houses have remained virtually unchanged since the currency reform, and rents in new buildings must not exceed the level of 1966 for households with monthly gross incomes of up to 2,000 Marks. In the Federal Republic, on the other hand, rents have been rising steadily, so that by the beginning of 1977 the ratio of GDR to West German rents had come down to between 20 and 25 per cent.

The prices of a number of services have been kept constant by subsidies in the GDR, while those in the Federal Republic followed the general trend of rising wages and prices. For comparable services, e.g. power supply, transport, mail, laundries, the GDR charges range between 25 and 50 per cent of the West German ones. But for radio and television licences and telephone calls the price levels in the two states are roughly the same (see table 51).

For other services, in fields such as culture (e.g. theatres), health (e.g. organised sport, holiday homes, health service) and finance (banks and insurance institutions), no valid comparison can be made between prices in the two states owing to differential subsidies and, in part, limited availability in the GDR.

212

Our price comparisons show that the purchasing power of the Mark in the GDR is superior to that of the Deutsche Mark in the Federal Republic so long as demand is confined to the necessities of life, but falls off rapidly the moment consumer demand in the GDR extends to high-quality, and thus as a rule, more expensive products.

5.3.2.2 Purchasing power With a few exceptions, the relative price levels in the two German states have since 1960 shifted in favour of the GDR, where prices remained relatively stable, while the Federal Republic experienced substantial price increases. But differences in the cost of living depend not only on prices but also on the type of goods purchased. In both parts of Germany the structure of consumption has markedly changed over the last decade as a result of a broadened and improved supply of goods. Such changes can be illustrated by comparisons of shopping baskets. The same method can be used to compare the cost of living in the GDR and the Federal Republic. The shopping basket, representing a particular pattern of consumption, reveals the comparative purchasing power of the two German currencies. The different expenditure patterns of West German and GDR employee households (shown in chart 47) reflect a composite picture of differences in incomes, price structure and the supply of goods and services, which condition the difference in the shopping baskets. To pinpoint the differences, each of the two shopping baskets, representative of the respective consumption patterns, has been priced in both parts of Germany.

The comparison of purchasing power is effected for a typical employee household of four persons. The GDR shopping basket, representing the consumption pattern of the majority of the population at the stated time, and thus allowing for structural shifts over the years, required the following expenditure at current prices in each of the two parts of Germany:

	in the GDR	in the Federal Republic
	Marks	DM
1960	650	500
1969	900	800
Jan. 1977	1,400	1,440

Thus, comparing the cost in Marks in the GDR with the cost of the same goods in DM in the Federal Republic, we find that expenditure in the GDR was at first considerably higher, but at the beginning of 1977

213

Chart 47
Expenditure pattern of four-person employee households

	FRG		GDR	
	1968	1975	1968	1975
Total consumption expenditure	100.0	100.0	100.0	100.0
Goods	70.9	68.2	84.7	85.7
Food, drinks and tobacco	37.6	29.8	47.7	43.4
food	31.8	25.5	36.7	32.6
alcoholic drink, coffee and tobacco	5.8	4.3	11.0	10.8
Industrial products	33.3	38.4	37.0	42.3
footwear and accessories	2.0	1.8	2.5	2.9
textiles and clothing	8.1	8.0	13.8	13.9
construction and housing requirements	5.5	5.9	4.0	5.4
electrical engineering products	1.5	2.8	3.3	3.2
other industrial goods	16.2	19.9	13.4	16.9
Services and repairs	29.1	31.8	15.3	14.3
Rents	13.2	12.0	3.9	3.3
Electricity, gas, all forms of heating	3.6	4.0	1.9	1.7
Transport	2.4	2.9	2.3	1.4
Culture, recreation, holidays	3.9	5.7	2.9	3.8
Other services and repairs	6.0	7.2	4.3	4.1

Sources: Specimen household accounts. FRG: Federal Office of Statistics, Preise, Löhne, Wirtschaftsrechnungen, Fachserie M, Reihe 13; GDR: GDR Statistical Yearbook.

somewhat lower than in the Federal Republic. Thus the purchasing power of the GDR Mark relative to the Deutsche Mark was for the GDR shopping basket:

		per cent
	1960	77
	1969	89
Jan.	1977	103

If the same calculation is made for a shopping basket representative of the far more copious West German consumption pattern, the relative purchasing power of the GDR Mark as a percentage of the purchasing power of the Deutsche Mark developed as follows:

	1960	75 per cent
	1969	83 per cent
Jan.	1977	90 per cent

Thus the relative purchasing power of the GDR is considerably lower when measured by the yardstick of West German consumer demand. It is clear in the light of these findings that the relative purchasing power of the GDR Mark is highest for the poorest, for instance pensioners' households, and lowest for households with higher incomes and correspondingly higher consumer demand.

Taking the mean of the results derived from the respective consumption patterns in the Federal Republic and the GDR ('crossed shopping baskets'), it emerges that the relative purchasing power of the GDR Mark, thus defined, rose from 76 per cent in 1960 to 86 per cent in 1969 and to 96 per cent in 1977.

Chart 48
Relative purchasing power of GDR Mark for an employee household of four (purchasing power of DM in the Federal Republic = 100)

| | For expenditure pattern typical of | | | | | |
| | FRG[1] | | | GDR[1] | | |
Expenditure on	mid 1960	mid 1969	beginning 1977	mid 1960	mid 1969	beginning 1977
Food	75	82	102	76	89	110
Alcoholic drink, coffee and tobacco	47	49	65	49	50	65
Housing	133	227	314	133	227	397
Heating and lighting	135	189	274	137	189	339
Household expenses	66	61	63	67	55	63
Clothing and footwear	51	65	58	52	67	62
Toiletry	101	83	94	100	100	100
Education and entertainment	96	79	81	105	115	113
Transport	103	66	66	105	95	77
Total consumer expenditure	75	83	90	77	89	103

1 The shopping baskets used in this calculation were compiled on the basis of available household accounts from both states and in the light of the shopping baskets and consumption patterns used for the official computation of cost-of-living indices, having regard also to the availability of goods and services in the GDR, as apparent from consumption statistics.

215

5.3.2.3 Real incomes

In the West, the term 'real incomes' usually denotes nominal incomes adjusted to the price levels of a base year. In the East European countries, on the other hand, real income is defined as the sum of nominal income plus the services rendered free of charge by the educational, health and social security institutions, etc. Here it is proposed to use the term in the Western sense: real incomes as the nominal incomes of the two territories, adjusted so as to eliminate disparities in the purchasing power of the two currencies. The adjustment is based on the results of the 'crossed shopping basket' comparison.

In 1960 the nominal incomes of employee households in the GDR were by a margin of over 10 per cent lower than those in the Federal Republic; allowing for the lower purchasing power of the GDR Mark,

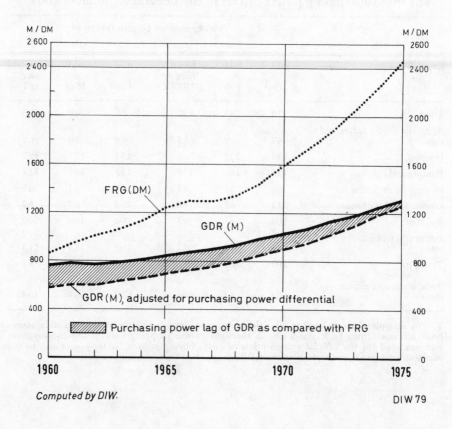

Computed by DIW.

DIW 79

Figure 32   Average net income of employee households in the GDR and the Federal Republic 1960-1975

216

the gap was over 30 per cent in real terms. After that the development was shaped by two opposing trends:

a) nominal incomes in the Federal Republic rose far more rapidly than in the GDR;
b) the gap in the purchasing power of the two currencies narrowed steadily.

On balance, the increase in nominal incomes clearly outweighed the diminution of the disparity in purchasing power. The gap continued to widen both in nominal and in real terms (as shown in figure 33): by 1969 it had increased to 40 per cent in real, about 30 per cent in nominal terms, and by 1975 the differential had reached 50 per cent for real, 45 per cent for nominal incomes.

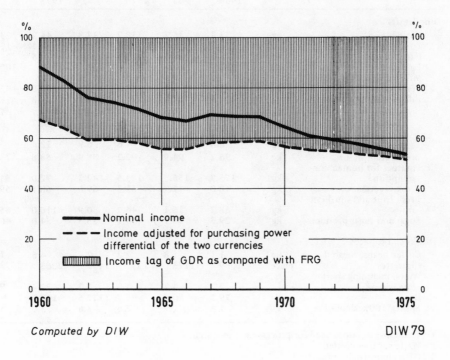

Computed by DIW   DIW 79

Figure 33 Average net income of employee households in the GDR 1960-1975 (in per cent
of corresponding West German figures)

217

5.3.3 Private consumption and savings

The standard of living of a population is not exclusively determined by the quantity and quality of purchased goods and the formation of private assets; it also depends on the supply of services by the state free of charge (e.g. educational and transport facilities) and on the system of social security. Owing to lack of data, a quantitative comparative assessment of those *welfare components of the standard of living* in the two Germanies must be dispensed with.

Chart 49
Per capita consumption of selected foodstuffs and products of the drink and tobacco industry

Goods	Multiples of	GDR				FRG	UK
		1960	1965	1970		1975	
Foodstuffs							
Pork	kg	33.3	36.2	38.7	47.8	44.2	23
Poultry	kg	3.7	4.0	5.1	7.6	9.1	12
Other meats	kg	18.0	18.5	22.3	22.4	29.5	27
Eggs and egg products	piece	197	211	239	268	289	300
Milk for drinking, 2.5% fat content	1	94.5	94.1	98.5	102.1	83.6	52
Edible fats, fat content	kg	27.4	27.9	27.7	25.5	24.8	18
butter	kg	10.4	9.6	11.2	10.2	5.7	7
margarine	kg	8.2	9.5	8.9	8.4	6.7	6
other animal and vegetable fats and oils	kg	8.8	8.8	7.6	6.9	12.4	5
Bread, grain, flour	kg	96.2	94.9	92.2	88.9	58.8	72
Potatoes for human consumption[1]	kg	173.9	156.5	153.5	142.3	92.0	84
Fresh vegetables	kg	48.0	47.9	61.3	69.6	68.5	69
Fresh fruit and southern fruits	kg	68.2	36.1	46.2	50.9	110.0	45
Sugar and sugar products[2]	kg	29.3	30.1	34.4	38.3	34.0	40
Drinks and tobacco							
Coffee beans, roasted	kg	1.1	1.8	2.2	2.4	4.6	1.6
Cigarettes	piece	1069	1123	1257	1452	2063	2422[4]
Wines, including sparkling wines[3]	1	3.2	4.2	5.0	7.2	22.4	9.3
Beer	1	79.5	80.6	95.7	117.6	148.1	*
Spirits, 100% alcohol	1	1.4	1.9	2.6	3.6	3.0	5.2

1 Excluding potatoes used for processing into starch.
2 White sugar equivalent.
3 GDR: industrially processed.
4 1973.
Sources: GDR Statistical Yearbook 1976; FRG: Statistisches Jahrbuch über Ernährung, Landwirtschaft und Forsten, 1976; UK: Agrarstatistisches Jahrbuch der EG, 1973-1976.

*No data available.

A quantitative investigation, then, must be confined to a number of characteristic *indicators of living standards*. Here, too, a number of factors which materially affect living standards, but cannot be quantified, must be left out of account. This refers above all to the consumer satisfaction derived from the regular availability of required goods in respect of volume, range and quality.

If these aspects were included in the comparison of living standards, it would be to the disadvantage of the GDR, where the supply of goods to the population is still beset by shortcomings. It appears that the planning authorities have not so far found a solution to the problem of estimating the shifts in demand for certain goods, such as textiles, footwear, clothing and furniture with any degree of accuracy, in the face of increasingly differentiated consumer preferences. The range of goods on offer, and this applies even to minor goods of daily use, continues to be unsatisfactory. Higher-grade consumer goods often require prolonged waiting times which, for instance for motor cars may extend to several years. The availability of repairs and other services also falls far short of demand.

In view of the high level of industrialisation of the GDR economy, the reason for these shortcomings must be sought in the system itself.

These weaknesses apart, it has to be noted that

a) from 1965 to 1975 the retail turnover of foodstuffs, drinks and tobacco goods increased by 47 per cent, and that of industrial consumer goods by 77 per cent;

b) per capita consumption of many foodstuffs is equal to that in the Federal Republic;

c) the equipment of households with durable consumer goods has steadily improved.

The GDR has thus reached a standard of living which in some respects is clearly superior to that of all East European countries (see section 5.3.5).

The 60 per cent increase in the *retail turnover*[1] from 1965 to 1975 was accompanied by considerable *structural shifts* between the main groups of commodities (as shown in table 32).

At first, *food consumption* was preponderant; but with growing affluence a declining portion of incomes was spent on food. There are

---

1 In the GDR, retail turnover, the most important indicator of private consumption, comprises all transactions involving the ultimate consumer, including sales of food and drinks in catering establishments and retail sales by artisan enterprises. About 3 per cent of the turnover is contributed by sales to enterprises, administrations and other organisations. Conversely, the population makes some purchases outside the retail trade (sales direct from the farm, peasant markets, etc.) to the extent of about 4 per cent of retail turnover.

signs that in terms of quantity, food consumption is approaching saturation. The continuing and steady increase in expenditure on food consumption in recent years is probably due in the main to a shift towards higher-grade products — protein-rich foodstuffs, such as meat, milk and eggs — and in part to a growing tendency to go out for meals.

The turnover of *drinks and tobacco goods* has gone up in the GDR as elsewhere with rising standards of living, but is still below the West German level, largely, it may be presumed, as a result of high prices.

Sales of *industrial goods* were at first concentrated in the sectors of shoes, textiles and clothing. Gradually other goods came to the fore, chiefly consumer durables and products catering for communications and leisure requirements, such as furniture, domestic appliances, audio equipment, television sets and motor cars. Nevertheless, the 48 per cent share of industrial goods in the total retail turnover is surprisingly small for an industrialised economy. Moreover, the official figures overstate the true proportion of industrial sales, since industrial goods, like drinks and tobacco goods, are burdened with high indirect taxes, whereas foodstuffs are subsidised.

The quality of industrial consumer goods has steadily improved. Even so, gaps in manufacturing programmes and long delays in deliveries are still part of everyday life in the GDR. In many instances, production fails to keep up with rapid changes in fashion. Thus the ranges of goods offered by the textile, clothing and footwear branches hardly ever matched demand.

The equipment of households with *durable technological consumer goods* has reached a relatively high level. In respect of some products,

Chart 50
Stocks of selected durable consumer goods
(number per 100 households)

	GDR					FRG	UK
	1960	1965	1970	1973	1975	1973	1975
Private cars[1,2]	3	8	16	21	26	55	57
Motorcycles[1,2,3]	*	33	42	46	50	7	*
Radio receivers[3]	90	87	92	95	96	99	*
TV receivers[3]	17	49	69	78	82	89	95
Electric domestic refrigerators	6	26	56	75	85	93	85
Electric domestic washing machines	6	28	54	67	73	75	72

1 Excluding vehicles used predominantly for business journeys.
2 Including scooters and mopeds.
3 Licensed receivers; in the FRG also combined receiving and sound reproducing equipment.

Sources: GDR Statistical Yearbook; FRG: Ergebnis der Einkommens- und Verbrauchsstichprobe 1973 (Federal Office of Statistics, Fachserie M, Reihe 18, no.1). UK: Annual Abstract of Statistics 1976.

*No data available.

radio and television receivers, demand appears to be approaching saturation. Other household appliances continue to have steady sales in spite of very high prices (e.g. 1,100 Marks for a refrigerator of 130 litres capacity, without deep-freeze compartment). In respect of most of these consumer goods the GDR has now attained the level reached by the Federal Republic at the beginning of the 1970s. More modern developments, such as hi-fi equipment, colour television receivers and dish-washers, are only beginning to gain ground.

As regards motor vehicles, there is a vast difference between the two German states. In the GDR, the motorcycle still predominates, but the number of motor cars is rapidly growing; it increased more than three-fold from 1965 to 1975. For a long time the GDR authorities endeavoured on the grounds of industrial and traffic policy to keep the number of motor cars down. This policy has *de facto* been abandoned, but high prices and long delivery periods tend to slow down the rate of increase in the ownership of motor cars.

Statements about the level of equipment give no clear indication of *differences in quality*. The utility of technological products and appliances depends to a considerable extent on their liability to breakdowns and the *need for repairs*. This aspect becomes particularly troublesome when, as is the case in the GDR, there is a long-term *shortage of spares* and repair facilities. The shortage of other service facilities, such as petrol stations, dry cleaning establishments and laundries, similarly tends to restrict the full use of consumer goods designed to save labour. This factor is all the more important, as so many women are at work. Since wider dissemination of appliances entails an increasing need for servicing and repairs, new bottlenecks are being created all the time.

As incomes increased, *savings* also rose. The annual savings rate — proportion of net income saved — in the GDR fluctuates between 5 and 7 per cent, as compared with 16 per cent in the Federal Republic in 1975. Per capita savings that year were 360 Marks in the GDR, 1765 DM in the Federal Republic.[1]

The bulk of savings in the GDR, 85 per cent, is deposited with the credit institutions by way of savings books or various types of special accounts. The remainder of savings goes into insurance schemes (provision for old age and accidents) and into purchases of securities, of which two types are still available in the GDR: mortgage bonds and housing construction debentures.

---

1 It must be borne in mind, however, that the high figure for the Federal Republic is due in part to the intense savings activity of the self-employed, whose per capita savings are much higher than those of wage and salary earners. In the GDR, on the other hand, the group of self-employed is hardly significant.

Saving for home building never played a significant part and was finally abolished in 1971. Thus the possibility of converting monetary into real assets has virtually disappeared. Saving in the GDR leads almost exclusively to the accumulation of financial assets, which in 1975 amounted to 5,250 Marks per inhabitant, no more than 40 per cent of the corresponding per capita sum in the Federal Republic (as shown in table 52).

5.3.4   Travel

5.3.4.1   Travel by GDR citizens As in all other countries, information about travel in the GDR is gathered by means of fact-finding inquiries organised at irregular intervals. From the results of the three major inquiries so far carried out[1] it emerges that holiday trips (defined as trips of at least seven days' duration) are frequent in the GDR and are growing in importance. The following proportions of the adult population did make holiday trips:

	Total	Foreign trips
1966	35 per cent	15 per cent of total
1972	50 per cent	15 per cent of total

The results of the 1976 inquiry are not strictly comparable, as they were set out in a different way, but they show that travel activity was continuing to rise. Day trips and short-distance trips are also on the increase.

Conditions generally have become more conducive to travel in recent years: incomes were rising, the minimum annual holiday was increased from 15 to 18 days, and the number of private motor cars went up at a rapid rate. Moreover, numerous administrative obstacles that had militated against foreign travel were cleared away in 1972.

Permission to travel to Western countries, on the other hand, is granted only in exceptional cases to GDR citizens of working age, in contrast to the practice of some other CMEA countries, such as Czechoslovakia, Poland and Hungary, whose citizens generally are allowed one journey to the West every three years and are granted foreign exchange allocations to this purpose.

As regards the propensity to travel (i.e. number of holiday trips per inhabitant of working age), there are no major differences between the two German states. In 1975 55 per cent of the West German population

1 See Werner Bischoff and Olaf Schmutzler, 'Zum Umfang der Ferientätigkeit der erwachsenen Bevölkerung der DDR', Mitteilungen des Instituts für Marktforschung, Leipzig, no.1, 1968; Wolfgang Stompler, 'Zur Urlaubsreisetätigkeit der DDR-Bevölkerung', ibid., no.1, 1974; idem, 'Dynamische Entwicklung des Freizeittourismus der DDR-Bevölkerung', ibid., no.4, 1976.

went on holiday away from home for five days or more.[1] The pattern of travel, however, is different: about 60 per cent of West German holiday makers, but only 15 per cent of those of the GDR spend their holidays abroad. Thus inland travel is still dominant in the GDR in respect of prolonged trips. In 1975, the FDGB holiday service and the individual enterprises between them handled about 35 per cent of all domestic holiday trips, each taking about 1.5 million persons to their own holiday homes. The services of the state travel agency DER were used in 1975 by 149,000 persons, no more than 2 per cent of holiday makers. The remainder went under their own steam, visiting friends and relations, going privately to tourist resorts, or camping. The Baltic coast and the Thuringian Forest were the most popular holiday regions.

Since 1972, between 12 and 15 million outward frontier crossings by GDR citizens have been recorded each year. Most of these were accounted for by day trips, which however are not listed separately. About 90 per cent of those foreign trips ended in the neighbouring countries: Poland, Czechoslovakia and the Federal Republic. This lively traffic is due to the easing of travel regulations in 1972, when travel to and from Poland and Czechoslovakia was largely liberalised, and when GDR pensioners, who until then had been allowed one annual visit of up to 30 days to friends or relatives in West Germany or West Berlin, were enabled to spread that 30-day allowance over several journeys.

5.3.4.2 Travel to the GDR Since the easing in 1972 of the regulations governing travel from and to the neighbouring countries, the GDR has become one of the most attractive countries for foreign visitors within the CMEA orbit. A peak number of 18.2 million visitors was recorded in 1972; in 1975 the number was 16.2 million visitors. The decline is due above all to travellers from Poland. After the Travel conventions of 1972, the influx of Polish visitors turned into a spring-tide, rising from 0.7 million in the preceding year to 10 million in 1972. This tourist onslaught was more than the GDR could cope with. Supply bottlenecks ensued, which prompted the authorities to impose new restrictions (concerning the exchange of foreign currency, etc.). After that, the spate of Polish visitors subsided, though the reduced number of 5.7 million in 1975 still constituted one third of all foreign visitors to the GDR in that year.

The agreements concluded in conjunction with the Basic Treaty between the two German states of December 1972 and with the Four-Power Agreement made visits by Federal citizens and West Berliners easier, and their number almost trebled in 1972 and 1973. A tightening

---

1 According to investigations by the Study Circle for Tourism, Starnberger. See: cf. Materialien für die Internationale Tourismus Börse, (West) Berlin 1977.

up of currency regulations at the end of 1973, doubling the minimum amount of West German currency that must be exchanged for GDR Marks per day per person to 20 DM for all visitors, including pensioners, led to a temporary decline in the following year. A year later the compulsory minimum was again reduced and altogether abolished for pensioners; in addition all restrictions on the entry of West German and West Berlin motorists were lifted. These measures boosted the influx of visitors from these parts. In 1975 they numbered 7.3 million, by far the largest contingent of visitors from any single country.

5.3.5 The standard of living of the GDR within the CMEA orbit

Any international comparative investigation of standards of living is faced with a fundamental difficulty: there is no generally recognised and universally valid definition of the term; hence there is no unambiguous yardstick by which the standard of living can be measured and quantified. Standards of living are composite entities of many factors, the selection and weighting of which must always contain a subjective element. In the following a number of data considered relevant in this context are presented.

Some social amenities and benefits provided by the state for the community cannot easily be related to the individual and do not lend themselves to international comparisons. These must be left out of account here, although they are important for the standard of living.

5.3.5.1 *Monetary incomes and savings as components of the standard of living* In all East European countries wage and salary earners constitute the numerically strongest group of the economically active population. Accordingly, the average earnings of this group may be accepted as a valid indicator in comparing standards of consumption. The second major group of the economically active population is represented by the co-operative peasants, who get no fixed wages but a share in the net profits of their co-operative (LPG, kolkhoz, etc.) by way of remuneration for their part in the collective production effort. The self-employed as a group are of negligible importance, except in Poland where substantial numbers of peasants continue to farm on their own account. In all CMEA countries money incomes are still supplemented to some extent by benefits in kind as a part of wages. In the GDR and Czechoslovakia, the most highly industrialised CMEA countries, payments in kind contribute only 5 per cent of net incomes of private households and are thus only of marginal importance, whereas in predominantly agrarian countries, such as Poland and Bulgaria, the proportion may be around 10 per cent. Chart 51 shows the average

224

monthly gross pay of wage and salary earners in the various CMEA countries, both in their national currencies and in GDR Marks, converted according to a key calculated by the CMEA for 'non-commercial payments'.[1]

Chart 51
Average gross monthly pay of employees
and savings deposits per inhabitant 1975

Country	Units of currency	Gross wage		Savings deposits M
		in national currency	in M	
Bulgaria	Lewa	146	531	3168
Czechoslovakia	Crown	2304	737	2521
GDR	Mark	889	889	4470
Hungary	Forint	2821	612	1672
Poland	Zloty	3562	662	1654
Rumania	Lei	1813	621	*
USSR	Rouble	146	466	1143

*No data available.

Source: CMEA Statistical Yearbook; DIW calculations.

The GDR full-time employee, with average monthly earnings of 889 Marks, is clearly at the head of this table. It may be noted in this context that average household incomes cannot be equated with average employee earnings, since in the socialist countries the majority of married women, including mothers of young families, go out to work, so that more often than not household incomes are provided by two wage or salary earners.

Private saving is encouraged in all CMEA countries. The predominant mode is the savings account. Both propensity and ability to save vary considerably from country to country. In Czechoslovakia and the GDR, for instance, virtually every inhabitant has a savings book, but in the Soviet Union and Rumania only one in three. The differences in the volume of savings are greater still, as can be seen from chart 51. It is not affluence alone, however, that determines the level of savings. Private households save for a variety of reasons: to accumulate funds

1 The conversion key makes allowance for the purchasing power of the various currencies and forms the basis for the computation of all payments outside the field of foreign trade, for instance in the conversion of earnings of employees working in another CMEA country.

for holiday travel or major purchases; to hold back from buying when the goods available are not those wanted by the consumer; to have a nest egg for emergencies and old age. But the psychological attitude towards the saver is different in the different countries. For these reasons volumes of savings cannot be accepted without reservations as yardsticks of affluence. Even so, the fact remains that any propensity to save becomes the more readily effective the higher monetary household incomes are. This relationship is confirmed by observations of savings activity: the highest income groups invariably have the largest savings deposits.

5.3.5.2 Goods and services as components of the standard of living

Comparisons of standards of living in terms of the consumption of goods and services are more straightforward, as they are not complicated by the problems of currency conversion. Consumption of foodstuffs and stocks of consumer durables can be compared directly. Yet, here too some caution is called for, above all because there is no way of making allowance for differences in quality, which are highly relevant, especially in the case of industrial consumer goods. Again, per capita consumption of particular foodstuffs depends largely on climatic conditions and traditional patterns of consumption. This applies notably to the consumption of potatoes and cereal products (bread, rice, flour, pasta). Here, the contrast is most marked between the GDR and Bulgaria. The Bulgarian consumption pattern, with the accent on cereals rather than potatoes is generally followed in Rumania and Hungary in the south-easterly part of the CMEA region whereas the more northerly member states, Soviet Union, Czechoslovakia, GDR, Poland, continue to depend largely on the potato as an indispensable staple food.

Habits of nutrition have changed both in the East and in the West over the last twenty years. The common trend which, irrespective of climate and tradition, accompanies rising incomes consists in a shift towards the consumption of animal products as primary sources of the nutritionally important proteins and fats, while the consumption of vegetable products, primary source of carbohydrates, goes down in relative or even in absolute terms. This general shift from a predominantly carbohydrate-based diet to one with a higher proportion of proteins and fats, together with a rising consumption of drinks and tobacco goods is manifest in all CMEA countries.

The share of foodstuffs, drinks and tobacco goods in the total consumption of goods is declining in the GDR, Czechoslovakia, Hungary and the Soviet Union. In these countries the sections of the population with the highest purchasing power are increasingly interested in the acquisition of consumer durables. The trend is present in all East European countries, but is most marked in those that are more affluent and more highly industrialised. Data on the distribution of consumer durables show relatively high densities in the GDR and Czechoslovakia, and for some items also in Poland and Hungary. The proportion of households with washing machines appears to be higher in Poland and Czechoslovakia than in the Federal Republic. In this field, however, the quality aspect is crucial: certain makes of washing machines in the CMEA countries cannot stand comparison with the types generally on sale in the Federal Republic. It may even be asked whether some of the appliances counted as washing machines in East European statistics would ever be classified as such in the West.

Not surprisingly, the differentials in stocks of consumer durables between the various CMEA countries and the gap separating them from Western consumption levels are widest for the most expensive products. This is clearly illustrated by the stock of motor cars. In 1975, the ratio of number of inhabitants to number of motor cars (passenger cars), including those used for business purposes, was as follows:

Rumania	91
Soviet Union	66
Poland	32
Bulgaria	23
Hungary	18
Czechoslovakia	10
GDR	9
Federal Republic	4

In the states of the Eastern Bloc as in the West the motor car is the most coveted consumer good, next to a home of one's own, not only for its utility as a means of transport, but also as a status symbol. The long-term target of private motorisation in all CMEA states is one motor car for every three to four persons, i.e. one for every family. The GDR and Czechoslovakia are planning to reach this target some time in the 1980s, the other CMEA countries have not yet committed themselves to any timetable in this respect.

5.3.5.3 Housing The provision of housing is an acute problem in all CMEA countries. The shortage is most pronounced in Poland and the Soviet Union, countries which suffered extensive war damage and where the population has grown at a particularly rapid rate. The housing policy of the CMEA countries is geared to the aim of providing every family with a self-contained dwelling of a size corresponding to the size of the household, with a floor space of 15 to 20 sq.m per person considered an optimum. So far, only the GDR and Czechoslovakia have been able to build up a housing stock meeting those conditions. In the GDR, which is at the head of the table, in 1975 each inhabitant had on average 22 sq.m of residential floor space (including domestic offices) at his disposal. The Soviet Union, where housing standards are lowest reported in the same year a housing stock of 12.2 sq.m per town dweller.[1] (No data are given for the rural population, but housing conditions are believed to be even more cramped in the countryside).

The housing situation of the GDR is relatively favourable, at least in quantitative terms, because it inherited a larger pre-war housing stock than most of the CMEA countries, war damage was less than in Poland and the Soviet Union, and the population has for many years been stagnant. In contrast, the Polish population increased from 1949 to 1975 by 9.6 million people, the Soviet population by 77 million. In countries with rapidly growing populations the pressure on the housing market made it imperative to embark on new housing construction projects, whereas the GDR was able to postpone investment in this sector for a long time. The price to pay for this temporary advantage has been a pronounced obsolescence of the housing stock in the GDR by comparison with other CMEA countries. Thus over two thirds of the urban housing stock in the Soviet Union was built after 1950, compared with only one quarter of the entire residential floor space in the GDR.

5.3.5.4 *Summing up* There can be no absolute answer to a question concerning a country's standard of living. The answer will always relate current standards either to those of an earlier age or to the current standards of another country. The subjective assessment of one's standard of living is likely to be most decisively influenced by an appraisal of the recent trend: are things getting better or worse?

The position may look very different to the outside observer who in an attempt to size up the standard of living of a population will always be swayed by ingrained personal attitudes and by the collectively held norms of his own country. Thus the West German citizen visiting the GDR will generally come away with a fairly negative impression of living conditions in the other part of Germany.

A very different impression will be formed by visitors from the other CMEA countries. In their eyes the GDR is an affluent country. In monetary terms (money incomes and assets), the GDR is clearly in the lead. In terms of the consumption of goods and services, the ranking of the CMEA countries is not uniform, but whatever criteria of consumption and stocks of goods are applied, the lead is always shared between the GDR and Czechoslovakia, with Hungary some distance behind.

1 According to Narodnoe Khozyaystvo SSSR 1975, pp 7 and 576.

228

Compared with this leading group, the other countries of the economic alliance, Bulgaria, Poland, the Soviet Union and Rumania, have much leeway to make up.

6 Foreign economic relations

Like every small and highly specialised region, the territory of what is now the GDR was always engaged in lively trading relations with territories outside its own boundaries. In 1936 this territory delivered 54 per cent of its entire industrial and agricultural output either to other German regions or abroad, and covered nearly the same proportion of its needs, 53 per cent, from outside.[1] The political partition of Germany was accompanied by a process of economic disaggregation, which prompted each of the two parts to turn to its partners in its respective bloc. The formerly close intra-German economic relations were severed. At the time, the strain on the Soviet Zone was particularly acute, since the rest of Germany had accounted for four fifths of its trade volume. This dependence on intra-German trade was far less pronounced in the territory of the present Federal Republic. Thus the Soviet Zone/GDR came off worst in the partition of Germany.

A precise assessment of the current *foreign trade involvement* of the GDR is hampered by a number of statistical incongruities. The GDR presents the results of its foreign trade not in terms of the domestic currency,[2] but in so-called Foreign-Exchange Marks (Valutamark, VM), a statistical unit.[3] The official rate of conversion to the domestic Mark is not known. Isolated data are available, however, concerning the value of exports and imports at domestic prices, and in this way it is possible to deduce an approximate conversion factor for the 'external' and 'domestic' currency units, and thus arrive at an estimate of the degree of foreign trade involvement. In 1965, the average conversion factor for imports and exports was 1 VM = 1.5 Marks. Since then the rate has shifted in favour of the domestic Mark, owing to the increase in world market prices.

The foreign trade of the GDR increased at a substantially faster rate

1 Cf. Bruno Gleitze, Ostdeutsche Wirtschaft, DIW, West Berlin 1956, p.8.
2 The GDR Mark is a purely domestic currency. Officially it has been assigned a gold parity for the purpose of conversion into other currencies, but that is purely fictitious. An exchange rate of 3.20 Marks to the Rouble has been introduced for non-commercial transactions with socialist countries. Western travellers pay the tourist rate of 1 Mark = 1 DM.
3 Up to 1964 GDR foreign trade results were given in Roubles, since then in VM. The value of the VM was that of the DM prior to the revaluation of 1961. Since then the conversion ratio has changed. In 1976, the VM was equivalent to 0.72 DM, and one US Dollar was worth 3.52 VM. The relation to the Rouble remained constant throughout at 1 Rouble = 4.667 VM.

than its domestic product: from 1960 to 1975, the foreign trade turnover increased at an average annual growth rate of 9.7 per cent, national income by 4.7 per cent. In 1975 the export ratio of the GDR (i.e. commodity exports as a proportion of gross domestic product defined according to the Western method) was over 25 per cent, precisely the same level as in the Federal Republic. Yet, before the war the trade involvement of the GDR's territory with the outside world was nearly twice that of the West German regions.

With exports worth 10,100 million US dollars, the GDR ranked fifteenth in world trade in 1975, behind Switzerland and Australia. It transacted 1.2 per cent of the volume of world trade. During the same year the Federal Republic had a share of 10.3 per cent in world exports. Among the countries of the East European economic bloc, the GDR holds a strong position, ranking with Poland second after the Soviet Union with its 3.7 per cent share in world trade. Czechoslovakia comes next.

The prospects of a major expansion of GDR foreign trade relations are not bright because of a number of factors, which apply generally to the foreign trade of socialist countries:

1   The potential role of foreign trade as an instrument of growth was not discovered until the mid-1960s. Up to that time, foreign trade was held to be merely a balancing device, with imports making up for the lack of indigenous raw materials and filling the yawning gaps in the range of domestic production (*stop-gap function*), while exports were considered a necessary evil, imports having to be paid for.

2   The *foreign trade monopoly* of the state and the restriction of foreign trade activities to bilateral arrangements, which are more readily amenable to rigorous planning and control, are impeding foreign economic relations to this day. The regimentation of foreign trade unduly curtails the role of the exporting enterprises in the planning and execution of foreign trade transactions, and thus destroys opportunities for initiative at the operational level.

3   The foreign trade administration is not flexible enough. Commercial agents and technicians have very limited freedom of action and access to information, owing to the frontier mentality of the authorities and their concern for security.[1] Thus the

1 Though not free of political mistrust, the West was able on the whole to adopt a fairly liberal attitude. Since the countries of the Eastern Bloc were in the majority of cases more dependent on East-West trade than the West, the Western countries were in a position to resort to the more primitive devices of trade policy: isolation and economic boycott (embargo policy).

state ordains a reduction in the efficiency of its foreign trade apparatus, giving rise to difficulties which the Western trade partners, too, cannot overcome: market inquiries of their own are virtually impossible, and they are not given adequate information about detailed plan targets and trading intentions of the GDR.

4   Foreign trade is still dominated by the primacy of politics. Priority is given on principle to economic relations with other socialist countries, whereas trade with Western countries is seen as potentially prejudicial to the independence of the state.

5   The absence of a *convertible currency* constitutes another obstacle to efficient foreign trading.

6   The products offered to the West, especially capital goods, are often not up to the latest technological standards. Potential customers have been deterred from purchasing Eastern products by poor experiences of servicing and spares availability. In the case of consumer goods, *marketing opportunities* and the possibility of profitable sales are sometimes lost when the selection of goods on offer, and their quality and styling, in the light of changing fashions, have not sufficient sales appeal.

7   *Marketing efforts* need to be improved. Publicity for GDR goods is generally neglected, and attempts to market branded products are rare. Acquaintance with market conditions is usually inadequate, and the sales organisations are not flexible enough to cope with the sometimes rapid shifts in demand.

8   In the Federal Republic the marketing of GDR products is often frustrated by *prejudices* on the part of potential consumers.

9   In other Western countries access to markets is impeded by *restrictive measures*, such as protective tariffs, import quotas, etc. This applies both to measures by individual states and those taken collectively by the EEC. Some of these restrictions are waived by the Federal Republic on the strength of the special status accorded to intra-German trade. Even so, some GDR export goods are still subject to quotas and other import restrictions in the Federal Republic.

The system of directing foreign economic relations, common to all centrally administered economies of the Eastern type, rests on the

232

foreign trade and foreign exchange monopoly of the state, which as an integral element of the economic system is actually enshrined in the Constitution of the GDR (clause 9, section 5). Planning, organisation and supervision of all foreign economic relations are entrusted to the Foreign Trade Ministry,[1] which to this end makes use of the services of specialised foreign trade organisations and ancillary agencies, which are either subordinated directly to the Ministry or authorised by it.[2] They discharge as a rule the functions of buying and selling for several manufacturing and trading enterprises. The manufacturing enterprises themselves are in principle cut off from the foreign markets as regards both organisation and pricing.

In order, then, to provide an incentive for enterprises to engage in intensified foreign trade activities, the so-called *'unified record of enterprise results'* (*einheitliches Betriebsergebnis*) was introduced in 1968, and extended to the whole of industry in 1971. It lists in addition to profits from domestic sales any export profits, as well as any 'export incentive payments' received from the state in the form of export subsidy, export compensation and export promotion bonuses (*Exportstützung, -vergütungen, -förderungsprämien*). The export result is converted into the domestic currency according to the official rates of exchange and is then adjusted by an official correction factor, the 'rectification coefficient' (*Richtungskoeffizient*). The result is considered the equivalent of the foreign currency earnings and determines the level of the export profit attributed to the enterprise. The rectification coefficients are regionally differentiated to allow for differences in domestic and foreign price structures, but they serve at the same time as an instrument to encourage the flow of trade in politically desirable directions.

It is the task of the authorities administering the foreign trade monopoly to co-ordinate the results of the domestic currency accounting procedure described in the foregoing with the foreign currency flows, for it may well happen that the foreign exchange accounts are balanced, while the domestic currency accounts show a deficit or a surplus, or vice versa. These differences are settled centrally by means of a clearing account (*Preisausgleichskonto*) forming part of the state budget. The price differences of all exports and imports are entered in this account,

1 Previously styled Ministry for Foreign and Intra-German Trade (up to 1967) and Ministry for External Economic Relations (up to 1973).
2 There are about thirty foreign trade enterprises (often referred to as foreign trade companies) in charge of handling commodity traffic with foreign countries. They are legally constituted as limited companies (GmbH). Their predecessors were the German Internal and Foreign Trade Sections set up in 1951. Other institutions are entrusted with specialised tasks, e.g. VEB Deutrans (international forwarding agents), 'Genex' (handling foreign gifts), and various export agencies, such as 'Agrima' for agriculture or 'Agema' for the establishment of general business contacts. There are other institutions, more directly supervised by the state, including the Chamber for Foreign Trade.

positive differences figuring as state revenue, negative ones as state subsidies. This method has the additional advantage of screening the domestic price system from inflationary foreign influences.

This system makes it possible, up to a point, to gain a foothold in certain markets by means of a consistent pricing policy or to attain a desired foreign trade balance. Yet, the scope of such an autonomous pricing policy is limited in the first place by the fact that the position of the GDR in foreign markets, at any rate in the trade with the West, is usually too weak to allow it to assume the role of a price leader, and in the second place by the response of the trade partners, such as the West German price scrutiny procedure, which frustrates attempts at deliberate dumping. Moreover, considerations of profitability have been given increasing weight in the making of import and export decisions by the GDR, as by all CMEA countries, in recent years.

Efforts which were undertaken during the period of the New Economic System to bring an element of decentralisation into foreign trade relations by entrusting foreign trade transactions to the manufacturing enterprises or their associations, never got beyond very modest beginnings. Under the procedure instituted after the demise of the New Economic System, the export business is transacted by the foreign trade enterprises in their own name, but on the account of the exporting enterprises (commission contract). Only a few enterprises and associations of publicly owned enterprises have been authorised to conduct their own export business, among them the Association of Publicly Owned Shipyards, VVB Schiffbau Rostock; VEB Carl-Zeiss-Jena; VEB Uhren- und Maschinenkombinat Ruhla (watches, machines); VVB Werkzeugmaschinenbau (machine tools); the Schwedt petrochemical combine; and VVB Energiewirtschaft (generating equipment). But these bodies, too, exercise monopolies over supply or demand and are guided by the state. In 1973, 85 per cent of exports were handled by foreign trade enterprises and manufacturing enterprises directly supervised by the Ministry of Foreign Trade. Another attempt to establish direct links between the enterprises and the foreign markets has been abandoned in the meantime: while this experiment lasted, manufacturing enterprises which overfulfilled their export targets were permitted under certain conditions to use part of their surplus earnings of foreign exchange for imports on their own initiative.

6.1   Foreign trade

6.1.1   Overall development

Until the world markets were destabilised by the turbulent price

234

developments of 1973, the balance of trade of the GDR was fairly stable. During the period from 1960 to 1973 a cumulative export surplus of about 3 per cent of total imports was recorded. These figures, however, conceal wide regional variations: export surpluses in trading with socialist[1] countries (9 per cent of imports) and developing countries (23 per cent of imports) had to compensate for trade deficits with the West (19 per cent of exports).

In the West, the surpluses achieved by the GDR in its trade with CMEA countries are often interpreted as credits. Actually the GDR needs some of those surpluses to pay for deficits in the balance of services. Thus, the trade surplus with Poland has to pay for the GDR deficit in the bilateral transport service balance of the two countries, while the trade surpluses with Bulgaria and Rumania are probably used to square the balance of tourist traffic. In dealing with other countries, certain developing countries and, at an earlier stage, Vietnam, the GDR export surpluses have the character of economic aid granted on political grounds.

As regards the flow of international payments, credits, revenue and expenditure related to services, etc., no specific statements can be made, as the GDR, like the other CMEA countries, publishes no balance of payments figures.

In the 1960s the foreign trade of the GDR was characterised by a slight downward trend of prices. Vis-à-vis the socialist countries, the GDR registered a minor improvement in its terms of trade, but in the trade with the rest of the world the opposite was the case, due to substantial reductions in export prices, which presumably served the object of expanding trade with the West.

But in 1973 the world market registered explosive price increases for several commodity groups, as shown in chart 52.

At first, the GDR was affected by the price increases only in respect of the goods which it bought from outside the CMEA region. Within that region the pricing rules agreed in 1958 continued for a while to be observed. These rules provided for price stability over the medium term, i.e. for five-year periods, prices to be based on the world market prices of a particular period of reference, though purged of the 'obnoxious influence of the cyclical factors of the capitalist market'. According to this set of principles, the increase in raw material prices should not have become effective until 1976, at the start of the 1976-

---

1 The countries classified in GDR statistics as socialist comprise the CMEA countries and a few others. The CMEA countries are Bulgaria, Czechoslovakia, GDR, Hungary, Poland, Rumania, USSR, as well as Albania (whose membership is purely nominal), Mongolia, Cuba (since 1972), Vietnam (since June 1978). The other socialist countries are China, Yugoslavia, North Korea, and prior to their admission as members, Cuba and Vietnam.

Chart 52
HWWA[1] index of world market prices[2]
(1952-1956 average = 100)

	1972	1973	1974	1975	1976
Unprocessed foodstuffs and animal feeds	114.6	170.4	273.5	225.3	218.1
Industrial raw materials including	120.6	181.8	311.1	294.6	320.1
Heating and motor fuels	129.8	159.8	438.8	470.9	495.8

1 Hamburger Weltwirtschafts-Archiv (economic research institute).
2 On US dollar basis, allowing for exchange rate fluctuations.

1980 quinquennium. Nonetheless, in view of the upheaval on the world market — and presumably as a result of pressure brought to bear by the Soviet Union which as a supplier of raw materials and energy sources had most to gain from an upward price revision — a new arrangement was agreed at the beginning of 1975. This provided for annual price adjustments on the basis of the preceding five years, and for an immediate price increase for 1975 on the basis of world market prices during the 1972-1974 period. This averaging out over a period the first half of which (up to the middle of 1973) still fell into the era of stable raw material and fuel prices, cushioned the impact of the world market price explosion on the CMEA countries.

In the light of these circumstances it has become increasingly difficult to present a clear picture of the GDR's foreign trade; indeed:

1   There are marked discrepancies between real and nominal trends.

2   The different price mechanisms applied in trading with the CMEA partners on the one hand, and the rest of the world on the other led to an irregular development of the regional trade pattern, since the price increases became effective at different times in the different regions.

3   As the extent of the price increases varied from product to product, the traditional commodity structure of the trade was altered.

4   As a raw-material importing country, the GDR suffered a deterioration of its terms of trade, and hence of its balance of payments situation.

236

In addition the foreign trade statistics released by the GDR have lost much of their usefulness owing to a number of reasons. In the first place, the official figures are often vitiated by a rapidly growing number of incongruities and inconsistencies; secondly, the information policy of the foreign trade authorities has become yet more restrictive; and finally, the revision of the rates of exchange since the early seventies has made comparisons more difficult. All these factors are especially relevant for the GDR's trade with the West.

Accepting the official data from the GDR, we get the following picture of salient trends since 1974:

1 Whereas during the period from 1960 to 1973 the GDR achieved a cumulative trade surplus of 5,700 million VM, 1974 and 1975 brought trade deficits totalling 7,300 million VM, due largely to the development of trade with the West. Indeed, according to GDR statistics, 6,700 million VM of that total was incurred in trading with Western countries. During the period from 1960 to 1973, the cumulative deficit with the West totalled 8,200 million VM.

2 From 1972 to 1975, prices in the foreign trade of the GDR rose on average by about one quarter: export prices by 17 per cent, import prices by 34 per cent. This meant a deterioration of the terms of trade of the GDR by 13 per cent. During the same period the price index of the entire trade turnover rose by no less than 39 per cent in the trade with non-socialist countries, and by 20 per cent for the CMEA countries. The highest annual increases were recorded in 1973 and especially 1974 for the non-socialist countries, i.e. the regions where the movements of world market prices were immediately effective, whereas in the trade with the CMEA partners the impact of the price increases began to be felt only in 1975, when the turnover price index rose in a single year by 18 per cent.

6.1.2   Regional structure

The regional (country-by-country) structure of the foreign trade of the GDR is characterised by the preponderance of trade with the CMEA countries, by the dominant position of the Soviet Union, and by the special role of intra-German trade.

In the 1950s and the early sixties, the socialist countries accounted for about three quarters of the foreign trade turnover of the GDR. In recent years, however, GDR trade with these countries has grown at a slower rate than its trade with the rest of the world. This applies in

237

particular to imports, where the share of the Western industrial countries increased. But these shifts are only a reflection of the price movements of recent years. In real terms the proportions have hardly changed.

The socialist countries outside the CMEA played only a minor part in the foreign trade of the GDR, to the extent of 5 per cent at the most. Until 1960, the aggregate share of these countries had been higher as a result of a fairly substantial trade with China.

The fluctuations of the joint share of the CMEA countries were due above all to the development of GDR trade with the Soviet Union. For a number of years the share of the Soviet Union in the foreign trade turnover of the GDR declined gradually and reached a low of 31 per cent in 1974. In 1975 it went up again, following the price increases instituted at the beginning of that year.

The remaining CMEA countries accounted in 1975 between them for well over one quarter of the foreign trade turnover of the GDR. In this group Czechoslovakia, Poland and Hungary are to the fore, ranking respectively third, fourth and fifth among the trade partners of the GDR. In 1975, the volume of trade with those three countries was larger than that with all Western countries, including the Federal Republic, taken together. Trade with Poland in particular showed an above-average growth rate in recent years. All in all, a slight shift away from the Soviet Union towards the other partners has been discernible in the pattern of GDR trade with the CMEA countries.

An assessment of the trade of the GDR with the Western industrial countries cannot be made with any degree of certainty owing to statistical difficulties, since the GDR data are both self-contradictory and inconsistent with the data supplied by the foreign trade partners. This applies in particular to the ranking of the individual countries, above all to the respective shares of the Federal Republic and the rest of the Western industrial countries in the foreign trade of the GDR, and to the relation of imports to exports in general.[1]

Wide divergencies arise especially in respect of GDR imports from the West since 1970. GDR statistics put them much higher than the figures given by the Western trade partners, and as a result the bilateral trade deficits of the GDR differ substantially in the two statistical

---

1 Experience has shown that the statistical methods applied by any pair of bilateral trade partners in stating the results of foreign trade are usually at variance. Valuation may or may not include transport costs (using c.i.f. or f.o.b. prices); export and imports via third countries may be listed in different ways; the periods for which data are given may vary. But the discrepancies apparent in GDR statistics on trade with the West are of a different order. Moreover, the GDR data are internally inconsistent, since the values stated for the individual countries do not add up to the value shown for the group as a whole. The discrepancies are particularly marked in respect of GDR trade with the Federal Republic, which is credited with too small a proportion of the GDR's entire trade with the West.

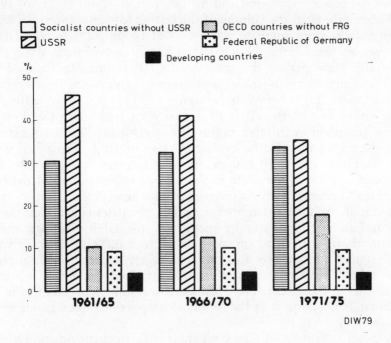

DIW79

Figure 34   Regional structure of GDR
            foreign trade (at current prices)

versions. Thus, the total cumulative deficit of the GDR in its trade with all Western countries, including the Federal Republic, for the period 1970 to 1975 was 14,000 million VM according to GDR statistics, but only 5,000 million VM according to the statistics of the GDR's Western trade partners.

The same statistical problems frustrate all attempts to estimate the level of indebtedness of the GDR in the West. The GDR publishes no balance of payments which would indicate the results of commodity trade, interchange of services and capital transactions with other countries. According to an estimate by the Bank for International Settlements, the net indebtedness of the GDR to the West (including the Federal Republic) was about 3,500 million dollars in mid-1976.

Disregarding the problematic data of the GDR statistics and turning to the data supplied by the Western trade partners (as set out in table

239

61), we find that trade with the OECD countries (not including the Federal Republic) increased during the period from 1960 to 1975 at a higher rate than the volume of the GDR's foreign trade as a whole. A particularly steep increase was recorded for imports by the GDR.

It can be seen, both from GDR statistics and Western data, that during the same period the growth of GDR trade with the Federal Republic (intra-German trade) was lagging behind the development of trade with the other Western countries. This is undoubtedly due to the endeavour of the GDR to diversify its trade with the West in regional terms, so as to relax exclusive ties gradually. To some extent, the development can also be explained as an overdue normalisation of trade relations: the GDR's share in West German foreign trade was just about 2 per cent; its share in the foreign trade volume of the rest of the OECD countries only a fraction of that percentage.

No doubt, trade with the other CMEA countries (intra-Bloc trade) will continue to dominate the picture of the GDR's foreign trade. Even so, the recent trend of an above-average increase in trade with the West may persist also. But this will largely depend on the success of the other CMEA countries in establishing closer economic relations with the West, for in that event the GDR would be relieved of some of the demands made on it as the foremost supplier of capital goods within the Bloc.

A general activation of East-West trade will affect the position of the GDR in the intra-Bloc trade. The GDR will have to contend then with the competition of Western industrial countries in its very own foreign markets, and as an importer it will have to compete more strenuously for its share in the still very modest volume of East European manufactures measuring up to world market requirements.

The *developing countries* are of minor importance in the external economic relations of the GDR, notwithstanding the authorities' repeated protestations of their desire to boost trade with those regions. During the period under review, the developing countries' share in the trade turnover of the GDR was 4 per cent. In this trade, the GDR achieved a cumulative export surplus of 1,700 million VM during the period 1961 to 1975, which represents 15 per cent of GDR imports from those countries.

GDR trade with the Third World is concentrated on a few countries, notably Egypt, with a trade volume of 627 million VM in 1975, India (320 million VM), Brazil (213 million VM) and Iraq (648 million VM). Iraq came into the picture only after the increase in oil prices. These four countries accounted for nearly 60 per cent of the entire trade of the GDR with the developing countries. In 1975, two thirds of GDR exports to the Third World was made up of engineering products.

Among the goods supplied by Third World countries, raw materials were predominant.

Chart 53
GDR foreign trade turnover with OECD countries[1]

Country	Ranking OECD statistics	per cent[2]	Ranking GDR statistics
		Annual average 1970-1975	
France	1	14.5	4
Sweden	2	12.6	5
Netherlands	3	11.1	1
UK	4	8.4	2
Italy	5	7.7	9
Austria	6	7.7	7
Belgium/Luxembourg	7	6.2	6
Japan	8	4.6	11
Switzerland	9	4.5	3
Denmark	10	4.3	10
USA	11	2.6	8
Others	–	15.2	–

1 Without intra-German trade.
2 OECD total = 100.

Sources: Statistics of OECD countries; GDR Statistical Yearbooks.

6.1.3 Commodity structure

The commodity structure of GDR foreign trade is characterised above all by the country's dependence on imports of raw materials and by the high ratio of manufactures, and in particular capital goods, in its exports. On balance, the GDR finances its requirements of raw materials and fuels through exports of machines, equipment, vehicles and industrial consumer goods. In these classes of goods it recorded substantial surpluses year after year. The commodity structure changed considerably over the period of review, especially as regards imports (as shown in table 60). Here, a marked increase in products of the metal processing industry is significant. The proportion of machinery and equipment went up from 13 per cent in 1960 to 31 per cent in 1975. Imports of raw materials and foodstuffs increased at a slower than average rate, but as a result of the explosive increases in raw material prices, this trend was reversed as from 1974.

The massive increase in imports of capital goods reflects an endeavour to use foreign trade more effectively than in the past as an instrument of economic growth, that is to say to reap more of the benefits of technological progress by importing highly advanced capital goods. A clear indication of this trend is given by the export/import ratio for machines, equipment and means of transport, which declined from 4:1 in 1960 to 1.5:1 in 1975.

The development of GDR exports advanced in parallel with the economy as a whole, and responded to the long-term need for changes in the structure of trade. Products resulting from higher stages of processing are gaining ground. Products of the metal processing industry were dominating the export pattern from the outset. In 1975, machines, equipment and means of transport accounted for nearly 18,000 million VM out of a total export volume of 35,000 million VM.

This commodity group comprises a vast array of different products; nevertheless, in spite of the wide range of machinery exports, some sectors are represented far more strongly than others. Thus, the sectors of engineering products and means of transport – the latter including chiefly ships, motor vehicles and rail vehicles – each contributed roughly 20 per cent of the total machinery exports in 1975. Machine tools made up about 10 per cent. Agricultural, office and textile machines also played a prominent part in the export programme. A large proportion of the total domestic output of engineering products is exported. In 1966, the last year for which these particular data are available, the export ratio in these industries varied from 30 to 60 per cent (shipbuilding 60 per cent, general engineering and vehicle construction about 35 per cent, heavy engineering 40 per cent), as compared with an export ratio of 23 per cent for industry as a whole.

The regional distribution of GDR machinery exports is markedly one-sided. The socialist countries took 90 per cent, the Soviet Union alone half of the total (as shown for 1974 in table 63). The level of machinery exports to the West was very modest. The leading items were waterborne craft and machine tools, which over a number of years accounted between them for one third of all exports to the West. As regards machinery exports to developing countries, the leading items were textile and printing machines and machine tools, which together contributed about 30 per cent of the total.

The regional pattern of machinery exports by the GDR is largely determined by the fact that its East European partners look to the GDR as a supplier of capital goods. This trend is reinforced by the lack of competitiveness of some GDR goods in this sector in Western markets and by the tendency of GDR export marketing executives to take the line of least resistance and fall for the lure of 'Eastern Europe, that vast and easy market'.

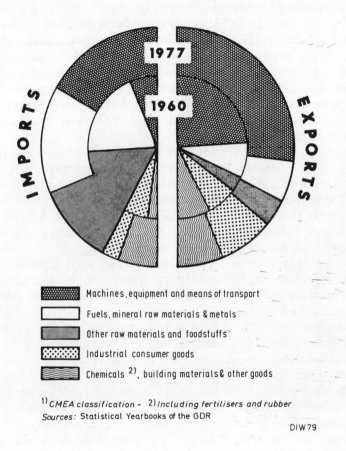

Figure 35   Commodity structure of GDR foreign trade[1]

The trade of the GDR with the Soviet Union is still characterised by the fact that the two economies complement each other so largely. The Soviet Union is the GDR's main supplier of industrial and agricultural raw materials and semi-manufactures (as shown in table 65). During the period from 1961 to 1975, the Soviet Union supplied on average well over 50 per cent of GDR imports of hard coal, 40 per cent of coke and meat, 60 per cent of vegetable fats and grain. GDR imports of sawn timber, mineral oil, natural gas and cotton came almost entirely from the Soviet Union. The Soviet Union also supplies a large proportion of GDR imports of iron ore, pig iron, tubes and non-ferrous metals such as zinc, aluminium and lead, although some of these items are not covered by the official statistics.

Conversely, the GDR, with its share of 16 per cent in the Soviet foreign trade turnover is not only the leading trade partner of the Soviet Union but also, and in particular, its foremost supplier of capital goods. One quarter of all Soviet imports of machinery and equipment comes from the GDR, and in some sectors the GDR share is considerably higher (as shown in table 66). By and large, the simplified description of Soviet-GDR trade as an exchange of raw materials for capital goods still applies, yet in recent years some notable changes in the composition of Soviet export goods can be discerned, among which capital goods have become increasingly prominent. This trend is to be intensified.

There has been little change in the structure of GDR exports to the Soviet Union. Textiles, chemicals and ships figure prominently, next to engineering products. An exceptionally steep rise was recorded for exports of agricultural machinery.

The commodity structure of GDR-Soviet trade, with its gradual shifts, presents a picture of economic benefits and necessities as well as difficulties. The benefits lie in the opportunity, offered to both countries, of complementing their potential. A secure basis for economic relations is given by the similarity of the two economic systems. Co-operation, reciprocal adjustment of long-term plans and trade projections, and the long-term trade agreements concluded on that basis have assured a development that is relatively immune to world market influences and marketing risks. The GDR, in particular, has in the Soviet Union a large and receptive market for capital and consumer goods.

Yet in spite of the generally concurring interests of the two partners, this trade raises problems, especially for the technologically more advanced partner, the GDR. Indeed, in order to benefit fully from the advantages of a division of labour, the GDR must be able to count not only on the necessary deliveries of raw materials, but also on supplies of some high-technology high-quality manufactures from the Soviet Union. It is this ability on the part of the Soviet Union that will determine the long-range growth prospects of an economically efficient bilateral trade. If, on the other hand, the rate of expansion is largely dictated by Soviet purchasing preferences, the trade between the two countries could well be balanced on paper by compensatory Soviet deliveries, but the relationship would in part run counter to the economic interests of the GDR. The development of world market prices in the 1970s has altered the terms of trade in favour of the Soviet Union. The GDR must pay for dearer raw materials with substantially increased export deliveries. The economic strain on the GDR is out of proportion to the gain derived by the Soviet Union with its vastly greater economic potential and its relatively minor dependence on foreign trade.

This does not mean, however, as has been frequently asserted, that the Soviet Union is 'exploiting' the GDR by charging excessive prices for raw materials and offering in return unduly low prices for GDR capital goods. Actually, as we have seen, current raw material prices in inter-Bloc trade lie below world market prices. It is true that earlier on, up to 1973, the prices of a number of raw materials were above those of the world market, but this in itself is no conclusive evidence of 'price exploitation', since it is quite possible that such price differentials were balanced by appropriate price levels for Soviet imports.

6.1.5   The remaining CMEA countries

GDR trade with the other CMEA countries (as set out in tables 67 to 69), with the exception of Czechoslovakia, generally follows the pattern of trade with the Soviet Union and gives rise to similar problems. These countries, too, are in the main suppliers of agricultural products and industrial raw materials. The GDR, with its deliveries of capital goods, plays an important part in their industrialisation, but derives from this relationship hardly any impulses conducive to improvements in technology and marketing. Nevertheless, these aspects are not as prominent as in the GDR's relationship with the Soviet Union, and they do not apply with equal force to all the countries concerned. The imports taken by the GDR from Poland, Czechoslovakia and, to a lesser extent, Hungary, already include relatively high proportions of manufactures (in particular capital goods), while the bulk of Bulgaria's exports still consists of agricultural products.

Among Polish exports to the GDR, machinery and equipment have replaced hard coal as the leading item. Machinery and equipment have also gained ground among Hungarian exports, with the greatest increases in deliveries of vehicles and electrical engineering products. Trade with Czechoslovakia, the only CMEA partner whose level of development is comparable to that of the GDR, is to a large extent evenly matched. Thus, mutual deliveries of machinery and equipment are far more nearly balanced than in the GDR's trade with the rest of the Bloc. According to official statistics, machinery and equipment made up about 40 per cent of the flow of goods in either direction. Czechoslovakia, then, is the only CMEA partner with whom the GDR has so far been able to establish a genuine division of labour.

6.1.6   Trade with the West

The list of GDR goods exported to the OECD countries, not including the Federal Republic, is headed by basic and intermediate materials (as shown in table 62), which in 1975 accounted for well over one third of the total, followed by capital goods (over one quarter), industrial consumer goods (about one fifth), and agricultural products/foodstuffs (over one sixth). There were some shifts in the commodity structure since the early 1960s, with exports of capital goods and agricultural products running ahead of the overall growth rate, and exports of basic and intermediate materials lagging behind. This development is due in part to stagnant sales of mining products and products of the iron and steel industry, whereas exports of chemicals were keeping step with the overall growth. From 1970 on, machinery exports went chiefly to France, Britain, Japan and Sweden. The leading item in this sector was machine tools, representing about one third of the total.

Basic and intermediate materials also come first in the list of GDR imports from OECD countries, followed by capital goods whose share in total imports increased at a remarkable rate. The same applied since 1973 to raw materials, a reflection of world market developments.

In spite of the steep rise in capital goods imports, their volume most probably still falls far short of the extensive needs of the GDR for the most up-to-date machines and installations. Consumer goods play a minor part in the GDR's trade with the West (and this also applies to intra-German trade). Even the 1971-75 Five-Year Plan, with its accent on consumption, did not change this position.

Imports of agricultural products, on the other hand, have lost in importance. At times in the early 1960s they accounted for half the total imports from OECD countries, but that proportion later dropped

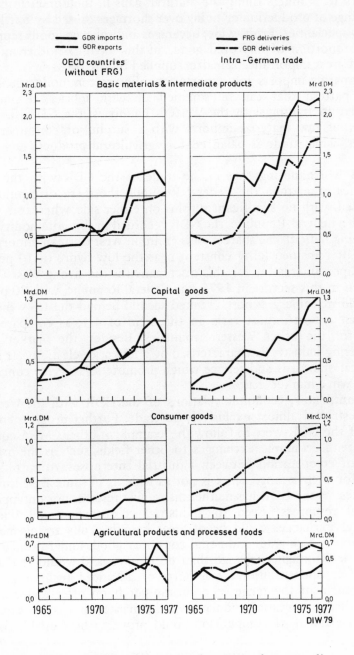

Figure 36   Western trade of the GDR by type of commodity

to about one fifth. Within the agricultural sector, the GDR confined its imports to products filling the 'natural' gaps in the domestically available range of production or tiding over shortages caused by bottlenecks, and to specialities. Fruit, wine, beverages and tobacco goods represent a large proportion of imported goods in this sector. Another individual item of great importance is maize, supplied by the USA.

Comparing imports and exports according to commodity groups, we get a pattern that can be summed up with a brief, if simplified, formula: in trading with the Western countries, the GDR finances a surplus of raw material imports with a surplus of consumer goods exports, while trade is balanced for agricultural products and capital goods.

It is worth noting that in the trade of the GDR with the OECD countries other than the Federal Republic the share of capital goods increased, with no significant surplus on either side, whereas in trading with the Federal Republic, the GDR recorded in this commodity group a growing deficit. The share of this group in West German imports from the GDR remained fairly constant near the low figure of 10 per cent. One important reason for this discrepancy is the strong West German position in this sector: in 1975, the Federal Republic, with 20 per cent of world machinery exports, ranked second behind the USA and registered an export/import ratio in this field of 4:1, as compared with 1.5:1 for the other Western countries. Besides, the market of the engineering industry is characterised by a low price-elasticity. It is technological standards and service which promote sales. Price concessions do not win a market share.

Up until now, economic relations of the GDR with the West have been restricted almost exclusively to trade. Further progress could be made if the GDR were to follow the example of other CMEA countries and extend economic exchanges to other fields, such as the manifold forms of co-operation between industrial enterprises. Admittedly, the scope for such arrangements is not as wide as in some East European countries, as the GDR has neither manpower reserves nor untapped raw material resources. Even so, industrial co-operation and scientific-technical exchanges could be of great benefit. Thus arrangements to manufacture high-grade industrial consumer goods under licence would require less foreign exchange than do imports and would at the same time offer opportunities for imports of advanced technology. They would augment the range of domestic goods on offer and might set standards for domestic producers. As the market approaches saturation such an element of competition could prove to be fruitful. Another advantage offered by co-operation arrangements is access to Western markets.

6.2   Intra-German trade

6.2.1   Contractual basis and procedures

The contractual basis of intra-German trade (*Innerdeutscher Handel*)[1] is the Interzonal Trade Agreement of 20 September 1951, known as the *Berlin Agreement*. Although this treaty itself, as well as the innumerable specific regulations issued within its framework have repeatedly been adjusted to changed circumstances, it still forms the legal basis of trade between the two parts of Germany, recognised as such by both parties. In their Basic Treaty of December 1972, the Federal Republic of Germany and the German Democratic Republic undertook to continue their bilateral trade 'on the basis of the existing agreements' and thus according to the rules in force at the time.

In the light of political considerations, the Berlin Agreement contained a 'currency region clause', i.e. the representatives of the two sides signed for their respective currency regions. As a result of this mode of signing, Berlin was automatically included in the Treaty. In addition it was agreed that an appropriate proportion of the trade volume was to fall to the city.[2] The Agreement was concluded for an indefinite period and can be terminated at the end of any year, subject to notice to this effect being served three months in advance. The Agreement regulates the exchange of goods, services and payments. The practical execution of the Agreement falls on the West German side within the competence of the *Trustee Office for Interzonal Trade* (*Treuhandstelle für den Interzonenhandel*, TSI), which has been based

---

1   Formerly known as 'Interzonal Trade', a term originally applied to trade between any two of the four post-war occupation zones, later restricted to trade of the Federal Republic with the GDR. In the GDR, intra-German trade is officially treated as part of the Republic's foreign trade. It is designated, and recorded in the statistics, as 'trade with West Germany and West Berlin', or even as 'external trade with the Federal Republic of Germany and the autonomous political entity of West Berlin'.
2   West Berlin's share in direct deliveries from the GDR fluctuated during the period from 1960 to 1976 between 16 and 27 per cent, whereas it contributed only between 3 and 9 per cent of direct deliveries to the GDR. No statistical data are available for the participation of East Berlin, which is economically as well as politically completely integrated in the GDR.

in West Berlin since 1949, while the Ministry of Foreign Trade is responsible on the GDR side.

Intra-German trade is conducted on the following lines:

1   The trade is 'two-sided' in the sense that deliveries in both directions must balance, at least in the long term.

2   Payments are effected exclusively by way of clearing between the two note-issuing banks. Debtors settle their obligations, and creditors receive payments through banks authorised to handle this trade in the territory of the respective state. The claims of the supplying firms are settled by the payments received from the purchasers.

3   Contracts for deliveries in either direction are concluded on the basis of the DM (West). According to the Agreement, payment is assessed in *'units of account'* (*Verrechnungseinheiten*, VE), which to all intents and purposes are identical with the Deutsche Mark of the Federal Republic.[1] In the GDR, the accounts are closed in its own domestic currency.

4   To avoid stoppages of the flow of goods in both directions as a result of time lags in settling claims, the two sides are permitted to overdraw their clearing accounts up to a certain limit, the *'swing'*. If the facility of the swing is constantly used by one side, as is the case with the GDR, it is tantamount to a permanent interest-free credit. This has been the situation since December 1968, when the Federal Government waived its claim to the annual settlement of balances as part of a pack-

---

1 The introduction of the unit of account did not establish a parity relationship between the DM and the GDR Mark, nor does its existence give any indication about the relative purchasing power of the two currencies (see section 5.3.2.2 above), any more than does the free exchange rate of the West Berlin exchange bureaux, denounced as 'fraudulent' by the GDR. This rate, fluctuating between 5 and 3 GDR Marks to the DM, merely reflects the supply-demand situation of the GDR currency. What drives GDR residents to the exchange bureaux are partly the enormous price differences for some goods (e.g. cheap tights or nylon shirts) and partly the unavailability of certain articles in the GDR. Thus, the currency drain is balanced by an influx of goods. The unfavourable free exchange rate, then, is an expression of the strong demand for Western goods on the part of GDR residents and the absence of a reciprocal urge in West Berlin. The limited amounts of convertible currency allowed to GDR travellers also tend to boost the demand for DM.

age of new agreements. After repeated adjustments of the swing to the current volume of trade it was agreed to introduce an automatic adjustment on the basis of 25 per cent of the deliveries of the previous year. This 'dynamised', sliding swing was replaced at the end of 1974 by an arrangement fixing the upper limit at 850 million DM up to the end of 1981.

5   For the clearance of payments, the two Central Banks are running a number of accounts, currently two *Commodity Accounts* (I and II)[1] and one *Service Account* (III).

6   The volume of trade in goods covered by Account I is agreed by the two sides in terms of value, while goods covered by Account II are in principle not subject to any limitation. In fact, however, the Federal Government, prompted by economic policy considerations, has secured for itself possibilities of intervening in this trade as well by instruments such as the tendering procedure[2] and the 'autonomous limitation of value' (i.e. quota system).

7   In addition to Accounts I to III, a special account, Account S, was instituted in 1958 in order to enable the GDR to import West German goods for settlement in cash. In practice, the GDR has made little use of this facility,[3] although it was certainly not short of West German currency, since there are several substantial sources of DM-revenue apart from the channels of intra-German trade. Charges for use of roads and visa fees alone yielded 235 million DM in 1973 and similar amounts in the subsequent years. Further DM-receipts are secured by the compulsory currency conversion quota imposed on visitors to the GDR[4] and by commercial ventures

---

1   Account I deals with 'hard commodities', comprising chiefly GDR deliveries of mining and engineering products and West German deliveries of iron and steel products as well as engineering manufactures. Account II records transactions in 'soft commodities'.
2   Before a deal can be concluded, the opportunity for an export or import contract must first be published in the Federal Republic (in the Bundesanzeiger), and the merchant must have been awarded the contract.
3   Up to 1972 inclusive, the GDR spent no more than a total of about 500 million DM in free currency on imports from the Federal Republic. In 1973, the transactions over Account S reached a peak of 300 million DM. The combined purchases of 1974 and 1975 over this account amounted to about 200 million DM.
4   It should be noted, however, that this source of DM-revenue is treated by the GDR as a political rather than fiscal matter, as was clearly shown by the doubling of the minimum conversion quota in November 1973 (cf. section 5.3.4 above). As was to be expected, and clearly desired by the GDR leadership, this measure led to a drastic decline in the number of visitors. It was received with dismay in the GDR, while in the Federal Republic it was considered to be a violation at least of the spirit of the Basic Treaty. In connection with renewed negotiations on the swing, the Federal Government was able to secure a partial repeal of the anti-travel regulations. The GDR authorities were at pains to obscure the connection.

251

such as *Intershop*, *Intertank*, *Genex-Geschenkdienst*.

8   In the Federal Republic, all intra-German trade deals are subject to a licensing procedure. (In the GDR, of course, they are transacted by the official foreign trade agencies of the state). To effect a transaction contracted by the two business partners in the GDR and the Federal Republic, purchasing licences or consignment notes must be produced in the Federal Republic. In 1969, the procedure was relaxed, and for a large number of transactions, approval is deemed to follow automatically upon registration.

6.2.2   *Special status*

In the Federal Republic, in contrast to the GDR, intra-German trade is not considered to form part of foreign trade. Goods delivered by the GDR accordingly get preferential treatment: manufactures come in duty-free, agricultural products are exempted from the compensatory levy imposed on imports by the CAP, and there are some tax concessions. The free entry of agricultural deliveries from the GDR has enabled the GDR export agencies to benefit at least in part from the agrarian prices ruling within the EEC. This special status has aroused the envy of the GDR's partners in the CMEA and also caused resentment in the West, even though the special status of intra-German trade was recognised by the EEC partners in the Treaty of Rome. Moreover the volume of intra-German trade is insignificant by comparison with the Federal Republic's trade with its partners in the EEC (in 1975 the proportion was 4 per cent, both overall and for GDR agricultural deliveries). Misuse of intra-German trade is virtually impossible, since the member states are obliged to exchange information and have a statutory right of intervention. Finally, it should be noted that GDR agricultural deliveries are used above all to supply West Berlin. Sugar deliveries, for instance, go exclusively to the city. In fact, agricultural products and foodstuffs supplied to West Berlin made up two fifths of all GDR deliveries within the framework of intra-German trade in 1975.

West German importers of goods from the GDR are entitled to tax relief on the turnover tax. In May 1970 this rebate was increased for manufactures from 5 to 11 per cent, while for agricultural products it remained unchanged at 2.5 per cent. Deliveries to the GDR, on the other hand, which at first, when value added tax was introduced at the beginning of 1968, had been zero-rated, were burdened with a 6 per cent tax in July 1970, and thus were more highly taxed than exports to other countries. From the angle of the Federal budget, then, intra-German trade involves some sacrifice of revenue on the one hand, and some additional tax revenue on the other.

The advantages derived by the GDR from the special status of intra-German trade cannot be quantified with any degree of accuracy, although the opposite has often been asserted and some attempts have been made to prove it. Apart from difficulties due to the inadequacy of the statistical data, any attempt at computation is bound to involve hypothetical assumptions. It may be asked, for instance: 'What burden would be imposed on whom if customs duties were charged and levies exacted?' To answer this question, it would be necessary to make a number of rough-and-ready assumptions about elasticities, competitive positions, etc., which could hardly do justice to the complexities and intricacies of the real world. What can be said in summing up is that the West German exchequer is sacrificing certain revenues. Some part of this loss, which, however, cannot be quantified, is a clear gain for the GDR; but there can be no doubt that the West German economy also benefits to some extent. Within the ambit of the economic process as a whole, it is a case of redistribution of income from the state to private individuals. The state's sacrifice of revenue entails income benefits for individual economically active persons, whether it be the first purchaser or the processing industry or the ultimate consumer.

6.2.3 Significance and commodity structure[1]

The significance of intra-German trade is different for the two sides. For the GDR, the Federal Republic is, after the Soviet Union, its second most important trade partner and, by a wide margin, its leading Western trade partner. According to Western statistics (presented in tables 61 and 70), West German trade with the GDR exceeds that of all other Western countries taken together. GDR trade statistics (table 58), on the other hand, puts the share of the Federal Republic in its foreign trade at only half that of the other Western countries combined. But seen from the Federal Republic, the picture looks very different. Here, the GDR ranks only 13th, behind Denmark, among its trade partners. The volume of intra-German trade corresponds to only 2 per cent of the Federal Republic's foreign trade.

Yet, as far as West Berlin is concerned, some of the supplies received from the GDR are of considerable importance. A substantial part of the city's requirements of fuel oil, diesel oil and petrol is supplied by the

---

1 Statistical data on intra-German trade are published by two official bodies in the Federal Republic, the Federal Office of Statistics and, under the auspices of the Federal Government and the Trustee Office for Interzonal Trade, by the Federal Office for Industry in Frankfurt. The two sets of statistics do not tally. GDR statistics, owing to the methodology chosen, give again different results, but are in any case of limited value, as the data are not specific enough.

GDR. In 1975, 31 per cent of all mineral oil products delivered to West Berlin (in terms of value) came from the GDR. But all round the GDR's share in the supplies of West Berlin is modest. Only about 4 per cent of the city's foodstuffs is delivered by the GDR, and as regards industrial products, too, the city's trade is geared to the West.

From the point of view of many involved West German firms, intra-German trade is a good business proposition, seen in a broader context it is in the first place of political significance. According to a widely held and frequently expressed opinion, intra-German trade has a part to play in safeguarding the transport link with West Berlin. It was with an eye to the security of this line of communications that the 'cancellation clause' was introduced in 1960, which enabled the West German trade partners to cancel deliveries of goods via Account I at short notice. However, the point and the possible consequences of this device, which in the end was never used, were controversial, and so the Federal Government dropped the clause in August 1967. The GDR authorities were also aware of the political implications. Their attitude is well documented.[1]

The commodity structure of intra-German trade (as set out in table 72) is not in keeping with the level of development attained by the two economies. Above all, it is not sufficiently differentiated. The flow of capital goods, in particular plant and machinery, is relatively low in both directions, while basic materials and semimanufactures, and above all products of agriculture and the food-processing industry, have a disproportionately high share. The low level of differentiation is most marked in respect of GDR deliveries, 40 per cent of which still consist of textiles and agricultural/food products. Evidently, the GDR was compelled to sell consumer goods, in order to bring in foreign exchange, as the prospects of expanding machinery sales in the Federal Republic were strictly limited. But in recent years a shift in the commodity structure towards products involving higher stages of processing has been noticeable. Within the range of chemicals delivered by the GDR, for instance, basic inorganic and organic materials have ceded their dominant position to plastics, plastic products and manmade fibres. A similar trend can be noted in the textiles and clothing sector.

For a long time, brown coal held a prominent place among GDR deliveries; lately it has been of minor importance. Deliveries of mineral oil products to the Federal Republic were subject to marked fluctuations. Initially they played a very important part; later, they experienced a strong decline; and in recent years they came into prominence again, ranking third among the range of GDR deliveries, after

1 Cf. 'Dichtung und Wahrheit über den Aussenhandel der DDR und BRD', Neues Deutschland, 7 June 1970.

textiles and agricultural products.

The structure of GDR deliveries is determined by a number of contrasting factors, including notably:

a) traditional trade relations in respect of certain consumer goods;
b) advantages of location: products with a high content of transport cost find receptive markets, especially in West Berlin;
c) lower costs resulting from regional concentration in respect of marketing activities, customer relations, etc.;
d) the preferential treatment accorded to GDR trade under the 'special status', which undoubtedly stimulates sales of certain GDR products.

6.2.4 Development

Over the long term, intra-German trade has shown a remarkable growth in volume: the turnover rose from 2,100 million DM in 1960 to 8.2 million DM in 1976, an average annual increase of 8.4 per cent. However, the rate of progress was rather uneven and not free of setbacks. During the period under review the changes from one year to the next ranged from – 16 per cent to more than +20 per cent. A steady trend as regards GDR deliveries can be observed for the period 1968 to 1971, when West German purchases increased year after year. The highest growth rates on both sides were registered in 1974. But an investigation by the DIW showed that this increase merely reflected rising prices.

The turnover declined substantially in 1961 and 1962, and to a lesser extent in 1967. On the first two occasions this was clearly due to political reasons, at a time when the GDR was blocking economic relations in the course of its 'Operation Stop Mischief' (*Aktion Storfreimachung*).[1] On the last occasion it was the procedural rules which had a retarding effect. They were duly revised by the Federal Government under the 'grand coalition'. In the subsequent years the rate of growth of intra-German trade was unusually high, but unbalanced, with West German deliveries running rapidly ahead of those from the GDR. A substantial imbalance resulted, with a growing deficit on the part of the GDR corresponding to the West German cumulative active balance,[2]

1 Western attitudes, too, played a part in the deterioration. Thus, when the GDR authorities imposed restrictions on traffic between the two parts of Berlin, the Federal Government responded by serving notice to terminate the Interzonal Trade Agreement by the end of 1960. This action failed in its purpose; the GDR authorities did not revoke the controversial measures.
2 Apart from the commodity trade, the state of the balance depends on the interchange of services and on cash payments. The balance is financed in the main by credit from banks or the importing firms, and only to a lesser extent by the swing.

which by the end of 1976 had amounted to 2,600 million DM. It is not the absolute debit or credit position, however, that is decisive but the current ratio of commodity flows in both directions (the so-called cover ratio) or the ratio of cumulative balance to annual deliveries. In these respects, the situation did not deteriorate in the 1970s up to 1976. During that period West German deliveries were covered to the extent of over 85 per cent by counter-deliveries. To settle the total deficit would require about two thirds of the proceeds of GDR deliveries in 1976.

In contemplating the future, it may be noted that both sides, however different their motives, are interested in a further intensification of economic relations. Nevertheless, there will be strong competition from the remaining Western countries. It is on the cards that GDR trade with the other Western countries will increase faster than intra-German trade. As in the past, economic dealings between the two German economies will to all intents and purposes be confined to trade. At the present stage, other forms of economic collaboration, such as enterprise-to-enterprise co-operation offer little prospect of fresh impulses for the invigoration of bilateral exchanges.

7 The GDR in the Council for Mutual Economic Assistance (CMEA)

7.1 Aims and development of the CMEA

7.1.1 Historical development

The CMEA[1] was founded in January 1949 in Moscow. The founder members were Bulgaria, Czechoslovakia, Poland, Rumania, Soviet Union and Hungary. Albania joined a month later, the GDR was admitted to full membership in September 1950. The foundation was first and foremost politically motivated as a counterblast to the Marshall Plan. Yet, at the time, the participating governments were lacking in the will for collective economic activity. That explains the low level of activity of the Council during the early years of its existence.

In the second half of the 1950s the activities of the CMEA became more lively. The importance of organisational rules for an improved functioning of the community was then recognised. This led at the end of 1959 to the adoption of the first statutes of the CMEA, in which aims, principles, functions and powers of the organisation as well as conditions of membership are defined.

1962 was a crucial year in the history of the CMEA:

1   The proposal for the institution of community economic planning at supra-state level, put forward by Khrushchev (Soviet Party chief at the time), failed to get through, owing to the opposition of Rumania.

2   The Heads of Party and Government of the CMEA countries passed the 'Fundamental principles of the international socialist division of labour', an important programme for the further development of the organisation.

3   A revision of the statutes laid the foundation for the present organisational structure of the community (for which see section 7.1.4 below).

---

1   In the West also known as Comecon.

4 With the admission of Mongolia, the CMEA lost its purely European regional character.

5 Albania, as a political gesture relating to the dispute between the Soviet Union and China, ceased to make use of her membership of the community.

Since the mid-fifties, Yugoslavia and other socialist countries, Cuba from 1963, China up to 1966, occasionally attended Council sessions as observers. There followed in 1964 an agreement conferring a status of 'partial association' on Yugoslavia, which is to participate in certain CMEA activities ('of common interest').

Since 1969 a debate on 'socialist economic integration' has been going on in the CMEA area. In an official CMEA document, the term was used for the first time in 1970. This debate reached a culminating point in July 1971 with the unanimous adoption by all member states of the 'Complex Programme for the Further Deepening and Perfecting of Collaboration and Development of Socialist Economic Integration of the Member Countries of the CMEA'.[1] It envisages a transitional period of fifteen to twenty years, during which the co-ordination of the East European economies is to be strengthened and deepened with the aim of eventual integration.

Since Cuba's accession to full membership in July 1972, the CMEA reaches out into the Western hemisphere, although this geographical extension is likely to be of little economic significance. The most striking feature of recent developments in the CMEA is the emergence of a common approach to third countries. In May 1973 an agreement on co-operation with Finland was concluded, which was followed in 1976 by similar agreements with Iraq and Mexico. Each of these agreements provides for the setting up of a joint commission whose task it is to define the spheres and forms of co-operation more precisely, and to supervise the working of the agreement. Other developing countries — Pakistan, India, Syria, Guyana — have announced their interest in establishing special relations with the CMEA. To meet such cases the CMEA statutes were revised once more in 1974, enabling the community to entertain relations with its member states, with third countries and with international organisations. Since the middle of 1973, the CMEA has sought official contacts with the EEC. In the course of these efforts, the CMEA submitted in February 1976 a draft treaty regulating the basic principles of relations between the two communities. It envisaged co-operation even in the field of trade and credit policies. In November 1976, the EEC presented its counter-proposals, suggesting a 'working

1 Cf. Neues Deutschland, 7 August 1971.

relationship' between the two communities, while matters of trade policy should be left to be settled bilaterally by appropriate agreements between individual CMEA countries on the one hand and individual EEC countries on the other.

7.1.2   Aims of integration

In the CMEA, as in the EEC, international co-operation was started without a theoretical basis. The strategic goal of 'socialist integration' is not defined in the Complex Programme. Integration itself is characterised with considerable vagueness as 'a process of international socialist division of labour fashioned and planned with deliberation' by the communist parties and governments of the member states. In the course of this process a number of separate economic and political aims, such as accelerated economic growth, higher living standards, enhanced defensive potential, expansion and stabilisation of intra-Bloc trade, are to be attained. Yet, relative priorities of these aims in terms of merit and timing are open to interpretation. The principal aim of the community in the coming fifteen or twenty years is the gradual convergence and equalisation of the levels of socio-economic performance of the participating states.

Yet, just which of the economies associated in the CMEA are underdeveloped and hence in a position to claim development aid from their partners is never hinted at, with the sole exception of Mongolia, nor is anything said about who would be rendering such aid, to what extent and in what form. The frequent naming of Mongolia in this context is probably due to three reasons:

1   Mongolia is clearly the least developed member country, the one with the greatest need.

2   It is also, in terms of population, the smallest country, so that the volume of aid need not be excessive, which suits the more affluent economies of the CMEA (that is to say, above all the GDR and Czechoslovak economies).

3   Lastly, in view of the dispute with China, it is in the interest of the Soviet Union to speed up the economic development of the Mongolian People's Republic.

In order to advance economic co-operation within the CMEA at all, it was necessary to formulate the aims of integration in a way acceptable to all members, in spite of their partly diverging interests (cf. section 7.1.5). Accordingly the stated aims of the Complex Programme,

259

which had been adopted unanimously, are formulated in very general terms. The Programme can therefore scarcely serve as a guideline for specific action; instead, measures to apply its principles in practice have to be negotiated afresh as each contingency arises.

7.1.3   Method of integration

In the face of diverging economic interests, agreement within the CMEA could only be reached on methods of integration that did not encroach on the member states' national sovereignty. This condition is met by the *co-ordination of plans*, described in the Complex Programme as the 'principal method for organising collaboration and intensifying the international division of labour'. The member states are to mutually adjust their medium-range and above all their major long-range economic-policy measures, on the one hand in the fields of structural policy and scientific-technological development, and on the other in the field of specialisation and co-operation in industrial production. The independence of the national governments is adequately safeguarded by the rule that only the 'interested' members need participate in arrangements for the co-ordination of activities in any particular sector, so that the mutual policy adjustments may be either bilateral or multilateral.

Plan co-ordination as the chief instrument of a far-reaching harmonisation of national economic policies was introduced in the CMEA as early as 1962. But the absence of economically sound rates of exchange made it impossible for national planning authorities to assess cost and benefits of economic-policy decisions with any accuracy as soon as factors outside their national frontiers were involved. Contrary to the original intention, therefore, plan co-ordination in practice is chiefly confined to trade. It may be noted, however, that according to the most recent practice trade agreements are drafted and mutually adjusted before the national Five-Year Plans are passed into law, so that a certain measure of co-ordination of national economic policies has been established.

The importance of this advance is somewhat diminished by the fact that trade between CMEA countries is on principle organised on a bilateral basis, because, in the words of a Polish economist, 'processes of multilateral co-ordination have not, and cannot have, decisive economic significance while the system of exchanges between the member countries is founded on bilateral accounting'.[1]

1   M. Deniszczuk, 'Planning co-ordination in the range of objectives of the socialist economic integration of the CMEA countries' (in Polish), Gospodarka Planowa, no.1, 1974, p.11.

260

If the provisions of the Complex Programme are followed, planning co-ordination will retain its bilateral character throughout the transition period until 1990, and will thus continue to be confined in the main to trade relations. The introduction of economically sound exchange rates is only envisaged for the 1980s. As things stand now, however, the indications are that this objective laid down in the Complex Programme will not be attained. For the intra-Bloc trade, the most important sphere of co-operation within the CMEA, the same principles that have governed trade policy in the past will continue to be decisive: bilateral exchanges of goods, largely on a strict quota basis; bilaterally negotiated prices; bilateral clearing.

A new form of economic linkage mentioned in the Complex Programme is the joint planning of specific industries or product types. But, by way of unequivocally safeguarding the rights of the individual states, this form of future co-operation was restricted from the outset in a threefold manner:

1 Participation in any joint planning arrangements is to be confined to the 'interested' countries.

2 The autonomous character of 'internal planning' must be preserved.

3 The relevant production plants and resources remain national property.

In approaching joint economic planning, the governments of all CMEA countries have to break fresh ground. From the point of view of the individual country, the benefit of such an experiment for its own economy is as uncertain in these circumstances as is the slice of economic self-determination that may have to be sacrificed in the process. It is this uncertainty that explains the more or less chary attitude of the CMEA countries in this question.

In addition, all CMEA countries accepted the obligation of *mutual consultations* on all basic issues of economic policy. This is the least demanding method of integration; the emphasis here is on mutual information concerning all problems of social-economic development as well as on national economic reform measures and their results.

7.1.4   Organisation and decision making

The main principles of the CMEA, as laid down in the statutes, were re-affirmed by the Complex Programme: 'Socialist economic integration

261

proceeds on an entirely voluntary basis and does not involve the setting up of supra-national authorities . . . '.

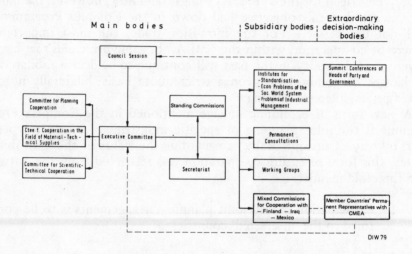

Figure 37   Organisational structure of the CMEA

The current *organisational structure* of the community (shown diagramatically in figure 37) features the following main elements:

Council Session: This is composed of representatives of the member countries delegated by the national governments. It is the supreme authority of the CMEA.

Executive Committee: The deputy heads of government form this Committee, the most important executive organ, which supervises all subordinate organs.

Standing Commissions: There are currently 22 such Commissions, either sectoral (e.g. for the chemical industry) or functional (e.g. for foreign trade). They are composed of representatives of the member countries, each delegation headed by the competent departmental Minister. Their task: development of further co-operation within their sphere.

Committee for Co-operation in the Field of Planning Activity: In this Committee the planning chiefs of the member countries discuss scope and measures of planning co-ordination.

Committee for Scientific-Technical Co-operation: Forum of the heads of the national departments of science and technology for the discussion and harmonisation of measures for the co-ordination of research.

Committee for Co-operation in the Field of Material-Technological Supplies: Composed of the heads of the State Offices for Material-Technological Supplies (in Western terminology: state-managed wholesale trade in producer goods, in particular economically important raw materials).

Secretariat: Permanent office of the CMEA (one General Secretary with a staff of 650), in charge of administrative work for all main and subsidiary departments.

This organisational structure (of which only a rough sketch has been given here) assures the member countries of a maximum of influence at community level. For the most the main bodies of the organisation are entitled to do — and the Secretariat has no right to do even that — is to issue recommendations in matters of economic co-operation. They are automatically declared 'Council recommendations'. The Secretariat which, more than any other CMEA body, would be in a position to pursue community interests cannot make recommendations; in the process of decision making within the CMEA it discharges the function of an initiator.

Even more important for the dominance of national over community interests is the *statutory form of decision making*: all recommendations must be adopted unanimously. The principle of unanimity, the crucial guarantee of the national sovereignty of the member states, is enshrined in the statutes of the CMEA.

To allow any progress at all to be made in fostering co-operation within the East European community against the background of the unanimity rule, an Executive Committee recommendation was approved in 1967, after two years of vehement controversy, which confines the rule to the members 'interested' in any particular issue: a country which declares its 'non-interest' in a specific measure is entitled to opt out (Rumania, for instance, is not a member of Interatom-instrument), but can no longer veto the adoption of a measure recommended with the approval of the interested countries.

The same principle holds for the Inter-State Organisations of the CMEA countries, set up by the member states on the basis of treaties with the force of international law and financed as a rule through contributions by the member states. It also holds for the International Economic Organisations of the CMEA countries (see below), which within their respective spheres of competence are in a position to make decisions with immediate legal effect (as shown in charts 54 and 55).

In the statute of the International Investment Bank, one of the Inter-State Organisations, the unanimity rule is qualified for the first time, though only in a marginal area. Decisions on 'fundamental questions' must still be adopted unanimously, but all other decisions can be passed by a majority vote.

A corresponding provision is found in the statutes of the International Economic Organisations, set up under the terms of the Complex Programme in order to take charge of 'the specific co-ordination of collaboration and project co-operation, and of joint economic activity in the fields of research and development, production, services and foreign trade'. In the meantime seven International Economic Associations have been formed. They are bodies corporate in the respective countries where they are based. Their members are economic organisations of the founder countries, which retain their complete independence in respect of assets and legal status. The Associations operate on a commercial basis, that is to say they are intended to become profitable after a trial period. They are supposed to advance co-operation of the CMEA countries in specific markets, notwithstanding all the difficulties and divergencies of interest. They are not yet, however, 'socialist multinational enterprises' (multinational capital integration). Only Interatominstrument began, five years after its foundation, to extend its activities by setting up its own enterprises on a multinational basis. All other joint enterprises of CMEA countries, the second form of the International Economic Organisations, are based on bilateral agreements; in other words, they constitute a form of foreign investment.

7.1.5 CMEA integration policy in the light of national disparities

In spite of their common party ideology and the basic uniformity of their social and economic orders, the CMEA countries have not yet succeeded in harmonising their conflicting economic interests. The main reason lies in the wide differences of level and structure. The potential of economic performance is very unevenly distributed within the CMEA. The Soviet Union alone produces 65 to 70 per cent of the (estimated) combined national products of the community. That fact sums up the current economic and political pre-eminence of the Soviet Union, and it foreshadows at the same time the inescapable trend of future development: any progress in integration is bound to intensify the dependence of the smaller CMEA countries on the Soviet Union, irrespective of the political will of the Soviet leadership.

Chart 54
Inter-state economic organisations of the CMEA countries
(December 1976)

Organisation	Founded seat	Purpose	Participants[1]
Permanent Conference of Chartering and Shipping Organisations	1952 Moscow	Co-ordination of chartering of sea-going ships; rationalisation of maritime transport	B, Cz, G, H, P, R, S
Permanent Conference of Managing Directors of Danube Navigation Companies	1953	Strengthening co-operation; improving utilisation of cargo space and of traffic-bearing capacity of Danube	State shipping lines of B, Cz, H, S
United Institute for Nuclear Research	1956 Dubna	Research in nuclear physics for peaceful use of nuclear energy	B, Cu, Cz, G, H, M, NK, P, R, S, V
Organisation for Co-operation of Socialist Countries in the Field of Rail Transport	1956 Warsaw	Improvement of railway passenger and goods transport; co-operation with international transport organisations	B, Cu, Cz, G, H, M, NK, P, R, S, V
Organisation for Co-operation of Socialist Countries in the Field of Postal and Tele-communication Services	1957	Improved utilisation of capacities and extension of international communications network	B, Cu, Cz, G, H, M, NK, P, R, S, V
Uniafrika	1960	Organisation of liner services and chartering between Baltic ports and West Africa	State shipping lines of G, P
Kubalko	1962 Gdynia	Co-operation in the field of cargo shipping between Cuba and the Baltic ports	State shipping lines of Cu, Cz, G, P, S
Central Load Co-ordinators' Administration of the Amalgamated 'Peace' Power Grid	1962 Prague	Co-ordination of planning and operation of national power grids with a view to exchanges of electric power	B, Cz, G, H, P, R, S
International Bank for Economic Co-operation	1963 Moscow	Multilateral clearing and arrangement of short-term credits for intra-bloc trade	B, Cu, Cz, G, H, M, P, R, S, V
Freight wagon pool	1963 Prague	More efficient utilisation of freight-carrying capacity and of railway network	B, Cz, G, H, P, R, S
Interpodshipnik	1964 Warsaw	Preparation of measures for improved supplies and more efficient utilisation of capacity in the field or roller bearings	B, Cz, G, H, P, R, S, Y
Intermetall	1964 Budapest	Preparation of measures for improved utilisation as well as expansion of the capacities of the iron and steel industry so as to meet demand more adequately and raise technological and economic level of production	B, Cz, G, H, P, S [R, Y]

Organisation	Founded seat	Purpose	Participants[1]
Agromash	1965	Co-ordination of development, production and marketing of equipment for the mechanisation of fruit and vegetable growing and viticulture	B, G, H, P, S
Intransmash	1965 Budapest Sofia	Research and development, production and distribution of mechanical handling equipment	B, H
Baltafrika	1967	Organisation of liner services and chartering between Baltic ports and East Africa	State shipping agencies of G, P
Baltamerika	1968	Organisation of liner services and chartering between Baltic ports and South America	State shipping agencies of G, P
International Shipping Association	1970 Gdynia	Co-operation in maritime transport; organisation of common services	State shipping agencies of 10 socialist countries
International Investment Bank	1970 Moscow	Financing of long and medium term credits for joint investments	B, Cu, Cz, G, H, M, P, R, S, V, [Y]
Interkhim	1970 Halle	Contributions towards development of specialisation and co-operation in production, and towards the co-ordination of production and supply plans	B, Cz, G, P, R, S, Y
Intercosmos	1970 Moscow	Joint outer space research projects	B, Cu, Cz, G, H, M, P, R, S
Intersputnik	1971	Co-operation in the field of satellite communications	B, Cu, Cz, G, H, M, P, R, S
Intertalonpribor	1972 Moscow	Joint research and development and production of measuring devices	B, Cz, G, H, M, P, R, S
Interelectro	1973 Moscow	Planning co-ordination and joint planning, specialisation and co-operation in production in selected branches of electrical engineering	B, Cz, G, H, P, R, S
Interport	1973 Szczecin	Co-ordination of utilisation of harbour capacities	Sea ports of G, P
Intercomponent	1973 Warsaw	Co-ordination of research and development, production and contracting of licences from third countries in the field of electronic components	Industrial associations of H, P

1   Abbreviations of participants: B, Bulgaria; Cu, Cuba; Cz, Czechoslovakia; G, GDR, H, Hungary; M, Mongolia; NK, North Korea; P, Poland; R, Rumania; S, Soviet Union; V, Vietnam; Y, Yugoslavia.

Square brackets [ ] indicate co-operation on a contractual basis.

Source: Jochen Bethkenhagen and Heinrich Machowski, Integration im Rat fur Gegenseitige Wirtschaftshilfe, Entwicklung, Organisation, Erfolge und Grenzen, 2nd augmented ed., West Berlin 1976, pp 90 ff.

Chart 55

International economic organisations of the CMEA countries

Organisation	Founded seat	Constituent Document Membership[1]	Legal Status Assets	Activities powers	Governing Bodies[2] mode of decision-making
		A. International Economic Associations			
1. Interatominstrument	1972 Warsaw	International agreement between B, Cz, G, H, P, S 15 industrial associations and enterprises; foreign trade enterprises	Body corporate, operating on commercial lines (from 1976). Statutory Fund 2.1 mill. TR, raised by equal contributions from members	Co-operation in research and development, production and marketing in the field of nucleonic equipment Authority to trade with third countries	MB: Council, each member country one vote; EB: Director; SB: Revision Commission Decisions on 'matters of principle' unanimous, otherwise by majority vote
2. Interatomenergo	1973 Moscow	International agreement between B, Cz, G, H, P, R, S, Y. One enterprise from each country	Body corporate, operating on commercial lines. Statutory Fund 8 mill. TR, raised by equal contributions from members.	Co-operation in research and planning for construction of nuclear power stations and organisation of supplies	MB: General Council, each member country one vote; EB: Director-General; SB: Revision Commission Decisions on 'matters of principle' unanimous, otherwise by majority
3. Assofoto	1973 Moscow	International agreement between G, S. One industrial association from each country	Body corporate	Joint planning for the photochemical industry	MB: Council; EB: Bureau of 10 members, five from each country
4. Intertextilmash	1973 Moscow	International agreement between B, Cz, G, H, P, R, S, [Y]. 26 industrial enterprises and design offices	Body corporate, operating on commercial lines (from 1976). Statutory Fund 5 mill. TR, raised by equal contributions; first instalment of 3 mill. TR paid up by 1.3.75	Co-operation in R & D, production and marketing in sections of the textile machine building industry Authority to trade with third countries 'envisaged for the future'	MB: Council, each member country one vote; EB: Director-General; SB: Revision Commission. Decisions on 'matters of principle' unanimous, otherwise by majority decision

Organisation	Founded seat	Constituent Document Membership[1]	Legal Status Assets	Activities powers	Governing Bodies[2] mode of decision-making
5. Mongol-sovtsvetmet	1973 Ulan Bator	International agreement between M, S		Co-ordination of prospecting, extraction and processing of non-ferrous metal ores	
6. Interkhim-volokno	1974 Bucharest	International agreement between B, Cz, G, H, P, R, S, [Y]	Body corporate, operating on commercial lines Amount and mode of payment of Statutory Fund to be determined later; first instalment of 0.5 mill. TR raised by equal contributions from all members	Co-operation in R & D, production and marketing of manmade fibres	MB: Council, each member country one vote; EB: Director General; SB: Revision Commission Decisions on 'matters of principle' unanimous, otherwise by majority vote
7. Domo-khim	1974 Moscow	International agreement between G, S One industrial association from each country	Body corporate	Joint planning in the field of household chemicals Retail outlets in the founder countries	MB: Council (on which the member industries as well as the trade and foreign trade authorities of the two countries are represented); EB: Bureau
		B. Joint enterprises			
1. Haldex	1959 Katowice	International agreement between H, P	Joint stock company; share capital 319 mill. Zl (nominal value of shares 250,000 Zl)	Extraction of coal and building materials from spoil dumps of coal mines	General Meeting; Supervisory Board (6 members from each country); Praesidium (Chairman, Deputy Chairman and two Chief Clerks)
2. Friend-ship	1972 Zawiercie (P)	International agreement between G, P	Body corporate, operating on commercial lines Cost of construction 78.5 mill. TR	Production of cotton yarns	MB: Administrative Council (4 members from each country); EB: Directorate, composed of Director General, three Directors and Chief Accountant

Organisation	Founded seat	Constituent Document Membership[1]	Legal Status Assets	Activities powers	Governing Bodies[2] mode of decision-making
3. Erdenet	1973 Erdenet (M)	International agreement between M, S	Body corporate, operating on commercial lines	Mining and dressing of copper and mlybdenum ores	MB: Council, parity of membership; EB: Director General; SB: Revision Commission
4. Servicing Enterprise	1976 Zielona Gora (P)	Branch enterprise of Interatom-instrument	Body corporate, operating on commercial lines	Technical servicing of nucleonic equipment imported by Poland	

1 Abbreviations as in chart 54.
2 MB, Managing Body; EB, Executive Body; SB, Supervisory Body.

Source: Heinrich Machowski, 'Internationale Wirtschaftsorganisationen der RGW-Lander; Stand, Probleme und Perspektiven', Vierteljahrsheft des DIW, no.2, 1977.

In terms of absolute size of the national product the GDR ranks third in the CMEA behind the Soviet Union and Poland. In terms of production per capita of the population, or per economically active person, the GDR is at the head of the table with a production record about 50 per cent above the community average, a lead that is comparable to the gap in living standards (cf. section 5.3.5). The Soviet Union, despite its position of leadership, is one of the less developed economies in the community. Within the CMEA, there are vast differentials in respect of nearly all economic indicators: productivity and standard of living, economic structure and relative weight of foreign trade (as shown in table 74). These differentials give rise to strongly divergent national growth targets. The situation is further complicated by different habits of consumption and production and different psychological attitudes to economic problems. Such are the circumstances a policy of integration has to contend with, and not only in Eastern Europe, as has been demonstrated within the EEC by endeavours to promote an Economic and Monetary Union.

One important structure problem of the CMEA is the wide variation in the degree of foreign trade involvement of the individual member countries. The smaller countries, whose dependence on foreign trade is relatively high, have external involvement ratios (i.e. export volume as a proportion of national product) ranging from 45 per cent for Hungary to 28 per cent for Poland. These countries clearly must take foreign economic relations into consideration in working out their economic policies. In contrast, with its external involvement ratio of only about 8 per cent, the Soviet Union, like the USA, can afford to embark on economic policy measures without regard for external repercussions.

The structural differences between the CMEA countries and the conflicts of interest entailed by them are long-term problems. The gradual elimination of structural features that stand in the way of integration, in other words the 'gradual convergence and equalisation of the levels of socio-economic performance of the participating states', envisaged as a 'principal aim' of the community, can be attained only by assuring differential growth rates.

Yet, it appears from the Five-Year Plans of the CMEA countries for 1976-80, that, provided the plan targets are reached, the income differentials separating the GDR from Hungary, Czechoslovakia, and above all from the Soviet Union will be wider in 1980 than they were in 1976. Poland and Bulgaria, on the other hand, may succeed in narrowing the gap. (As for Rumania, the situation in the aftermath of the disastrous earthquake of 1977 is too uncertain to allow a forecast).

Under such conditions, the goal of gradually ironing out differentials in productivity and income is unlikely to be attainable, and thus a major obstacle to closer links between the economies of the CMEA countries will continue to hamper progress during the current planning period.

Chart 56
Growth of national product per inhabitant of CMEA countries
(average annual growth rate in per cent)

	1961/65	1966/70	1971/75	1976/80 (Plan)
Bulgaria	5.9	8.0	7.3	7.0
Czechoslovakia	1.1	6.8	4.9	4.4
GDR	3.7	5.1	5.7	5.4
Hungary	3.7	6.5	5.7	5.1
Poland	4.8	5.4	8.7	6.0
Rumania	8.3	6.5	10.3	9.9
USSR	4.8	6.8	4.7	3.9

7.2   The GDR as economic partner of the CMEA countries

7.2.1   Trade

Within the East European economic community the GDR is the country with the most highly developed level of economic performance. It is thus the one partner to whom the others must be looking for assistance in stimulating technological progress. The relatively high capacity of the GDR economy is reflected in its strong participation in intra-Bloc trade. In 1975 its share in the total internal trade volume of the community was 15 per cent, ranking second after the Soviet Union, with 36 per cent. In 1960, the GDR share was even higher, 18 per cent. As an *exporter*, the GDR is represented on the CMEA market chiefly by industrial goods, above all machinery and equipment, chemical products and industrial consumer goods. Over the years, however, it lost its absolute supremacy as a supplier of engineering products. In 1975, its share in the total volume of intra-Bloc machinery exports was still a respectable 20 per cent, running a close second to the Soviet Union, but this must be compared to its 36 per cent share in 1960.

One reason for this relative decline is the growing industrial capacity, and hence export potential, of some of the less developed countries, in particular the Soviet Union, Poland and Bulgaria.

The significance of the GDR as a supplier of capital goods is demonstrated by the following figures relating to 1975: in that year the GDR supplied 11 per cent of all Soviet imports, but no less than 22 per cent of its imports of machinery and equipment. As regards individual subsectors, the following percentages of Soviet and Czechoslovak imports came from the GDR:

	Soviet Union	Czechoslovakia
Agricultural machinery	42	34
Office machines	*	43
Rail vehicles	30	50
Metal-working machines	30	23

*No data available.

The GDR chemical industry also holds a strong competitive position. Next to the Soviet Union, it is the biggest exporter of potash fertilisers, which are so important in the drive for higher agricultural productivity in the CMEA countries. In 1975, Czechoslovakia took a full 75 per cent of its imports of potash fertilisers from the GDR, Hungary 35 per cent, Poland 38 per cent.

While importing chiefly engineering products from the GDR, the other CMEA countries, with the exception of Czechoslovakia, deliver in return mainly raw materials and semifinished articles. Thus the GDR is largely dependent on Western sources for its technology imports. It is not surprising, then, that over the fifteen-year period from 1960 to 1975 the Western industrial countries were able to increase their exports to the GDR more rapidly than were the GDR's partners in the CMEA.

7.2.2   Specialisation and project co-operation

The CMEA countries are confronted with the problem of selecting the export markets in which to force expansion. In the years ahead this problem will become yet more acute: on the one hand, they can get from the West know-how and high-grade consumer goods. On the other hand, the difficulty of financing such desirable imports through exports of their own is even greater in dealing with Western countries than with the GDR.

An intensification of trade between the GDR and its partners in the CMEA presupposes a steady increase in the exports of those countries. Agreements on industrial co-operation and specialisation can provide a positive impulse for such a development. The agreements so far concluded within the CMEA refer mostly to specialisation, while manufacturing co-operation (division of labour in the manufacture of components) exists only on a very minor scale, although some agreements in this field have been concluded. The object of specialisation agreements is to achieve long production runs and thus low unit costs. It has been calculated that a 50 per cent increase in the level of specialisation in the engineering industry would allow labour productivity to be raised by at least 20 per cent.[1] The large majority of specialisation agreements is concerned with the manufacture of types of plant and machines. Up to 1976, 5,000 such agreements were concluded. It appears, however, that most of them were not new departures, but merely reaffirmations in formal terms of traditional practices. Otherwise it is hardly possible to account for the brisk increase in the volume of 'specialised' products as a proportion of total GDR exports to CMEA countries from 1 per cent in 1970 to 17 per cent in 1974. By 1980 it is envisaged that 50 per cent of GDR intra-Bloc exports of products of the machine-tool and engineering industries should be covered by specialisation agreements. The major part of these agreements concerns deliveries to the Soviet Union. In this trade, the share of products covered by specialisation agreements in the total volume of GDR export to the Soviet Union is scheduled to rise from 27 per cent in 1975 to 35 per cent in 1980.

The industry of the GDR concentrates its efforts on the traditional export production: instruments manufactured by the precision engineering/optical industry, electronic equipment, plant for chemical, cement and metal-processing factories, lifting and conveying gear, as well as ships, rail vehicles and agricultural machinery.

One instance of specialisation is the joint development and co-ordinated manufacture of the 'unified system of electronic calculating technology' (*einheitliches System elektronischer Rechentechnik*, ESER), a project in which all European CMEA countries, with the exception of Rumania, are participating. Examples of specialisation linked with co-production are the manufacture of the KS6 sugar beet combine, carried out jointly by the Soviet Union, the GDR and Bulgaria, or the manufacture of truck-mounted cranes in the GDR, with special axles and cylinders supplied by Hungary and clutches and gearboxes made in Czechoslovakia. Examples of the utilisation of the benefits of long production runs are provided by the division of labour in the manufacture of rail vehicles and buses, with the GDR specialising in passenger coaches and refrigerator wagons, while Hungary's Ikarus buses can be found in all CMEA countries. The two countries thereby became export leaders in their respective fields.

Especially in the plant and machinery sector, the GDR still has a wide range of export goods to offer. This indicates that the possibilities of further productivity gains through international specialisation are by no means exhausted. Two circumstances impede the intensification of

---

1 According to Wolfgang Jahn, Hans-Jurgen Lemm, Werner Probbig, Sozialistische Integration zum Wohle unserer Volker, East Berlin 1974, p.37.

industrial co-operation in the CMEA:

1 Since the currencies of the CMEA countries are of a purely domestic nature, and in the absence of rates of exchange of any relevance for foreign trade transactions, both costs and benefits of co-operation agreements are difficult to measure.

2 The interests of the various countries diverge. The Soviet Union, with its vast home market, is in a position to embark on mass production and long production runs in many branches. Moreover, the less developed CMEA countries, and Rumania in particular, are keen on building up a broadly based industry and prefer to leave specialisation to a later stage.

A further factor which tended to retard specialisation was the inadequate response to Council recommendations for standardisation. In the meantime, the CMEA countries, with the exception of Rumania, have agreed that endorsement of a Council recommendation on standards shall imply an undertaking to accept such standards as binding. But the number of agreed CMEA standards is still small.

7.2.3   Co-operation in other spheres

The GDR is increasingly involved in the opening up of basic resources in other CMEA countries, above all in the Soviet Union. At their 29th Council session in 1975, the member countries passed a *'dovetailed plan of multilateral integration measures'*, providing for GDR participation in the following construction projects: Ust-Ilimsk cellulose combine, Kiyembay asbestos combine, Kursk metallurgical works, natural gas pipeline Orenburg-Soviet Western frontier (length 2,750 Km), 750 kV power transmission line from the Soviet Union to Hungary, and a nickel smelter in Cuba. On these projects, the GDR is to incur an expenditure totalling 8,000 million Marks during the current Five-Year Plan. The GDR is thus shouldering at least one third of the total investment expenditure of the CMEA countries (without the Soviet Union).

Payment for the deliveries and interest on the credits granted (generally at a rate of interest of 2 per cent) is to come out of the production of the new enterprises. This may not represent the highest conceivable stage of international co-operation between industrial countries, but it can be regarded as a first step in that direction.

At the 30th Council Session in July 1976, the CMEA countries launched another attempt to intensify their co-operation with a decision on the drawing up of long-term target programmes. The decision envisages the preparation of long-term demand forecasts for selected sectors (power and raw materials, engineering, staple foods, industrial consumer goods and transport), to be followed by the working out of joint measures to satisfy the estimated demand.

In view of the unresolved currency problems of the CMEA, community projects will have to be executed in the foreseeable future on a barter basis, for in the absence of a supra-national capital market, the socialist planned economies can finance their supra-national investment projects only through the direct provision of goods and services. The *International Investment Bank*, founded in 1970, can discharge the functions of a capital market only to a limited degree. The basic capital of 1,070 million Transfer-Roubles (TR) to be raised by the member countries, 30 per cent of the contributions to be paid in convertible currency or gold, is to be used for the Bank's credit operations. By the beginning of 1976, a little over one third of the statutory basic capital, 370 million TR, was paid up. In addition the Bank contracted credits on the Euro-dollar market, which at the end of 1976 totalled 1,000 million dollars. The GDR's share in the basic capital of the Bank is 16.5 per cent (176 million TR). Up to the end of 1975 40 projects were supported by the Bank with credits totalling 577 million TR. Only two GDR projects of any significance benefited from credits to a total of 25 million TR. The GDR is thus a net creditor. The biggest community project so far supported by the Bank is the natural gas pipeline from Orenburg to the Soviet western frontier. Since 1976, the support programme has been concentrated on the fuel and power sector, which absorbs about 80 per cent of the credits granted by the Investment Bank.

Liberalisation of the *labour market* is not one of the aims of the CMEA. Trans-national movements of manpower are accordingly minimal in quantitative terms. The number of foreign workers currently employed in the GDR (most of them from Poland and Hungary) may be estimated at about 50,000. About 10,000 Hungarians are working in the GDR under an agreement, concluded in 1967 and extended in 1973 until 1980, 'on the temporary engagement of young Hungarian workers in socialist enterprises of the GDR in order to give them practical experience in their trades'. It is not likely that this number will be increased, since Hungary has manpower problems of her own and finds it difficult to provide the number of workers foreseen in the agreement. The largest contingent of foreign workers appears to be contributed by Poland. Apart from the regular 'frontier crossers' of the border regions, a substantial proportion of Polish workers active in the GDR have been sent there by their firms. In spite of its tight manpower situation, the GDR, according to official statements, has no intention of recruiting labour on a major scale in other CMEA countries. Instead, it is GDR policy to create employment opportunities where manpower reserves exist.

This objective could be attained by direct investment abroad, that is to say, by the transfer of capital through the founding of new enterprises. Within the EEC, this possibility is assured by the right of companies to establish foreign branches. In the CMEA region, such arrangements must be agreed by the central authorities of the countries concerned, to assure the inclusion of such enterprises in the economic plan. According to the Complex Programme, interested countries may 'set up joint enterprises which shall have assets of their own; shall be treated as bodies corporate under civil law; shall operate on a commercial basis; and shall be fully liable with their assets for any obligations entered into'.

Poland and the GDR made use of this provision when, in 1972, they jointly decided to set up a cotton spinning mill at Zawierce, near Katowice. The works came on stream in mid-1975, with a labour force of about 2,000 and an annual output of 12,500 tonnes of yarns spun from Soviet cotton. The enterprise is jointly managed and utilised by Poland and the GDR. Shares in capital and profits are apportioned between the two countries according to the contribution made by each to the performance of the enterprise. Supreme authority in the running of the enterprise is vested in the Board of Management, composed of four representatives of each country. Decisions must be unanimous.

This form of organisation may be regarded as a suitable instrument for overcoming the disproportions manifest in the demand for labour and capital within the community, while safeguarding the decision-making role of each participating country. It is doubtful, however, whether this model has come up to expectations, and thus can serve as an example for the establishment of similar enterprises. Plans for the setting up of further joint enterprises by Poland and the GDR have been under discussion, but steps to implement them are slow in coming.

Appendix

Table 1
Development of the residential population of the GDR by selected age groups[1]

Year	Children under 15	Persons of working age			Persons of pension-able age[2]	Sum total	of which female
		Men aged 15 to 64	Women aged 15 to 59	Total			
			'000				
1939[3]	3,275	5,721	5,588	11,310	1,860	16,745	8,555
1946	4,535	4,736	6,816	11,552	2,401	18,488	10,629
1950	4,202	5,185	6,461	11,646	2,540	18,388	10,227
1955	3,718	5,153	6,116	11,269	2,845	17,832	9,863
1960	3,678	4,931	5,552	10,483	3,028	17,188	9,443
1965	4,067	4,734	5,074	9,808	3,165	17,040	9,260
1970	3,970	4,815	4,958	9,773	3,325	17,068	9,203
1971	3,939	4,835	4,946	9,781	3,334	17,054	9,181
1972	3,879	4,856	4,929	9,785	3,347	17,011	9,145
1973	3,798	4,885	4,916	9,801	3,352	16,951	9,100
1974	3,696	4,922	4,921	9,843	3,352	16,891	9,056
1975	3,591	4,970	4,958	9,928	3,303	16,820	9,003
1976	3,542	4,995	4,989	9,984	3,260	16,786	8,978
			Prospective development[4]				
1980	3,125	5,248	5,196	10,444	2,898	16,468	8,735
1985	2,921	5,521	5,202	10,723	2,580	16,224	8,512
1990	2,914	5,580	5,105	10,685	2,402	16,002	8,301
			Per cent of total population				
1939	21.4	34.2	33.4	67.5	11.1	100	51.1
1946	24.5	25.6	36.9	62.5	13.0	100	57.5
1950	22.9	28.2	35.1	63.3	13.8	100	55.6
1955	20.8	28.9	34.3	63.2	16.0	100	55.3
1960	21.4	28.7	32.3	61.0	17.6	100	54.9
1965	23.8	27.8	29.8	57.6	18.6	100	54.3
1970	23.3	28.2	29.0	57.3	19.5	100	53.9
1971	23.1	28.4	29.0	57.4	19.5	100	53.8
1972	22.8	28.5	29.0	57.5	19.7	100	53.8
1973	22.4	28.8	29.0	57.8	19.8	100	53.7
1974	21.9	29.1	29.1	58.3	19.8	100	53.6
1975	21.3	29.5	29.5	59.0	19.6	100	53.5
1976	21.1	29.8	29.7	59.5	19.4	100	53.5
			Prospective development				
1980	19.0	31.9	31.6	63.4	17.6	100	53.0
1985	18.0	34.0	32.1	66.1	15.9	100	52.5
1990	18.2	34.9	31.9	66.8	15.0	100	51.9

1 The 1939, 1946 and 1950 figures refer to the respective census dates, those of 1976 to the state at the end of June, the remainder to the year end.
2 Men over 65, women over 60.
3 In the territory of today's GDR.
4 Including migrations across national frontiers.

Sources: GDR Statistical Yearbooks, Statistisches Taschenbuch der DDR 1977, Wochenbericht des DIW, no.23/1976.

Table 2

The population of the GDR and FRG and its prospective development by age group and sex[1]

GDR

Age groups	'000 persons			%		
	male	female	total	male	female	total
1960						
under 15	1,883	1,794	3,677	24.3	19.0	21.4
15-60	4,461	5,552	10,013	57.6	58.8	58.3
60-65	469	659	1,128	6.1	7.0	6.6
over 65	932	1,438	2,370	12.0	15.2	13.8
Sum total	7,745	9,443	17,188	100	100	100
1970						
under 15	2,033	1,934	3,967	25.9	21.0	23.3
15-60	4,367	4,953	9,320	55.6	53.8	54.6
60-65	438	665	1,103	5.6	7.2	6.5
over 65	1,019	1,648	2,667	13.0	18.0	15.6
Sum total	7,858	9,199	17,057	100	100	100
Prospective development 1980[2]						
under 15	1,600	1,525	3,125	20.7	17.5	19.0
15-60	5,037	5,196	10,233	65.1	59.5	62.1
60-65	211	366	577	2.7	4.2	3.5
over 65	884	1,648	2,532	11.4	18.9	15.4
Sum total	7,733	8,735	16,468	100	100	100
1990[2]						
under 15	1,492	1,422	2,914	19.4	17.1	18.2
15-60	5,200	5,106	10,306	67.5	61.5	64.4
60-65	380	466	846	4.9	5.6	5.3
over 65	629	1,307	1,936	8.2	15.7	12.1
Sum total	7,701	8,301	16,002	100	100	100

FRG

Age groups	'000 persons			%		
	male	female	total	male	female	total
1960						
under 15	6,042	5,746	11,788	23.8	20.2	22.0
15-60	15,749	17,549	33,288	62.0	61.9	61.9
60-65	1,289	1,669	2,958	5.1	5.9	5.5
over 65	2,314	3,398	5,712	9.1	12.0	10.6
Sum total	25,394	28,362	53,756	100	100	100
1970						
under 15	7,230	6,873	14,103	24.9	21.5	23.1
15-60	17,163	17,931	35,094	59.0	56.2	57.5
60-65	1,545	2,140	3,685	5.3	6.7	6.1
over 65	3,134	4,985	8,119	10.8	15.6	13.3
Sum total	29,072	31,929	61,001	100	100	100
Prospective development 1980[2]						
under 15	5,500	5,229	10,729	18.9	16.8	17.8
15-60	19,397	18,760	38,157	66.5	60.1	63.2
60-65	973	1,450	2,423	3.3	4.6	4.0
over 65	3,296	5,768	9,064	11.3	18.5	15.0
Sum total	29,165	31,207	60,372	100	100	100
1990[2]						
under 15	4,865	4,631	9,496	17.1	15.5	16.3
15-60	19,031	18,101	37,132	67.0	60.7	63.8
60-65	1,643	1,755	3,398	5.8	5.9	5.8
over 65	2,851	5,338	8,189	10.0	17.9	14.1
Sum total	28,390	29,825	58,215	100	100	100

1 State at year end, except 1980 and 1990 figures for FRG, which refer to mid-year. 2 Including migrations across frontiers.

Sources: GDR and FRG Statistical Yearbooks; Federal Office of Statistics (ed.), Fachserie A. Bevölkerung und Kultur, Reihe 1, Gebiet und Bevölkerung, II. Alter und Familienstand der Bevölkerung 1970; Wochenberichte des DIW, nos 23 and 46/1976; DIW calculations.

Table 3
Demographic development in the GDR and FRG: selected data for 1976[1]

		GDR	FRG
Birth rate	Live births per 1,000 inhabitants	11.6	9.8
Death rate	Deaths per 1,000 inhabitants	14.0	11.9
Excess of births	per 1,000 inhabitants	−2.3	−2.1
Fertility rate	Live births per 1,000 women aged 15 to 45	55.6	47.5[2]
Decline of birth rate by comparison with 1965	per cent	−30.4	−42.3
Infant mortality	Deaths during first year of life per 1,000 live births	14.1	17.4
Marriage rate	per 1,000 inhabitants	8.6	5.9
Divorce rate	per 1,000 inhabitants	2.7	1.6[3]
Expectation of life[4]	years: male	68.8	68.6
	female	73.8	74.8

1 Provisional figures
2 1975
3 1974
4 For children after the first year of life; FRG: 1972/74, GDR: 1971/72

Sources: GDR Statistical Yearbooks, Statistisches Taschenbuch der DDR 1977; FRG Statistical Yearbooks; Federal Office of Statistics, Fachserie I, Reihe 1.3. (**Bevölkerung nach Alter und Familienstand** 1977); Wirtschaft und Statistik, no.5/1977.

Table 4
Demographic development in the GDR: selected data

Year	Mean population ('000)	Change in per cent	Percentage share of persons of working age[3]	Females per 100 males	Live births	Deaths	Excess of births (+) or deaths (−)	Fertility rate	Infant mortality rate
						'000			
1939[1]	16,745	−	67.5	104	18.7	12.6	+ 6.1		
1946	18,057	+ 7.8	62.5	135	10.4	22.9	− 12.4	40.2	31.4
1950	18,388	+ 1.8	63.3	125	16.5	11.9	+ 4.6	71.3	72.2
1955	17,944	− 2.4	63.2	124	16.3	11.9	+ 4.4	77.0	48.9
1960	17,241	− 3.9	61.0	122	17.0	13.6	+ 3.4	85.3	38.8
1965	17,020	− 1.3	57.6	119	16.5	13.5	+ 3.0	85.2	24.8
1970	17,058	+ 0.2	57.3	117	13.9	14.1	− 0.2	70.8	18.5
1971	17,061	+ 0.02	57.4	117	13.8	13.8	± 0	69.7	18.0
1972	17,043	− 0.11	57.5	116	11.8	13.8	− 2.0	58.8	17.6
1973	16,980	− 0.37	57.8	116	10.6	13.7	− 3.0	52.7	15.6
1974	16,925	− 0.32	58.3	116	10.6	13.5	− 3.0	52.0	15.9
1975[2]	16,850	− 0.44	59.0	115	10.8	14.3	− 3.5	52.4	15.9
1976[2]	16,786	− 0.38	59.5	115	11.6	14.0	− 2.3	55.6	14.1

1 In the territory of today's GDR.
2 Provisional figures.
3 Males aged 15 to 64, females aged 15 to 59.

Sources: GDR Statistical Yearbooks; Statistisches Taschenbuch der DDR 1977; DIW calculations

Table 5
GDR settlement structure (state at year end)

Year Area	Residential population '000	per sq.km	Population distribution by size of communes or municipalities (per cent of total population) under 500 inhabitants	500 to 2,000	2,000 to 10,000	10,000 to 20,000	20,000 to 50,000	over 50,000	Size distribution of communes and municipalities (per cent of total) under 500 inhabitants	500 to 2,000	2,000 to 10,000	10,000 to 20,000	20,000 to 50,000	over 50,000
1939	16,745	155	11.3	16.5	20.7	8.1	11.3	32.1	66.4	24.4	7.2	0.8	0.5	0.2
1946	18,488	170	10.1	22.2	23.2	8.4	11.5	24.6	53.1	36.5	8.7	0.9	0.6	0.2
1950	18,360	171	6.9	22.1	22.9	9.0	13.6	25.5	42.0	44.9	10.9	1.2	0.8	0.2
1960	17,188	159	7.8	20.2	21.8	9.7	13.9	26.6	47.2	40.4	10.1	1.3	0.8	0.2
1965	17,040	158	7.9	19.0	20.9	9.1	15.2	28.0	49.0	38.8	9.9	1.2	0.9	0.3
1970	17,068	158	7.4	18.8	20.2	9.5	15.3	28.8	48.3	39.3	9.8	1.3	0.9	0.3
1975	16,820	155	5.9	18.6	20.1	8.8	15.4	31.0	42.3	43.6	11.3	1.4	1.1	0.4
1976[1]	16,786	155	6.0	18.5	20.0	8.8	15.2	31.5	42.6	43.3	11.2	1.4	1.1	0.4
by Area 1975														
Berlin	1,098	2,725	–	–	–	–	–	100.0	–	–	–	–	–	100.0
Cottbus	873	106	12.0	17.0	23.5	4.3	24.4	18.8	61.5	28.5	7.9	0.5	1.3	0.3
Dresden	1,836	272	3.1	17.4	20.5	7.2	19.5	32.3	26.7	53.4	16.6	1.5	1.5	0.3
Erfurt	1,242	169	7.2	26.2	16.5	4.5	19.4	26.2	42.6	47.3	8.1	0.6	1.0	0.4
Frankfurt	689	96	10.7	17.0	24.3	9.2	28.3	10.5	58.2	29.9	9.4	1.1	1.1	0.2
Gera	738	184	12.9	14.0	17.9	12.1	13.9	29.2	69.6	21.7	6.5	1.3	0.5	0.4
Halle	1,876	214	2.9	21.9	21.6	4.4	21.6	27.6	23.3	58.4	14.9	0.9	1.7	0.7
Karl-Marx-Stadt	1,977	329	2.3	16.0	28.1	13.4	12.0	28.2	24.5	47.8	22.5	3.1	1.5	0.6
Leipzig	1,446	291	2.9	15.6	19.0	8.6	11.1	42.8	25.3	56.4	14.1	2.1	1.6	0.5
Magdeburg	1,290	112	6.2	22.8	19.5	11.1	18.9	21.5	37.4	49.0	10.9	1.4	1.1	0.2
Neubrandenburg	626	58	12.5	28.2	19.6	17.8	11.6	10.2	46.9	45.4	5.3	1.6	0.6	0.2
Potsdam	1,121	89	12.1	17.1	24.7	12.8	14.3	19.0	59.8	28.9	8.8	1.4	0.8	0.3
Rostock	869	123	4.7	21.5	15.1	12.9	–	45.8	31.2	54.9	10.6	2.2	–	1.1
Schwerin	590	68	10.0	27.3	18.4	10.5	15.7	18.2	42.6	49.0	6.1	1.3	0.8	1.1
Suhl	549	142	7.7	29.0	31.4	10.9	21.0	18.2	38.4	45.3	14.1	1.1	1.1	0.2

1 State at end of June.

Sources: GDR Statistical Yearbooks, Statistisches Taschenbuch der DDR 1977

Table 6
Economically active persons[1] in the GDR by sector

Economic sector	1960	1965	1970	1971	1972	1973	1974	1975[2]
	Annual average ('000)							
Industry[3]	3,580	3,510	3,595	3,630	3,695	3,685	3,705	3,710
Construction	515	535	660	665	655	640	645	660
Agriculture[4]	1,445	1,230	1,060	1,025	975	965	965	950
Transport, posts, telecommunications	570	575	605	610	615	615	625	625
Trade	920	900	885	865	880	865	875	885
Service sectors[5]	1,530	1,735	1,915	1,970	2,000	2,055	2,095	2,125
All sectors	8,560	8,485	8,720	8,765	8,820	8,825	8,910	8,955
	Percentage shares							
Industry[3]	41.8	41.4	41.2	41.4	41.9	41.7	41.6	41.4
Construction	6.0	6.3	7.6	7.6	7.4	7.3	7.3	7.3
Agriculture[4]	16.9	14.5	12.2	11.7	11.0	10.9	10.8	10.6
Transport, posts, telecommunications	6.7	6.8	6.9	6.9	7.0	7.0	7.0	7.0
Trade	10.7	10.6	10.1	9.9	10.0	9.8	9.8	9.9
Service sectors[5]	17.9	20.4	22.0	22.5	22.7	23.3	23.5	23.7
All sectors	100.0	100.0	100.0	100.0	100.0	100.0	100.0	100.0

1 Including apprentices and economically active persons omitted from official statistics.
2 Provisional figures.
3 Including manufacturing artisan trades, and persons engaged in industry, but omitted from official statistics (e.g. uranium mining).
4 Including forestry and fisheries, as well as family members working on private plots of members of agricultural producer co-operatives.
5 Economic services, banking, insurance, other producing sectors and State (including soldiers and members of other military organisations).

Sources: GDR Statistical Yearbooks; Central State Administration for Statistics, Ergebnisse der Volks- und Berufszählung am 31. Dezember 1964, East Berlin 1967; DIW calculations and estimates.

Table 7
Female economically active population[1] in the GDR by sector

Economic sector	1960	1965	1970	1971	1972	1973	1974	1975[2]
	Annual average ('000)							
Industry[3]	1,360	1,380	1,495	1,515	1,520	1,535	1,555	1,560
Construction	45	50	80	85	90	90	90	95
Agriculture[4]	680	570	460	440	420	405	395	390
Transport, posts, telecommunications	185	200	215	220	225	230	235	235
Trade	595	605	615	605	605	615	625	630
Service sectors[5]	855	1,015	1,165	1,200	1,240	1,270	1,300	1,320
All sectors	3,720	3,820	4,030	4,065	4,100	4,145	4,200	4,230
	Percentage share of total economically active population							
Industry[3]	38.0	39.3	41.6	41.7	41.1	41.7	42.0	42.0
Construction	8.7	9.3	12.1	12.8	13.7	14.0	14.0	14.4
Agriculture[4]	47.1	46.3	43.4	42.9	43.1	42.0	40.9	41.1
Transport, posts, telecommunications	32.5	34.8	35.5	36.1	36.6	37.4	37.6	37.6
Trade	64.7	67.2	69.5	69.9	68.8	71.2	71.4	71.2
Service sectors[5]	55.9	58.5	60.8	60.9	62.0	61.8	62.1	62.1
All sectors	43.4	45.0	46.2	46.4	46.5	47.0	47.1	47.2

1   Including apprentices and economically active persons omitted from official statistics.
2   Provisional figures.
3   Including manufacturing artisan trades, and persons engaged in industry, but omitted from official statistics (e.g. uranium mining).
4   Including forestry and fisheries, as well as family members working on private plots of members of agricultural producer co-operatives.
5   Economic services, banking, insurance, other producing sectors and State (including soldiers and members of other military organisations).

Sources: GDR Statistical Yearbooks; Central State Administration for Statistics, Ergebnisse der Volks- und Berufszählung am 31. Dezember 1964, East Berlin 1967; DIW calculations and estimates.

Table 8
Economically active population[1] of the GDR by socio-economic group

Economically active persons	1960	1965	1970	1975[2]	1960	1965	1970	1975[2]
	Annual average ('000)				Percentage share			
Employees (wage and salary earners)	6,610	6,680	7,000	7,535	77.2	78.7	80.3	84.1
Industry[3]	3,140	3,060	3,130	3,340	36.7	36.1	35.9	37.3
Construction	395	385	460	530	4.6	4.5	5.3	5.9
Agriculture[4]	325	265	255	270	3.8	3.1	2.9	3.0
Transport, posts, telecommunications	530	545	565	580	6.2	6.4	6.5	6.5
Trade	785	790	790	795	9.2	9.3	9.1	8.9
Service sectors[5]	1,435	1,635	1,800	1,020	16.8	19.3	20.6	22.5
Apprentices	335	365	430	430	3.9	4.3	4.9	4.8
All employees (actually working)	6,945	7,045	7,430	7,965	81.1	83.0	85.2	88.9
Members of co-operatives	845	1,070	1,010	790	9.9	12.6	11.6	8.8
Agricultural producer co-operatives (LPGs)[6]	710	875	760	645	8.3	10.3	8.7	7.2
Artisan producer co-operatives	135	195	250	145	1.6	2.3	2.9	1.6
Self-employed	440	260	210	150	5.1	3.1	2.4	1.7
Family workers[7]	330	110	70	50	3.8	1.3	0.8	0.6
Economically active population	8,560	8,485	8,720	8,955	100.0	100.0	100.0	100.0

1   Including apprentices and economically active persons omitted from official statistics.
2   Provisional figures.
3   Including manufacturing artisan trades, and persons engaged in industry, but omitted from official statistics (e.g. uranium mining).
4   Including forestry and fisheries, as well as family members working on private plots of members of agricultural producer co-operatives.
5   Economic services, banking, insurance, other producing sectors and State (including soldiers and members of other military organisations).
6   Including members of horticultural and fishery producer co-operatives.
7   Including those working on private plots of LPG members.

Sources: GDR Statistical Yearbooks; Central State Administration for Statistics, Ergebnisse der Volks- und Berufszählung am 31. Dezember 1964, East Berlin 1967; DIW calculations and estimates.

285

Table 9
Capital assets[1] in the GDR economy by sector
(Bn. M at 1962 prices)

Sector	1960	1965	1970	1971	1972	1973	1974	1975	1975 (1960= 100)
Producing sector without infra-structure	162.0	217.5	276.0	292.5	308.5	326.6	345.7	366.7	226
of which buildings	*	*	136.6	145.5	153.0	158.4	165.5	175.7	*
including: Processing trades[2]	96.3	132.4	170.1	180.5	191.2	203.3	216.6	231.1	240
of which buildings	*	*	78.6	84.1	88.7	90.7	95.1	101.6	*
Construction	2.8	4.6	7.5	8.0	8.6	9.2	9.8	10.6	379
of which buildings	*	*	2.4	2.6	2.8	3.7	3.9	4.2	*
Agriculture[3]	20.5	28.4	37.5	39.6	41.5	43.9	45.7	47.9	234
of which buildings	*	*	25.8	27.6	28.8	30.4	31.6	33.0	*
Transport[4]	33.1	40.1	45.5	47.6	49.3	51.1	53.5	56.0	169
of which buildings	*	*	20.6	21.3	22.0	22.3	22.9	24.2	*
Trade[5]	8.7	11.2	14.1	15.1	16.0	16.9	17.7	18.6	214
of which buildings	*	*	8.6	9.1	9.8	10.3	10.9	11.5	*
Remaining producing branches[6]	0.6	0.8	1.3	1.7	1.9	2.2	2.4	2.5	417
of which buildings	*	*	0.6	0.8	0.9	1.0	1.1	1.2	*
Other capital assets	162.9	175.0	190.7	194.3	197.8	201.5	205.7	210.2	129
Total	324.9	392.5	466.7	486.8	506.3	528.1	551.4	576.9	178

1 Including equipment under the value of 500 M in new plants to complete them for the first run.
2 Industry, including mining, power and manufacturing artisan enterprises but without building trades.
3 Including forestry.
4 Including posts and telecommunications, without roads and waterways.
5 Including catering, without foreign trade.
6 Leading economic bodies and institutes of all producing branches, project-planning and computing enterprises, publishing houses, repair combines and dry cleaning.

Sources: GDR Statistical Yearbooks, Statistisches Taschenbuch der DDR 1977; building assets calculated by DIW for entire GDR economy by extrapolating official figures for centrally managed publicly owned economy.

*No data available.

Table 10
Regional structure of GDR industry in 1975: selected data

Area	Mean residential population — Percentage share	Persons economically active in industry[1] — Per 1,000 inhabitants	Per sq.km.	Percentage of economically active population	Percentage share	Industrial gross output[2] — 1965 = 100	Marks per inhabitant
Berlin	6.5	147	400	26.6	5.7	168	10,563
Cottbus	5.2	214	23	42.2	5.4	211	12,557
Dresden	10.9	223	61	44.1	12.1	176	13,336
Erfurt	7.4	209	35	41.8	7.3	214	11,896
Frankfurt	4.1	123	12	28.6	4.6	257	13,551
Gera	4.4	231	43	45.4	4.8	206	13,192
Halle	11.1	227	49	45.3	14.3	180	15,399
Karl-Marx-Stadt	11.8	259	86	50.5	14.4	180	14,716
Leipzig	8.6	200	58	39.9	8.5	173	11,876
Magdeburg	7.7	162	18	32.8	6.5	177	10,193
Neubrandenburg	3.7	86	5	18.9	1.7	232	5,494
Potsdam	6.7	142	13	30.6	6.1	219	11,021
Rostock	5.2	120	15	24.5	3.2	184	7,477
Schwerin	3.5	108	7	23.1	2.4	213	8,238
Suhl	3.3	271	39	50.8	3.1	192	11,442
GDR	100	193	30	38.6	100	187	12,037

1 Including apprentices.
2 At constant 1967 prices.

Source: DIW calculations based on GDR Statistical Yearbook 1976.

Table 11
Gross capital assets of GDR industry 1960-1975
(annual mean in Bn. M at 1962 prices)

Industrial sector	1960	1965	1970	1971	1972	1973	1974	1975	1975 (1960 = 100)
Fuel and power	22.4	32.9	40.6	42.8	45.2	47.7	50.9	54.3	242
Chemicals	17.2	23.4	31.9	34.1	36.3	38.9	41.9	45.6	265
Metallurgy	5.3	7.5	10.2	10.6	11.2	11.8	12.6	13.4	253
Building materials	3.4	4.9	6.1	6.6	7.0	7.6	7.9	8.2	241
Water resources	7.9	10.1	12.5	13.0	13.6	14.1	14.7	15.4	195
Mechanical engineering/vehicle building	13.0	19.6	25.5	27.3	29.4	31.4	33.4	35.5	273
Electrical engineering, electronics, instrument building	3.7	5.6	8.6	9.7	10.7	11.6	12.4	13.3	359
Light industry (without textiles)	7.7	9.9	12.1	12.7	13.6	14.6	15.7	16.8	218
Textile industry	6.2	7.3	8.1	8.4	8.8	9.4	10.0	10.6	171
Food processing	7.9	9.2	12.0	12.8	13.6	14.4	15.2	16.1	204
All industry	94.7	130.4	167.6	178.0	189.4	201.5	214.7	229.3	242

Sources: GDR Statistical Yearbooks, Statistisches Taschenbuch der DDR 1977

Table 12
Origin of GDR gross domestic product[1] (Bn. M)

Sector	1960	1965	1970	1971	1972	1973	1974	1975[2]
Commodity producing trades	51.3	64.2	86.5	91.2	96.0	101.6	108.0	114.6
Power, mining, water resources	4.7	4.7	5.8	6.0	6.3	6.6	6.9	7.4
Processing trades	41.1	52.3	70.2	74.2	78.2	83.0	88.4	93.9
Basic materials	8.4	11.1	15.1	16.0	17.3	18.6	20.2	21.7
Capital goods	12.4	18.4	27.3	29.2	30.8	32.9	35.3	37.8
Consumer goods	20.4	22.9	27.8	28.9	30.1	31.4	32.9	34.5
Construction	5.4	7.2	10.5	11.1	11.5	12.1	12.7	13.3
Agriculture and forestry	11.9	12.2	13.5	13.0	14.7	14.8	16.0	15.6
Trade and transport	13.9	16.5	21.6	22.9	24.0	25.4	27.1	28.5
Services	4.1	4.5	5.0	5.2	5.2	5.4	5.5	5.6
Health, education, State	9.3	11.0	13.3	13.8	14.2	14.8	15.4	15.9
All sectors	90.4	108.4	139.8	146.1	154.1	162.0	171.9	180.2
Corrective adjustment[3]	0.0	1.2	2.1	2.1	2.4	2.3	2.3	2.5
Gross domestic product	90.4	107.2	137.7	144.0	151.7	159.7	169.6	177.7

1 Western method, at 1967 prices.
2 Provisional figures.
3 Add general overhauls, deduct officially declared price subsidies.

Source: DIW calculations

289

Table 13
Origin of GDR net domestic product[1] (Bn. M)

Sector	1960	1965	1970	1971	1972	1973	1974	1975[2]
Commodity producing trades	46.6	58.2	78.0	82.0	86.1	90.9	96.5	102.3
Power, mining, water resources	2.8	2.8	3.4	3.5	3.6	3.7	3.9	4.1
Processing trades	38.6	48.6	64.8	68.2	71.7	76.0	80.9	85.8
Basic materials	7.4	9.7	13.1	13.8	14.9	16.0	17.3	18.6
Capital goods	11.5	17.0	25.3	27.0	28.4	30.3	32.5	34.7
Consumer goods	19.6	21.8	26.4	27.5	28.5	29.7	31.1	32.5
Construction	5.2	6.8	9.8	10.3	10.7	11.2	11.7	12.3
Agriculture and forestry	11.0	11.2	12.1	11.6	13.0	13.0	14.0	13.5
Trade and transport	12.7	14.8	19.0	20.2	21.2	22.5	23.9	25.2
Services	3.8	4.1	4.6	4.7	4.7	4.9	5.0	5.1
Health, education, State	8.8	10.4	12.5	13.0	13.4	13.9	14.4	14.9
All sectors	82.9	98.8	126.2	131.5	138.4	145.2	153.9	161.0

1 Western method, at 1967 prices.
2 Provisional figures

Source: DIW calculations

Table 14
Origin of GDR national income[1] (Bn. M)

Sector	1960	1965	1970	1971	1972	1973	1974	1975[3]
Industry[2]	41.2	51.9	68.8	72.4	76.2	80.8	85.9	91.2
Construction	5.1	6.4	9.3	9.8	10.1	10.6	11.1	11.7
Agriculture and forestry	12.0	12.1	13.2	12.6	14.2	14.1	15.2	14.7
Transport, posts, tele-communications	4.0	4.8	5.9	6.3	6.4	6.6	6.9	7.2
Domestic trade	9.5	11.0	14.3	15.1	16.1	17.3	18.6	19.5
Remaining producing branches	1.2	1.5	1.8	1.8	1.9	2.1	2.3	2.4
Net product	73.1	87.7	113.3	118.1	124.9	131.5	139.9	146.7
Price subsidies	2.0	3.5	4.6	4.5	4.8	4.7	4.9	5.0
Produced national income	71.0	84.2	108.7	113.6	120.1	126.8	135.0	141.7

1 Eastern method, official data at 1967 prices.
2 Including manufacturing artisan enterprises without building trades.
3 Provisional figures.

Source: GDR Statistical Yearbook.

Table 15
Use of GDR gross national product[1] (Bn. M)

	1960	1965	1970	1971	1972	1973	1974	1975[2]	1976[2]
Private consumption	54.9	61.8	75.4	78.1	81.6	85.9	90.7	94.0	98.0
Commodities	45.5	51.3	63.9	66.3	69.6	73.5	77.9	80.6	84.0
Services	6.9	7.9	9.2	9.6	10.0	10.4	10.8	11.3	11.9
Consumption of natural produce by producer	2.5	2.6	2.3	2.2	2.0	2.0	2.0	2.1	2.1
Investment	20.5	26.7	39.4	39.8	40.9	43.5	46.6	48.3	50.0
Gross capital investment[3]	18.1	22.8	35.2	35.4	36.7	39.4	41.2	42.8	45.7
Equipment	8.9	12.0	18.7	18.3	18.9	20.9	21.5	22.1	
Buildings	8.0	9.5	14.4	14.7	15.2	15.9	16.7	20.7	
Investment in stock	2.4	3.9	4.2	4.4	4.2	4.1	5.4	4.5	4.3
State consumption and net exports	15.0	18.7	22.9	26.1	29.2	30.3	32.1	35.4	36.3
Gross national product	90.4	107.2	137.7	144.0	151.7	159.7	169.4	177.7	184.3

1 Western method, at 1967 prices.
2 Provisional figures.
3 Including general overhauls.

Source: DIW calculations.

Table 16
Gross national product of the GDR and FRG 1967-1976
(Bn. DM at current West German prices)

	GDR 1967	GDR 1973	GDR 1976[3]	FRG 1967	FRG 1973	FRG 1976[3]
ORIGIN						
Agriculture and forestry	8	10	10	21	27	30
Commodity producing trades	62	109	140	258	489	564
Trade and transport	18	33	43	96	164	203
Services	24	47	65	123	260	354
Gross domestic product[1]	111	195	255	497	928	1,137
USE						
Private consumption	56	90	115	285	496	627
Investment[2]	28	53	65	113	238	250
State consumption and foreign contribution	27	52	75	97	194	258
Gross national product	111	195	255	496	928	1,135

1 The difference between the total and the sum of the contributions is due in the GDR to part of the price subsidies minus general overhauls, in the FRG to the different rates of value added tax, depending on whether the taxed purchases are consumption − or investment − related.
2 Including general overhauls.
3 Provisional figures.

Source: DIW calculations

Table 17
GDR industrial output in 1975 (by sector)

Sector	Industrial gross output		Contribution of processing trades[2] to gross domestic product	
	Bn. M	1975 (1960=100)	Bn. M	1975 (1960=100)
Fuel and power, water resources	11.2	170	7.4	156
Chemicals	30.5	315	15.8	292
Metallurgy	15.9	230	3.8	174
Building materials	4.1	260	2.1	273
Mechanical engineering/ vehicle building	48.9	266	24.9	290
Electrical engineering/ electronics/instrument building	22.7	386	12.9	340
Light industry	22.9	219	13.7	164
Textile industry	13.3	181	6.2	172
Food processing	33.4	192	14.6	172
All industry	202.8	247	101.3	221

1 At 1967 prices.
2 Including producing artisan trades and production omitted from official statistics.

Sources: GDR Statistical Yearbook; DIW calculations

Table 18
Sectoral structure of GDR industry[1] 1936 and 1950 to 1975
(in per cent)

Sector	1936[2]	1950	1955	1960	1965	1970	1975
Fuel and power	9.0	11.7	8.3	6.8	6.4	5.6	5.1
Chemicals	6.4	11.2	12.0	12.1	13.5	14.5	15.1
Metallurgy	10.5	6.2	8.8	8.4	7.8	7.8	7.9
Building materials	2.6	2.3	1.7	2.0	2.1	2.1	2.0
Mechanical engineering/ vehicle building[3]	16.1	17.4	19.1	22.1	24.1	24.9	24.2
Electrical engineering/ electronics/instrument building[4]	2.7	4.4	5.1	6.8	8.2	9.5	11.2
Light industry[5]	13.6	14.7	12.4	12.0	11.3	11.2	11.3
Textile industry	10.6	10.2	9.6	8.8	7.6	7.0	6.6
Food processing	28.5	21.9	23.0	21.0	19.0	17.4	16.6
All industry	100	100	100	100	100	100	100

1 Without water industry. Calculated on the basis of gross output at 1967 prices.
2 1936 gross production in the territory of today's GDR at 1967 prices.
3 Including foundries and forges, shipbuilding and metal goods industry.
4 Including precision engineering/optical industry, data processing and office machines industry.
5 Without textile industry.

Sources: GDR Statistical Yearbooks; DIW calculations.

Table 19

Selected data on the GDR power economy

	Unit	1960	1965	1970	1971	1972	1973	1974	1975
Output of primary energy sources									
Brown coal	Mill. t	225.5	250.8	261.6	262.8	248.5	246.2	243.5	246.7
Hard coal	Mill. t	2.7	2.2	1.0	0.9	0.7	0.8	0.6	0.5
Natural gas	Bn. Nm^3	0.0	0.1	1.0	2.8	5.0	7.0	8.0	8.0
Crude oil	Mill. t	*	0.1	0.1	0.1	0.1	0.1	0.1	0.1
Hydroelectric power	Bn. kWh	0.6	0.8	1.3	1.3	1.2	1.3	1.3	1.3
Crude oil imports[1]									
total	Mill. t	1.9	5.1	10.3	10.9	14.9	16.0	16.4	17.0
of which from the USSR	Mill. t	1.8	4.9	9.2	9.8	11.2	13.0	14.1	15.1
Natural gas imports from USSR	Bn. Nm^3	–	–	*	*	*	0.8	2.9	3.3
Export[1] of									
brown coal	Mill. t	6.3	6.0	3.8	2.8	2.5	2.3	2.6	2.3
mineral oil products	Mill. t	1.0	1.7	1.3	1.0	2.3	2.4	2.9	2.8
Installed power generating capacity	MW	7,842	10,350	12,569	13,339	14,182	14,940	15,808	16,928
of which nuclear fuelled	MW	–	–	75	75	75	75	515	955
Electric power output	Bn. kWh	40.3	53.6	67.7	69.4	72.8	76.9	80.3	84.5
of which by brown-coal fired plant	per cent	79.5	82.5	85.0	84.7	83.4	84.0	82.3	83.8
Electric power consumption	Bn. kWh	39.9	53.7	68.1	69.9	73.8	78.2	81.4	85.2
of which by industry[2]	per cent	79.8	78.5	76.3	76.5	77.1	77.0	76.8	76.0
households and other small consumers	per cent	18.3	19.6	21.6	21.4	20.8	20.9	21.2	22.0
Transport	per cent	1.9	1.9	2.1	2.1	2.1	2.1	2.0	2.0
Town gas output	Bn. Nm^3	*	3.5	4.4	4.5	4.8	4.8	4.9	5.1

Sources: GDR Statistical Yearbooks; CMEA Statistical Yearbook; DIW estimates.

1 Including intra-German trade.
2 Including power losses by electricity supply industry.
*No data available.

Table 20
Building volume in the GDR and FRG 1960-1975
(at 1967 prices)

| Year | GDR | | | | | FRG | |
	Total[1]	Building repairs[2]	Building investment[3]	Other building output[4]	Total per capita	Total	per capita
	Bn. M				M	Bn. DM	DM
1960	9.66[5]	2.14	7.16	0.36	560	60.80	1,097
1965	12.51[5]	3.61	8.50	0.40	735	81.66	1,393
1970	18.58	4.57	13.20	0.81	1,089	91.58	1,510
1971	19.64	5.12	13.50	1.02	1,151	96.24	1,570
1972	20.89	5.74	14.25	0.90	1,226	100.44	1,629
1973	21.85	5.87	14.85	1.13	1,287	100.31	1,618
1974	23.62	6.28	15.60	1.74	1,393	92.57	1,492
1975	25.12	6.51	16.78	1.83	1,491	85.75	1,387

1 Building output of all economic sectors (including heavy steel structures used in building and bridge construction, lightweight metal structures and export of building output); not including corrective reworking and work under guarantee, nor hoists, escalators, electrical installations in industrial buildings or preliminary project planning for domestic investment or export.
2 Including general overhauls.
3 Without general overhauls.
4 Rubble clearance, demolition work (except residential), supervision of project execution by architects, etc.
5 Without heavy steel structures used in building and bridge construction, light metal structures, export of building output as well as certain project planning contributions. The total of the output omitted in this way may be estimated at 250 to 300 mill. Marks in 1965.

Sources: GDR and FRG Statistical Yearbooks; DIW computation of building output for the FRG; DIW calculations and party estimates.

Table 21
Development of housing construction volume in the GDR and FRG

Year	Total[1]	GDR of which Building investment (without general overhauls)[2]	Building repairs[3]	Share in total building volume	Per capita	FRG Share in total building volume	Per capita
		Bn. M at 1967 prices		%	M at 1967 prices	%	DM at 1967 prices
1960	2.88	2.00	0.88	29.8	167	43.1	472
1965	3.20	1.92	1.28	25.6	188	41.5	577
1970	3.86	2.34	1.52	20.8	226	38.3	578
1971	4.05	2.43	1.62	20.6	237	40.3	633
1972	4.61	2.78	1.83	22.1	270	43.5	708
1973	5.27	3.25	2.02	24.1	310	43.9	710
1974	5.64	3.57	2.07	23.9	333	41.0	611
1975	6.00	3.75	2.25[4]	23.9	356	40.1	557

1 Building work for housing construction and maintenance of housing stock.
2 Calculated by multiplying the floor area of the new dwellings built in any one year with the building cost per sq.m.
3 Building repair work on residential buildings, including general overhauls (modernisations).
4 Estimated.

Sources: GDR and FRG Statistical Yearbooks; DIW computation of building output for the FRG; DIW calculations and party estimates.

Table 22
Selected data on GDR housing construction

Year	Completed dwellings[1]	of which by Modernisation	of which by Conversion or extension	New constructions Total	New constructions by assembly method	New constructions by individual dwelling construction	Floor space of completed dwellings[2]	Building costs[3] Total	Building costs[3] per sq.m. floor space[4] (at 1967 prices)	Total expenditure per sq.m.[5] (at 1967 prices)
	'000	'000	'000	'000	%	%	'000 sq.m.	Bn. M	M	M
1960	80.5	*	8.6	71.9	32.1	*	4,447	2.00	494	523
1961-65	400.0	*	37.3	362.7	69.0	*	21,694	10.50	498	564
1966-70	364.0	*	67.3	296.7	90.8	*	19,583	10.70	547	698
1971	86.8	10.7	11.1	65.0	88.1	3.4	4,398	2.43	588	719
1972	117.0	31.1	16.3	69.6	86.6	3.5	4,905	2.78	573	775
1973	125.8	29.5	15.6	80.7	84.3	6.4	5,573	3.25	574	776
1974	138.3	35.1	14.9	88.3	79.6	10.8	6,201	3.57	573	755
1975	140.8	29.8	15.0[6]	96.0	80.1	11.7	6,523	3.75	555	777
1971-75	608.7	136.2	72.9	399.6	83.3	7.7	27,600	15.78	571	762
1976	150.6	47.5		103.1	82.6	10.8	6,869	*	*	*
Plan 1976-80	750.0	200.0		550.0	*	10.0	7,097	*	*	*

1 New buildings, conversion, extension and modernisation.
2 Floor space of dwellings completed by new construction, conversion or extension.
3 Without consequential costs.
4 Based on adjusted total building price.
5 Expenditure on housing construction, including consequential and site preparation costs, but without expenditure on maintenance of housing stock.
6 Estimate.

*No data available

Sources: GDR Statistical Yearbooks; Statistisches Taschenbuch der DDR 1977; DIW calculations.

Table 23
The GDR's socialist agriculture: selected data

	1955	1960	1965	1970	1975	1976
	Number of enterprises					
I Traditional method						
LPGs	6,047	19,313	15,139	9,009	4,621	3,582[1]
incl. Type III	4,652	6,337	6,166	5,524	4,260	*
VEGs	540	669	572	511	463[2]	424
II Industrial method						
KAPs	–	–	–	283[3]	1,210	1,024[4]
ZGEs	–	–	376	803	1,869	
	AL					
Total ('000 ha)[5]	6,480	6,420	6,358	6,286	6,296	6,293
	Percentage shares					
Socialist agriculture	27.3	91.9	93.1	93.6	94.0	94.4
I LPGs	18.6	84.2	85.8	85.8	85.9	14.8
incl. Type III	17.8	52.7	58.7	72.0	79.9	*
VEGs	4.4	6.2	6.7	7.0	7.5	1.9
II KAPs	–	–	–	13.3[3]	79.4	74.3[4]
	Average size of production units (ha. AL)					
I LPGs	205	280	360	599	1,170	*
incl. Type III	248	534	605	819	1,180	*
VEGs	524	591	743	866	1,023[2]	283
II KAPs	–	–	–	2,950[3]	4,130	4,564[6]
	Livestock					
Cattle ('000 head)[5]	3,760	4,675	4,762	5,190	5,532	5,471
	Percentage shares					
LPGs	15.6	91.1	91.7	88.7	83.4	82.4
incl. Type III	*	54.3	59.0	72.9	82.0	*
VEGs	2.8	6.3	6.8	8.6	9.7	10.2
High-level co-operative institutions	–	–	–	1.3	5.8	6.4
Pigs[5] ('000)	9,029	8,316	8,878	9,684	11,501	11,291
	Percentage shares					
LPGs	15.8	82.9	81.6	80.5	72.1	71.1
incl. Type III	*	52.8	57.5	69.9	71.3	*
VEGs	6.8	8.1	9.3	12.5	14.9	15.6
High-level co-operative institutions	–	–	–	2.0	9.5	9.9

1 Including 161 specialised crop-farming LPGs averaging 929,749 ha AL.
2 Including six specialised crop-farming VEGs averaging 5,267 ha AL and six stock-farming VEGs.
3 1971.
4 Without ZGEs of forestry and construction.
5 All agriculture.
6 KAPs and crop-farming ZBEs.   *No data available.

Sources: GDR Statistical Yearbooks; Statistisches Taschenbuch der DDR 1977; DIW calculations.

Table 24
Factors of production in GDR and FRG agriculture

	GDR 1960	GDR 1965	GDR 1970	FRG 1975	GDR 1976
	Labour force[1] per 100 ha AL				
Personnel[2]	*	17.6	15.1	13.4	18.0	13.1
of which: permanent[3]	*	16.4	14.4	12.8	10.2	12.3
Whole time equivalent[4]	*	15.9	13.6	12.0	8.9	11.8
	Capital per member of labour force[7]				
Gross capital investment[8] (M/DM)[9]	1,480	2,349	4,361	5,702	2,165[10]	*
Capital assets (M/DM)[9]	15,316	24,455	36,356	52,129	39,761[11]	*
	Agricultural machines				
Tractors ('000)	71	124	149	140	1,437	138
Tractors ('000 hp)	2,283	4,338	6,441	7,575	47,311	*
Lorries	9,312	13,115	27,186	42,518	6,867	44,025
Manure spreaders	8,542	8,773	16,076	15,136	*	14,346
Combine harvesters	6,409	15,409	17,911	11,235	170,800	12,277
Potato combines	6,386	6,843	12,000	9,174	*	8,867
Beet combines	3,665	4,742	5,276	4,949	*	4,536
	per 100 ha AL				
Tractors (units)	1.2	2.1	2.5	2.4	10.8	2.3
Tractors (hp)	39	73	110	128	356	130
	Livestock ('000)				
Cattle	4,675	4,762	5,190	5,532	14,493	5,471
of which: cows	2,175	2,169	2,163	2,155	5,535	2,146
Pigs	8,316	8,878	9,684	11,501	19,805	11,291
Total livestock ('000 livestock units)[13]	5,319	5,244	5,396	5,769	13,491	5,708
	Livestock per 100 ha AL[12]				
Cattle	72.8	74.9	82.6	87.9	109.1	86.9
of which: cows	33.9	34.1	34.4	34.2	41.6	34.1
Pigs	129.5	139.6	154.0	182.7	149.2	179.4
Total livestock (livestock units)[13]	82.9	82.5	85.8	91.6	101.4	90.7
	Fertiliser consumption (kg/ha AL)[14]				
Nitrogen N	38.5	66.4	83.7	104.0	90.0	115.3
Phosphate P_2O_5	35.1	47.7	64.3	71.6	65.7	63.8
Potash K_2O	82.3	92.8	99.1	113.2	87.7	108.6
Lime CaO	117.1	226.2	197.7	199.2	56.9	206.5
	Inhabitants per 100 ha AL				
Inhabitants per 100 ha AL	269	268	271	268	465	267

1 Without apprentices
2 Including Agrochemical Centres.
3 Without Agrochemical Centres.
4 GDR: strength of labour force multiplied by 0.9.
5 1974/75.
6 1974/75, including only agricultural enterprises with over 2 ha AL.
7 Including forestry.

8 Excluding general overhauls and livestock.
9 M at 1967 prices.
10 1973/74, without forestry.
11 At 1962 prices.
12 State at year end.
13 DIW calculations, using GDR abridged livestock unit key.
14 Harvest years (1.7.-30.6.) 1960/61 to 1975/76.

Sources: GDR and FRG Statistical Yearbooks; FRG Statistical Yearbook on Food, Agriculture and Forestry; Statistisches Taschenbuch der DDR 1977; DIW calculations.

Table 25
Structure of agricultural land (quinquennial averages)

	GDR				FRG
	1956-1960	1961-1965	1966-1970	1971-1975	
	'000 ha				
Agricultural land[1]	6,477	6,380	6,314	6,290	13,412
of which: arable	4,916	4,750	4,657	4,651	7,550
meadows and pastures	1,309	1,427	1,453	1,420	5,332
other areas[2]	222	203	204	219	530
	Percentage shares				
Agricultural land[1]	100.0	100.0	100.0	100.0	100.0
of which: arable	76.2	74.4	73.8	73.9	56.3
meadows and pastures	20.3	22.4	23.0	22.6	39.7
other areas[2]	3.5	3.2	3.2	3.5	4.0
Grain	37.9	35.4[4]	36.6	38.1	39.4
of which: wheat	6.5	6.7	8.7	8.7	11.9
barley	5.4	6.9	9.3	11.7	12.1
rye	16.4	12.9	11.5	10.1	5.6
Potatoes	12.1	11.4	10.5	10.1	3.6
Sugar beet	3.4	3.6	3.2	3.7	2.7
Oil crops	3.0	2.4	2.1	2.1	0.8
Pulses	1.4	1.5	1.0	0.9	0.2
Fodder root crops	3.4	2.7	2.8	1.7	2.2
Green fodder crops	11.8	14.4	14.8	13.7	4.9

1 FRG: Agricultural land in actual use for agricultural purposes.
2 Gardens attached to dwelling houses; other small gardens; orchards; vineyards; tree plantations, including osieries.
3 Including green and silage maize.
4 1964 and 1965: without shelled (grain) maize.

Sources: GDR Statistical Yearbooks; FRG Statistical Yearbook on Food, Agriculture and Forestry.

Table 26
Development of agricultural yields (quinquennial averages)

	GDR			FRG[1]
	1956-1960	1961-1965	1966-1970	1971-1975
	Crops ('000 t)			
Grain	6,043	5,846	6,896	8,679	21,255
of which: wheat	1,307	1,357	2,006	2,797	7,132
barley	994	1,291	1,913	2,966	6,482
rye	2,231	1,741	1,718	1,774	2,642
Oil crops	191	190	231	278	220
Pulses	87	122	95	81	73
Potatoes	13,369	12,066	12,283	10,806	13,858
Sugar beet	5,852	5,522	6,310	6,481	15,925
	Yields (q/ha)			
Grain	24.8	25.8	29.8	36.2	40.2
of which: wheat	31.2	31.3	36.4	40.7	44.7
barley	28.8	29.5	32.4	37.3	39.8
rye	21.2	21.2	23.7	27.8	35.0
Potatoes	171.3	165.7	184.8	170.8	286.2
Sugar beet	262.5	243.7	313.4	279.0	444.1
	Gross crop production			
Output ('000 t GE)[2]	19,736	19,474	22,731	24,244	61,257
Yield (q GE/ha AL)	30.6	30.5	36.0	38.5	45.7
	Animal products ('000 t)			
Fat stock[3]	1,274	1,410	1,763	2,124	6,081
of which: pigs	847	852	1,060	1,258	3,382
poultry	57	86	107	159	342
cattle[4]	307	414	554	651	2,334
Eggs (mill.)	2,962	3,517	4,114	4,691	15,325
Milk	5,497	5,704	7,036	7,715	21,549
	Milk yield per cow			
Milk production (kg)[5]	2,585	2,675	3,255	3,607	4,325
	Total animal production			
Output ('000 t GE)[2]	13,080	14,209	17,635	20,421	58,317
Yield (kg GE/livestock unit)[6]	2,549	2,735	3,280	3,612	4,380

1 Total animal production for harvest years 1971/72-1974/75.
2 DIW calculations based on GDR conversion keys, in particular GE key.
3 Live weight.
4 Including calves.
5 In terms of 3.5% fat content.
6 DIW calculations based on abridged livestock unit key used in GDR.

Sources: GDR Statistical Yearbooks; FRG Statistical Yearbooks on Food, Agriculture and Forestry; DIW calculations.

Table 27
Agricultural market production and sales proceeds
(quinquennial averages)

	GDR				FRG[1]
	1956-1960	1961-1965	1966-1970	1971-1975	1971/72-1974/75
	'000 t GE[2]				
Market production (total)[3,4]	14,596	16,922	21,131	25,155	68,736
	Percentage shares				
Vegetable products[3]	31.3	27.0	24.0	23.2	21.2
grain	13.3	11.5	10.6	10.8	12.9
oil crops	2.3	2.2	2.1	2.2	0.6
potatoes	6.0	5.4	4.7	4.5	2.0
sugar beet	9.5	7.6	6.5	5.6	5.7
Animal products[4]	68.7	73.0	76.0	76.8	78.8
fat stock[5] (animals for slaughter)	35.2	37.5	40.5	42.6	44.4
pigs	22.7	21.2	22.5	23.4	21.8
poultry	0.5	1.6	2.0	3.3	2.8
cattle[6]	12.0	14.7	16.0	15.9	19.8
milk	28.3	29.9	30.1	28.7	28.2
eggs	2.8	3.6	3.7	3.9	5.9
wool[7]	2.4	2.0	1.7	1.6	0.3
	Mill. M (DM)				
Sales proceeds (total)[3,4]	6,991	9,841	14,830	20,369	33,660
	Percentage shares				
Vegetable products[3]	19.4	18.3	15.7	14.7	17.2
grain	7.9	7.6	6.3	5.4	10.4
potatoes	4.1	5.1	4.7	5.5	2.9
sugar beet	5.0	3.7	3.0	2.4	3.4
Animal products[4]	80.6	81.7	84.3	85.3	82.8
fat stock[5]	42.9	43.6	47.3	49.5	47.6
pigs	32.1	29.6	30.2	30.4	25.1
poultry	0.9	2.3	2.6	3.7	1.8
cattle[6]	9.9	11.7	14.5	15.4	20.7
milk	28.8	28.9	28.9	28.2	27.9
eggs	7.2	7.7	6.8	6.4	7.3

1 Average over four harvest years (1.7.-30.6.).
2 According to GE conversion key of the GDR.
3 Without pulses for human consumption, fruit, vegetables, wine, hops, tobacco, arboricultural products, seed establishments, etc.
4 Without honey.
5 Live weight; excluding horses and rabbits.
6 Including calves, sheep and goats.
7 Washed.

Source: DIW calculations.

Table 28
Transport and telecommunications in the GDR: principal data

	1960	1965	1970	1972	1974	1975
Transport sector's percentage share in:						
net domestic product	5.5	5.4	5.2	5.1	4.9	4.9
investment	10.7	9.5	8.8	8.3	12.7	12.7
capital assets[1]	20.4	18.4	16.5	16.0	15.5	15.3
personnel	6.6	7.1	7.2	7.5	7.6	7.6
Railway data[2]						
personnel ('000)	307	295	273	267	270	268
mode of traction[3]						
steam locomotives (per cent)	94.4	88.4	42.3	35.9	27.5	21.1
diesel locomotives[4] (per cent)	0.7	3.0	41.5	47.5	56.6	62.5
electrical locomotives (per cent)	4.9	8.6	16.2	16.6	15.9	16.4
turn-round period[5] (days)	3.57	3.59	4.04	3.92	3.89	3.89
number of trains ('000)	5,637	5,532	5,297	5,409	5,398	5,390
containers carried ('000)	—	—	186	258	333	358
Inland shipping data						
personnel ('000)	6.7	6.8	6.1	5.0	5.0	5.0
ship types[6]						
motor barges (per cent)	8.9	33.6	32.3	31.9	34.6	33.5
motor tugs (per cent)	12.2	8.5	6.1	5.9	6.2	5.6
pusher tugs (per cent)	—	6.9	42.8	48.6	52.3	54.7
barges (per cent)	78.9	51.0	18.8	13.6	6.9	6.1
Maritime shipping data						
personnel ('000)	5.1	10.9	17.2	18.3	20.0	20.5
number of vessels[7]	47	127	175	194	194	198
tonnage ('000 grt)	197	570	940	1,028	1,152	1,200
Civil aviation data						
personnel ('000)	*	2.7	4.4	5.1	5.9	6.1
air services	18	24	39	41	51	52
total length of routes ('000 km)	13	19	64	61	81	85
Urban local traffic data[8]						
personnel	31.1	27.7	26.7	26.9	28.7	29.2
tram cars[9] ('000)	4.8	4.7	4.6	4.4	4.4	4.5
trolley-buses ('000)	0.3	0.4	0.3	0.3	0.1	0.1
buses ('000)	1.1	1.2	1.5	1.6	1.8	1.9
Licensed vehicle stock ('000)						
lorries [10]	118	147	186	206	226	239
passenger and estate cars	299	662	1,160	1,400	1,703	1,880
motorcycles[11]	848	1,187	1,374	1,373	1,361	1,363
mopeds	477	1,145	1,538	1,699	1,942	2,076
Radio receivers[12] (per 100 households)	89.9	86.5	91.9	94.5	95.5	96.3
Television receivers[12] (per 100 households)	16.7	48.5	69.1	75.3	79.6	81.6

1 Mean values of the producing sector.
2 Deutsche Reichsbahn.
3 Shares in volume of operations.
4 Including diesel coaches.
5 Average time during which a goods wagon is in use until ready for the next trip.
6 Share in the volume of goods transport.

7 Excluding maritime and coastal passenger vessels.
8 Excluding taxis.
9 Pilot cars and trailers.
10 Excluding special vehicles and wheeled or track-laying tractors.
11 Including scooters.
12 Number of licences.

Source: GDR Statistical Yearbooks.

*No data available.

Table 29
GDR transport performance by sector

	1960	1965	1970	1972	1974	1975
GOODS TRANSPORT						
Volume (Mill.t)	522	628	764	837	881	935
Railways[1] (per cent)	45.5	41.4	34.4	32.8	32.5	30.9
Inland shipping (per cent)	2.4	1.9	1.8	1.6	1.7	1.6
Road transport[2] (per cent)	51.8	55.0	60.7	61.9	61.5	62.9
Long-distance traffic (per cent)	1.3	1.8	3.0	3.0	3.4	3.7
Short-distance traffic (per cent)	50.3	53.2	57.7	58.9	58.1	59.2
Maritime shipping (per cent)	0.3	1.0	1.1	1.2	1.3	1.2
Long-distance pipelines (per cent)	–	0.6	2.0	2.5	3.0	3.4
Performance (bn. tkm)	50.6	78.6	128.0	134.4	147.2	152.7
Railways[1,3] (per cent)	64.9	49.5	32.4	33.3	33.4	32.5
Inland shipping (per cent)	4.4	2.8	1.8	1.7	1.6	1.5
Road transport[2] (per cent)	9.9	9.2	9.5	10.1	10.3	11.0
Long-distance traffic (per cent)	2.4	2.6	3.3	3.6	4.0	4.3
Short-distance traffic (per cent)	7.5	6.6	6.2	6.5	6.3	6.7
Maritime shipping (per cent)	20.8	38.4	54.5	52.6	52.0	52.2
Long-distance pipelines (per cent)	–	0.1	1.7	2.3	2.6	2.8
PASSENGER TRANSPORT[4]						
Number of passengers (Mill.)	4,397	4,847	5,486	5,941	6,457	6,739
Public transport (per cent)	82.0	72.7	63.5	60.8	57.8	56.8
Railways (per cent)	12.0	9.2	7.5	7.2	6.6	6.5
Berlin S-bahn (per cent)	9.5	5.0	4.0	3.6	3.1	2.9
Tramways[5] (per cent)	37.5	31.4	24.3	22.6	20.6	19.9
Buses (per cent)	23.0	27.1	27.7	27.4	27.5	27.5
local traffic[6] (per cent)	7.3	7.6	7.0	6.8	7.3	7.5
long-distance traffic[2] (per cent)	15.7	19.5	20.7	20.6	20.2	20.0
Air transport (per cent)	0	0	0	0	0	0
Personal transport[7] (per cent)	18.0	27.3	36.5	39.2	42.2	43.2
Performance (Bn. pkm)	52.3	64.9	82.5	92.7	103.9	110.0
Public transport (per cent)	74.6	59.5	51.5	50.4	48.0	46.7
Railways (per cent)	29.4	21.3	17.2	17.9	17.1	16.6
Berlin S-bahn (per cent)	11.2	5.5	4.2	3.6	2.9	2.8
Tramways[5] (per cent)	11.2	8.0	5.5	4.9	4.6	4.5
Buses (per cent)	21.9	23.5	23.1	22.5	21.8	21.2
local traffic[6] (per cent)	2.9	2.7	2.1	2.0	2.1	2.1
long-distance traffic[2] (per cent)	19.0	20.8	21.0	20.5	19.7	19.1
Air transport (per cent)	0.3	0.6	1.1	1.2	1.3	1.4
Personal transport[7] (per cent)	25.4	40.5	48.5	49.6	52.0	53.3

1 Excluding railway service consignments.
2 Including commuter traffic.
3 Tonne-kilometre charged.
4 Without shipping

5 Including subways.
6 Including trolleybuses.
7 By passenger and estate cars, motorcycles and mopeds.

Sources: GDR Statistical Yearbooks; DIW calculations.

Table 30
GDR artisan trades: principal data by form of ownership

	1960	1965	1970	1973	1974	1975
Private businesses	173,243	146,764	116,478	99,418	93,636	88,635
Producer co-operatives (PGHs)	3,878	4,198	4,458	2,782[1]	2,791	2,793
Economically active persons ('000)	596.6	573.8	607.7	444.8[1]	430.4	417.5
private ('000)	434.1	368.5	347.5	303.0[1]	287.1	272.3
PGHs ('000)	162.5	205.3	260.2	141.8[1]	143.3	145.2
share of PGHs (per cent)	27.2	35.8	42.8	31.9[1]	33.3	34.8
Gross production (Mill.M)	9,926.8	12,559.4	17,763.1	13,460.5[1]	13,594.2	13,638.1
private (Mill.M)	7,005.8	7,513.4	8,902.8	8,670.4[1]	8,574.3	8,418.1
PGHs (Mill.M)	2,920.9	5,046.0	8,860.3	4,790.1[1]	5,019.9	5,220.0
share of PGHs (Mill.M)	29.4	40.2	49.9	35.6[1]	36.9	38.3

1 Decline due to conversion of producer co-operatives into publicly owned enterprises of the industrial sector in 1972.

Source: GDR Statistical Yearbooks.

Table 31
Performance of GDR artisan trades by type of activity

Year	Gross pro- duction	Manufacturing output			Construc- tion	Services	Repairs/ Manu- facturing output	Services/ Gross pro- duction
		total	new pro- duction	repairs				
	Mill. Marks						%	
1960	9,926.8	7,264.6	5,935.3	1,329.3	2,111.2	550.9	18.3	5.5
1965	12,559.4	9,069.2	7,151.7	1,917.5	2,852.2	637.9	21.1	5.1
1970	17,763.1	12,882.7	10,184.5	2,698.2	4,073.6	806.8	20.9	4.5
1973	13,460.5	9,517.8	6,779.2	2,738.6	3,086.8	855.9	28.8	6.4
1974	13,594.2	9,552.6	6,749.7	2,802.9	3,146.4	895.1	29.3	6.6
1975	13,638.2	9,555.0	6,701.2	2,853.8	3,155.9	925.7	29.9	6.8

Sources: GDR Statistical Yearbooks; see also section 4.5 above.

Table 32
Development of retail trade turnover in the GDR

	1960	1965	1970	1971	1972	1973	1974	1975	1976
					Bn. M				
Food, drinks and tobacco goods	24.9	28.9	35.8	36.8	38.3	39.6	41.2	42.5	44.0
Food	17.2	19.8	24.1	24.6	25.5	26.3	27.3	27.9	28.9
Drinks and tobacco goods	7.7	9.1	11.7	12.2	12.8	13.2	14.0	14.5	15.1
Industrial goods	20.0	22.2	28.3	29.7	32.2	35.1	37.9	39.4	41.7
Footwear	1.0	1.5	1.8	1.9	2.0	2.2	2.3	2.2	2.4
Textiles and clothing	7.2	7.2	8.8	9.2	9.9	10.8	11.3	11.4	11.6
Other industrial goods	11.8	13.5	17.7	18.7	20.2	22.1	24.3	25.7	27.7
Total	45.0	51.1	64.1	66.6	70.5	74.6	79.2	81.9	85.7
					per cent				
Food, drinks and tobacco goods	55.4	56.5	55.8	55.3	54.3	53.0	52.1	51.9	51.3
Industrial goods	44.6	43.5	44.2	44.7	45.7	47.0	47.9	48.1	48.7

Sources: GDR Statistical Yearbooks; Statistisches Taschenbuch der DDR 1977

Table 33
Development of gross capital investment in the GDR and FRG

Year	GDR							FRG[5]	
	Gross capital investment[1]	Investment in buildings	Investment in equipment	Other types of investment[2]	Building ratio[3]	Equipment ratio[4]	Gross capital investment per capita	Gross capital investment[1]	Gross capital investment per capita
	Bn.M at 1967 prices				%		M at 1967 prices	Bn. DM at 1967 prices	DM at 1967 prices
1950	4.21	2.37	1.56	0.28	56.3	37.1	229	36.2	722
1955	9.30	4.42	3.46	1.42	47.5	37.2	518	65.8	1,255
1960	18.12	7.73	8.91	1.48	42.7	49.2	1,051	90.5	1,633
1965	22.76	9.45	11.97	1.34	41.5	52.6	1,337	124.4	2,122
1970	35.22	14.34	18.68	2.20	40.7	53.0	2,065	153.4	2,529
1971	35.38	14.61	18.34	2.43	41.3	51.8	2,074	160.5	2,618
1972	36.68	15.35	18.76	2.57	41.9	51.1	2,152	165.6	2,685
1973	39.43	16.00	20.74	2.69	40.6	52.6	2,322	166.1	2,681
1974	41.05	16.75	21.27	3.03	40.8	51.8	2,426	153.1	2,467
1975	42.50	17.85	21.86	2.79	42.0	51.4	2,522	146.2	2,369

1 Including general overhauls.
2 Project planning, geological surveys, land purchase, outlay for feasibility studies by outside experts, site preparation, land use charges.
3 Investment in buildings as a percentage of gross capital investment.
4 Investment in equipment as a percentage of gross capital investment.
5 1950 and 1955: Federal territory without Saarland and West Berlin.

Sources: GDR Statistical Yearbooks; DIW calculations and estimates for GDR; West German Statistical Yearbooks; current investment accounting by DIW.

Table 34
Gross capital investment in the GDR by sector

Sector	1960	1965	1970	1971	1972	1973	1974	1975	1975 (1960=100)	Percentage shares (disregarding general overhauls)	
				Mill. Marks at 1967 prices						1960	1975
Industry[1]	8,005	11,290	17,075	17,620	18,720	20,715	20,380	20,220	253	49.7	50.5
Construction	425	410	1,065	860	860	855	1,050	1,240	292	2.6	3.1
Agriculture and forestry	1,930	2,770	4,345	4,390	4,320	4,380	4,890	5,100	264	12.0	12.7
Transport, posts and telecommunications	1,725	1,950	2,875	2,785	2,850	3,115	3,830	4,320	250	10.7	10.8
Trade[2]	475	895	1,565	1,480	1,410	1,410	1,465	1,590	335	3.0	4.0
Other producing branches[3]	65	85	490	310	290	330	355	380	585	0.4	0.9
Cultural and social institutions[4]	565	640	1,305	1,480	1,630	1,655	1,720	1,810	320	3.5	4.5
Extension of housing stock[5]	2,095	2,030	2,550	2,565	3,000	3,430	3,780	3,950	175	14.1	9.9
Other non-producing branches[6]	810	420	1,530	1,505	1,205	1,140	1,120	1,440	223	4.0	3.6
Total (without general overhauls)	16,095	20,490	32,800	32,995	34,285	37,030	38,600	40,050	249	100.0	100.0
General overhauls[7]	2,020	2,270	2,420	2,380	2,390	2,400	2,450	2,450	121	–	–
Total gross capital investment	18,115	22,760	35,220	35,375	36,675	39,430	41,050	42,500	235	–	–

1 Including power, mining and water resources.
2 Including publicly owned collection and purchasing agencies (for agricultural produce) and catering establishments.
3 Leading economic bodies and institutes of all producing branches, project-planning and computing enterprises, publishing houses, repair combines and dry cleaning.
4 Education, culture, art, health and social affairs, sports and hiking.
5 Computed by multiplying residential floor space of new dwellings completed in the current year by building cost per sq.m. and by estimating expenditure on project-planning and equipment.
6 Economic services, state administration, state agencies and social organisations.
7 Estimated as from 1970.
Sources: GDR Statistical Yearbooks; DIW calculations and estimates.

309

Table 35
GDR investment in buildings by economic sector

Sector	1960	1965	1970	1971	1972	1973	1974	1975	1975 (1960=100)	Percentage shares (disregarding general overhauls)	
	Mill. Marks at 1967 prices									1960	1975
Industry[1]	2,120	3,395	5,250	5,360	5,560	5,940	5,860	6,140	290	29.6	36.6
Construction	105	105	365	290	290	235	330	415	395	1.5	2.5
Agriculture and forestry	1,175	1,450	2,470	2,395	2,435	2,435	2,735	2,900	247	16.4	17.3
Transport, posts and telecommunications	570	450	495	530	595	740	825	875	154	8.0	5.2
Trade[2]	180	485	705	710	705	605	665	690	383	2.5	4.1
Other producing branches[3]	15	20	115	105	95	105	90	125	833	0.2	0.7
Cultural and social institutions[4]	225	285	805	960	1,095	1,080	1,115	1,175	522	3.2	7.0
Extension of housing stock[5]	2,005	1,915	2,340	2,430	2,775	3,250	3,565	3,745	187	28.0	22.3
Other non-producing branches[6]	760	390	655	720	700	465	410	715	94	10.6	4.3
Total (without general overhauls)	7,155	8,495	13,200	13,500	14,250	14,855	15,595	16,780	235	100.0	100.0
General overhauls[7]	570	950	1,140	1,110	1,100	1,145	1,155	1,075	189	–	–
Total investment in buildings	7,725	9,455	14,340	14,610	15,350	16,000	16,750	17,855	231	–	–

1 Including power, mining and water resources.
2 Including publicly owned collection and purchasing agencies (for agricultural produce) and catering establishments.
3 Leading economic bodies and institutes of all producing branches, project-planning and computing enterprises, publishing houses, repair combines and dry cleaning.
4 Education, culture, art, health and social affairs, sports and hiking.
5 Computed by multiplying residential floor space of new dwellings completed in the current year by building cost per sq.m.
6 Economic services, state administration, state agencies and social organisations.
7 Estimated as from 1970.

Sources: GDR Statistical Yearbooks; DIW calculations and estimates.

310

Table 36
GDR investment in equipment by economic sector

	1960	1965	1970	1971	1972	1973	1974	1975	1975 (1960=100)	1960	1975
			Mill. Marks at 1967 prices							Percentage shares (disregarding general overhauls)	
Industry[1]	5,180	7,100	10,360	10,515	11,295	12,875	12,365	12,010	232	66.4	58.2
Construction	285	280	665	500	525	585	695	800	281	3.7	3.9
Agriculture and forestry	680	1,150	1,695	1,850	1,740	1,780	1,985	2,095	308	8.7	10.1
Transport, posts and telecommunications	995	1,435	2,300	2,135	2,140	2,210	2,790	3,280	330	12.8	15.9
Trade[2]	230	365	755	670	595	705	685	800	348	2.9	3.9
Other producing branches[3]	50	60	365	190	165	220	235	250	500	0.6	1.2
Cultural and social institutions[4]	265	245	430	460	435	515	540	580	219	3.4	2.8
Extension of housing stock	80	70	130	105	115	50	65	115	144	1.0	0.6
Other non-producing branches[5]	40	30	740	685	500	555	660	710	1,775	0.5	3.4
Total (without general overhauls)	7,805	10,735	17,440	17,110	17,510	19,495	20,020	20,640	264	100.0	100.0
General overhauls[6]	1,105	1,230	1,240	1,230	1,245	1,245	1,250	1,220	110	–	–
Total investment in equipment	8,910	11,965	18,680	18,340	18,755	20,740	21,270	21,860	245	–	–

1 Including power, mining and water resources.
2 Including publicly owned collection and purchasing agencies (for agricultural produce) and catering establishments.
3 Leading economic bodies and institutes of all producing branches, project-planning and computing enterprises, publishing houses, repair combines and dry cleaning.
4 Education, culture, art, health and social affairs, sports and hiking.
5 Economic services, state administration, state agencies and social organisations.
6 Estimated as from 1970.

Sources: GDR Statistical Yearbooks; DIW calculations and estimates.

311

Table 37

Gross capital investment (without general overhauls) of GDR industry[1] by branch

Branch	Mill. Marks at 1967 prices						1975 (1960=100)	Percentage shares		Investment intensity[4] in Marks	
	1960	1965	1970	1973	1974	1975		1960	1975	1960[5]	1975[6]
Fuel and power	3,080	3,610	3,330	5,680	5,280	5,200	169	38.5	25.7	14,000	25,100
Chemicals	1,460	2,485	3,620	4,145	3,745	3,360	230	18.3	16.6	4,600	9,400
Metallurgy	450	825	740	1,065	1,140	1,210	268	5.6	6.0	3,900	9,000
Building materials	380	350	925	710	780	870	228	4.8	4.3	4,000	8,700
Water resources	525	725	885	970	990	1,080	206	6.5	5.3	39,200	50,000
Mechanical engineering/ vehicle building[2]	855	1,545	2,930	2,985	3,205	3,350	392	10.7	16.6	1,200	3,600
Electrical engineering/ electronics/instrument building[3]	300	495	1,690	1,225	1,150	1,150	386	3.7	5.7	900	2,500
Light industry (without textile industry)	450	495	1,310	1,710	1,770	1,770	396	5.6	8.8	900	3,300
Textile industry	275	300	615	990	920	750	273	3.4	3.7	800	2,900
Food processing	230	460	1,030	1,235	1,400	1,480	646	2.9	7.3	1,100	5,700
All industry	8,005	11,290	17,075	20,715	20,380	20,220	253	100.0	100.0	2,800	6,200

1 Including power, mining and water resources.
2 Including foundries and forges, shipbuilding and metal goods manufacture.
3 Including precision engineering/optical industry, data processing and manufacture of office machines.
4 Gross capital investment per employee (including apprentices); annual mean, rounded to nearest hundred Marks.
5 In computing investment intensities, it was necessary to recalculate the employment data, published only for the old classification of industries, in terms of the new system of classification; the figure for employment in the water industry was estimated.
6 For the purpose of computing the investment intensities, the global figure for the number of apprentices has been distributed among the various branches in accordance with the corresponding pattern in the preceding years.

Sources: GDR Statistical Yearbooks.

Table 38
Revenue and expenditure of the GDR state budget 1970 to 1975

	1970	1971	1972	1973	1974	1975	1975 (1970 = 100)	1970	1975
	Bn. Marks							Percentage shares	
REVENUE, total	70.6	80.2	86.9	94.9	104.6	114.7	162	100	100
Revenue from VEBs, combines and VVBs	38.0[1]	43.2	48.2	52.5	60.1	70.5	186	54	61
of which:									
production fund and trade fund levies	5.9	9.4	10.7	11.3	12.4	13.3	225	9	12
net profit levy	12.7[2]	11.2	14.0	15.1	19.4	26.7	210	18	23
product-related levies	19.4[2]	19.6	23.1	25.8	27.9	30.3	156	27	26
other taxes	*	0.3	0.4	0.2	0.3	0.3	*	*	0
Contributions from the banks	*	1.4	1.5	2.7	3.1	3.4	*	*	3
Dues from agriculture	1.2	1.1	1.1	1.1	1.2	1.3	108	2	1
Revenue from artisan and other producer co-operatives	3.0	3.7	3.3	3.4	2.5	2.6	87	4	2
Revenue of private artisans and traders	6.8[3]	7.7[3]	4.7[3]	2.4	2.4	2.4	35	10	2
Wages tax of employees and tax paid by self-employed professionals	3.6	3.8	4.3	4.5	4.9	5.3	147	5	5
Revenue from state institutions (education, health and social affairs, culture) and state apparatus	4.3	4.9	5.3	5.6	6.3	6.7	156	6	6
Social insurance contributions	8.8	10.0	10.5	10.9	11.4	11.8	134	12	10
Local taxes	0.5	0.5	0.5	0.5	0.5	0.5	100	1	0
Other revenue[4]	4.4	4.0	7.6	11.3	12.2	10.2	232	6	9

1 Without 'other taxes'.
2 Levies on production and consumption.
3 Revenue from semi-state (partnership) and private enterprises.
4 Residual item.

*No data available.

Table 38 (cont.)

	1970	1971	1972	1973	1974	1975	1975 (1970 = 100)	1970	1975
	Bn. Marks							Percentage shares	
EXPENDITURE, total	70.0	79.1	85.7	93.3	103.9	114.2	163	100	100
Research	2.5	2.4	2.6	1.8	1.8	1.8	72	4	2
Investment in the publicly owned economy[7]	1.5	2.4	2.7	3.7	4.6	*	*	2	
Investment in the state sector	2.5[5]	2.8	2.9	3.1	3.1	3.4	136	4	3
Transport	1.5[6]	2.8	3.1	3.3	3.3	3.5	233	2	3
Subsidies for the publicly owned economy	3.6	3.9	3.6	4.9	4.8	5.0	139	5	4
Grants for agriculture	2.6	2.7	2.8	2.4	2.5	3.0	115	4	3
Price support for consumer prices, fares and public utility charges	7.3	8.5	9.6	10.2	10.6	11.2	153	10	10
of which for: foodstuffs	4.8	5.5	6.1	6.4	6.8	7.2	150	7	6
industrial consumer goods	0.4	0.8	1.0	1.0	1.1	1.2	300	1	1
public passenger transport	1.1	1.7	1.8	1.8	1.9	2.2	200	2	2
drinking-water purification and sewage treatment	0.5[8]	0.3	0.5	0.5	0.5	0.5	100	1	0
repairs and services	0.5[9]	0.2	0.2	0.2	0.2	0.1	20	1	0
Housing and rent subsidies	2.4[5]	2.5	3.3	3.7	3.8	4.3	179	3	4
Education	5.8	6.4	6.8	7.3	7.6	8.1	140	8	7
Health and social affairs	5.9	6.1	6.5	6.9	7.3	7.8	132	8	7
Social insurance	15.0	16.2	17.7	19.8	20.6	21.4	143	21	19
Culture and sport (including radio, television and recreation)	0.7	1.0	1.1	1.8	2.2	2.4	343	1	2
State apparatus and economic administration	3.1	3.0	3.0	3.1	3.3	3.5	113	4	3
Defence	6.7	7.2	7.6	8.3	8.7	9.6	143	10	8
Other expenditure[4]	8.9	11.5	12.4	13.0	19.7	29.2[10]	328	13	26

5 Estimate.
6 Roads.
7 For the formation of enterprise funds; for product-related price support; for raw materials, basic materials, etc.

8 Drinking water, brown coal briquettes and coke.
9 Services and building work.
10 Includes investment in the publicly owned economy (not separately shown).
*No data available.

Sources: 1970 to 1976 budget accounts: Anlagen zur Volkskammerdrucksache der DDR — 5. und 6. Wahlperiode (discrepancies in sum totals due to rounding)

314

Table 39

Public income transfers to private households (social income) in the GDR

Benefit	Bn. M								per cent							
	1960	1965	1970	1971	1972	1973	1974	1975	1960	1965	1970	1971	1972	1973	1974	1975
Social insurance and old age pensions	5.28	6.76	8.93	9.59	10.54	11.98	12.32	12.41	62.0	67.4	70.0	71.3	71.8	73.5	74.5	73.8
Social insurance pensions[1]	5.15	6.46	8.41	8.87	9.80	11.23	11.57	11.63	60.5	64.4	66.0	65.9	66.8	68.9	70.0	69.2
Old age pensions of the intelligentsia and provision for special groups[2]	0.13	0.18	0.30	0.51	0.53	0.55	0.55	0.58	1.5	1.8	2.3	3.8	3.6	3.4	3.3	3.4
Honour pensions[3]	–	0.12	0.22	0.21	0.21	0.20	0.20	0.20	–	1.2	1.7	1.6	1.4	1.2	1.2	1.2
Pensions for war victims[4]	0.24	0.17	0.14	0.12	0.12	0.12	0.11	0.10	2.8	1.7	1.1	0.8	0.8	0.7	0.7	0.6
Short-term financial benefits	1.23	1.35	1.67	1.73	1.97	2.17	2.13	2.33	14.4	13.5	13.1	12.9	13.4	13.3	12.9	13.9
Other transfers	1.77	1.75	2.01	2.02	2.05	2.03	1.98	1.97	20.8	17.4	15.8	15.0	14.0	12.5	11.9	11.7
Family benefits[6]	1.24	1.28	1.57	1.57	1.57	1.53	1.48	1.45	14.6	12.8	12.3	11.7	10.7	9.4	8.9	8.6
Social welfare benefits	0.16	0.10	0.07	0.07	0.08	0.08	0.07	0.07	1.9	1.0	0.6	0.5	0.6	0.5	0.4	0.4
Other benefits[7]	0.37	0.37	0.37	0.38	0.40	0.42	0.43	0.45	4.3	3.6	2.9	2.8	2.7	2.6	2.6	2.7
Total social income	8.52	10.03	12.75	13.46	14.68	16.30	16.54	16.81	100	100	100	100	100	100	100	100

1 Old age, disablement, old-age disabled, miners' and accident pensions, including widows' and orphans' pensions as well as old age pensions for railway and postal service employees and pensions accruing under the voluntary supplementary pension scheme.
2 Includes special retirement pensions for senior state officials, etc.
3 Granted to 'fighters against fascism' and 'victims of fascism'.
4 Includes pensions for 'victims of Nazi persecution'.
5 Sickness benefit, household allowance, pocket money, monetary post-natal maternity benefits, single parent allowances, etc.
6 Maternity grants, children's allowances, allowances for spouses.
7 Study and educational grants, removal grants, other monetary benefits.

Sources: GDR Statistical Yearbooks; DIW calculations and estimates.

Table 40
Public income transfers to private households (social income)
by type of benefit in the GDR and FRG[1]

Type of benefit	1960	1965	1970	1971	1972	1973	1974	1975
	GDR (Bn.M)							
Old age, disablement, accident and widows' and orphans' pensions[2]	5.28	6.64	8.71	9.38	10.33	11.78	12.12	12.21
Monetary sickness benefits[3]	1.23	1.35	1.67	1.73	1.97	2.17	2.13	2.33
Benefits consequent upon the war[4]	0.24	0.29	0.36	0.33	0.33	0.32	0.31	0.30
Other transfers[5]	1.77	1.75	2.01	2.02	2.05	2.03	1.98	1.97
Total social income	8.52	10.03	12.75	13.46	14.68	16.30	16.54	16.81
1960 = 100	(100)	(118)	(150)	(158)	(172)	(191)	(194)	(197)
	FRG (Bn.DM)							
Old age, disablement, accident and widows' and orphans' pensions	24.83	39.82	63.16	69.32	78.76	88.84	102.03	115.15
Monetary sickness benefits[3]	3.08	4.33	3.58	4.66	5.03	5.66	5.86	6.32
Benefits consequent upon the war[7]	5.57	6.75	8.00	8.55	8.78	9.01	9.88	10.72
Other transfers[8]	2.59	5.02	7.15	9.10	11.40	12.63	15.94	34.85
of which: unemployment insurance	0.61	0.91	2.43	3.33	3.80	4.78	7.11	13.32
children's allowance	–	2.75	2.84	3.21	3.19	3.12	3.05	14.41
Total social income	36.07	55.92	81.89	91.63	103.97	116.14	133.71	167.04
1960 = 100	(100)	(155)	(227)	(254)	(288)	(322)	(371)	(463)
	Per capita							
	GDR (M)							
Old age, disablement, accident and widows' and orphans' pensions[2]	306	390	510	550	606	693	716	724
Monetary sickness benefits[3]	71	79	98	101	116	128	126	140
Benefits consequent upon the war[4]	14	17	21	19	19	19	18	18
Other transfers[5]	103	103	118	119	120	120	117	117
Total social income	494	589	747	789	861	960	977	999
	FRG (DM)							
Old age, disablement, accident and widows' and orphans' pensions	448	671	1,041	1,131	1,277	1,434	1,644	1,862
Monetary sickness benefits[3]	56	73	59	76	82	91	95	102
Benefits consequent upon the war[7]	100	114	132	140	142	145	159	173
Other transfers[8]	47	85	118	148	185	204	257	564
of which: unemployment insurance	11	15	40	54	62	77	115	215
children's allowance	–	46	47	52	52	50	49	233
Total social income	651	943	1,350	1,495	1,686	1,874	2,155	2,701

Notes to table 40

1 East Berlin included in GDR, West Berlin in FRG.
2 Including old age pensions for intelligentsia, provision for special groups and supplementary pensions.
3 Sickness benefit, household allowance, pocket money, post-natal sickness benefits, death grants, etc.
4 Pensions for war victims and victims of Nazi persecution, honour pensions.
5 Social welfare, unemployment benefit, maternity grants, children's allowances, allowances for spouses, study and educational grants.
6 Social insurance pensions, civil service pensions (net), supplementary insurance, agricultural age relief.
7 Pensions for war victims and ex-prisoners of war, restitution payments.
8 Unemployment and social assistance benefits, pre-natal and maternity grants, educational and training grants, grants to private non-profit making organisations, less transfers of income from private households to the state.

Sources: GDR: Statistical Yearbooks, Statistisches Taschenbuch der DDR 1977, Wochenbericht des DIW, no.23/1976; FRG: Deutsche Bundesbank

Table 41
Private household incomes and their use in the GDR (Bn. Marks)

	1960	1965	1970	1971	1972	1973	1974	1975
					Income			
Gross money incomes	65.4	74.1	90.5	94.3	98.5	102.9	107.9	112.3
deduct: social insurance contributions	3.7	4.0	4.6	5.2	5.3	5.5	5.7	5.9
direct taxation	4.2	4.9	6.6	7.2	6.6	5.9	6.2	6.6
Net money incomes[1]	57.5	65.2	79.3	81.9	86.6	91.5	96.0	99.8
Income in kind	2.5	2.6	2.3	2.2	2.0	1.9	1.9	1.8
Net income	60.0	67.8	81.6	84.1	88.6	93.4	97.9	101.6
					Use			
Purchases of commodities[2]	45.4	51.2	62.5	65.0	68.0	72.0	76.0	78.8
Payment for services[3]	6.9	7.9	9.2	9.6	10.0	10.4	10.8	11.3
Consumption of income in kind	2.5	2.6	2.3	2.2	2.0	1.9	1.9	1.8
Private consumption	54.8	61.7	74.0	76.8	80.0	84.3	88.7	91.9
Other expenditure[4]	1.1	1.3	2.8	2.9	3.0	3.2	3.4	3.6
Savings	4.1	4.8	4.8	4.4	5.6	5.9	5.8	6.1
Net income	60.0	67.8	81.6	84.1	88.6	93.4	97.9	101.6

1 From 1971 on, GDR statistics include contributions to the Voluntary supplementary pension scheme in the official figure for gross money incomes. Since this is, in spite of its name, to all intents and purposes a compulsory scheme, the figures shown in this table have been obtained by deducting those contributions from the GDR figures for net money incomes and for 'other expenditure' and adding them to the item 'social insurance contributions'. In the years 1971 to 1975 the contributions under this scheme amounted (in Bn. M) successively to: 0.1, 0.3, 0.4, 0.5 and 0.6.
2 Including purchases made not through the retail trade (canteen and school meals, ex-farm sales, etc.).
3 Artisans', transport and postal services, housing rents, electricity, gas and water, education, entertainment, travel, other services.
4 Stamp duties, etc., interest payments, private insurance premiums, lotteries, other taxes.

Sources: DIW calculations and estimates; GDR Statistical Yearbooks and reports on plan fulfilment; budget accounts and elucidations issued by the People's Chamber; Heinrich Birner, 'Zur Entwicklung des materiellen Lebensniveaus der Bevölkerung der DDR im Jahr 1965', Statistische Praxis, no.8, 1966, pp 336 ff.; Alfred Keck, Die Bilanz der Geldeinnahmen und -ausgaben der Bevölkerung der DDR, East Berlin 1968; Elvir Ebert, 'Reale Umsatz- und Warenfondsplanung für 1969', Der Handel, no.6, 1968, pp 240 ff.; Horst-Dieter Randow, 'Zur Entwicklung der Ausgaben der Bevölkerung für entgeltliche Leistungen', Mitteilungen des Instituts für Marktforschung (MIM), no.2, 1973; Karl-Heinz Dalichow, 'Zu einigen Problemen der Grundstruktur der Konsumtion der Bevölkerung', MIM, no.4, 1975.

Table 42
Personal incomes of the GDR and FRG population by socio-economic group

	Gross income				Deductions			Net income
	Income from work	Social income[2]	Other income	Total	Taxation[3]	Social insurance contributions	Total	
GDR (Bn. M)								
Employees[1]	74.1	6.6	4.1	84.8	5.3	4.9	10.2	74.6
Self-employed and members of co-operatives	14.9	1.0	3.2	19.1	1.3	1.0	2.3	16.8
Pensioners	0.7	9.0	0.5	10.2	–	–	–	10.2
Total	89.7	16.6	7.8	114.1	6.6	5.9	12.5	101.6
FRG (Bn. DM)								
Employees[1]	475.0	44.2	22.3	541.5	74.6	58.3	132.9	408.6
Self-employed	2.8	3.8	195.5	202.1	45.2	9.7	54.9	147.2
Pensioners	1.8	128.2	5.3	135.3	2.1	–	2.1	133.2
Total	479.6	176.2	223.1	878.9	121.9	68.0	189.9	689.0

1 Including apprentices and working pensioners.
2 Pensions, sickness benefit, household allowance for the hospitalised, death grants, maternity grants, children's allowances, allowances for spouses, social welfare benefits, other social insurance cash benefits.
3 Wages tax and direct taxes levied on entrepreneurial activities and capital assets.

Sources: DIW calculations and estimates; Heinrich Birner, loc. cit. (table 41); Alfred Keck, op. cit. (table 41); Eberhard Kurnoth, 'Unser sozialistisches Programm wird zielstrebig verwirklicht', Einheit, no.10, 1973; Lexikon der Wirtschaft, volume Versicherung, East Berlin 1976, p.410; Budget accounts and elucidations, issued by the People's Chamber; reports on plan fulfilment; DIW income computation.

Table 43
Development of employee incomes in the GDR 1960-1975

	1960	1965	1970	1971	1972	1973	1974	1975
					Bn. M			
Gross wages and salaries	41.8	46.7	57.7	60.6	64.6	67.1	70.7	74.1
Deduct: social insurance contributions	3.2	3.3	3.8	4.1	4.3	4.5	4.7	4.9
wages tax	2.4	2.7	3.7	3.8	4.3	4.5	4.9	5.3
Net wages and salaries	36.2	40.7	50.2	52.7	56.0	58.1	61.1	63.9
Social income	3.5	4.2	5.1	5.3	5.8	6.2	6.4	6.6
Other receipts[1]	1.5	2.1	2.9	3.0	3.4	3.6	3.9	4.1
Total net income	41.2	47.0	58.2	61.0	65.2	67.9	71.4	74.6
			per working employee[2], monthly, M					
Gross wages and salaries	501	552	647	672	699	718	746	775
Deduct: social insurance contributions	38	39	43	46	47	48	49	51
wages tax	29	32	41	42	46	48	52	56
Net wages and salaries	434	481	563	584	606	622	645	668
Social income	42	50	57	59	63	66	68	69
Other receipts[1]	18	25	33	33	37	39	41	43
Total net income	494	556	653	676	706	727	754	780

1 Including receipts in kind.
2 Wage and salary earners, including apprentices.

Sources: DIW calculations and estimates; Heinrich Birner, loc.cit. (table 41); Alfred Keck, op. cit. (table 41); Eberhard Kurnoth, 'Unser sozialistisches Programm wird zielstrebig verwirklicht', Einheit, no.10, 1974; Lexikon der Wirtschaft, vol. Versicherung, East Berlin 1976, p.410; Budget accounts and elucidations, issued by the People's Chamber; reports on plan fulfilment.

Table 44
Development of employee incomes in the FRG 1960-1975

	1960	1965	1970	1971	1972	1973	1974	1975
					Bn. DM			
Gross wages and salaries	123.4	201.0	303.2	341.4	372.5	419.6	458.9	475.0
Deduct: social insurance contributions	11.6	18.5	32.4	36.2	41.0	48.5	53.1	58.3
wages tax	7.9	15.7	36.1[2]	45.7[2]	48.3[3]	62.7[4]	73.3[4]	72.0
Net wages and salaries	103.9	166.8	234.7	259.5	283.2	308.4	332.5	344.7
Social income	10.6	14.0	16.0	19.0	21.2	23.7	28.3	44.2
Other receipts[1]	2.1	4.3	11.0	12.2	13.2	16.1	19.0	19.7
Total net income	116.6	185.1	261.7	290.7	317.6	348.2	379.8	408.6
			per working employee[5], monthly, DM					
Gross wages and salaries	508	770	1,135	1,270	1,383	1,550	1,726	1,848
Deduct: social insurance contributions	48	71	121	135	152	179	200	227
wages tax	32	60	135	170	179	232	275	280
Net wages and salaries	427	639	879	965	1,052	1,139	1,251	1,341
Social income	44	54	60	71	79	88	106	172
Other receipts[1]	9	16	41	45	49	59	72	77
Total net income	480	709	980	1,081	1,180	1,286	1,429	1,590

1 Predominantly investment income.
2 Including repayable cyclical adjustment surcharge.
3 After repayment of surcharge.
4 Including 'stabilisation surcharge'.
5 Wage and salary earners, including apprentices.

Source: DIW income computation.

Table 45
Imposts on employee incomes in the GDR and FRG:
social insurance contributions and wages tax
as percentages of gross remuneration

Year	GDR			FRG		
	Social insurance contributions	Wages tax	Total	Social insurance contributions	Wages tax	Total
1960	7.7	5.7	13.4	9.4	6.4	15.8
1965	7.1	5.8	12.9	9.2	7.8	17.0
1970	6.6	6.4	13.0	10.7	11.9[1]	22.6
1971	6.8	6.3	13.1	10.6	13.4[1]	24.0
1972	6.7	6.7	13.4	11.0	13.0[2]	24.0
1973	6.7	6.7	13.4	11.6	14.9[3]	26.5
1974	6.6	6.9	13.5	11.6	16.0[3]	27.5
1975	6.6	7.2	13.8	12.3	15.2	27.4

1 Including the repayable cyclical adjustment surcharge.
2 After repayment of surcharge.
3 Including stabilisation surcharge.

Sources: Federal Office of Statistics, Fachserie N, Reihe 1; DIW calculations.

Table 46
Rates of wages tax in the GDR (in M) and the FRG (in DM)

Gross monthly income	Single persons[1]		Married persons			
			without children[2]		with two children[3]	
	GDR	FRG	GDR	FRG	GDR	FRG
200	3.–	–	–	–	–	–
300	18.–	–	10.50	–	–	–
400	38.–	–	28.–	–	10.50	–
500	62.–	13.70	50.–	–	28.–	–
600	92.–	32.40	77.–	–	50.–	–
700	126.–	51.–	109.–	–	77.–	–
800	148.50	69.20	137.30	9.80	109.–	9.80
900	171.–	88.–	159.80	28.50	137.30	28.50
1,000	193.50	107.20	182.30	46.10	159.80	46.10
1,200	238.50	147.90	227.30	83.50	204.80	83.50
1,400	280.–	188.50	270.–	121.–	249.80	121.–
1,600	320.–	228.70	310.–	157.10	290.–	157.10
1,800	360.–	282.90	350.–	194.60	330.–	194.60
2,000	400.–	347.40	390.–	233.10	370.–	231.–
3,000	600.–	739.70	590.–	440.–	570.–	429.–
4,000	800.–	1,196.50	790.–	752.60	770.–	735.–
5,000	1,000.–	1,680.20	990.–	1,131.30	970.–	1,111.30

1 Tax category I.
2 GDR: Tax Category II; FRG: Tax category III.
3 Tax category III. Tax allowances in respect of children are low in both German states, both paying children's allowances in cash instead.

Sources: GDR: Heinz Balling, Nettolohnabrechnung, East Berlin 1971; FRG: Bundessteuerblatt, Teil I, no.29a of 5 December 1974.

Table 47
Net monthly incomes of employee households in the GDR and FRG

Year	Average house-hold income	All house-holds	Percentage of households within the income bracket of						
			under 600	600 to 800	800 to 1,000	1,000 to 1,200	1,200 to 1,400	1,400 to 2,000	over 2,000
			GDR (M)						
1960	758	100	34.2	25.2	21.9	10.8	4.9[1]	3.1[1]	
1964	807	100	28.5	23.6	24.4	13.8	5.9[1]	3.8[1]	
1970	1,031	100	14.9	14.3	19.0	22.0	14.4	13.4	2.0
1974	1,253	100	7.7	9.9	11.8	17.0	19.6	28.2	5.8
			FRG (DM)						
1960	852	100	38.2	21.1	12.4	9.5	6.5	8.9	3.4
1964	1,126	100	17.8	19.1	16.6	12.3	10.0	16.1	8.1
1970	1,589	100	5.7	9.3	11.6	12.4	11.7	24.8	24.6
1974	2,254	100	0.3	1.9	4.9	7.8	9.6	29.3	46.2

1 Estimate.

Sources: GDR: Statistical Yearbooks; DIW estimates. FRG: DIW income computation.

Table 48
Consumer prices in the GDR and FRG
in mid-1969 and January 1977 –
foodstuffs, drinks and tobacco goods

Commodity	Unit	mid-1969		Jan. 1977		DM = 100	
		DM	M	DM	M	mid-1969	Jan. 1977
Potatoes[1]	5 kg	1.90	0.85	3.40	0.85	45	25
Carrots[1]	1 kg	0.97	0.49	1.35	0.52	51	39
Red cabbage[1]	1 kg	0.89	0.49	1.38	0.53	55	38
Apples, medium grade, home-grown[1]	1 kg	0.80	1.77	1.26	1.97	221	156
Lemons	1 kg	1.87	5.00	2.28	5.00	267	219
Jam, per pound-jar	450 g	1.17	1.08	1.70	1.08	92	64
Wheat flour, type W 405	1 kg	1.04	1.32	1.20	1.32	127	110
Rolled oats, packaged (1969: loose)	1 kg	1.48	0.98	3.00	1.60	66	53
Semolina (wheat)[2]	1 kg	1.44	1.34	2.30	1.34	93	58
Egg noodles, packaged[2]	1 kg	1.93	2.80	2.75	2.80	145	102
Rye bread (mixed flour)	1 kg	1.18	0.52	2.20	0.52	44	24
White bread	1 kg	1.56	1.00	2.75	1.00	64	36
Wheat rolls, etc.[2]	1 kg	2.13	1.00	3.00	1.00	47	33
Refined sugar, packaged	1 kg	1.21	1.64	1.65	1.64	136	99
Full-cream milk chocolate	100 g	0.80	3.85	1.04	3.85	481	370
Cocoa powder	125 g	1.04	4.00	1.45	4.00	385	276
Beef, for frying	1 kg	9.74	9.80	14.85	9.80	101	66
Pork cutlets	1 kg	7.88	8.00	11.00	8.00	102	73
Belly pork	1 kg	3.97	4.60	6.34	4.60	116	73
Spring chicken for roasting, deep frozen[2]	1 kg	3.98	4.75	4.88	4.75	119	97
Braunschweiger sausage	1 kg	6.97	6.80	11.40	6.80	98	60
Full-cream milk, bottled[3]	½ l	0.37	0.36	0.51	0.36	97	71
Edam or Gouda cheese, 40-45% fat content[2]	1 kg	6.48	10.00	9.50	10.00	154	105
German butter, top grade	1 kg	7.72	10.00	9.00	10.00	130	111
Lard, home produced	1 kg	2.08	3.10	3.20	3.10	149	97
Margarine, top grade[2]	1 kg	2.52	4.00	4.00	4.00	159	100
Eggs	1 piece	0.20	0.36	0.26	0.34	180	131
Aerated fruit drinks[2]	1 l	1.07	0.90	1.15	0.90	84	78
Pipe tobacco, fine cut	50 g	1.50	3.00	2.30	3.00	200	130
Filter cigarettes, medium quality	10	0.91	1.60	1.35	1.60	176	119
Brandy, 38%	0.7 l	6.40	17.50	11.80	17.30	225	147
Roast coffee	1 kg	15.56	70.00	23.60	70.00	450	297
Tea	50 g	1.32	1.20	1.45	1.20	91	83
Sparkling wine	1 bottle	6.83	21.00	6.00	21.00	308	350

1 Annual average.
2 Figures based on unofficial observation.
3 Fat content in the GDR 2.5 per cent, in the FRG 3 per cent in 1969, 3.5 per cent in 1977.

Sources: Federal Office of Statistics, Fachserie M, Preise, Löhne, Wirtschaftsrechnungen, Reihe 6; GDR Statistical Yearbooks; diverse press reports.

Table 49
Consumer prices in the GDR and FRG
in mid-1969 and January 1977 —
leather and textile goods

	mid-1969		Jan. 1977		DM = 100	
	DM	M	DM	M	mid-1969	Jan. 1977
Man's walking shoes, ox hide, rubber sole[1]	35.10	41.75	*45.90	*59.50	119	130
Children's shoes, ox hide, rubber sole	25.10	16.30	*28.20	*18.00	65	64
School satchel, grained leather	23.10	25.50[2]	*42.90	*66.00	110	154
Brief case, ox hide[3]	45.50	111.25	*17.90	*31.85	245	178
Man's suit, two-piece, single-breasted, manmade fibre	139.00	188.00	*189.00	*265.00	135	140
Man's trousers, corduroy	27.50	54.30	29.50	47.00	198	159
Lady's jersey dress, manmade fibre	56.00	79.20	*65.00	*116.00	141	178
Boy's suit, wool[4]	78.00	59.20	*98.00	*70.80	76	72
Man's shirt, manmade fibre	22.00	75.00	*19.90	*46.80	340	235
Man's shirt, cotton[5]	24.20	45.00	*24.90	*50.00	186	201
Man's underwear set, fine-ribbed cotton	**	**	14.50	10.75	**	74
Lady's underwear set, two-piece, cotton	7.00	7.25	9.95	11.20	104	113
Lady's stockings, seamless, 20 den.	2.50	7.47	3.45	7.00	299	203
Lady's tights, sheer, stretch nylon or dederon silastik	4.35	31.60	3.65	18.00	726	493
Man's socks, stretch acrylic	3.30	7.45	3.95	6.90	226	175
Tea cloths, 50% linen, set of three	5.49	10.50	6.85	11.70	191	171
Hand towel	4.00	7.50	4.50	6.90	188	153
Bed sheet[6]	11.23	17.40	13.75	17.40	155	127

1 Leather lining and sole.
2 Pig skin.
3 1977: imitation leather, case with handle.
4 1977: manmade fibre.
5 1977: cotton 33 per cent, manmade fibre 67 per cent.
6 FRG: heavy fabric, 150 by 250 cm; GDR, cotton, 140 by 230 cm.

*Not strictly comparable with the previous period.

Sources: Federal Office of Statistics, Fachserie M, Preise, Löhne, Wirtschaftsrechnungen, Reihe 6; GDR Statistical Yearbooks; diverse press reports.

**No data available

Table 50
Consumer prices in the GDR and FRG
in mid-1969 and January 1977 —
other industrial goods

	mid-1969		Jan. 1977		DM = 100	
	DM	M	DM	M	mid-1969	Jan. 1977
Brown coal briquettes, free sale, 50 kg [1]	6.37	4.10	11.30	3.51	64	31
Brown coal briquettes, controlled, 50 kg	6.37	1.70	11.30	1.70	27	15
Heavy duty detergent, 1 kg	4.13	3.00	3.34	3.00	73	90
Detergent for fine fabrics, small-size packet, 1 kg	6.83	8.33	7.80	10.09	121	140
Preserving jar, without ring, 1 l[2]	0.75	0.46	*1.60	*2.10	61	130
Cutlery set, stainless steel, plain[3]	7.50	13.65	8.25	*17.65	182	214
China soup plate, 24 cm diameter[4]	1.46	1.40	2.15	2.85	96	133
Pressure cooker, aluminium, 7 l[3]	**	**	69.00	62.10	**	90
Household bucket, plastic, 10 l	2.13	8.80	2.75	9.00	413	327
Automatic washing machine, front-loading, for 4 kg of dry washing	**	**	498.00	1,450.00	**	291
Electric iron, with thermostatic control dial and indicator lamp, light weight[3]	24.60	35.50	26.50	36.80	144	139
Kitchen chair, tubular metal, plastic covered	**	**	39.90	54.00[5]	**	135
Wardrobe, two-door, with linen shelf	181.00	340.00	270.00	370.00	188	137
Vacuum cleaner, wheeled[6]	159.00	195.00	165.00	195.00	123	118
Hand mixer	48.50	98.00	44.90	98.00	202	218
Electric cooker, 3 boiling rings	295.00	642.00	319.00	688.00	218	216
Refrigerator[7]	301.00	1,250.00	338.00	1,400.00	415	414
Television receiver, 59 cm picture tube[8]	**	**	530.00	2,050.00	**	387
Portable radio receiver, transistorised[9]	**	**	135.00	475.00	**	352
Gramophone record, 30 cm, long-playing	16.46	12.00	18.50	12.00	73	65
Camera	98.00	106.00	*89.00	*79.00	108	89
Miniature film, 36 exposures, black and white	2.90	2.15	4.05	2.15	74	53

Table 50 (cont.)

	mid-1969		Jan. 1977		DM = 100	
	DM	M	DM	M	mid-1969	Jan. 1977
Daily paper, monthly subscription	5.93	3.50	11.70	3.50	59	30
Man's bicycle, leading makes	159.00	242.00	155.00	242.00	152	156
Moped, 1.6 hp, 50 cu.cm	**	**	498.00	695.00	**	140
Motorcar, 500-900 cu.cm cubic capacity, Trabant/Fiat	3,400.00	7,850.00	6,000.00	8,050.00	231	134
Petrol, 1 l	0.57	1.40	0.87	1.50	246	172
Portable typewriter	205.00	430.00	220.00	430.00	210	195
Lady's wrist watch, 17 jewels, gold-plated case, stainless steel base	70.50	135.00	79.00	145.00	191	184
Electric razor, oscillating armature, adjustable for trimming or close shave	81.80	105.00	69.00	72.00	128	104

1 Annual mean; FRG: including delivery.
2 1977: Plastic food container for refrigerator.
3 Comparable models from mail order catalogues.
4 Coffee set for two; FRG: china, GDR: patterned sintolan.
5 Stool.
6 1969: FRG — 300 to 350 W, GDR — WS 900; 1977: FRG — 500 W or WS 1600, GDR — 550 W or WS 1325.
7 1969: FRG with deep-freeze compartment, automatic temperature regulator, 150 l; GDR without deep-freeze compartment, 130 l; 1977: 170 l with automatic defrosting; freezer compartment: FRG — 18°C, GDR — 12°C.
8 Picture tubes of different size.
9 Four wavebands, battery or mains operated.

*Not strictly comparable with previous period.

Sources: Federal Office of Statistics, Fachserie M, Preise, Löhne, Wirtschaftsrechnungen, Reihe 6; GDR Statistical Yearbooks; diverse press reports.

**No data available.

Table 51
Consumer prices in the GDR and FRG
in mid-1969 and January 1977 —
services

	mid-1969		Jan. 1977		DM = 100	
	DM	M	DM	M	mid-1969	Jan. 1977
Electricity, 75 kWh, including meter charge	13.25	8.00	21.40	8.00	57	37
Railway journey, slow train, 2nd class, 50 km	4.25	4.00	5.60	4.00	94	71
Weekly railway season ticket, 2nd class, 15 km	9.00	2.50	13.00	2.50	28	19
Single tram or trolley-bus journey	0.65	0.20	1.20	0.20	31	17
Inland postage for long-distance letter	0.30	0.20	0.50	0.20	67	40
Inland postage for long-distance postcard	0.20	0.10	0.40	0.10	50	25
Telephone call from public call-box	0.20	0.20	0.20	0.20	100	100
Radio and television receiving licence for multi-channel television network	7.00	7.00	10.50	10.00	100	95
Cleaning of man's two-piece suit	7.85	5.75	9.75	5.50	73	56
Man's hair-cut, medium length[1]	3.30	0.90[2]	6.50	3.00	27	46
Resoling man's shoes, leather sole, including cost of material[3]	7.95	5.77	19.40	8.00	73	41

1 1977: fashion styling.
2 Price group II; East Berlin: 1.40 M.
3 1969 without, 1977 with heels.

Sources: Federal Office of Statistics, Fachserie M, Preise, Löhne, Wirtschaftsrechnungen, Reihe 6; GDR Statistical Yearbooks; diverse press reports.

Table 52
Private monetary assets in the GDR and FRG 1975

	GDR			FRG		
	Bn. M	M per capita	%	Bn. DM	DM per capita	%
Savings deposits[1]	75.3	4,478	85	498.7	8,090	62
Securities[2]	5.3[4]	315	6	164.5	2,669	21
Insurance credits[3]	7.7	455	9	137.8	2,235	17
Total	88.3[5]	5,248	100	801.0[6]	12,994	100

1 GDR: Savings and other accounts, sight deposits; FRG: savings deposits and certificates, bearer bonds, term deposits, building society deposits.
2 FRG: shares (at current quotation), fixed-interest stock and money market securities.
3 GDR: deposits of policy holders; FRG: money deposited with insurance institutions and pension funds.
4 1969.
5 Disregarding changes in money supply.
6 Without sight deposits and cash.

Sources: GDR: 1976 Statistical Yearbook; Hannsjörg Buck, 'Sparen und Vermögensbildung in beiden Teilen Deutschlands', Bank-Betrieb, no.7-8, 1971, p.275; FRG: Monatsbericht der Deutschen Bundesbank, May 1976.

Table 53
Foreign travel to and from the GDR 1965 to 1976

Country of destination or origin	1965	1970	1971	1972	1973	1974	1975	1976	1965	1975
	1,000 persons								per cent[1]	
Foreign travel by GDR citizens										
All countries	2,275	2,849	3,000	14,550	12,443	12,479	13,401	11,724	*	8.2
Socialist countries	1,275	1,749	1,900	13,400	10,191	9,973	10,757	8,929	51.5	10.2
of which:										
Bulgaria	85	125	120	138	161	153	181	146	54.1	45.3
Czechoslovakia	694	520	750	5,900	4,222	4,058	4,527	4,283	64.6	14.0
Poland	330	519	510	6,760	5,208	5,118	5,343	3,787	23.3	3.2
Rumania	18	15	30	40	*	*	*	*	77.8	35.0[2]
USSR	60	221	230	250	266	285	310	328	68.3	46.3
Hungary	50	236	240	290	278	294	324	319	54.0	15.4
Western countries	1,000	1,100	1,100	1,150	2,252	2,506	2,644	2,796	*	0.2
of which:										
FRG[3]	*	1,010	1,020	986	1,900	2,200	2,300	*	*	*
Entry by foreigners										
All countries	*	5,600[4]	5,900[4]	18,650	16,852	15,229	16,183	17,312	*	2.6
Socialist countries	707	1,400	1,700	11,550	8,599	9,176	8,245	9,420	56.4	3.0
of which:										
Bulgaria	26	27	53	60	96	95	114	105	30.8	14.0
Czechoslovakia	451	596	750	1,177	1,221	1,570	1,733	1,719	63.6	5.9
Poland	129	615	660	10,034	6,706	7,000	5,675	6,869	51.9	0.7
Rumania	4	11	14	14	*	*	*	*	50.0	71.4[2]
USSR	35	45	59	100	176	204	251	234	34.3	21.5
Hungary	60	71	112	150	201	217	287	288	35.0	5.2
Western countries	*	2,800	3,300	7,100	8,253	6,054	7,938	7,893	*	2.2
of which:										
FRG[3]	*	2,500	2,620	6,800	7,100	5,100	7,260	*	*	*

1 Share of journeys arranged by travel bureau.
2 1972.
3 Including West Berlin.
4 Includes in 1970 1.4 mill., in 1971 0.9 mill. travellers whose nationality was not stated.

Sources: GDR Statistical Yearbooks; Statistisches Taschenbuch der DDR 1977; IUOTO (International Tourism Union, Geneva) statistics; statistics of the countries of destination and origin; GDR press reports.

*No data available.

Table 54
FDGB holiday trips

Year	Total	Stays at health resorts	Foreign tours
	'000	Percentage shares	
1960	1,156	–	1.0
1965	1,089	3.3	1.5
1970	1,190	3.3	0.9
1971	1,238	3.6	1.1
1972	1,342	3.4	1.1
1973	1,413	3.8	1.0
1974	1,461	3.7	1.4
1975	1,532	4.3	1.2

Source: GDR Statistical Yearbooks

Table 55
Average gross monthly pay of wage and salary earners in the CMEA countries 1975

Country	Currency unit	National currency	M	DM
Bulgaria	Lewa	146	531	510
Czechoslovakia	Crown	2,304	737	708
GDR	Mark	889	889	853
Poland	Zloty	3,562	662	636
Rumania	Lei	1,813	621	596
USSR	Rouble	146	466	447
Hungary	Forint	2,821	612	588

Sources: GDR Statistical Yearbooks; DIW calculations; cf. section 5.3.5 above.

Table 56
Food consumption in East European countries and the FRG: ranking of countries in respect of per capita consumption of staple foods in 1975

Country	Meat[1] kg	Country	Eggs
Czechoslovakia	82	Czechoslovakia	295
GDR	78	Hungary	270
Poland	78	GDR	268
Hungary	71	USSR	215
Bulgaria	61	Poland	209
Rumania	60	Rumania	182
USSR	58	Bulgaria	146
FRG	83	FRG	298

	Potatoes kg		Edible fats kg
Poland	173	Hungary	28
GDR	142	GDR	28
USSR	120	Poland	21
Czechoslovakia	98	Czechoslovakia	20
Rumania	97	USSR	19
Hungary	65	Bulgaria	19
Bulgaria	23	Rumania	14
FRG	92	FRG	25

	Sugar[1] kg		Flour[1] kg
Poland	43	Rumania	159
USSR	41	Bulgaria	157
Hungary	40	USSR	142
Czechoslovakia	39	Poland	120
GDR	38	Hungary	118
Bulgaria	33	Czechoslovakia	107
Rumania	23	GDR	94
FRG	36	FRG	67

1 Includes products processed therefrom.

Sources: CMEA Statistical Yearbook; FRG Statistical Yearbook.

Table 57
Stock of durable consumer goods in the CMEA countries 1975
(number per 100 households)

Country	Radio	Tele-vision	Refriger-ators	Washing machines	Private motorcars
	Licences				
Bulgaria	52	56	54	53[1]	14
Czechoslovakia	77	87	79	110	30
GDR	96	82	80	70	26
Poland[2]	74	64	73	92	9
Rumania	34	39	29	21	4
USSR	78	74	62	65	5
Hungary	76	70	68	71	17

1 1973.
2 Workers' households.

Sources: Statistical Yearbooks of the CMEA countries; Statisticke Prehledi 1976/6; Die Länder des RGW 1960-1975, Warsaw; DIW calculations.

Table 58
GDR foreign trade[1] by groups of countries and individual countries (Mill. Valuta-Marks[2])

Countries	1960	1965	1970	1973	1974	1975[9]
			Imports			
All countries	9,217	11,801	20,357	27,330	33,570	39,289
Socialist countries[3]	6,788	8,595	14,119	17,616	20,219	26,157
CMEA countries[4]	6,125	8,010	13,452	16,970	19,324	24,944
USSR	4,024	5,061	8,170	8,638	10,147	14,064
Czechoslovakia	785	1,103	1,920	2,360	2,517	3,323
Poland	457	589	1,230	2,236	2,408	3,323
Hungary	393	521	931	1,618	1,685	*
Other socialist countries[5]	663	585	667	646	895	1,213
Other countries[6]	2,429	3,206	6,238	9,714	13,350	13,133
Western industrial countries[7]	2,028	2,681	5,444	8,898	11,463	11,415
FRG[8]	898	1,107	2,162	2,436	2,987	3,287
Developing countries	401	524	794	816	1,888	1,718
			Exports			
All countries	9,271	12,893	19,240	26,171	30,443	35,105
Socialist countries[3]	7,011	9,646	14,221	19,164	20,836	25,688
CMEA countries[4]	6,373	9,139	13,207	18,320	19,739	24,324
USSR	3,884	5,505	7,315	9,889	9,956	12,475
Czechoslovakia	807	1,226	1,850	2,637	3,035	3,590
Poland	773	1,132	1,673	2,576	2,640	3,297
Hungary	396	532	1,124	1,155	1,703	*
Other socialist countries[5]	638	507	1,014	844	1,097	1,364
Other countries[6]	2,260	3,247	5,019	7,008	9,607	9,416
Western industrial countries[7]	1,869	2,665	4,212	6,006	8,328	7,880
FRG[8]	1,014	1,235	1,888	2,499	3,010	3,188
Developing countries	390	582	807	1,002	1,279	1,536

1 At current prices, fob; includes processing of foreign customers' materials, re-exports, etc.
2 The Valuta-Mark (VM) is a statistical unit of account used in GDR foreign trade returns; its value is fixed at 4.667 VM to the Rouble (cf. chapter 6, p.230 above).
3 CMEA countries and other socialist countries.
4 USSR, Poland, Czechoslovakia, Hungary, Bulgaria, Rumania, Mongolia, Albania (lapsed in 1961), Cuba (admitted in 1972).
5 Yugoslavia, China, North Korea, North Vietnam (in 1978 the united Vietnam was admitted to CMEA membership), Cuba (up until 1971).
6 Western industrial countries and developing countries.
7 All Western industrial countries in Europe (including the FRG), as well as Australia, New Zealand, Canada, Japan and the USA.
8 Including West Berlin.
9 Import and export figures according to Poland's Foreign Trade Yearbook for 1976.

Sources: GDR Statistical Yearbooks.

*No data available.

Table 59
Regional structure of GDR foreign trade (percentage shares)

Countries	1961-65[1]	1966-70[1]	1971-75[1]	1973	1974	1975
			Imports			
Socialist countries	76.0	72.2	65.0	64.5	60.2	66.6
CMEA countries	71.7	68.4	62.1	62.1	57.5	63.5
USSR	47.4	42.3	33.9	31.6	30.2	35.8
Czechoslovakia	9.4	9.4	8.6	8.6	7.5	8.5
Poland	4.9	5.8	7.5	8.2	7.2	8.5
Hungary	4.3	4.8	*	5.9	5.0	*
Other socialist countries	4.3	3.8	2.9	2.4	2.7	3.1
Other countries	24.0	27.8	35.0	35.5	39.8	33.4
Western industrial countries	20.1	23.9	30.9	32.5	34.2	29.0
FRG	9.0	10.2	9.4	8.9	8.9	8.4
Developing countries	3.9	3.9	4.1	3.0	5.6	4.4
			Exports			
Socialist countries	76.9	74.6	72.7	73.2	68.4	73.2
CMEA countries	72.9	69.3	68.9	70.0	64.8	69.3
USSR	44.7	39.9	36.6	37.8	32.7	35.5
Czechoslovakia	9.1	9.8	9.8	10.1	10.0	10.2
Poland	8.9	8.2	9.3	9.8	8.7	9.4
Hungary	4.4	5.1	*	4.4	5.6	*
Other socialist countries	4.0	5.3	3.8	3.2	3.6	3.9
Other countries	23.1	25.4	27.3	26.8	31.6	26.8
Western industrial countries	19.0	20.8	23.2	23.0	27.4	22.4
FRG	9.3	9.1	9.5	9.5	9.9	9.1
Developing countries	4.1	4.6	4.1	3.8	4.2	4.4

1   Annual average

Source: GDR Statistical Yearbooks.

*No data available.

Table 60
Commodity structure of GDR foreign trade

Goods by group	1960	1970	1973	1974	1975	1976
	Bn. Valuta-Marks					
Total imports	9.2	20.4	27.3	33.6	39.3	45.9
Machines, equipment, means of transport	1.2	6.9	9.0	10.2	12.1	14.5
Fuels, mineral raw materials, metals	3.5	5.6	6.7	8.9	12.0	13.3
Other raw materials[2] and foodstuffs	3.6	5.7	6.8	8.3	8.9	11.4
Industrial consumer goods	0.5	0.9	2.3	2.2	2.2	2.2
Chemical products,[3] building materials and other goods	0.4	1.1	2.6	3.9	4.1	4.5
Total exports	9.3	19.2	26.2	30.4	35.1	39.5
Machines, equipment, means of transport	4.5	9.9	13.5	14.7	17.8	20.2
Fuels, mineral raw materials, metals	1.5	1.9	2.8	4.3	4.2	4.5
Other raw materials[2] and foodstuffs	0.5	1.4	2.4	2.8	3.2	4.1
Industrial consumer goods	1.4	3.9	4.5	4.9	5.5	5.7
Chemical products,[3] building materials and other goods	1.3	2.0	3.1	3.7	4.4	5.0
BALANCE[4], ALL COMMODITIES	0.1	−1.1	−1.2	−3.1	−4.2	−6.4
Machines, equipment, means of transport	3.4	2.9	4.4	4.5	5.8	5.7
Fuels, mineral raw materials, metals	−2.1	−3.7	−3.8	−4.7	−7.7	−8.8
Other raw materials[2] and foodstuffs	−3.1	−4.3	−4.4	−5.5	−5.7	−7.3
Industrial consumer goods	0.9	3.0	2.2	2.7	3.2	3.5
Chemical products,[3] building materials and other goods	0.9	0.9	0.5	−0.2	0.3	0.5
	percentage shares					
Total imports	100.0	100.0	100.0	100.0	100.0	100.0
Machines, equipment, means of transport	12.7	34.2	33.0	30.3	30.8	31.5
Fuels, mineral raw materials, metals	38.5	27.6	24.4	26.8	30.5	28.9
Other raw materials[2] and foodstuffs	39.2	28.1	24.7	24.7	22.6	24.9
Industrial consumer goods	5.3	4.5	8.4	6.6	5.6	4.8

Table 60 (cont.)

	1960	1970	1973	1974	1975	1976
	percentage shares					
Chemical products,[3] building materials and other goods	4.3	5.6	9.5	11.6	10.5	9.9
Total exports	100.0	100.0	100.0	100.0	100.0	100.0
Machines, equipment, means of transport	49.0	51.7	51.4	48.2	50.7	51.2
Fuels, mineral raw materials, metals	15.7	10.1	10.8	14.2	12.1	11.3
Other raw materials[2] and foodstuffs	5.9	7.4	9.0	9.3	9.1	10.4
Industrial consumer goods	15.1	20.2	17.1	16.2	15.6	14.4
Chemical products,[3] building materials and other goods	14.3	10.6	11.7	12.1	12.5	12.7

1 CMEA classification.
2 Agricultural and other industrial raw materials.
3 Including fertilisers and rubber.
4 Exports minus imports.

Sources: GDR Statistical Yearbooks, Statistisches Taschenbuch der DDR 1977.

Table 61
GDR trade with selected OECD countries[1] 1960 to 1976

Countries	1960	1965	1970	1973	1974	1975	1976
				Mill. DM			
				OECD imports			
OECD total	690	1,030	1,506	1,790	2,464	2,546	2,707
Belgium-Luxembourg	69	104	118	137	168	200	237
France	31	64	155	288	324	402	473
Italy	64	56	129	153	246	214	236
Netherlands	82	131	167	178	213	193	221
UK	78	136	141	172	264	212	270
Sweden	69	100	171	216	290	398	390
Denmark	64	96	80	88	150	150	135
Austria	86	105	102	142	187	173	189
Switzerland	26	30	49	53	69	57	52
Japan	5	5	142	43	123	71	35
USA	13	26	34	28	37	28	33
Other OECD countries	102	177	218	292	393	448	436
				OECD exports			
OECD total	719	1,180	1,658	2,010	2,572	2,771	3,257
Belgium-Luxembourg	58	48	58	126	151	184	192
France	62	276	218	218	245	443	541
Italy	30	64	97	129	214	215	207
Netherlands	51	80	143	326	387	314	335
UK	88	90	149	89	235	177	202
Sweden	121	128	284	242	292	383	418
Denmark	83	99	62	85	72	63	91
Austria	89	114	96	192	229	285	251
Switzerland	25	33	93	150	154	177	215
Japan	3	4	54	103	119	121	123
USA	17	50	119	75	54	42	163
Other OECD countries	92	194	285	275	420	367	519
	GDR share in OECD countries' foreign trade (per cent)						
Imports	0.21	0.21	0.18	0.17	0.17	0.16	0.16
Exports	0.21	0.24	0.20	0.20	0.22	0.19	0.21

1 Without intra-German trade.

Sources: Foreign trade statistics of the OECD countries, rearranged by the Federal Office for Industry.

Table 62
Commodity structure of GDR trade with OECD countries[1]

Commodity groups	1961-65[2]	1966-70[2]	1971-75[2]	1973	1974	1975
			Mill. DM			
IMPORTS						
Total	824	1,439	2,230	2,010	2,572	2,771
			Percentage shares			
Basic materials and producer goods[3]	27.6	27.8	39.6	32.9	48.7	46.2
Iron and steel	12.8	8.6	8.2	6.8	8.3	9.3
Chemical products	7.2	8.0	19.2	14.9	28.7	24.6
Capital goods	20.1	33.2	31.4	25.6	24.9	32.7
Machines, equipment, means of transport	10.3	19.6	16.5	17.6	14.4	16.3
Consumer goods	5.2	5.0	7.8	11.2	9.6	7.9
Textiles, clothing	3.4	2.5	4.9	6.2	6.8	5.3
Agriculture, processed foods[4]	43.6	28.8	17.6	21.1	16.4	13.0
Agriculture	28.7	22.6	12.3	13.3	11.6	9.6
Processed foods	14.9	6.2	5.3	7.7	4.6	3.1
Unspecified commodities	3.5	5.2	3.6	9.2	0.4	0.2
			Mill. DM			
EXPORTS						
Total	796	1,413	1,993	1,790	2,464	2,546
			Percentage shares			
Basic materials and producer goods[3]	44.0	39.6	33.3	26.1	38.1	36.5
Mining	17.6	9.0	6.3	5.2	6.5	6.7
Mineral oil products	1.9	3.1	3.3	2.4	4.2	4.8
Iron and steel	7.6	9.3	6.1	5.0	8.2	6.6
Chemical products	12.6	12.0	13.5	10.2	14.5	14.5
Capital goods	23.4	25.0	28.8	29.0	27.5	26.2
Machines, equipment, means of transport	11.7	8.9	9.2	8.7	9.5	8.0
Consumer goods	19.5	16.5	19.5	19.0	18.6	19.1
Textiles, clothing	7.0	5.4	5.6	5.9	5.2	4.8
Agriculture, processed foods[4]	9.7	13.6	15.0	16.7	15.2	17.7
Agriculture	4.4	7.4	9.0	11.6	9.8	8.0
Processed foods	5.3	6.2	6.0	5.1	5.4	9.7
Unspecified commodities	3.4	5.3	3.4	9.2	0.6	0.5

1 Without intra-German trade.
2 Annual average.
3 Including mining products, excluding wood and paper products and printing industry products.
4 Including forestry, hunting and fisheries.

Sources: Foreign trade statistics of the OECD countries, arranged by the Federal Office for Industry in accordance with the classification of West German industrial statistics.

Table 63
GDR engineering exports[1] 1974

Products	Total	Socialist countries			Western industrial countries	Developing countries
		All	CMEA	USSR		
	Mill. VM	Percentage shares				
All engineering products	14,113	86.9	83.0	42.6	7.9	5.2
Non-electrical machinery	8,731	90.0	87.0	44.6	5.1	4.9
Machines and apparatus for power generation	259	90.1	75.6	36.3	4.8	5.1
Agricultural machines	1,241	98.7	98.4	52.3	0.9	0.4
Office machines	1,318	95.1	93.8	41.7	3.0	1.9
Calculating machines	1,027	97.7	96.2	43.5	1.5	0.8
Metal-working machines	1,575	81.4	77.0	50.9	9.7	8.9
Machine tools	1,159	80.7	76.2	48.0	11.9	7.4
Machines for the textile and leather industries	718	87.7	84.9	19.9	4.8	7.5
Textile machines	576	85.4	82.3	19.0	5.5	9.1
Machines for individual industries	1,190	83.3	77.2	25.7	7.0	9.7
Printing, stitching and binding machines	259	64.4	61.9	29.1	23.4	12.2
Food processing machines	299	92.2	89.4	39.5	2.0	5.8
Construction and mining machines	409	91.4	83.0	9.1	3.8	4.8
Ore dressing machines	201	76.9	64.9	34.6	0.3	22.8
Other special machines	2,430	92.6	90.5	55.7	4.4	3.0
Refrigerating machines	205	93.7	92.7	56.5	4.6	1.7
Lifting and haulage machines	579	93.3	90.3	59.0	2.8	3.9
Electrical machinery and equipment	2,315	76.4	73.2	32.7	16.0	7.6
Electrical machines	544	63.9	60.6	28.7	20.7	15.4
Generators, motors, transformers	238	56.1	52.2	25.2	32.8	11.1
Machines for the distribution of electric power	324	77.7	75.5	54.5	16.5	5.8
Wires and cables	279	77.6	75.2	62.2	16.2	6.2
Telephone, telegraph, television and radio apparatus	566	82.5	79.4	42.1	10.4	7.1
Transport vehicles	3,067	85.8	79.0	44.2	10.0	4.2
Rail vehicles	775	93.4	88.7	61.1	5.7	0.9
Passenger coaches and special rail cars	367	97.6	97.6	59.1	2.3	0.1
Goods wagons and repair vehicles	248	90.0	90.0	85.1	10.0	–
Motor vehicles	1,124	85.3	76.1	7.8	8.0	6.7
Passenger motorcars	284	74.8	60.9	–	25.2	–
Waterborne craft	1,051	80.3	73.7	72.5	15.6	4.1

1 Grouping of products according to UN classification of export goods (SITC).

Source: GDR Statistical Yearbook.

Table 64
Development of GDR trade with the USSR (annual averages)

Commodity groups	1961-65	1966-70	1971-75
		Mill. VM	
IMPORTS			
Total	4,961	6,707	9,733
		Percentage shares	
Basic materials, producer goods[1]	55.6	50.7	52.4
Mining products	18.3	15.8	19.9
Crude oil	4.5	7.1	11.5
Iron and steel[2]	23.2	20.4	19.2
Non-ferrous metals[3]	6.3	6.2	4.5
Capital goods	5.9	13.4	19.1
Machines, equipment, means of transport	2.9	7.1	15.4
Consumer goods	9.0	6.4	3.5
Textiles	8.3	5.9	3.3
Agriculture, food processing[5]	17.7	12.3	6.3
Grain	8.1	6.0	4.0
Unclassified goods	11.8	17.2	25.0
		Mill. VM	
EXPORTS			
Total	5,019	6,427	9,990
		Percentage shares	
Basic materials, producer goods[1]	10.0	8.5	9.1
Chemical products	9.1	7.6	8.2
Capital goods	59.2	58.8	55.9
Machines, equipment, means of transport	31.9	32.5	30.3
Steel constructions	9.2	8.9	5.1
Waterborne craft	7.8	8.6	7.9
Electrical engineering products	6.5	6.4	5.0
Precision engineering/optical products	3.1	2.7	2.5
Consumer goods	16.0	17.3	15.0
Wood products	3.0	3.6	3.0
Textiles, clothing	10.0	10.5	8.0
Unclassified goods	14.8	15.4	20.0

1 Including mining products.
2 Including foundry products.
3 Excluding copper, including non-ferrous semi-manufactures.
4 Including steel construction and vehicles.
5 Including forestry and hunting.

Sources: USSR trade statistics, arranged by the Federal Office for Industry in accordance with the classification of West German industrial statistics.

Table 65
GDR imports of selected goods, total and from the USSR
(annual averages)

Commodity groups	1961-65	1966-70	1971-75
	Total imports ('000 t)		
Hard coal	9,108	7,736	7,511
Blast furnace coke	3,111	2,971	3,067
Mineral oil	3,483	8,262	15,051
Sheet and plate metal[1]	867	963	592
Sawn timber[2]	1,218	1,425	1,593
Cotton	101.0	89.3	93.2
Wool[3]	22.9	20.4	16.6
Meat[4]	126.3	75.3	41.0
Vegetable oils	126.4	117.6	115.8
Grain[5]	1,912	2,111	3,139
	Percentage share of imports from USSR		
Hard coal	63.1	52.1	58.5
Blast furnace coke	47.1	45.0	36.2
Mineral oil	94.6	92.3	84.0
Sheet and plate metal[1]	78.4	72.9	80.7
Sawn timber[2]	90.4	93.6	96.4
Cotton	84.4	90.5	91.7
Wool[3]	62.7	64.9	38.6
Meat[4]	39.4	46.1	—
Vegetable oils	54.2	67.4	60.6
Grain[5]	80.7	66.2	39.5

1 1961 to 1964 only steel plate and sheets.
2 In '000 cu m.
3 In tonnes.
4 Including meat products and sausages.
5 Including pulses for human consumption and rice.

Sources: GDR Statistical Yearbooks.

Table 66
GDR share in USSR imports of selected goods
(per cent, annual averages)

Commodity groups	1961-65	1966-70	1971-75
Machinery and equipment	28.2	25.8	22.5
Metal-cutting machine tools	32.5	27.0	28.7
Forging and pressing equipment	65.2	68.4	37.8
Plant for the food-processing industry	24.5	32.2	28.5
Agricultural machines	43.8	35.0	41.0
Railway rolling stock	37.2	33.5	32.3
Ships, ships' fitments, cargo-handling gear	22.7	24.0	29.5
Clothing, including underwear	17.5	17.5	14.1

Source: USSR trade statistics.

Table 67
GDR trade with Czechoslovakia

Commodity groups	1965	1968	1970	1974
		Mill. VM		
IMPORTS				
Total	1,103	1,381	1,920	2,517
		Percentage shares		
Basic materials and producer goods[1]	38.2	27.2	17.7	17.9
Solid fuels	13.7	8.9	7.9	5.6
Ores and metals	16.5	10.3	6.6	0.5
Chemical products	5.2	5.2	3.2	4.0
Capital goods	41.0	41.6	37.1	63.7
Machines, equipment, means of transport	21.5	23.6	13.0	39.4
Land vehicles (excepting rail vehicles)	12.2	10.9	12.9	10.0
Electrical engineering products	3.7	3.7	5.1	10.4
Precision engineering/ optical products	3.2	2.8	2.2	1.5
Consumer goods	8.3	9.1	5.3	10.4
Textiles and clothing	4.0	3.6	2.7	5.2
Agricultural products[2]	2.8	2.2	0.9	1.5
Unclassified products	9.7	19.9	39.0	6.5
		Mill. VM		
EXPORTS				
Total	1,226	1,689	1,850	3,035
		Percentage shares		
Basic materials and producer goods[1]	24.3	22.9	17.4	15.9
Solid fuels	3.4	2.8	3.0	1.2
Chemical products	15.3	14.5	12.7	8.6
Capital goods	60.5	55.5	53.3	67.3
Machines, equipment, means of transport	42.0	34.2	49.1	39.3
Land vehicles (excepting rail vehicles)	6.6	7.2	14.4	8.2
Electrical engineering products	5.6	5.2	19.6	9.0
Precision engineering/ optical products	4.9	7.1	8.6	3.8
Consumer goods	5.9	6.6	7.9	8.8
Textiles and clothing	3.2	4.2	3.9	6.1
Agricultural products[2]	0.5	0.9	0.2	3.9
Unclassified products	8.8	14.0	21.2	4.1

1 Including mining products.
2 Including forestry and food processing.

Source: Czechoslovak foreign trade yearbooks, arranged in accordance with the classification of West German industrial statistics by the Federal Office for Industry.

Table 68
GDR trade with Poland

Commodity groups	1965	1968	1970	1974
		Mill. VM		
IMPORTS				
Total	589	942	1,230	2,405
		Percentage shares		
Basic materials and producer goods[1]	50.7	40.2	21.9	32.1
Hard coal	19.9	15.1	7.2	6.9
Iron and steel	4.4	6.0	2.3	1.2
Chemical products	0.9	3.2	2.6	10.4
Capital goods	20.7	29.7	39.4	42.0
Machines, equipment, means of transport	11.1	20.9	23.5	23.1
Electrical engineering products	4.2	3.6	6.8	10.7
Consumer goods	2.3	3.0	1.9	3.1
Textiles and clothing	1.4	1.4	1.3	2.2
Agricultural products[2]	8.0	11.8	3.9	4.6
Unclassified products	18.4	15.3	32.9	18.2
		Mill. VM		
EXPORTS				
Total	1,132	1,224	1,673	2,640
		Percentage shares		
Basic materials and producer goods[1]	25.6	28.0	27.3	23.4
Brown coal	3.2	0.6	1.1	–
Iron and steel	0.9	4.2	6.6	3.4
Chemical products	15.0	16.3	14.0	12.2
Capital goods	51.8	44.8	56.3	67.0
Machines, equipment, means of transport	32.9	25.3	29.5	36.0
Electrical engineering products	5.2	5.1	8.3	8.7
Precision engineering/ optical products	5.4	5.0	2.4	2.7
Land vehicles (excluding rail vehicles)	5.8	5.1	2.7	7.4
Consumer goods	11.5	12.6	14.2	6.1
Textiles and clothing	6.6	7.0	8.6	2.9
Agricultural products[2]	2.4	1.3	0.7	1.1
Unclassified products	8.7	13.2	1.5	2.4

1 Including mining products.
2 Including forestry and food processing.

Source: Polish foreign trade statistics, arranged in accordance with the classification of West German industrial statistics by the Federal Office for Industry.

Table 69
GDR trade with Hungary

Commodity groups	1965	1968	1970	1974
		Mill. VM		
IMPORTS				
Total	521	720	931	1,685
		Percentage shares		
Basic materials and producer goods[1]	5.4	5.4	3.7	4.3
Chemical products	4.9	2.7	2.6	2.1
Capital goods	24.7	32.2	32.5	46.9
Machines, equipment, means of transport	5.8	16.3	13.7	12.6
Land vehicles, excluding rail vehicles	18.9	9.8	11.0	16.4
Electrical engineering products	–	5.6	7.0	13.9
Consumer goods	5.5	7.2	4.8	6.8
Textiles and clothing	2.9	3.7	3.2	3.1
Agricultural products[2]	32.2	26.7	19.6	25.6
Unclassified products	32.2	28.5	39.4	16.4
		Mill. VM		
EXPORTS				
Total	532	813	1,124	1,703
		Percentage shares		
Basic materials and producer goods[1]	15.8	20.5	10.5	17.9
Brown coal briquettes	7.4	4.4	3.0	2.4
Chemical products	8.0	8.6	7.0	11.4
Capital goods	30.9	38.3	37.8	52.9
Machines, equipment, means of transport	13.3	16.4	14.9	20.4
Land vehicles, excluding rail vehicles	7.9	11.1	15.5	22.1
Electrical engineering products	3.8	2.3	1.8	4.9
Consumer goods	5.2	4.7	4.4	6.2
Wood products	2.4	2.1	1.9	0.4
Agricultural products[2]	1.9	0.0	3.4	5.8
Unclassified products	46.2	36.5	43.9	17.2

1 Including mining products.
2 Including forestry and food processing.

Sources: Hungarian statistical yearbooks, the data arranged in accordance with the classification of West German industrial statistics by the Federal Office for Industry.

Table 70
Development of intra-German trade[1] volume

Year	Mill. DM			Annual growth rate (%)	
	Deliveries[2]		FRG Balance	Deliveries[2]	
	to FRG	to GDR		to FRG	to GDR
1960	1,123	960	−163	26.2	−11.0
1961	941	873	− 68	−16.2	− 9.1
1962	914	853	− 62	− 2.8	− 2.3
1963	1,022	860	−163	11.8	0.8
1964	1,027	1,151	124	0.5	33.9
1965	1,260	1,206	− 54	22.7	4.8
1966	1,345	1,625	280	6.7	34.8
1967	1,264	1,483	219	− 6.1	− 8.8
1968	1,440	1,432	− 7	13.9	− 3.4
1969	1,656	2,272	616	15.1	58.6
1970	1,996	2,416	420	20.5	6.3
1971	2,319	2,499	180	16.2	3.4
1972	2,381	2,927	546	2.7	17.2
1973	2,660	2,998	338	11.7	2.4
1974	3,252	3,671	419	22.3	22.5
1975	3,342	3,921	579	2.8	6.8
1976	3,877	4,269	392	16.0	8.9

1 Between FRG, including West Berlin, and GDR, including East Berlin; the trade includes transactions for processing raw materials or semi-finished goods supplied by the partner, as well as commodity traffic on foreign account.
2 The West German distinction between intra-German and foreign trade is reflected in the official terminology, which refers to Bezüge and Lieferungen rather than the customary Einfuhr and Ausfuhr for imports and exports respectively.

Source: Federal Office of Statistics, Fachserie F, Reihe 6.

Table 71
Development of intra-German trade by commodity groups

Commodity groups	1961-65[1]	1966-70[1]	1971-75[1]	1973	1974	1975	1976
				Mill. DM			
DELIVERIES BY FRG							
Total	989	1,844	3,203	2,998	3,671	3,922	4,269
of which: West Berlin	51	125	207	203	255	288	350
				Percentage shares			
Basic materials and producer goods[2,3]	56.6	51.8	53.8	47.6	57.9	60.1	53.5
Iron and steel[4]	29.5	16.0	12.8	12.2	15.6	14.2	12.2
Chemical products[3]	16.8	21.3	23.2	23.1	25.4	23.8	21.3
Non-ferrous metals[5]	3.0	9.1	8.6	4.3	9.7	8.5	5.0
Capital goods	17.3	22.8	23.8	28.6	21.8	22.7	28.9
Machines, equipment, means of transport	11.1	16.4	17.3	21.2	15.6	15.3	20.2
Consumer goods	7.3	8.3	9.5	10.5	9.8	7.4	7.5
Agricultural products, processed foods[7]	18.5	16.5	11.7	12.2	9.6	8.5	8.9
Total[8]	100	100	100	100	100	100	100
of which: West Berlin	5.2	6.8	6.5	6.8	6.9	7.3	8.2
				Mill. DM			
DELIVERIES BY GDR							
Total	1,033	1,540	2,791	2,660	3,252	3,342	3,877
of which: West Berlin	206	334	673	708	803	864	1,039
				Percentage shares			
Basic materials and producer goods[2,3]	51.0	30.9	38.9	38.3	43.7	39.0	42.4
Iron and steel[4]	0.9	4.7	7.7	6.1	9.0	8.0	7.1
Mining products	22.7	8.1	3.4	3.3	3.5	2.7	3.0
Mineral oil products	14.3	2.9	9.8	10.2	13.7	13.2	15.2
Chemical products[3]	7.8	8.3	9.0	9.4	9.4	9.3	10.0
Capital goods	10.5	13.6	10.7	9.7	9.7	9.9	10.5
Machines, equipment, means of transport	5.9	5.8	3.5	3.2	3.4	2.7	3.5
Consumer goods	22.0	29.4	30.6	28.7	29.0	31.6	29.3
Textiles	10.1	10.4	10.5	10.3	9.9	10.5	11.0
Clothing	4.8	8.3	8.7	7.4	8.9	9.6	8.4
Wood products	1.6	4.2	4.9	4.7	4.5	5.2	3.8
Agricultural products, processed foods[7]	16.2	25.6	19.5	22.7	17.1	18.0	17.2
Total[8]	100	100	100	100	100	100	100
of which: West Berlin	19.9	21.7	24.1	26.6	24.7	25.8	26.8

1 Annual average.
2 Including mining products.
3 Including plastic, rubber and asbestos products.
4 Including castings as well as products of cold rolling mills, wire drawing and steel forming plants.
5 Including non-ferrous castings and semi-manufactures.
6 Including office machines and EDP equipment.
7 Including drinks and tobacco goods, and fishery, hunting and forestry products.
8 Including commodities not fitting into any of the above categories.

Source: Federal Office of Statistics, Fachserie F, Reihe 6.

Table 72
Development of intra-German trade: selected commodities
(Mill. DM)

Commodities	1965	1970	1974	1975	1976
DELIVERIES BY GDR					
Brown coal	208	104	99	70	87
Petrol	19	13	84	*	*
Diesel oil	31	29	169	*	*
Fuel oil	1	15	143	*	*
Quarrying products	26	41	89	78	84
Rolled steel	2	62	125	92	81
Metal working machines	27	90	31	40	53
Electrical consumer goods	6	20	34	37	26
Radio and television receivers, audio equipment	10	24	35	36	41
Precision engineering/ optical products	23	28	33	38	40
Chemical fibres	1	16	62	51	59
Plastic products	15	45	29	20	26
High-grade ceramics products	21	48	37	38	44
Toys	7	17	21	25	29
Furniture and other wood products	47	38	147	173	148
Knitwear	49	113	141	163	198
Textile fabrics (cut)	20	58	130	57	82
Outer garments	49	73	126	187	327
Underwear	22	49	104	45	55
Fat stock, other livestock	5	73	115	128	67
Fresh pig meat	84	75	*	*	*
Sugar, confectionery	45	71	72	84	71
DELIVERIES BY FRG					
Iron and steel plate	67	81	63	53	63
Steel tubes	108	121	122	146	87
Cold strip	21	24	28	26	23
Drawn wire	18	27	33	37	43
Metal working machines	26	200	149	152	198
Rubber and plastics processing machines	17	25	57	30	31
Food processing machines	4	19	23	80	217
Machines for the chemical industry	15	90	30	10	21
Paper and printing machines	4	23	32	28	24
Textile machines, sewing machines	26	47	93	53	65
Electrical engineering products	26	70	100	129	128
Precision engineering/ optical products	8	17	33	31	29
Metal goods and hardware	7	22	49	64	69
Fertilisers	140	60	91	119	46
Plastics, synthetic rubber	28	46	121	124	121
Chemical fibres	13	4	98	71	71
Plastic products	14	35	67	50	48
Leather, leather products, footwear	2	6	72	32	31
Textile fabrics (cut)	33	43	133	131	141
Clothing and knitwear	14	35	66	61	41

Source: Federal Office of Statistics, Fachserie F, Reihe 6

*No data available.

349

Table 73
Development of intra-German trade: reciprocal services[1]

	1961-65[2]	1970	1973	1974	1975
	Mill. DM				
Services extended by FRG	94	266	314	522	505
Freight charges	*	149.9	144.7	293.7	317.6
Harbour dues	*	5.1	28.4	21.7	4.5
Commission payments	*	26.6	41.2	57.7	52.1
Assembly costs	*	4.8	13.3	72.6	31.0
Licence fees	*	11.9	8.0	8.6	5.2
Services accepted by FRG[3]	24	148	161	161	166
Licence fees	*	2.0	6.0	10.3	8.7
Other agreed payments[4]	*	42.7	98.7	107.3	117.2
Balance	70	118	153	361	339
Turnover as a percentage of commodity trade	5.8	9.4	8.4	9.9	9.2

1 Transacted via the Service Account; not including transport costs and other services subsidiary to commodity trade and included in the commodity trade accounts.
2 Annual average.
3 Including postal service equalisation (at the annual rate of 30 mill. DM).
4 Freight charges, assembly costs, commission payments, etc.

*No data available.

350

Table 74
The CMEA countries[1] : selected economic data 1975

	Unit	Bulgaria	Czecho-slovakia	GDR	Mongolia	Poland	Rumania	USSR	Hungary
Population	Mill. pers.	8.7	14.8	16.9	1.4	34.0	21.2	254.4	10.5
Economically active population	Mill. pers.	4.3[2]	7.4	8.9	0.45[2]	16.9	10.2	130.8[2]	5.1
of which in									
Industry[3]	per cent	41.5	47.7	49.5	20.8	39.7	38.7	37.9	43.9
Agriculture	per cent	28.1	15.2	11.4	45.1	30.6	38.1	22.7	22.7
Women's share	per cent	48[4]	47.8	49.2[2]	45[2]	48.9[4]	49.0[4]	50.3[4]	48.4
Activity ratio[5]	per cent	44.1	50.2	49.9	32.1	49.8	48.1	51.4	44.0
Shares in produced national product									
Industry	per cent	51.0	64.4	62.2	24.7	52.1	57.1	52.7	47.0
Agriculture	per cent	22.0	8.3	10.0	22.4	12.6	16.6	16.8	16.3
Shares in used national product									
Personal consumption	per cent	64.2[2]	54.5	67.5	62.4	52.5	65.9[6]	64.2	65.7
Social consumption	per cent	3.3[2]	19.5	10.6		9.7	34.1[6]	9.4	9.1
Accumulation	per cent	32.5[2]	26.0	21.9	37.6	37.8		26.4	25.2
Share of retail trade in personal expenditure	per cent	93.2	72.9	78.8	*	86.1	*	90.2[7]	75.9
Shares in gross industrial output:									
Producer goods	per cent	58.6	63.2	71.5	49.5	65.7	72.2	74.0	64.8
Consumer goods	per cent	41.4	36.8	28.5	50.5	34.3	27.8	26.0	35.2
Shares in gross agricultural production:									
Crop production	per cent	56.7	44.6	39.7	23.9	51.9	57.0	45.4	56.1
Animal production	per cent	43.3	55.4	60.3	76.1	48.1	43.0	54.6	43.9
Average gross monthly wage	Marks	531	737	889	104	662	621	466	612
Per capita meat consumption	kg	61	82	78	—	78	60	58	71
Foreign trade turnover	Bn. TR	7.4	12.1	15.9	0.35	17.1	8.0	50.7	8.7
of which in									
CMEA countries	per cent	73.8	66.0	66.2	96.2	49.7	38.0	51.8	66.1
Western industrial countries	per cent	17.0	22.4	25.9	1.1	41.3	36.7	31.3	24.4
Developing countries	per cent	7.2	7.0	4.4	0.0	6.5	18.5	12.4	6.5
Foreign trade volume per capita	TR	864	822	943	249	502	375	199	823
Foreign trade volume with CMEA countries (intra-Bloc trade) per capita	TR	656	581	657	246	262	168	112	568

Table 74 (cont.)

NOTES TO TABLE 74

1 Without Cuba, for which little comparable data is available.
2 Estimate.
3 Including artisan trades.
4 Percentage of potentially active population (economically active population plus unemployed).
5 Economically active as a percentage of whole population.
6 Average 1971/75.
7 Relating to personal consumption of used national product.

Sources: Statistical yearbooks of the CMEA countries; Die Länder des RGW 1960-1975, Warsaw 1976; Statisticke Prehledi 1976/6, Prague; DIW calculations.

*No data available.

Table 75

Intra-Bloc trade of the CMEA countries[1] 1960 and 1975 (in TR)

	Bulgaria	Czecho-slovakia	GDR	Cuba[2]	Mongolia[2]	Poland	Rumania	USSR	Hungary	CMEA
1960										
Bulgaria	–	56	63	–	1	19	8	299	10	456
Czechoslovakia	51	–	178	1	5	100	58	567	85	1,045
GDR	49	168	–	4	2	98	47	862	84	1,314
Cuba[2]	1	9	2	*	*	4	–	64	1	81
Mongolia[2]	1	6	4	*	–	3	0	75	1	90
Poland	18	114	168	9	2	–	19	419	42	791
Rumania	8	58	47	–	0	21	–	239	23	396
USSR	269	587	836	93	51	348	252	–	223	2,659
Hungary	12	101	91	0	1	45	37	273	–	560
CMEA	409	1,099	1,389	107	62	638	421	2,798	469	7,392
1975										
Bulgaria	–	130	290	80	5	200	100	1,960	60	2,825
Czechoslovakia	160	–	774	47	9	606	178	2,035	333	4,142
GDR	200	710	–	85	5	750	200	2,980	420	5,350
Cuba[2]	55	38	50	–	*	11	13	1,351	27	1,545
Mongolia[2]	5	9	10	*	–	5	3	475	6	513
Poland	139	506	704	17	4	–	151	2,375	198	4,094
Rumania	82	193	235	6	3	159	–	687	110	1,475
USSR	1,931	1,892	2,643	1,448	125	2,406	824	–	1,616	12,885
Hungary	69	353	488	22	5	232	167	1,649	–	2,985
CMEA	2,641	3,831	5,194	1,705	156	4,369	1,636	13,512	2,770	35,814

*No data available.

1 On the basis of import statistics of the CMEA countries.
2 Based on trade partner statistics.

Sources: Statistical yearbooks of the CMEA countries; CMEA Statistical Yearbook.

Table 76
CMEA countries' foreign trade structure: percentage shares of total imports and exports

	Bulgaria	Czecho-slovakia	GDR	Cuba	Mongolia	Poland	Rumania	USSR	Hungary	CMEA
Imports 1960										
Socialist countries	83.2	71.3	73.9	18.7	100.0	63.5	73.1	70.7	70.4	69.1
CMEA countries	79.5	63.9	66.4	15.3	93.8	58.1	67.7	50.7	63.6	58.4
Other socialist countries	3.2	7.4	7.5	3.4	6.2	5.4	5.4	20.0	6.8	10.7
Western industrial countries	13.9	19.6	20.6	70.9	–	29.8	23.5	19.8	25.6	23.2
Developing countries[1]	2.9	9.1	5.5	10.4	–	6.7	3.4	9.5	4.0	7.7
Imports 1975										
Socialist countries	72.8	70.1	66.6	50.7	99.3	45.8	43.6	52.4	65.8	56.8
CMEA countries	71.3	65.5	63.5	47.3	98.0	43.7	37.0	48.3	63.2	53.2
Other socialist countries	1.5	4.6	3.1	3.4	1.3	2.1	6.5	4.1	2.6	3.5
Western industrial countries	23.1	24.8	24.2	38.9	0.7	49.5	42.2	36.6	27.0	35.1
Developing countries[1]	4.1	5.1	9.2	10.5	0	4.7	14.2	11.0	7.2	8.1

Table 76 (cont.)

	Bulgaria	Czecho-slovakia	GDR	Cuba	Mongolia	Poland	Rumania	USSR	Hungary	CMEA
Exports 1960										
Socialist countries	83.9	72.2	75.8	24.7	100.0	62.7	72.9	75.7	71.5	71.9
CMEA countries	80.4	63.5	68.7	20.1	93.8	54.9	65.6	56.8	61.3	60.4
Other socialist countries	3.5	8.7	7.1	4.6	6.2	7.8	7.3	18.9	10.2	11.5
Western industrial countries	12.9	17.2	19.3	67.2	0	29.1	21.3	18.4	22.5	21.6
Developing countries[1]	3.2	10.6	4.9	8.1	—	8.2	5.8	5.9	6.0	6.5
Exports 1975										
Socialist countries	80.2	71.5	73.2	67.9	99.4	59.9	46.0	60.8	72.3	64.6
CMEA countries	77.5	66.2	69.3	64.2	96.8	56.9	38.6	55.6	68.4	60.1
Other socialist countries	2.7	5.3	3.9	3.7	2.4	3.1	7.4	5.1	3.9	4.5
Western industrial countries	9.4	20.0	19.2	23.5	0.6	31.5	35.0	25.7	19.3	24.6
Developing countries[1]	10.4	8.5	7.6	8.6	—	8.6	19.0	13.5	8.4	10.8

1 Including countries not listed and re-export.

Sources: Statistical yearbooks of the CMEA countries; Die Länder des RWG 1960-1975, Warsaw 1976.

Table 77
CMEA countries' shares in intra-Bloc trade 1960 and 1975

Country	1960	1975	1960	1975
	Exports		Imports	
	Mill. TR			
Intra-Bloc trade	7,545	35,598	7,392	35,814
	Percentage shares			
Bulgaria	5.5	7.5	6.2	8.0
Czechoslovakia	14.8	10.9	14.1	11.7
GDR	18.2	14.6	17.8	15.0
Cuba	1.5	4.8	1.1	3.9
Mongolia	0.8	0.4	1.2	1.1
Poland	8.7	12.3	10.7	11.5
Rumania	5.6	4.3	5.4	4.2
USSR	38.5	37.5	36.0	36.3
Hungary	6.4	7.7	7.6	8.4

Sources: Statistical yearbooks of the CMEA countries.

Table 78
GDR share in CMEA countries' foreign trade 1960 and 1975
(per cent)

Country	1960	1975	1960	1975
	Exports		Imports	
	GDR share in foreign trade volume			
Bulgaria	11.3	7.3	9.9	7.3
Czechoslovakia	10.9	12.2	10.1	12.3
Cuba[1]	0.5	1.7	0.7	3.2
Mongolia[1]	4.5	2.5	2.8	3.2
Poland	12.5	7.5	9.4	9.2
Rumania	8.1	5.9	7.6	5.0
USSR	16.5	9.9	18.9	12.4
Hungary	10.4	10.3	11.6	10.8
CMEA	11.5	8.1	12.0	9.4
	GDR share in intra-Bloc trade			
Bulgaria	13.8	10.3	12.3	9.4
Czechoslovakia	17.0	18.7	15.8	18.5
Cuba[1]	2.7	3.7	3.8	5.0
Mongolia[1]	4.8	2.5	3.0	3.3
Poland	21.3	17.2	17.0	16.2
Rumania	11.9	15.9	11.6	13.1
USSR	31.4	20.5	32.6	22.3
Hungary	16.3	16.4	18.8	15.8
CMEA	19.1	15.2	19.2	15.7

1 Based on statistics of the trade partners.

Sources: Statistical yearbooks of the CMEA countries; CMEA Statistical Yearbook.

Index

Bank for Industry and Commerce (*Industrie-und Handelsbank*), 66

Bank for International Settlements, 239

Banking and credit sector, 65-8; building investment in, 124; contributions from, 179

Basic industries, 3, 5, 8, 13

Basic Treaty 1972, 223, 249

'Bassow initiative', 58

Berlin Wall, 8, 14, 26

Birth rate, 21, 25

Bonuses, 200-1

Bonus fund, 41, 61-4; allocations from, 80, 200

Brown coal, 107, 108-9, 155; exports, 254; price, 212; production, 19

Building materials, 114, 155, 176

Building sector, 122-30; investment, 124; labour productivity, 92; output rate, 88, 122, 296; transport bottlenecks in, 156

Bureaucratisation, 81

Burial grant, 188-9

Capital assets, 288; growth, 92, 105; sector distribution, 31-5, 100, 286

Capital goods, exports, 241, 242, 244-7, 271-2; imports, 246-7

Capital intensity, 91, 105, 108, 154, 176

Capital productivity, 92-3, 105-6

Central Institute for Manufacturing Techniques, 35-6

Central planning and control, 4-5, 39, 44, 46-8; of decision-making, 81; recentralisation, 10, 42, 59, 65, 68, 77, 172

Central Supply Plan, 56-7

Chambers of Industry and Commerce, 166

Chemical industry, 7, 13, 107, 111-13; exports, 246, 272; investments, 175-6; labour productivity, 106; output rate, 88, 103, 112

Children's allowances, 195-6

Civil aviation, 159

Clearing account (*Preisausgleichskonto*), 233

Clothing, 220

CMEA (Comecon), 3, ch.7, 351-2; 'Complex Programme', 51, 258-61, 264; consumption patterns, 226; decision-making, 263-4; economic integration of member states, 7-8, 54, 73, 117, 122, 170, 258-60, 264-71; foreign and inter-Bloc trade, 234-5, 237-8, 240, 270, 353-6; historical development, 257-9; housing, 227-8; industrial co-operation, 272-4, 276; interested members rule, 260, 261, 263; International Economic Organisations, 263-4, 267-9; Inter-State Organisations, 263-4, 265-6; labour mobility, 275; living standards, 224-9, 270; long-term planning, 52, 274-5; methods of integration, 260-1; organisation, 261-3; plan co-ordination, 260-1; statutes, 257; and third countries, 258-9

Code of Labour Law, 195

Collectivisation, 4, 8, 14

Combat Groups of the Working Class, 193

Combines (*Kombinate*), 36, 47, 48-51; concentration of managerial powers in, 101; formation of, 15

Commercial accounting (*Wirtschaftliche Rechnungsführung*), 48, 49, 65